DEMAGOGUES IN THE DEPRESSION

DEMAGOGUES
IN THE
DEPRESSION

AMERICAN RADICALS
AND THE UNION PARTY,
1932–1936

By DAVID H. BENNETT

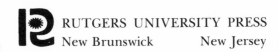 RUTGERS UNIVERSITY PRESS
New Brunswick   New Jersey

To Linda

Acknowledgments

A number of former teachers and students helped me develop the theme and shape the material for this book; their interests and insights were invaluable aids at different stages of its preparation. Professor Walter Johnson, particularly, read early versions of the manuscript and I have profited from his suggestions for revisions.

The librarians at the University of Chicago were helpful in securing obscure materials. The staffs of the Franklin D. Roosevelt Library at Hyde Park, New York, and the University of North Dakota Library helped make my extended manuscript searches there profitable.

My greatest debt is to my wife Linda, a discerning editor who has been deeply involved in this manuscript throughout its development.

D. H. B.

Contents

DEMAGOGUES IN THE DEPRESSION

Prologue: The Alliance
of the Demagogues

For Cleveland, Ohio, the summer of 1936 was a time to remember. In the steaming months of July and August there came to the lakefront city two great quasi-political conventions which captured the interest of the nation in that presidential election year. Both conventions met in the same hall that had housed, earlier in the season, the national meeting of the Republican Party. Both had at least two advantages over the Republicans: they were bigger and they were livelier.

In July, the second national gathering of the Old Age Revolving Pension Plan, founded and led by Dr. Francis E. Townsend, attracted eleven thousand delegates to Cleveland. In August, the first annual meeting of the National Union for Social Justice, the creature of Father Charles E. Coughlin, drew ten thousand followers of the radio priest to the midwestern metropolis. Both the Townsend Plan and the National Union numbered their membership in the multimillions. The leaders were demagogic, the followers fanatic. Of all the radical movements organized in the United States during the 1930's, these two were perhaps the most formidable. And with the election still some weeks away, the founders of these groups had decided — along with two other radical leaders — to join forces in an effort to defeat President Franklin D. Roosevelt and promote their own bizarre panaceas. The new political force that was the product of this curious coalition was the Union Party. The two conventions in Cleveland became, in effect, the means of promoting the Union Party, and because of the nature of this party, they marked the high point of the demagogues' appeal in the Depression decade.

The great economic crisis of the 1930's provided the setting for the growth of many kinds of extremist movements. Triggered by the stock market crash in the last year of the "roaring twenties," it sent the national

3

income, over $83 billion in 1929, plummeting down under $40 billion
in 1932. As the number of unemployed edged above fifteen million by
the first months of 1933, fear, hunger, and finally desperation became
the inevitable facts of life in an emergency that had no precedent in
United States history. Across America and across class lines spread privation. Men stood on bread lines, selling apples on street corners, sleep-
ing in subways and parks and city incinerators. Armies of homeless
youths roamed the land while relief agencies, running out of money
and morale, had to stand helplessly by while thousands suffered. Violence erupted in some communities, as men chose to steal rather than
watch their children starve.

Following the election of Franklin D. Roosevelt and the reforms in-
stituted by his administration, the crisis abated somewhat. But FDR was
not a miracle worker. Unemployment remained high, and huge pockets
of social discontent and economic distress remained as festering sores
across the nation. As the Depression lingered on throughout the years of
Roosevelt's first term, the setting remained a congenial one for the
demagogue.

Many men and movements appeared in these years, offering to solve
the pressing and perplexing problem of privation in the midst of plenty
in affluent America. These men were true demagogues. Stirring up the
prejudices and passions of the population by tricks of rhetoric and sensational charges, by specious arguments, catchwords and cajolery, the
demagogue tried to play on discontents and to intensify the original
irrational elements within them. By so doing, he sought to seduce his
followers into an emotional attachment to his person that would effectively block any group awareness of either the real sources of unhappiness or the real means of solution.

Among those who bid for demagogic leadership in the Depression
decade were James R. Cox of Pittsburgh, who led the Jobless Party in
1932, and William H. "Coin" Harvey, organizer of the Liberty Party in
that same year. William Dudley Pelley founded the Nazi-like Silver
Shirt Legion of America in 1933, "General" Art J. Smith, another emu-
lator of Hitler, set up his Khaki Shirts a few months later, and Philip
Johnson and Alan Blackburn, inspired by the fascistic writings of Lawrence Dennis, created their elitist National Party in 1934. Alexander
Lincoln and his Sentinels of the Republic, George E. Deatherage and
the Knights of the White Camellia, Seward Collins and Gerold Winròd
were others who clamored for attention.

Most of these would-be saviors were ignominious failures. Their "movements" amounted to little more than a fanatic and a letterhead. Pelley, for example, at his high point of popular appeal, polled less than sixteen hundred votes in the 1936 presidential election. The National Party never had more than 150 followers. The others listed above were equally insignificant.

But as the Cleveland conventions of 1936 demonstrated, not all the radical movements and their leaders made so little impact. Coughlin, the radio priest from Royal Oak, Michigan, utilized the new tool of mass communications so effectively that by 1933 he had an audience numbering in the tens of millions listening to his weekly political sermons. With the creation of his quasi-political National Union for Social Justice, Father Coughlin was, by 1935, a force to be reckoned with in the United States.

Townsend's rise was even more meteoric. First organized in California in 1933, the Old Age Revolving Pension Plan was soon sweeping the country. The Townsend movement had several million members at the time of the climactic events in the summer of 1936.

But the priest and the old doctor were not alone in their success. The Share-Our-Wealth Society, founded by Senator Huey P. Long of Louisiana, also won nationwide political significance in these years. The Society had a membership of approximately six million, when, in 1935, Long was killed and the Reverend Gerald L. K. Smith took over its leadership. The Share-Our-Wealth clubs, proliferating across the land in the midthirties, were especially popular in poor-white farming regions of the South, similar to those areas in Louisiana in which the founder had first built his political empire. But it was not only in Dixie that discontented farmers of these times found an articulate champion of their interests.

Representative William Lemke of North Dakota, a leader of the Nonpartisan League earlier in the century, was perhaps the most powerful spokesman for the northern plains agrarian interests. As chief draftsman of the three Frazier-Lemke bills, which were designed to relieve the suffering of farmers stricken by the Depression, Lemke commanded a large audience throughout the Midwest.

It was these four most successful radical leaders, then, who gathered their followings under the banner of the new political party, the Union Party, and chose William Lemke as its presidential candidate.

In some ways, there is a striking similarity among these four men. All offered plans which would, it was claimed, solve most of the nation's economic and social problems. Their proposed panaceas depended upon the manipulation of money, and in this sense they were following in the path of those American radical reformers of the past, the Populists and the Greenbackers.

Father Coughlin would take the control of the nation's money out of the hands of private bankers and issue large amounts of unbacked currency from a new central bank. Huey Long and Gerald L. K. Smith would confiscate all large fortunes in the United States and redistribute the wealth, guaranteeing every family a comfortable minimum income. William Lemke would save the threatened farmers of America by having the government pay their mortgages through the issuance of billions of dollars of "printing press" money, with a fortuitous by-product being the stimulation and recovery of the nation's economy. Dr. Townsend would also save the nation while helping a special interest group — the large monthly pensions he proposed to give each old citizen would have to be spent each month by the recipient, and as a result of this dollar circulation, the American economy would revive and prosper.

In addition to the commonalities in their plans to save America, these radical leaders followed approximately the same pattern in their relations with Franklin D. Roosevelt and his administration. Coughlin, Long, and Lemke were all strongly pro-FDR in the 1932 election and campaigned widely in support of his candidacy. Townsend, appearing on the political scene too late to be a factor in 1932, also at first looked hopefully to Roosevelt for support of his crusade for the aged. All of them soon turned on the President, however, when they discovered that he was not prepared to do their bidding.

But among these leaders were many crucial dissimilarities as well, particularly in regard to the nature of their followings, the style of their personal and political operations and their basic motivations.

Father Coughlin's audience ranged across the spectrum of ethnic and economic groups in America, but dominating the ranks of his followers were Irish and German Catholics in the larger cities. Huey Long and Gerald L. K. Smith were best received in southern and lower midwestern agricultural regions. William Lemke appealed particularly to the populistic radicals among the farmers of the northern Great Plains. Dr. Townsend was popular among the aged of the West and, by 1936, was making strong inroads among these groups in the East and Middle West.

The variance in the political styles of these leaders also reflects the differences among their followers. Coughlin's pioneering artistry in the use of the radio enabled him to disseminate his ideas and stir emotions across a wide segment of the nation and to penetrate densely populated urban areas. Long and Smith were most effective at that crossroads-meeting type of oratory upon which southern rabble-rousers had depended for many years to generate a following among poor-white "redneck" farmers. Lemke was a less impressive speaker, but he was able to manipulate the symbols of populism well enough to persuade his audience. Townsend did not have to be an outstanding orator to spread his gospel; he merely had to look and act the part of a sincere old man who had an idea which could save the nation.

The fact that Lemke and Townsend were relatively inferior speakers is suggestive. For these two men owed their success to their programs— to the particular and powerful appeals that brought them a following despite their uninspired oratory. Coughlin, Long, and Smith were of a different breed. They were charismatic leaders whose rhetoric and personalities won them an audience for their programs—programs designed to appeal to the urgent needs of searchers for a panacea.

This difference is underlined by an examination of the careers of these men. Lemke and Townsend spent the rest of their lives fighting for the causes which brought them to national attention in the mid-thirties. Smith and Coughlin were always chamaeleon-like men in search of a movement that would bring them fame and power. Their names have been associated with many causes since the days of their greatest success.

The differences among the radical leaders of this period thus were striking. But in the summer of 1936 these points of variance were somehow suppressed and a coalition formed in which the men and movements could pool their strength. When these "little foxes," as James MacGregor Burns has called them, decided to strike for power through the vehicle of the Union Party, the whole nation took note. The strategists of the major parties eyed the new alliance with suspicion, and, in some cases, with fear.[1]

The radical leaders' growing distaste for Roosevelt and the New Deal had made the coalition possible. The compatibility of their monetary reform programs made it plausible. It was supposed that the differences among them could serve to divide and weaken the alliance, but that the wide diversity of their following and their campaign techniques might make the new party an even more attractive vote-winner. In the history of the United States, third parties had traditionally been

[1] James MacGregor Burns, *Roosevelt: The Lion and The Fox* (New York: Harcourt, Brace and Company, 1956), p. 209.

unsuccessful. But occasionally they had succeeded in swinging the balance of power from one major party to the other, and sometimes they had been responsible for a change in the political climate of the nation. Operating as they did in what was still a depression setting in 1936, the founders of the new Union Party had high hopes for their venture.

As the election campaign that summer got under way, the new party was widely considered to be a potentially important factor in the eventual outcome. If the Unionites could not sweep to victory themselves, they might at least deny the prize to the hated FDR. Certainly the Republicans could not be expected to do the job alone; indeed, the tired old party of Hoover and Landon had met in dreary convention only a few weeks before the exuberant Townsendites, and their uninspired performance showed that they would need much help.

But if the Union Party was to be truly effective in stopping Roosevelt, it would have to show its strength early and prove to the country that the strange alliance of the mass leaders was viable and enduring. So it was that journalists from every corner of the land converged on Cleveland in the convention summer of 1936. For it was in the meetings of the Townsend and Coughlin organizations that the power and problems of the new party would be exposed. Not only would the two great social action groups exhibit themselves before their largest national audience, but the curious political offspring of these angry men of the Depression, the new Union Party, would have the opportunity of dramatizing its own program and its own promise. Would it prove to be foolish or formidable?

The Townsendites met first. The procession of people—gray, simple, sixtyish, and poor—converged on Cleveland from all across the nation. Arriving in busses and railroad coaches and broken-down Fords, they came bringing battered suitcases and found dollar-a-night lodgings, rooms without baths in tourist camps in the city's outskirts. They traveled to the downtown convention hall in trolleys, eating fruit out of paper bags to save lunch money. Penniless but respectable, they had come as to a revival meeting to reaffirm their dedication to the cause.

The eleven thousand delegates who trekked in were, like the seven thousand at the previous year's Chicago convention, nondrinking, nonsmoking and Bible-reading people. Appropriately, they were greeted by a banner stretched across the width of the mammoth Cleveland Auditorium: "I Am Tired Of Overlords And Poverty. God Said: 'My People Shall Be Free.'" And everywhere the deification of Dr. Townsend was in evidence. Banners proclaimed "The Three Emancipators: Washington, Lincoln, Townsend." One speaker suggested that "God Almighty placed this great idea in the mind of one of his servants." Another enthusiast wondered why no star hung over Dr. Townsend's birthplace to "guide Wise Men of that generation to his side." The Townsend Plan, the promise of a $200 monthly pension to each of the nation's old people intoxicated the elderly physician's followers, and as the convention opened, the old folks were in a festive mood.[2] They talked excitedly of what they would purchase when the pension checks started coming through. Few of these delegates, the true believers of the organization, expressed any doubt about the successful outcome of their crusade. Yet for the present they remained poor old people. The men, coatless in the summer heat, wore wide suspenders holding up light-colored wash pants. The women wore cotton print dresses and out-moded hats. The city's merchants were complaining at the week's end that these people had bought record quantities of picture post cards, but almost nothing else.[3]

On the first day of the meetings, good fellowship overflowed. One man on the rostrum told everybody to shout "God bless you." Another instructed each member of the crowd to shake hands with the neighbor sitting at each side. The Reverend Clinton Wunder, Eastern Regional Director, proudly announced that two million new Townsendites had been recruited in his district in the preceding year. Another speaker boasted that one-quarter of a million new members had joined within the last month. The crowd beamed and applauded each cheering prog-ress report.[4]

But the warm glow was not to last. The convention's second day found Norman Thomas accepting an invitation to address the throng. The Socialist Party leader, after boldly telling the thousands of hard-core Townsendites that their precious plan was "a quack remedy which could not possibly work," was roundly booed for his efforts. But the next speaker did not fare so poorly. Representative Gomer Smith (D.-Oklahoma), a famous Midlands lawyer of Indian blood and a stirring orator, came forward to touch on the most sensitive issue of all.[5]

Smith was a power in the movement and had played a prominent

---

[2] Harry Thornton Moore, "Just Folks in Utopia," *New Republic*, LXXV, No. 1093 (November 13, 1935), 10; and Richard L. Neuberger and Kelley Lee, *An Army of the Aged* (Caldwell, Idaho: The Caxton Printers, 1936), pp. 37, 230.

[3] *Ibid.;* and Thomas L. Stokes, *Chip Off My Shoulder* (Princeton, N.J.: Princeton University Press, 1940), p. 414.

[4] *New York Times,* July 16 and July 18, 1936.

[5] *Ibid.,* July 17, 1936.

role in the Chicago meetings of the year before. Now he was angry at the recent developments in the organizational hierarchy and lashed out at the "evil forces" at work in the Plan. He blasted Father Coughlin and Gerald L. K. Smith, accusing them of trying to use Dr. Townsend for their own sinister purposes. He boasted that he could "out rabble-rouse" either one and even hinted that these "newcomers" had been sent to the Townsend Plan by the Liberty League for the purpose of sowing discord in the ranks. Bitterly attacking the Union Party and calling on the convention to rebuff the new party's nominee and endorse instead Franklin D. Roosevelt, he conveniently forgot that he had led the assault on the President at the 1935 gathering. He now called FDR a "church-going, Bible-reading, God-fearing, golden-hearted man who has saved the country from Communism."[6]

The crowd gave Gomer Smith a rousing ovation. A chagrined Dr. Townsend immediately took the microphone to insist that "poor Gomer" was a "troublemaker" and should not be applauded, and the permanent chairman of the convention stated that "there will be no more free speech at these meetings." But the trouble was not over. Martin F. Smith, a Washington Townsendite and a Democrat, told the delegates, "My friends, we are not going to 'lose with Lemke,' we are going to 'triumph with Townsend.'" Thus the whole delicate question of the pension movement's position in the coming campaign had been opened. By the end of the day, some fifteen state delegations had caucussed and voted against endorsement of Lemke.[7]

Townsend and Gerald L. K. Smith were prepared for this revolt. They had already decided on the course that the dissenters were now demanding: no official support by the movement of the new party. The leaders quickly pushed through a resolution stating that the Townsend organization could not endorse any presidential candidate of any party. But then the old doctor himself made it clear that he did not consider official endorsements important. He emphasized that no specific prohibition had been passed on the endorsement of a candidate by the Townsend Plan's founder. And there was to be no mystery about where the founder stood in the coming campaign. The remainder of the convention program had been scheduled well in advance: it consisted of a series of powerful speeches by the four principals in the Union Party.

Gerald L. K. Smith was the first of these speakers. A veteran organizer in several other mass movements who had only recently joined forces

[6] *Ibid.*

[7] *Ibid.;* and Celeste Strack, "Whither Townsendism?" *New Masses,* XX, No. 5 (July 28, 1936), 8–9.

with Dr. Townsend, Smith was having a fine time at the convention. He roamed the floor of the auditorium, shaking hands with the delegates and looking the part, as one newsman put it, of "the irrepressible young man smashing his way into the leadership of the plan." He joked with the reporters and even allowed one group to interview him from his bathtub. He obviously enjoyed giving interviews filled with explosive remarks certain to be quoted in the day's dispatches. He called the Democrats "peanut-headed Jim Farley stooges" and said that "if Roosevelt does win and then goes back again with his threats and his bribery, I'll impeach him. . . . I mean, I'll head a movement to impeach him." [8]

Smith's speech was perhaps the best of a career that had been built upon rhetoric; it was an oratorical tour de force. He had the old folks ringing their cowbells and shouting themselves hoarse at what a prominent journalist called "one of the finest rabble-raising, Bible quoting harangues ever given at a national convention." Even the men in the press section abandoned their posts and leaped upon their rickety desks to cheer the performance.[9] An astounded H. L. Mencken wrote:

His speech was a magnificent amalgam of each and every American species of rabble-rousing, with embellishments borrowed from the Algonquin Indians and the Cossacks of the Don. It ran the keyboard from the softest sobs and gurgles to the most ear-splitting whoops and howls, and when it was over the thousands of delegates simply lay back in the pews and yelled. Never in my life, in truth, have I heard a more effective speech.[10]

Smith spoke clutching a Bible in his left hand. Coatless, broad-shouldered, sweat plastering his shirt to his barrel chest, he roared words of hate about Wall Street bankers, millionaire steel magnates, Chicago wheat speculators and New Deal social engineers who "sneezed at the doctor's great vision." He issued a call to arms: "Too long," he shouted, "have the plain people of the U.S. let Wall Street and Tammany rule them. There are enough good people who believe in the flag and the Bible to seize and control the government of America." Reaching the climax, he bellowed:

We must make our choice in the presence of atheistic Communistic influences: It is Tammany or Independence Hall! It is the Russian primer or the

---

[8] Gerold Frank, "Huey Long the Second," *The Nation*, CXLIII, No. 4 (July 25, 1936), 94.

[9] *Ibid.*, p. 93.

[10] H. L. Mencken in Milton Crane (editor), *The Roosevelt Era* (New York: Boni & Gaer, Inc., 1941), pp. 193–94.

Holy Bible! It is the Red Flag or the Stars and Stripes! It is Lenin or Lincoln! Stalin or Jefferson! James A. Farley or Francis E. Townsend! [11]

As the crowd gave Gerald Smith a standing, screaming ovation, Father Coughlin, the next speaker, fidgeted nervously while awaiting his turn. Coughlin had sulked at the back of the auditorium through most of Smith's address. He had, of course, been pleased by the minister's attacks upon their common enemies, but he was clearly discomforted by the effective way in which his fellow leader captured the crowd. Smith carried on in the tradition of the crossroads evangelist of the rural South; he had mastered all the tricks of manipulating an audience.

Dr. Francis E. Townsend, the Rev. Gerald L. K. Smith, and the Rev. Charles E. Coughlin after speaking at the convention of Townsend followers in Cleveland, Ohio, August, 1936. *United Press International*

Coughlin's long training at the microphone had given him a velvet voice and a flair for the spoken word, but he was totally lacking in that dramatic gesturing which made Smith so compelling face-to-face. Jealous of his supposed ally's platform delivery, he now looked upon Smith as a rival in the struggle for the affection of the crowd—this crowd

[11] *Ibid.*

and the ones to follow throughout the campaign. And so, as Smith concluded, the priest prepared for some histrionics of his own.

Coughlin strode to the rostrum not from the rear, but down the center aisle of the convention hall. He began speaking slowly and calmly enough, telling the delegates in his luscious brogue that he had come not to persuade or dictate to them, but to say some things about the National Union for Social Justice and the Union Party. But midway through the forty-minute speech he began to step up the speed and volume of his voice as well as the tone of his content. He denounced the "money changers" of the Federal Reserve System and lashed out at the President for not fulfilling the promises of his inaugural address. Now sweating as freely as had Smith, he stopped for a shocking pause. Stepping back from the microphone, Father Coughlin peeled off his black coat and Roman collar, literally unfrocking himself before the audience of 10,000 people. Striding back to the rostrum he roared:

As far as the National Union is concerned, no candidate who is endorsed for Congress can campaign, go electioneering for, or support the great betrayer and liar, Franklin D. Roosevelt. . . . I ask you to purge the man who claims to be a democrat from the Democratic Party — I mean Franklin Double-Crossing Roosevelt.[12]

After a moment of stunned silence, the delegates stamped and shouted their approval of this vicious assault upon the nation's President. The long years of the Depression, the golden promises of Dr. Townsend, and the bitter frustrations that attended the blocking of the pension plan by the New Deal had turned these older Americans away from their elected governors. They had been told repeatedly to hate the White House, and now, at the pinnacle of the emotional buildup of the movement, they did what they had been told. They kept on shouting as Coughlin accused Roosevelt of "driving the farmers off their homesteads" and dismissed the Republican candidate as "poor Mr. Landon, the creature of three newspaper editors, who doesn't know whether he's coming or going." The din in the hall did not recede as the priest set up Townsend, Smith, and himself as a "trinity of hope" against the "unholy trinity of Roosevelt, Landon and Browder."[13]

[12] "Recovery Pensions," *Literary Digest*, CXXII, No. 4 (July 25, 1936), 6; and *New York Times*, July 17, 1936.

[13] *Time*, XXVIII, No. 4 (July 27, 1936), 18. The Browder referred to is Earl Browder, General Secretary of the Communist Party of the United States and the Communist Party candidate for President in 1936.

Now Father Coughlin made his bid for support of the new party. He said,

Ladies and gentlemen, you haven't come here to endorse any political party. . . . But there is Dr. Townsend and there is the Reverend Gerald L. K. Smith. By these two leaders I stand four-square. . . . The principles of the National Union, the principles of Dr. Townsend and the principles of Dr. Smith have been incorporated in the new Union Party. You are not asked to endorse it. Your beloved leader endorses it — how many of you will follow Dr. Townsend? [14]

The Townsendites stood almost to a man in response to Coughlin's question. Triumphantly the priest called his cohorts to his side. He wrapped his arm around Townsend's narrow shoulders and poked Smith playfully in the ribs. As they stood standing for group pictures, the four leaders of the Union Party vowed to win in the fall.[15]

Beside the oratorical pyrotechnics of Coughlin and Smith, Dr. Townsend's speech was tepid stuff. But his adoring followers did not seem to care. Mencken rightly called Townsend "one of the dullest speakers on earth," yet the delegates wildly cheered the old man as he praised the National Union for Social Justice and the Share-Our-Wealth organization and attacked the Administration, calling the New Deal the "antithesis of democracy." Demonstrating once again that beneath his wildly inflationist ideas concerning the plan there was rooted a deep conservatism, he lamented the fact that the national debt had risen to over $35 billion "under Roosevelt." But he said that in spite of FDR, "we are on the eve of a great world surge toward an ideal civilization . . . and the Townsend Plan has started this contagion of idealism." [16]

Yet the old doctor told his audience that "I do not want to wait fifteen years for the plan to go into effect . . . and the only guarantee against that is to elect a President who will sign the bill when Congress passes it." He said he "would never vote for Roosevelt; . . . it would be insincere to do so." He said that he would not vote for Landon. Making his position in the coming election clear to all of his supporters, he proclaimed:

Congressman William Lemke is an outstanding member of Congress. I did not put him in the field as a candidate. I did not organize the Union Party. I did not organize the National Union for Social Justice, the Share-Our-Wealth movement or the great Farmers' Union, all of which support him. . . . William Lemke voted for the Townsend Plan in Congress. In our national office we have his

[14] Social Justice (Royal Oak, Michigan), July 22, 1936.
[15] New York Times, July 17, 1936.
[16] Crane (ed.), p. 194; and New York Times, July 16, 1936.

signed pledge . . . to do everything in his power to secure the enactment of the Townsend Plan. . . . As the founder of the organization and the leader of millions of sincere men and women who desire the Townsend Plan enacted into law, I cannot do otherwise than support, work, and vote for William Lemke for President of the United States.[17]

At his speech's conclusion Dr. Townsend expressed the hope that "millions" of his followers would join him in backing candidate Lemke. And it was William Lemke who was the featured speaker on the last day of the convention. The meeting's organizers had hoped for a large crowd for the finale and had hired cavernous Cleveland Municipal Stadium. But many Townsendites decided to head home early and so the Union candidate faced a disappointing gathering of five thousand people who seemed lost among the 85,000 seats of the lakefront arena.

But Lemke was not speaking for only the Townsendites in the audience; he was speaking to every malcontent in the land. He had something for everyone—for the Coughlinites, he promised a Bank of the United States and the issuance of $5 billion worth of greenbacks. For the followers of Smith, he promised to "make every man a king." He assured the Townsend Plan members that "I am 100 per cent for an old age revolving pension," adding that he "stood four square with Dr. Townsend in his battle for the common people."[18]

Lemke's address marked the conclusion of the Townsend Plan convention, the high point of the year of the old folks' crusade and the first of the two huge meetings at which the Union Party alliance was cemented. Thus for Cleveland, the bizarre season of political evangelism was only half over. In mid-August, only a few weeks after the old folks had departed, more than 10,000 rabid followers of Father Charles E. Coughlin poured into town for the first annual gathering of the National Union for Social Justice.

Both the strengths and the weaknesses of the new Union Party were in evidence at Coughlin's convention, just as they had been at Townsend's. The leaders of the party praised each other and each other's programs; they hailed their new political organization and vowed to support it. Yet the air was faintly charged with tension and jealousy.

Father Coughlin arrived in Cleveland on August 13. He had to take two floors of a downtown hotel to accommodate the clerical staff of thirty who had accompanied him on the steamer trip from Detroit. Reporters

[17] *Ibid.;* and Francis E. Townsend, *Dr. Townsend Tells Why He Is Supporting William Lemke* (Chicago: J. W. Brinton, 1936), pp. 1–2, 12.

[18] *New York Times,* July 19, 20, 1936.

noted that at his first press conference he was nervous and uneasy. He apologized for having called FDR a "double crosser" and said that the President "of course should be respected for his office." When a news-man suggested that Roosevelt was trying to steal his thunder by visit-ing Cleveland on the first day of the convention for the ostensible pur-pose of viewing the site of the Great Lakes Exposition and touring some WPA projects, the priest angrily brushed aside the implication and termed the visit "merely a coincidence." [19]

His affability toward his old enemy was in stark contrast to the irri-tation exhibited toward his new friends. Asked if Townsend and Smith would be speaking at various National Union rallies around the country, Coughlin snapped, "I don't know why they should be tagging after me all the time." Only in discussing his first love, the radio, did his obvi-ous tension dissipate slightly on this opening day. He observed lightly of Landon that "every time he makes a radio speech he throws a mil-lion votes to Roosevelt. I mean that honestly." [20]

The priest's spirits raised perceptibly when the conventioneers be-gan pouring into the city. As he began to talk of his party's chances in the fall, his old fire returned and his mood became expansive: He an-nounced to the press, "If I can't deliver my radio audience—and that's 9 million voters—if I can't deliver them for Lemke and O'Brien in No-vember, I'm through. . . . I'll be a washout and I'll quit broadcasting. That's a promise." It was quite a promise.[21]

Coughlin was cheered by the sight of the ten thousand National Union representatives who greeted him on the first day of the meeting. Ap-proximately 40 per cent of the delegates were women, and the majority of them were Roman Catholic urbanites from the eastern and north-central states. Most had come very many miles just to see their beloved leader in the flesh. They wasted little time in turning the convention into an orgy of affection for Charles Edward Coughlin.[22]

When the priest first entered the packed auditorium, a huge portrait of him was lowered from the flag-draped rafters while thousands shouted themselves hoarse and hundreds paraded in the aisles carry-ing effigies of detested New Dealers. There followed a series of extrav-agant testimonials to Coughlin: One delegate shouted out, "Father Coughlin, test us, try us, LEAD us!" A man from Indiana seized the

[19] *Detroit News*, August 13, 1936.
[20] *Ibid.*, August 14, 1936.
[21] Jonathan Mitchell, "Father Coughlin's Children," *New Republic*, LXXXVII, No. 1134 (August 26, 1936), 73.
[22] *Ibid.*, p. 72; and *Time*, XXVIII, No. 8 (August 24, 1936), 23.

rostrum to point out that the priest's father was born in that state. A Kentuckian called him a second Lincoln. And an artist from Kalamazoo, Michigan, reported that in a thirty-six-hour period he had sold 11,500 reproductions of Father Coughlin's portrait at a quarter apiece, each done in "misty, saint-like pastels." Some speakers compared him to Christ; all endorsed a resolution proclaiming him to be "The Greatest American of All Times."[23]

Finally a Maryland delegate, amid frantic applause and obviously in the grip of almost unbearable emotion, proposed: "Resolved, that we give thanks to the mother of the Reverend Charles E. Coughlin for bearing him." The priest's hypnotic influence was everywhere in evidence. His followers cried, shrieked and moaned. Most of them were people to whom a radio was perhaps the only luxury and the greatest comfort. Week after week, Father Coughlin had scathingly explained that their Depression-born suffering was not their fault, that it had been caused by evil and mysterious forces personified by international bankers and brain trusters. They had wanted to believe him, and now they leaped up to vote for what was surely one of the most extraordinary resolutions ever passed by a national political organization in the American democracy:

In the conduct of the affairs of the National Union for Social Justice, we endorse, without any exception whatsoever, all the acts of our president and great leader, Father Charles E. Coughlin. . . . Finally, lest specification detract from the fullness of our sanction, we publish our unreserved and unqualified endorsements of all public acts, radio addresses and statements of our leader, pledging our resources and our activities in his support and in support of our 16 principles, even as he has thrown into the battle every ounce of his endurance.[24]

With such a display of adoration on the record, it was not surprising that the priest had things his own way in the business sessions of the convention. After being unanimously elected president of the organization, he found no opposition to packing the newly formed board of trustees with friends and subordinates, including his personal secretary. He easily pushed through resolutions attacking the League of Nations, supporting the Frazier-Lemke Farm Re-finance Bill, and denouncing American Federation of Labor President William Green, who

[23] *New York Times,* August 16, 1936; and Gerold Frank, "Father Coughlin's Fish Fry," *The Nation,* CXLIII, No. 8 (August 22, 1936), 208.
[24] *Ibid.;* and Heywood Broun, "Broun's Page," *The Nation,* CXLIII, No. 8 (August 22, 1936), 213.

had had the bad taste to criticize the Coughlin monetary program.[25]

Shortly before the convention, Coughlin had talked darkly of "up-starts" in the ranks of his movement "who are on kissing terms with Roosevelt, who . . . wish to make of me a Victrola disk . . . and who wish to relegate me to the graveyard of the has-beens." But the "up-starts" did not materialize. The only note of discord at the meetings— and a pathetic note it was—came on the vote to endorse William Lemke for President. John H. O'Donnell, an alternate on the Pennsylvania delegation, cast the only dissenting vote, and he was outnumbered 8,152 to 1. Coughlin made the most of the moment by forcing O'Don-nell to speak from the rostrum and then sending him from the hall, escorted by policemen, as the faithful shouted "Judas" and "How much did Farley pay you."[26]

In setting up the vote of confidence for Lemke, the priest made it clear that the National Union was endorsing a candidate and not a party. He took this action not so much because he wanted to avoid the stigma resulting from a bad defeat for the Union Party, but because a cutting little journalists' joke—that William Lemke was but a tool of the radio priest and that the candidate had been nominated "from a phone booth" with Coughlin on the other end of the line—had irritated him. Through withholding official endorsement he hoped to impress the na-tion that the new party was not the creature of any one movement.[27]

When the business of the movement had been attended to, the speak-ers took over. Coughlin had promised that "this convention is not go-ing to be an oratorical contest," but in a very real sense it was. The first speaker was the keynoter, Senator Rush Dew Holt (R.-W.Va.), a non-member of the National Union but one who claimed to "think its prin-ciples are essentially good." Holt held forth for ninety minutes on the evils of the New Deal and the glories of the sixteen points of social jus-tice. He was followed by Father Tobin of Verona, New York, who gave an illustrated lecture on the pitfalls of a private banking system, com-plete with lighted bulbs flashing in sockets on a large display board.[28]

But the convention began to move into high gear with the addresses by the four Union Party leaders, although Dr. Townsend, the first of the four, was unexceptional. The doctor's speech was very long and he read it in a monotone. By the time Townsend finished, it was about din-ner hour, and the delegates were tired and hungry. Coughlin, it seems,

[25] *New York Times,* August 16, 1936; and *Cleveland Plain Dealer,* August 16, 1936.

[26] *Social Justice,* August 10, 1936; and *Detroit News,* August 13, 1936.

[27] *Cleveland Plain Dealer,* August 16, 1936; and *New York Times,* June 21, 1936.

[28] *Ibid.,* August 15, 1936; and *Detroit News,* August 13, 1936.

had planned it that way. Gerald Smith had been scheduled to speak at this time and the priest, remembering the Townsend convention, hoped that his audience would be too weary to care what the explosive minister had to say. But Father Coughlin had underestimated his supposed ally. Within minutes, the sleepy Coughlin following had forgotten their fatigue.[29]

It was an exemplary demagogic performance. Said Smith:

> You sit and take it while I pour it to you; I'll tell you when to clap. I come to you 210 pounds of fighting Louisiana flesh, with the blood memory of Huey Long who died for the poor people of this country still hot in my eyes. . . . I'll show you the most historic and contemptible betrayal ever put over on the American people. . . . Our people were starving and they burned the wheat . . . hungry, and they killed the pigs . . . led by Mr. Henry Wallace, Secretary of Swine Assassination . . . and by a slimy group of men culled from the pink campuses of America with friendly gaze fixed on Russia . . . beginning with Frankfurter and all the little frankfurters. . . . They told the workers to organize under section 7a, and the U.S. government became the biggest employer of scab labor in the world — hold on now, I'll tell you when — and they had the face to recognize Russia, where two million Christians had been butchered and the churches were still burning. . . . This election to me is only an incident. . . . My real mission is to see that the red flag of bloody Russia is not hoisted in place of the Stars and Stripes — Give that a hand![30]

The crowd did give him a hand, and Coughlin was angry. Throughout the torrid speech he had squirmed in his seat, talked to his friends, grinned slyly at those around him, and elaborately pretended to go to sleep — anything to detract attention from the spellbinding Smith. But seldom had the Coughlinites heard all their favorite devils excoriated so neatly and so thoroughly. When Smith roared that a "kerenskyized" FDR was leading the nation down the road to "inflation, repudiation, and chaos," and added that "only the Union candidate" could save the nation, the crowd marched about and stamped its feet, shouting "We Want Lemke!" Smith had disturbed the radio priest, but he had provided a fine introduction for the next day's speaker, William Lemke.[31]

Lemke had been getting mixed press notices at the convention. Reporters were irritated when he told them that they would be "allowed to visit the new President in the White House" after March 4, despite

---

[29] *Ibid.*, August 16, 1936.

[30] *New York Times,* August 16, 1936. Smith's speech was so effective that Mark Sullivan, a well-known syndicated columnist, was won over. Said Sullivan: "Under the spell of his oratory, one felt that there was something fine and . . . justified in his indignation." See Broun, *The Nation,* CXLIII, No. 8, 213.

[31] Mitchell, *New Republic,* LXXXVII, No. 1134, 74; and *New York Times,* August 16, 1936.

the fact that "your newspapers don't let you print the truth." Yet they enjoyed hearing him make wildly boastful claims, and reprinted his vow that "I shall poll 15 million. . . . An underground swell is now becoming a tidal wave. . . . It will sweep me into the White House and Roosevelt and Landon into discard."[32]

For his formal address Lemke had been placed on the last day of the program, immediately preceding Father Coughlin's final speech. He had, as one observer put it, been "spotted next to closing like the star turn on a vaudeville bill." Over thirty thousand people were on hand in the Cleveland Municipal Stadium when Lemke, a bald-pated, grinning figure in striped galluses and a baggy gray suit, stood to speak.[33]

"The American people," said the North Dakota Congressman, "are going back to the democracy of Jefferson and Lincoln in November." He promised, when elected President, that "if Congress hesitates too much in going through with the mandate of the people, I'll keep them in continuous session for four years until they do. Oh, I'll let them go home once in a while to get acquainted with the constituents instead of Wall Street." The candidate was doing his best and the crowd cheered, but Coughlin spoiled the effect by walking across the grass to the platform in the middle of the ovation. When his followers spotted the priest, they turned their applause on him.[34]

Coughlin's speech was not in keeping with the tone of the convention. Most observers agreed that the emotional pitch at these meetings had been even higher than at the Townsend Plan gathering. The wrathful words of the Union Party leaders had swept across the auditorium, welding the thousands of delegates into a single angry spirit. When Coughlin had called for the audience to stand up, they had risen in one surging wave. When he called for clapping, the sound was deafening. When he called for an oath to uphold the National Union's constitution, ten thousand right arms shot stiffly out in a Nazilike salute while the words were repeated. But in his final address, Coughlin's energies seemed depleted. He spoke in the manner of a professor of economics delivering a lecture to freshmen. Obviously feeling that even with his exertions before the Townsendites, he had been unable to "out-rabble-rouse" Gerald Smith, the priest now returned to the pedantry which sometimes marked his radio speeches.[35]

[32] Frank, *The Nation,* CXLIII, No. 8, 204.
[33] *Ibid.*
[34] *New York Times,* August 17, 1936.
[35] *Ibid.,* August 15, 1936; and *Newsweek,* VIII, No. 8 (August 22, 1936), 11–12.

There were no surprises in the text of the address but there was a shock at the finish. As the priest was building to his climax, telling his audience that Roosevelt and Rexford Guy Tugwell were "communistic," warning them that the present political campaign would be a "war," and asking them to "go to your homes as to a trench," he suddenly wilted under the hot sun, stepped back from the microphone and collapsed with his speech still uncompleted. Father Coughlin was not seriously ill, but he was too ill to continue, and the convention was over.[36]

The meeting of the National Union, like its predecessor, had exposed strains in the alliance of the radical leaders. But it had also served to strengthen the new Union Party, and with its conclusion the organizers of the party could turn their thoughts and energies to winning votes in the coming election. John Nystul, the Unionites' political manager, announced to the press that last day in Cleveland that "the campaign can now officially get under way." This campaign, and all that went with it, was to be a memorable one.[37]

The threat posed by the Union Party was clear enough. When the great Depression cast its black shadow across America it was inevitable that many men would seek to build empires in the ashes of the old order by presenting themselves as messiahs and their programs as panaceas. But that any of these would-be saviors could master the art of mass leadership as effectively as did Coughlin, Townsend, and Smith shocked many citizens who had always felt that Americans, unlike Europeans, were impervious to the siren song of the demagogue. And when the radical leaders joined forces in a new party, the danger to democracy seemed all the more dire.

Yet it was not only that these demagogues offered a stern test for democracy's viability in the difficult Depression years. The nature of each of the radical movements—their economic, social and psychological appeals as well as their political programs—was suggestive of discontents in various sectors of the nation's life which went far beyond the material dislocations of the 1930's. In this sense, the social conflict stimulated by the movements was, in the words of one sociologist, both realistic and unrealistic. For it was not only the frustration of specific group demands that led to political confrontation but also the need for tension release occasioned by the strain of life in a highly mobile and competitive society.[38]

[36] *Detroit News,* August 16, 1936.
[37] *New York Times,* August 13, 1936.
[38] Lewis Coser, *The Functions of Social Conflict* (New York: The Free Press, 1964), pp. 49–50.

The muted rage of farmers who saw themselves losing out in the new urban and industrial society—a society which ridiculed the independent agrarian who had been honored in an earlier America—was one such strain. The anxiety and frustration which darkened the lives of second- and third-generation citizens who felt that their ethnic origins blocked movement upward was another problem. Yet another was the fear and despair experienced by elderly Americans, who confronted not only the privations of a Depression which devoured their savings but also rapid changes in a nation which they had helped build but no longer understood.

All across the United States the drama was acted out. The economic crisis had opened old sociopsychological wounds and helped create new ones, and into this scene of unhappiness and confusion moved the radical leaders. They served not only as salesmen of Utopia—promising quick solutions for the nation's ills—but also as merchants of revenge. For they would win the economic war and identify the aggressors as well. They would provide scapegoats for the hurt and bewildered. And they offered to right not only the new wrongs of the Depression but the older wrongs that so many felt had long existed in the social and economic arrangements in the land.

To study the demagogues' appeal in the 1930's is thus to probe a shadowy corner of the American character. One is tempted, of course, to draw the inevitable parallel between the growth of radicalism at home and the victory of the radicals abroad. It is true that Hitler's Nazi Germany and Mussolini's Fascist Italy were dramatizing the triumph of dictatorial rule in the very years that the American demagogues were making their bid for power. And certainly the world-wide Depression which gave the home-grown extremists their opportunity also provided the setting for extremists' rise to power in other great industrial states. But to push the comparison too far is probably to miss the point. For the radicals in the United States operated in a uniquely American arena in these years. All the tragic dissonances in American life—the polyglot nature of the population, the tensions and jealousies among economic, racial, religious and sectional groups, and the by-products of revolutionary alterations of major social and economic institutions—were involved in the rise of radicalism at home. To see the phenomenon as a reflection of what happened abroad is to reveal what is interesting, but to conceal what is vital.

For the rise of the demagogues in the Depression can shed light on the disturbing and continuing recurrence of radicalism in American life. The men and women who responded to the appeals of Coughlin,

Smith, and Townsend in the thirties were not necessarily the same as those who endorsed the Know-Nothings or welcomed the Red Scare in an earlier America, or who followed Senator Joseph R. McCarthy or joined the John Birch Society in more recent times. But many of the themes played out in the mass movements of the Depression can be found in those other extremist organizations. The economic crisis was a great time of testing for democracy. In marshaling support for their messianic programs, the radical leaders of the time capitalized on the weak points in the society. In forming their new political party, they sought to convert these weaknesses into power for themselves and their followers. Radicals have appeared and reappeared down through the decades of American history. But rarely have they offered such a crucial challenge.

BOOK ONE

THE ORIGINS
OF THE UNION PARTY:
THE LEADERS AND THEIR
MOVEMENTS

How does it happen that the masses sell their souls to leaders and follow them blindly? On what does the power of attraction of leaders over masses rest? — Franz Neumann, 1955

PART I

FATHER COUGHLIN
AND THE NATIONAL UNION
FOR SOCIAL JUSTICE

I glory in the fact that I am a simple Catholic priest endeavoring to inject Christianity into the fabric of an economic system which was woven together upon the loom of greed. . . . This pulpit does not and will not maintain a craven silence in the presence of protected iniquity. — Charles E. Coughlin, 1933

1

The Road to National Fame

The Reverend Charles E. Coughlin's rise to national prominence was meteoric. In 1927 he was an obscure Catholic priest living near Detroit, Michigan. Six years later his name was a household word throughout the country and prominent men sought his advice and support. His was a success story so typical of the recent past in America. For here was a boy of modest means whose quick wit and Gallic charm, fueled by a driving ambition, brought him fame and power at an early age.

But this spectacular and controversial career started not in the United States but in Canada, where Charles E. Coughlin was born on October 25, 1891, in Hamilton, Ontario. His father, Thomas Coughlin, was an Indiana native and a citizen of the United States but a member of a wandering family of lumberjacks and steamboaters. Son of an Irish immigrant of the midnineteenth century, he was working as a sailor on the St. Lawrence River when he fell ill and settled in Ontario to search for a job ashore. It was in Hamilton, where he was working as a church sexton at St. Mary's Cathedral, that he met the Irish seamstress who was to be his wife. Charles E. Coughlin was their only surviving child.[1]

Young Coughlin was raised in lower middle-class surroundings and imbued with the Irish-Catholic culture of his parents. He attended church schools in Hamilton and then St. Michael's College in Toronto, one of three sectarian institutions federated with the University of Toronto.

[1] Ruth Mugglebee, *Father Coughlin of The Shrine of The Little Flower* (Garden City, N.Y.: Garden City Publishing Co., 1933), pp. 8–9; and The Unofficial Observer (John Carter Franklin), *American Messiahs* (New York: Simon and Schuster, 1935), p. 37.

His academic record was brilliant. Particularly excelling in dramatics, religion, and philosophy, he was such an outstanding extemporaneous speaker that his classmates dubbed him "the orator." His senior term was largely devoted to the study of Pope Leo XIII's famous encyclical, *Rerum Novarum,* and other writings of socially conscious church leaders. His special interests, of course, would be particularly useful in later years. But if there were a fatal intellectual flaw in his early training, it was the meager scope of his formal study of American history and politics. The man who sought to change the course of American history and to make a revolution in American politics would come to his task unprepared.[2]

But the youthful Charles Coughlin was certainly not thinking in these terms when he graduated valedictorian of his college class and when, after a brief trip to Europe, he entered St. Basil's Seminary in Toronto in preparation for the priesthood. Once in the Basilian Seminary he plunged immediately into a deeper study of those questions which had fascinated him as an undergraduate. The Basilian Fathers' strict adherence and dedication to medieval philosophy was especially significant in the realm of economics. Coughlin's teachers defined usury as sin, insisting that economic relations be governed by the dictates of the Scriptures. It may have been from such views that Coughlin later derived his argument relating the evils of modern capitalism to the misuse of money. Also, the missionary zeal with which the man was to approach his role as a social and political leader of the masses almost certainly was developed in his years of priestly training.

After being ordained in June, 1916, Father Coughlin's first assignment was as a teacher of English and Classics at Assumption College in Sandwich, Ontario, a suburb of Windsor in the Detroit metropolitan area. But the 1918 Canon Law disbanding the Basilian Order soon forced a new clerical path on the young Coughlin, who chose to remain a secular priest and joined the Detroit diocese. Thus, in addition to his duties at the college, Father Coughlin now served as an assistant to pastors in various parishes in and around Detroit. Articulate and dynamic, he was soon in demand as a speaker at Rotary Clubs and Chambers of Commerce.[3]

In the autumn of 1923, Coughlin became assistant pastor of St. Leo's

---

[2] Victor C. Ferkiss, "The Political and Economic Philosophy of American Fascism." (Unpublished Ph.D. dissertation, Department of Political Science, University of Chicago, 1954), p. 168.

[3] Charles J. Tull, "Father Coughlin, The New Deal, and the Election of 1936." (Unpublished Ph.D. dissertation, Department of History, Notre Dame University, 1962), p. 2.

Cathedral in Detroit, the center of Catholic life in a city—the nation's fifth largest—which was 52 per cent Catholic. His sermons immediately won the praise of the Bishop of Detroit, Michael J. Gallagher. Few could doubt that this young cleric was destined to make his mark. In 1926, after having served for six months in the little farming community of North Branch, Michigan, the first pastorate of his own, Father Coughlin was called back to Detroit by Bishop Gallagher. There was a special task awaiting him.[4]

The Bishop had recently returned from the Vatican, where he had attended the ceremony of canonization of Saint Therese, a Carmelite nun of Lisieuz, France, who had died in 1879. This sainthood had fired religious fervor among Catholics everywhere, and Bishop Gallagher wanted to build a temple to Saint Therese's "childlike faith, humility, littleness." He chose Father Coughlin as the pastor of this new church in honor of the "Little Flower of Jesus." In view of his later career, it is ironic that Coughlin was chosen as the spiritual leader of a church dedicated to a saint who stood for the "little way" and who implored people to "remain little . . . [and] not be disquieted about anything."[5]

Royal Oak, Michigan, a suburb thirteen miles north of Detroit, was the site chosen for the Shrine of the Little Flower. This was a poor town, pockmarked by vacant lots, and located in the center of an area of current Ku Klux Klan activity. The ignorant and frustrated men who flocked to the Klan in the 1920's preyed on small groups of Catholics, and the tiny congregation of thirty-two Catholic families in Royal Oak were a natural target.[6]

Father Coughlin soon discovered that building the shrine would be his greatest challenge. The few parishioners could not supply sufficient funds to run the church and the Klansmen announced their presence by planting fiery crosses on its lawn. Desperate to increase the meager membership of his congregation and eager to strike out at the bigotry of the Klan, Coughlin searched about for a forum. Perhaps the driving ambition and love of public speaking that had marked his youth and training influenced his search. In any case, the young priest hit upon the idea of reading his sermons on the radio. Along the airwaves lay an invisible but potentially vast audience.

In some ways it was a curious decision. Radio was still in its infancy in 1926, and few clerics had ever used it. But when Father Coughlin's

[4] Raymond Gram Swing, *Forerunners of American Fascism* (New York: Julian Messner, Inc., 1935), p. 38.
[5] Mugglebee, pp. 152–54.
[6] "Father Coughlin," *Fortune*, LX, No. 2 (February, 1934), 35.

friend, Leo J. Fitzpatrick, manager of Detroit's WJR, a small and at that time independent station, suggested that Coughlin go on the air, the priest agreed. Bishop Gallagher gave his approval.

Fitzpatrick squeezed Father Coughlin into WJR's Sunday litany of jazz bands and ballad singers and cut the costs of buying radio time to accommodate the financial situation of the priest. Coughlin went before the microphone for the first time on October 17, 1926. Almost overnight it became obvious that what had begun as an experiment was to become an institution.

The mail response mounted rapidly. After a few weeks, five hundred letters following a Sunday sermon were considered routine, and by early 1927, an exultant Father Coughlin had to hire clerks to handle a flow of mail that was soon to reach four thousand weekly letters. The young clergyman's modest idea had tapped an enormous wellspring of public interest.[7]

Capitalizing on this interest, Coughlin organized the Radio League of the Little Flower to solicit contributions. Soon he was receiving more than enough money to support his church, whose membership grew rapidly, and to pay for radio time and clerical staff.

But the success which crowned Father Coughlin's early radio efforts was limited. Detroit newsmen did journey to Royal Oak to photograph the "radio priest" amidst his bagsful of mail, but this response was still only a shadow of what was to come. Coughlin's greatest achievements lay in the future. True fame and power awaited his entry into the political arena.[8]

From 1926 through the summer of 1929, the priest was little known outside the Detroit area, for in this period Coughlin's role was that of an orthodox, if extraordinarily articulate, cleric who happened to have access to a large audience due to the wonders of radio. His sermons were concerned only with religious topics. Weekly he would launch scathing attacks on hypocrisy or moral degeneration. His words, though warmly received, certainly did not make headlines. In those days of material prosperity and political apathy, Coughlin's listeners might have turned a deaf ear to stronger themes. But until he was prepared to address himself to political and economic questions, the radio priest would not become a national figure.[9]

All this was to change with the stock market crash in October, 1929.

[7] *Ibid.*, p. 36.

[8] Louis B. Ward, *Father Charles E. Coughlin: An Authorized Biography* (Detroit: Tower Publications, Inc., 1933), p. 30.

[9] Herbert Harris, "That Third Party," *Current History*, XLV, No. 1 (October, 1936), 77.

With the whole nation soon fixated on falling economic indices and turning in need and fear to its political leadership, Father Coughlin recognized an opening and quickly moved to take advantage of it. That fall he began to attack political and socioeconomic problems. His appeal thus broadened, his audience began to multiply. He purchased radio time in Chicago and Cincinnati and thus addressed a network of three stations when he spoke on Sunday afternoons. In 1930 he signed a contract with the Columbia Broadcasting System for a twenty-seven-week series of radio sermons over a chain of sixteen stations spread across the country. Now the parish priest seemed ready to play the role of a powerful political figure.[10]

Attacks upon Communism constituted a major theme during the 1929–30 broadcasting season, which ran from November to April. Listeners noted that his Sunday speeches had become punctuated with warnings and exhortations about political ideologies. On one occasion he admonished his audience that the great issue of the age was "Christ or the Red Fog." [11]

The following season, 1930–31, found Coughlin basing many of his texts upon the writings of Popes Leo XIII and Pius XI. These discussions of economic morality were mixed with others in which he vehemently attacked birth control and Prohibition, dual themes which disturbed his more liberal listeners.[12]

But the priest at first moved only slowly and tentatively toward political controversy. His first objects of attack were conventional scapegoats, and indeed, in late 1930 he lamented that "too many pulpits have become political rostrums, openly taking sides with party or government as if Jesus Christ Himself, were He living today, would be either a Democrat or a Republican. . . ." That Coughlin would hesitate before taking sides became apparent the next spring, when he told his listeners, "In these gentlemen [President Hoover and his Cabinet] we have lost no faith whatsoever." [13]

This timidity, however, was only a passing phase. All the radio priest needed was encouragement. When his audience responded with enthu-

---

[10] *Fortune,* p. 36.

[11] Ward, pp. 56–57.

[12] *Ibid.,* pp. 73–77. See also the reminiscences of John F. Patt, American radio pioneer and a WJR (Detroit) employee at the time of Father Coughlin's early broadcasts. Oral History Research Project, Columbia University, New York, N.Y., No. 59 (Radio Unit), p. 49.

[13] Charles E. Coughlin, *By the Sweat of Thy Brow* (Detroit: The Radio League of the Little Flower, 1931), pp. 56, 149.

siasm to sharper political thrusts, Coughlin made it clear that he felt no compunctions about turning his own pulpit into a political rostrum.

In 1932 he turned on Herbert Hoover. Coughlin at this time was developing his economic philosophy, in which the Wall Street banker was the devil. On February 14, 1932, he assailed the President as "the banker's friend, the Holy Ghost of the rich, the protective angel of Wall Street." The listeners loved it. Over 1,200,000 letters poured into Royal Oak following a sermon entitled "Hoover Prosperity Breeds Another War." [14]

It was now open season on everything associated with Hoover or Hooverism. Secretary of the Treasury Andrew Mellon was likened to Judas Iscariot for paying millions of dollars to bankers while the poor veterans were denied their bonuses. The President and his friends were seen as a "concrete example of the exploitation of the few by the insiders." [15]

So successful were these political sermons that two years after going on the national network, the priest was employing 96 clerks to struggle with an average of 80,000 letters per week. If there were any doubt that Father Coughlin's popularity was growing at an astonishing rate, it was dispelled by the response to a single announcement on KSTP (St. Paul, Minnesota) asking if the audience wanted to hear the Sunday programs. In a metropolitan area with a population of some one million, 137,882 people wrote and phoned the station and of them only some 400 said no.[16]

Coughlin suddenly had become a new shooting star in the American political firmament. Why had his impact been felt so quickly and so dramatically? One factor was that the cleric was riding the crest of a wave of public interest in radio. Radio prices had been drastically reduced as a result of technological advancements as well as the Depression in the early thirties. Between 1931 and 1935 these prices had been halved, making it possible for almost 70 per cent of American homes to be radio-equipped by the middle of the decade.[17]

Charles E. Coughlin was well prepared to exploit the medium's growing popularity. His years before the microphone had served as a

[14] Quoted in Mugglebee, p. 297.

[15] Nick Arthur Masters, "Father Coughlin and Social Justice — A Case Study of a Social Movement." (Unpublished Ph.D. dissertation, Department of Political Science, University of Wisconsin, 1955), p. 48.

[16] Ward, p. 30.

[17] Irving Kolodin, "Propaganda on the Air," *American Mercury*, XXXV, No. 139 (July 1939), 293, 298.

training ground for the development of oratorical techniques designed to make the most of this new means of mass communication. He was very much attuned to the problems and promises of radio speech. Every word in his discourse was written to be heard, not read. The imagery was carefully selected, and the priest's vague but powerful style was used to fullest advantage. Radio transmitted nuances and subtle emotions denied to print while at the same time tending to arrest in the listener the critical impulses that often would lead a reader to turn back to the dubious or imperfectly understood. Coughlin learned to manipulate his unseen audience as effectively as other mass leaders aroused their live audiences.

As his following grew larger, his technique grew more effective. His oratorical style became a blend of biting irony and well-ordered rhetoric, with a few popular wisecracks and vulgarisms thrown in along with the usual run of Biblical references. He found that the use of words such as "damn," "hot," "swell" and "lousy" added zest to his speech, his hearers enjoying them all the more because they came from the lips of a priest. These words gave warmth to his discussions of economic problems and brought him closer to his disembodied audience.

Finding that ringing assertions and righteous fury brought a far better response than the balanced and objective statement, he became a master at the coining of phrases designed to alarm his listeners, such as "Christ or chaos," or, somewhat later, "Roosevelt or ruin." He once even attempted to tie Communism to free love by proclaiming, "It is either the marriage feast of Cana or the brothel of Lenin!" [18]

Naming names was another important part of his radio technique. It was more dramatic and persuasive to assail J. P. Morgan or Kuhn and Loeb than simply "bankers," and better to point at Hoover and Mellon than "politicians." He discovered that personalities were attention-getters, and soon they were filling his speeches.[19]

But of all his oratorical tools, his musical voice was by far the most powerful. Warmed by a touch of Irish brogue, it could be high and plaintive or deep and solemn. He could use it like a violin, running arpeggios with it and making the listening experience a memorable one long after the trilled rrr's had faded away.

[18] Forrest Davis, "Father Coughlin," *Atlantic Monthly*, CLVI, No. 6 (December, 1935), 660–61.

[19] Coughlin justified the use of personalities on the ground that he was but imitating the Fathers of the Church who, in extirpating heresy, invariably made the heretic as uncomfortable as possible.

One listener called it

> . . . a voice of such mellow richness, such manly, heart-warming, confidential intimacy, such emotional and ingratiating charm, that anyone turning past it almost automatically returned to hear it again. . . . It was without doubt one of the great speaking voices of the twentieth century.[20]

With such a voice — "a voice made for promises" — Coughlin could give his florid rhetoric and smooth style tremendous impact. It enabled him to be first and foremost among that new genre of personalities created by the rise of the radio.

So it was that as the Depression deepened and the Hoover Administration dragged to a close in 1932, Charles E. Coughlin began his drive for national fame and power. Still a relatively young man of forty-one, he retained the stocky but powerful athlete's physique developed by years of playing and coaching football. His round face was still unlined behind the rimless glasses which had become a trademark. With his great personal charm and that magnificent voice, he was truly a striking figure as he moved from pulpit to politics.

The spirited response to this new political personality included money along with letters of praise for the radio priest of Royal Oak. By 1933 his listeners were contributing approximately $5 million yearly to the Radio League for the Little Flower — enough cash to pay all his bills and plan bold new ventures. (No one thought it unusual one Tuesday when he walked into a Detroit bank to deposit $22,000 in one-dollar bills which had arrived in the Monday mail following his weekly broadcast.[21])

Coughlin repeatedly reminded his audience that without contributions he would be forced off the air. Indeed, as his national network expanded to carry his message to more cities across the country, the bill for rental of radio lines climbed to $50,000 a week. With clerical staff salaries to pay and mailing costs to cover, Father Coughlin needed the generous support of his followers.[22]

But so generous was this support that after operational payments were met, the priest had enough funds to set up the God's Poor Society as a relief center to which Royal Oak's Depression victims could come for

---

[20] The quotation is from Wallace Stegner. See "The Radio Priest and His Flock," in Isabel Leighton (ed.), *The Aspirin Age, 1919–1941* (New York: Simon and Schuster, 1949), p. 234.

[21] *Fortune*, p. 34.

[22] Raymond Gram Swing, "Father Coughlin: The Wonder of Self Discovery," *The Nation*, CXXXIX, No. 3625 (December 26, 1934), 731–33.

food and clothing. He also found the means to build a huge Crucifixion Tower at his Shrine—a tower 111 feet high and made of granite and marble, costing over one-half million dollars. Plans were laid also for the construction behind the tower of a mammoth new Shrine Church, large enough to seat 3,500. There was, indeed, fame and money in radio sermons on politics.[23]

But there was also trouble. Radio networks, then as now, sought to avoid controversy, and Father Coughlin was rapidly becoming a troublesome figure. Although hundreds of thousands of his adherents wrote in his support, the Columbia Broadcasting System seemed more concerned with the much smaller number of protesting listeners, who were disturbed by his vitriolic attacks on the men and institutions they admired.

In late 1931, officials of CBS suggested that he tone down his sermons. Coughlin replied on his next program with an appeal for freedom of speech and a denunciation of censorship. More than 350,000 letters praising the priest swamped the network the following week. Despite this impressive display, CBS quietly dropped Father Coughlin from the program lists several months later. Network officials decided it would be safer to have nonpolitical preachers alternate on a new program, the Church of the Air.[24]

Coughlin was angry, and his fury was intensified when the National Broadcasting Company brushed aside an overture he made in its direction. He thought briefly of a lawsuit against CBS but dropped the idea when he found it feasible to rent time from a number of independent stations for the weekly sermons. This private network, organized by 1932, soon was reaching more listeners than ever were reached by the Columbia Broadcasting System.[25]

Father Coughlin used this radio rostrum to support Franklin D. Roosevelt. The broadsides the priest had fired at the Hoover Administration during the 1932 presidential campaign had helped the Roosevelt bandwagon. After the election, Coughlin drew ever closer to the new Chief Executive. He visited the White House on his frequent trips to the East and was a regular correspondent.[26]

---

[23] Mugglebee, pp. 177, 205, 265–67.

[24] *Fortune*, p. 37.

[25] Tull, p. 10.

[26] Coughlin continued to see the President after inauguration despite his reported statement, "You won't see me any more. This Roman collar won't do you any good around the White House." Marquis W. Childs, "Father Coughlin, A Success Story of the Depression," *New Republic*, LXXVIII, No. 1013 (May 2, 1934), 327.

His letters were exercises in adulation. In them he termed the President "magnificent" and "fearless" and affectionately addressed him as "the boss" or "the chief." Coughlin told Roosevelt, "You have done more than any person in the history of America to break down the barriers of prejudice." He prepared a form letter which he asked his followers to copy and send to FDR in their own writing containing such phrases as "I stand solidly behind you," "I appreciate what a terrific sacrifice you personally are making," and even, "I love you." Coughlin himself wrote the President that "unless you are a success I can never be considered one." [27]

But even in his wild flights of praise, the priest could not resist delivering lectures. He dispatched lengthy letters and telegrams to the White House filled with opinions on many presidential matters. Coughlin strongly supported most of the early New Deal measures, including the National Recovery Act, the relief acts, the public works program, and stock exchange regulation. He did not like the Agricultural Adjustment Act, damning the "Wallace-Tugwell slaughter of five million pigs." [28]

Most of all Charles Coughlin was concerned with what he called "the money problem," the issue he considered central to the Depression and its causes. In the vital area of monetary and banking arrangements, the radio priest convinced himself that Roosevelt agreed with his increasingly radical views.

The President, for his part, received the messages from his new and ebullient supporter warmly but cautiously. Franklin D. Roosevelt knew how many men sought the glamour and reflected glory attending a personal relationship with the supreme commander. Sensitive to the perils of commitment to individual admirers, Roosevelt, as shrewd and forceful a figure as any who had occupied his office, carefully parceled out his time and power. He welcomed the help of the influential Coughlin, but he certainly did not reciprocate in kind. And he made no promises to the priest concerning any specific policy.

Circumstances, however, would soon create the coincidence which seemed to give substance to Father Coughlin's fantasies. The President was searching for ways to stimulate an economy experiencing its darkest hours. He began to experiment with some policies, such as gold revaluation, which appeared to square with Coughlin's theories. But

[27] Letter of Charles E. Coughlin to Franklin D. Roosevelt, November 17, 1933, Coughlin to Marvin McIntyre, November 13, 1933, and Coughlin to Roosevelt, June 14 and September 24, 1933, in Franklin D. Roosevelt Papers (Franklin D. Roosevelt Library, Hyde Park, N.Y.) Official File 306 (Charles E. Coughlin). Cited hereafter as Roosevelt Papers.

[28] Coughlin to Roosevelt, August 5, 12, 16, and September 24, 1933, *ibid.*

the priest misread the signs, attributing the New Deal programs to his own influence. Convinced that FDR would do his bidding, he began to fancy himself the Richelieu of the Roosevelt era. And believing that as the power behind the throne, he should build popular support for the titular leader, he filled his sermons with praise of Franklin D. Roosevelt.

In 1934, Father Coughlin was still supporting Roosevelt and "Christian capitalism." *Wide World*

One of the distinguishing features of Charles E. Coughlin's political style was extravagance. Whether commending or condemning a man or institution, he always went too far. In 1933 and into 1934, Coughlin, in his own words, was "going the limit" for the President.[29]

[29] Coughlin to McIntyre, November 23, 1933, *ibid.*

"It is either Roosevelt or ruin," proclaimed the radio priest. FDR was leading the nation in the "Wall Street battle" next to which the Runnymeade of the Magna Carta and the Gettysburg of slavery were "indifferent happenstances." The President was "the new Lincoln leading the fight against financial slavery," and gathered around him were "enlightened men" such as Vice-President Garner and "the impressive, dynamic James Farley." [30]

Coughlin's followers were warned to expect no miracles, to allow time to take its course. Veterans were asked to refrain from demanding their bonuses and to give FDR time to straighten out other affairs of state. All were asked to pray for President Roosevelt, who was "America's unquestioned leader in the propagation of the faith." [31]

Enemies of the Administration, of course, were shown no mercy. Wealthy capitalists, laissez-faire economists and Al Smith were all denounced as trying to "stop Roosevelt, which equals stop progress." For the priest told his audience that everyone must get behind the President. "His is to lead. Yours and mine to follow. Lift aloft the flag of unity." [32]

Father Coughlin's outspoken support of Roosevelt and his Administration led many people to suspect some official connection between them. Angry letters arrived at the White House complaining that an inflammatory Catholic priest had been made "the mouthpiece of the Administration." Some Congressmen seemed to give substance to this charge when they suggested, in June, 1933, that Coughlin be appointed an economic adviser to the American delegation at the forthcoming London Economic Conference. Senators Elmer Thomas, William Gibbs McAdoo, and Huey P. Long and Representatives Emanuel Celler and Everett M. Dirksen were listed among the eighty-five members of Congress who petitioned the President on this issue.[33]

Despite the efforts of his friends in Congress, Father Coughlin was never considered by the Administration to be anything more than a helpful propagandist. As long as he was useful he was humored. But when he attempted to assume the role of an official spokesman for the New Deal, he was gently but firmly rebuffed. This was the case in the Detroit banking crisis of late March, 1933.

[30] Charles E. Coughlin, *The New Deal in Money* (Royal Oak, Mich.: The Radio League of the Little Flower, 1933), pp. 5, 75, 86, 116.

[31] Charles E. Coughlin, *Driving Out the Money Changers* (Detroit: The Radio League of the Little Flower, 1933), pp. 76, 80, 83–86.

[32] *Ibid.*, pp. 91–93.

[33] Henry C. Dietrick to Roosevelt, March 27, 1933, and Elmer Thomas to Roosevelt, June 9, 1933, Roosevelt Papers, OF 306.

The Union Trust Company, one of Detroit's major banks, had failed — thus endangering the city's banking community. Coughlin had gone on the air to oppose Reconstruction Finance Corporation loans to the still solvent banks, charging that the bankers involved had approved fraudulent loans to themselves in order to protect personal investments after the 1929 crash. Subsequent to these attacks, Secretary of the Treasury William H. Woodin appointed federal conservators to take charge of the resources of the two major banks.[34]

Father Coughlin decided that the Administration needed him to defend its policies in this controversy. He approached both Secretary Woodin and Presidential Secretary Marvin McIntyre, asking if they wanted him to respond to charges against the New Deal. Both gave equivocal answers. Nonetheless, the priest went before the microphones and boldly stated that he had been asked to speak for the President on this banking issue.[35]

McIntyre and others at the White House, embarrassed by the reaction, made it clear that Coughlin had taken "considerable liberties with the facts and had misstated the case." After the bank crisis experience, the Administration ignored subsequent Coughlin communications except for the most perfunctory acknowledgments, and even this courtesy was occasionally neglected.[36]

But there was no open split at this time between the radio priest and the Roosevelt Administration. With pro-Coughlin mail flooding the White House and with the priest's strength still unmeasured and hence impressive, the New Dealers did not want to alienate him but hoped simply to demonstrate by inaction the limitations on his influence.

Charles Edward Coughlin, rebuffed but not estranged by the Roosevelt forces, was content to go along with the President for a while. He would still call the New Deal "Christ's Deal." [37] For his economic theories and political aspirations were still being shaped. But once they were full grown, there could be no doubt that if he found it personally or politically useful, he would turn on Roosevelt as he had on Hoover. Every day he was growing more aware and confident of his power. He told a con-

[34] The affected banks were the Guardian National Bank of Commerce and the First National Bank of Detroit. The First National's President, E. D. Stair, was also publisher of the influential *Detroit Free Press*. Charges and counter-charges flew between Coughlin and Stair in a war of words. Stair called the priest "a religious Walter Winchell"; Coughlin said the publisher was "vicious and immoral." See Ward, pp. 97–98.

[35] McIntyre to Louis M. Howe, March 27, 1933, Roosevelt Papers, President's Personal File 2338 (Charles E. Coughlin), and *Detroit Free Press*, March 24, 1933.

[36] McIntyre to Howe, March 27, 1933, Roosevelt Papers, PPF 2338.

[37] *New York Times*, November 27, 1933.

gressional committee, "I think I know the pulse of the nation. . . . I get 150,000 letters a week." He told his radio audience that "the dictionary defines demagogue as 'the leader of the people.' I plan to be a demagogue in the original sense of the word." [38]

[38] Mugglebee, p. 325; and Ward, p. 190.

2

Shaping the Panacea

Before Father Coughlin could lead the people, he had to determine where to lead them. This decision was no small task, for consistency in political and economic thought was never one of his virtues. Indeed, he was one of the really prominent equivocators of the era—a few months or even a few hours often would find him taking both sides of many important issues. His early church training had taught him that the key to politico-economic reform was "the money problem," but even within that limited area he flirted with several panaceas before achieving the synthesis which became his economic philosophy of social justice.

Coughlin first called for the revaluation of gold as the only sure road out of the Depression. Later he dropped this theme, switching to a plea for the remonetization of silver. This cure-all was also discarded when the priest decided that only a publicly owned central bank, issuing large amounts of unbacked paper currency, could save the nation.

Although he kept changing the remedies, Coughlin's diagnosis of the disease did remain constant. The United States, he felt, was suffering from a starvation diet of money. The need was for more money and for cheap money. All of his economic nostrums were inflationary.

Coughlin's devils were as unchanging as his diagnosis. They were always the international bankers of Wall Street and Europe and the politicians serving these manipulators of money. The priest described them as selfish, heartless, and satanic creatures who cared not at all for the common man but were interested only in power and money for themselves.

These themes are, of course, recurring ones in the history of Ameri-

43

can reform movements. They are also familiar to readers of the more famous Papal Encyclicals of modern times. It was to these two traditions that Father Coughlin looked for inspiration and documentation.

On several occasions the radio priest praised the leaders of those movements in the past that had sought a managed and inflated currency to improve the economic status of debtor groups. He looked to the men who had fought brave but hopeless battles against the entrenched interests of their times as his historical forebears.[1]

Coughlin's radicalism was, indeed, indigenous to America. In this nation of democratic institutions and almost unlimited natural resources, discontented groups rarely advocated, as in Europe, class conflict and forcible overturning of the existing form of government. Instead, American radicals, eschewing revolution and feeling they could improve their lot by their own hands if opportunity were to be equalized, had often thought in terms of monetary reform. Believing that prosperity was denied them only because certain men made money and credit hard to obtain, these radicals had always been fascinated by the miracle of cheap money.

In the 1870's, the debtor community of the Middle Border, feeling, in Parrington's words, that "to allow the bankers to erect a monetary system on gold was to subject the producer to the money broker," turned in significant numbers to the National Independent or Greenback Party. Two decades later, the People's or Populist Party was to argue for the unlimited coinage of silver, which, like the Greenbacker's paper money, would inflate the economy. The Populist flailed the same devils as had their predecessors, pronouncing in the platform of their first national convention that "a vast conspiracy against mankind has been organized on two continents," leading to "colossal fortunes for a few . . . usurers." Populist leader "Sockless Jerry" Simpson and later, William Jennings Bryan, both spoke of the struggle between "the robbers and the robbed" and "the toiling multitude versus the money power."[2]

Coughlin's theories appeared to be grounded in good Catholic doctrine as well as in American history. Pope Leo XIII's encyclical, *Rerum Novarum*, was issued in 1891, the year of Charles E. Coughlin's birth. This encyclical replied to the challenge of Marx, bidding Catholic labor-

[1] *Social Justice*, April 3, 1936.

[2] Vernon Louis Parrington, *Main Currents in American Thought* (New York: Harcourt, Brace and Company, 1930), III, pp. 273, 281–82; John D. Hicks, *The Populist Revolt* (Minneapolis: The University of Minnesota Press, 1931), p. 440; and Richard Hofstadter, *The Age of Reform* (New York: Alfred A. Knopf, 1956), pp. 64–65, 70.

ing classes return to the mother Church. It reminded employers that labor was not chattel, that the worker possessed human dignity, and that wealth was a stewardship and not a right. Pope Pius XI forcefully restated this theme in his 1931 *Quadragiesmo Anno*. In it, Pius noted the "immense power and despotic economic domination . . . concentrated in the hands of a few" and called for more state control over bankers and industrialists.[3]

Coughlin made innumerable references to these papal pronouncements. He claimed that as a priest he must follow the papal lead and propagate the philosophy of social justice. He noted that some would term him "a clerical dabbler in economics and politics," but insisted that he did "not exceed the doctrine of Jesus Christ." He went so far as to say, "If I be a demagogue, so must be Leo and Pius."[4]

The papal encyclicals were, of course, much more sophisticated than the radio priest's interpretation implied. Coughlin used them only as a support for his rather simplistic antibanking harangues. His achievement lay not in twisting Church doctrine, but in wedding this doctrine to the radical thought of the American past. Thus he gave the appearance of operating in both a historical and a doctrinal setting. His arguments were additionally strengthened by the seeming corroboration of his ideas in recent economic thought and government action.

For over two decades public and private investigators had been raising questions concerning the ever-increasing concentration of economic power in the hands of a few Americans. Both the 1911 investigation of the money trust by the House of Representatives' Pujo Committee and the important Berle and Means study issued some twenty years later had alerted the nation to this potential danger. When the Senate Banking and Currency Committee in 1933 reported, after lengthy hearings, that some of the country's foremost bankers had been guilty of unscrupulous transactions and personal greed, the sinister pattern seemed to be clearly exposed. Thus could President Roosevelt attack the "economic royalists."[5]

Certainly the monetary shortage and credit freeze that marked the first part of the Depression decade gave Coughlin's followers a first-hand reason to doubt and distrust the banking system. Not only had millions of Americans lost their homes to banks in mortgage foreclosures, but

[3] Forrest Davis, "Father Coughlin," *Atlantic Monthly*, CLVI, No. 6 (December, 1935), pp. 661–63.

[4] Ward, p. 252; and Coughlin, *The New Deal in Money*.

[5] Adolf A. Berle, Jr. and Gardner C. Means, *The Modern Corporation and Private Property* (New York: The Macmillan Company, 1933), pp. 18–47.

even more millions had lost their deposits in the closing of banks. To these people, the system's slow and cautious response to the crisis, involving a reluctance to lend even to sound credit risks, was evidence not only of the incompetence but also the pernicious behavior of the financial leaders of the nation, the leaders Coughlin accused of obstructing social justice.

Indeed, the priest's belief in inflation as the way out of the Depression was more sound than the predilection of orthodox economists for deflationary action. Yet Coughlin's ideas were not to be confused with those of competent professional economists, led by the noted Englishman, John Maynard Keynes, who argued for controlled inflation. The radio priest thought that all the nation's ills could be cured merely by printing more dollar bills. The Keynesians, on the other hand, were concerned with one central idea, dazzling in its stark simplicity, that had to do with the behavior of capitalist economies during periods of depression. Keynes and his followers disputed the dictates of classical economics, pointing out that low wages, low prices and budget balancing would not necessarily save an ailing economy caught in a serious depression. Instead, Keynesians advocated strong government action to unbalance the budget through heavy spending and low taxes which would, in turn, stimulate consumer purchases and investment by private capitalists.

Coughlin was blind to the complexities of the new economics. He had had no solid training in the discipline, and his economic arguments were often vague and incoherent. But he fancied himself an expert: "I do not know everything, . . . Only as an economist am I sure." Thus could he approach with sublime confidence his search among economic programs for a panacea.[6]

His first fascination was with gold revaluation. During the 1932–33 broadcasting season he told his listeners that the United States monetary system was seriously distorted in two ways. First, there were not enough currency dollars in circulation for the amount of gold held in the national treasury. Second, the total of all debts was dangerously high, the result of the manipulations of international bankers who had fostered war loans, bond flotations and stock speculation. He explained that the top-heavy debt had caused currency hoarding leading to deflation and depression. The only way out, he argued, was the revaluation of the gold ounce.[7]

---

[6] Quoted in Walter Davenport, "The Shepherd of Discontent," *Collier's*, XCV, No. 18 (May 4, 1935), 13.

[7] Joseph E. Reeve, *Monetary Reform Movements* (Washington, D.C.: American Council on Public Affairs, 1943), pp. 138–39.

Coughlin turned the plea for revaluation into a crusade, listing Lincoln, Washington, and Bryan as his predecessors in the war against the gold brokers. When President Roosevelt finally decided to revalue gold, the priest called it the "dawnlight of a new era of economic independence" as a result of a battle "more important than a dozen Château Thierrys or a hundred Marnes." [8]

Devaluation, however, did not bring the massive dehoarding of currency and consequent inflation that Father Coughlin had predicted, and soon he was contradicting his earlier statements, denouncing gold revaluation for having "multiplied by billions the gold in the hands of the internationalists—the European Warburgs, Rothschilds and the rest of the . . . notorious financial Dillingers." In the fall of 1933, he turned to a campaign for the nationalization and free coinage of silver.[9]

Silver schemes were popular at this time. Columnist Walter Lippmann, veteran inflationist William H. "Coin" Harvey, foreign exchange specialist Rene Leon, and agrarian leader Milo Reno were toying with ideas for employing the "other" metal. Coughlin argued for symmetallism, the coining of silver and gold, explaining that by such a plan, the basic money stock would expand by several billion dollars and would help to nullify the domination of the international bankers who fattened, allegedly, on the gold scarcity.[10]

With his usual zest and colorful metaphor, the priest waded into the battle for silver. He lauded Senators Elmer Thomas and Burton K. Wheeler of the prosilver forces, and roasted the opposition, including Bernard Baruch and the "Tory press." Bryan-like phrases, such as "the god of gold must be destroyed," earned him the nickname, "Silver Charlie." [11]

Coughlin believed that President Roosevelt shared his penchant for silver. "Here is the prophecy: I believe the President is about to remonetize silver!" he proclaimed to his radio audience. But the priest was wrong. The President was adamantly against any mandatory silver-purchase programs and stripped such provisions from measures brought before the Senate by the inflationist bloc. Indeed, Secretary of the Treasury Morgenthau published lists of individuals and firms holding silver on January 31, 1934, successfully demonstrating that many of

---

[8] Coughlin, *The New Deal . . .* , pp. 41–43, 64; and Charles E. Coughlin, *Eight Lectures on Labor, Capital and Justice* (Royal Oak, Michigan: The Radio League of the Little Flower, 1934), p. 66.

[9] A. B. Magil, "Can Father Coughlin Come Back?" *The New Republic*, LXXXVII, No. 1125 (June 24, 1936), 197.

[10] Reeve, pp. 140–41, 243; and Charles E. Coughlin, "Inflation and Silver," *Today*, I, No. 11 (January 6, 1934), 7, 22.

[11] Coughlin, *The New Deal . . .* , pp. 38–49.

Father Coughlin, during one of his many visits to Washington, discusses inflationary legislation with Senators Elmer Thomas of Oklahoma (center) and Patrick McCarran of Nevada. *Wide World*

those who argued that the nationalization of silver would be good for the country really meant that it would be good for them. Prominent on this list was Miss Amy Collins, holder of five million ounces of silver futures and treasurer of Father Charles E. Coughlin's Radio League of the Little Flower.[12]

Coughlin was shocked by what he considered an unprovoked attack by the Administration. Bitterly complaining that Secretary Morgenthau's investigation "smelled to high heaven," he insisted that silver holdings were just one of many League investments. But soon after the disclosure, the radio priest turned his attention from silver.[13]

As he prepared to launch the drive for his next and last inflationary scheme, the final formulation of his economic panacea, Coughlin gathered around him his own brain trust of money reformers. These advisors helped provide the statistics, names of enemies, and economic arguments with which his speeches bristled.

Father Coughlin's boyhood friend, foreign exchange broker Frank Keelon, introduced him to the principal members of the brain trust,

[12] Coughlin, *Eight Lectures* . . . , p. 114; and Reeve, p. 69.
[13] Masters, p. 109.

namely, George L. LeBlanc and Robert M. Harriss. LeBlanc, sometime Wall Street banker regarded as a visionary in financial circles, was associated with many "cheap" money plans in the Depression period. So, too, was Harriss, a wealthy New York commodity broker with an interest on the cotton market. These two men saw in the radio priest an articulate spokesman for their ideas.[14]

Coughlin also profited by contacts with several other inflationist thinkers. He met with members of the Committee of the Nation, a pro-inflation group headed by business executives Frank A. Vanderlip and James H. Rand. Two radical monetary spokesmen from Congress, Senator Elmer Thomas and Representative Louis McFadden (D.-Penna.) frequently had his ear. Miss Gertrude M. Coogan, author of *Money Creators,* and the Reverend Dennis Fahey, Irish college professor and money reformer, also helped shape his notions on economics.[15]

Armed with this plethora of advice and undismayed by the failures of his gold and silver campaigns, Father Coughlin turned at last to the crusade for a central bank and the issuance of currency unbacked by precious metal.

The radio priest had always detested private bankers. Their purpose, he argued, was to create a money scarcity. It was they who had caused the great Depression by inflating the economy with "check book" money and then recalling their so-called loans. These loans had cost the bankers nothing, for they were made with "stage money" created by "the purple fountain pens" of financial manipulators. Yet when the loans were recalled, hard currency was demanded, and if that were not available, then the houses, farms and factories which were held as security. But the bankers didn't care. These heartless men never visited hospital wards or even liked babies; there were no "pictures of the cradle in their offices." "Oh rob, steal, exploit and break your fellow citizens," Coughlin cried. "Every time you lift a lash of oppression you are lashing Christ!"[16]

[14] Jonathan Mitchell, "Father Coughlin's Children," *New Republic,* LXXXVII, No. 1134 (August 26, 1936), 73; and *Fortune,* pp. 37–38.

[15] A. B. Magil, *The Truth About Father Coughlin* (New York: Workers Library Publishers, 1935), p. 24; John McCarten, "Father Coughlin: Holy Medicine Man," *American Mercury,* XLVII, No. 186 (June, 1939), 139; and Gertrude M. Coogan, *Money Creators* (Chicago: Sound Money Press, 1935), pp. 42–53, 173–310. McFadden is best remembered for having delivered the only anti-Semitic speech in the history of the House of Representatives and for having been impeached. Miss Coogan later charged that Coughlin took her ideas and gave her neither credit nor royalties. See Leighton, p. 242.

[16] Charles E. Coughlin, *A Series of Lectures on Social Justice, 1935–1936* (Royal Oak, Michigan: The Radio League of the Little Flower, 1936), p. 154; Coughlin, *Driving Out . . . ,* pp. 22, 37–39; and Coughlin, *Eight Lectures . . . ,* p. 30.

Of all the banking culprits, by far the most dangerous and despicable were the international usurers, those "sellers of foreign bonds and establishers of bank balances in various countries." He told his followers that these men were incredibly powerful; indeed, they were "the rulers of the world, dominating and controlling the economic and social life of any nation." [17]

The priest demanded government action to check the international bankers. He dismissed as "fraud" the public representation on the board of the Federal Reserve System, charging that its banks were under the control of the House of Morgan and a few other giant private institutions, which were in turn the "hired servants" of English international bankers. Moreover, the Federal Reserve System operated in "violation of constitutional law," which provided that Congress should control the coining of money.[18]

As an alternative, Coughlin proposed a government-owned central bank with an elected board of directors which would represent every state in the union. This new Bank of the United States would have jurisdiction over all private banks and would possess sole authority to issue currency. The priest insisted that only his bank could preserve a stable price level, for, after calling in all other forms of currency, it would print and circulate new money, backed not by gold but by "the real wealth of the nation." To the charge that the new dollars would be worthless, Coughlin replied, "It is just a pure absurdity to say that you cannot have currency money if you have not got gold upon which to base it." [19]

Professional economists were unimpressed by the radio priest's arguments, noting that he could not possibly be aware of the complexity of money control problems if he blamed all the ups and downs of the business cycle upon the deliberate manipulations of the credit supply by a small coterie of international bankers. They certainly rejected his thesis that these bankers had caused the Depression. As one prominent economist has written, "Bankers yielded, as did others, to the blithe, optimistic and immoral mood of the times, but probably not more so." Large numbers of economists did endorse reforms in the banking system, such as the ones effected by the President in the first months of

---

[17] Charles E. Coughlin, *Money! Questions and Answers* (Royal Oak, Michigan: Social Justice Publishing Company, 1936), pp. 156–60.

[18] *Ibid.,* p. 34; and Coughlin, *The New Deal . . .* , pp. 29, 60, 81, 114.

[19] Wilfrid Parsons, "Father Coughlin and the Banks," *America,* LIII, No. 7 (May 25, 1935), 150; and Reeve, p. 142.

his Administration, but few if any would support the radical changes growing out of simplistic and sometimes absurd notions of the amateur from Royal Oak.[20]

But opposition would not still the voice or blunt the enthusiasm of Charles E. Coughlin. As part of his "frontal attack upon the depression," he vowed that the private bankers would be beaten and hinted darkly, "If we cannot do it one way, I swear to God that we will accomplish it another way." Not that the priest was advocating undemocratic methods in combatting his enemies. At this juncture in his career he continued to give lip service to the idea of democracy. He did occasionally warn, however, that American democracy was becoming a "plutocracy in which . . . the power of wealth dominates."[21]

In arguing for his reforms, the priest also maintained that he was not rejecting capitalism; indeed, he claimed to be "no Socialist, no Communist, no Fascist and against . . . any un-Americanism." But capitalism, while "perhaps the best system of economics provided it does not run counter to the laws of morality," was being corrupted in the United States. The capitalist now refused to share profits with the laborer. The few at the top were becoming ever more wealthy and powerful while labor and agriculture lay at their mercy. With monopoly the rule and free competition only a memory, capitalism had been transformed into a vicious caricature of its former self. If modern capitalism were not quickly reformed, Coughlin warned, there would be "bloody revolution" and a consequent Communist takeover.[22]

The radio priest's invocation of the spectre of Communism was both confused and confusing. The cleric despised Communism because of its rejection of religion and its domination by "internationalists." Yet he feared that capitalists, "privately sustaining in some instances the worst elements of Communism," would in a mysterious way provide the setting for a Communist coup. The only way to ward off this disaster was to wrench power from the international capitalists and create a system which he called "state capitalism." This program would have Coughlin's monetary reform scheme at its center, but would also involve the public ownership of those things which were "too important to be entrusted in private hands." He neglected to define just what

[20] *Ibid.*, pp. 140–45; Wilfrid Parsons, "Father Coughlin's Ideas on Money," *America*, LIII, No. 8 (June 1, 1935), 174; and John Kenneth Galbraith, *The Great Crash* (Boston: Houghton Mifflin Company, 1954), p. 184.
[21] Charles E. Coughlin, "How Long Can Democracy and Capitalism Last?" *Today*, III, No. 10 (December 29, 1934) 6–7.
[22] Coughlin, *The New Deal . . .* , p. 55; and Coughlin, *Money . . .* , pp. 79–85.

these things might be; in fact, he opposed the Tennessee Valley Authority, although the reason was not entirely clear. His plans were obviously vague and inconsistent in all areas outside the "money problem." [23]

In shaping his panacea, Father Coughlin tried to make specific appeals to several special interest groups. Farmers were told that they would be freed from the tyranny of Wall Street and the financial East. He declared to veterans that they were being made sport of by bankers, and that when his plan was implemented, they would at last be appreciated and paid their well-deserved bonuses. Labor was courted in a variety of ways. The priest promised to improve the working man's status by leading the fight for an annual living wage and for a shorter work week. But Coughlin did not support the existing union power structure. He attacked the American Federation of Labor for "class bigotry" and for failure to abolish child labor. He even attempted to start his own union during the labor strife which accompanied the A.F. of L.'s attempt to organize Detroit's auto factories.[24]

Part of Coughlin's appeal to special interest groups lay in his provision of scapegoats. Bankers, big businessmen and European intriguers were, of course, his favorite devils. But the priest also occasionally made use of the traditional anti-Semitic stereotypes. It would not be until November, 1938, that Coughlin would begin his all-out campaign against the American Jewry. Yet in the early and midthirties, the cleric's associates knew him to be personally anti-Semitic and a possessor of an elaborate library on the subject. He might claim to be the friend of the Jew and on occasion brag about his Jewish listeners, but statements such as "don't forget this is a Christian nation — let's not overwork this democracy," and labels such as "bad international Jews," and "gentile silver" (as opposed to Jewish gold) make it clear where he stood on the subject.[25]

But Coughlin carefully avoided going too far down the road of anti-Semitism. He did not want to offend those liberals who might still remain in his audience in 1934 and 1935, and he certainly did not want to bring upon himself the opprobrium which the inevitable comparisons with Adolf Hitler would invite. He therefore masked his anti-Semitism and rarely did more than hint at a "Jewish problem." Some Jewish

---

[23] Coughlin, *Eight Lectures* . . . , pp. 69–90; and Wilfrid Parsons, "Father Coughlin and Social Justice," *America*, LIII, No. 6 (May 18, 1935), 131.

[24] Coughlin, *Eight Lectures* . . . , pp. 81–127; *New York Times*, January 26, 1936; and "Coughlin vs. A.F. of L.," *Business Week*, I, No. 306 (July 13, 1935), 15.

[25] Coughlin, *Driving Out* . . . , pp. 56–58; and Dale Kramer, "The American Fascists," *Harper's Magazine*, CLXXXI, No. 9 (September, 1940), 390.

organization protested his veiled allusions, but this did not become a real issue until 1938.[26]

The radio priest was as skillful in his manipulation of hate symbols as he was in his appeal to pressure groups. His political style, like his economic program, was not evolved overnight, but was years in the shaping. By late 1934, the Coughlin personality and the Coughlin panacea were full grown. The new question: What would be the public's response to its appeal?

[26] *New York Times,* March 17, 1935.

3

Father Coughlin and
His Followers

To Americans of the midthirties, Charles E. Coughlin was a conspicuous figure. Like him or not, everyone had heard of the radio priest. *Fortune* magazine reported, "So far as the response of his audience is concerned, Coughlin is just about the biggest thing that ever happened to radio." [1]

Radio men estimated that up to thirty million people listened to the priest each Sunday—if only ten million did so, this still would have been the largest radio audience in the world. No clergyman since time began had regularly addressed a following of such dimensions. One observer noted that by 1934 Coughlin already had reached more people than all of Christ's disciples. [2]

Father Coughlin attracted far more listeners than did Gracie Allen or Rudy Vallee; and his mail exceeded that of such other radio preachers as S. Parkes Cadman or Harry Emerson Fosdick by one thousand to one. He bragged that he had on file the names of two million correspondents, adding, "I believe I possess in them the greatest human document in our time." [3]

To handle a greater volume of mail than that of any contemporary American private individual or institution, the priest had to increase his stenographic staff to 145. (The basement of his Shrine tower looked like a modern post office for a middle-sized city.) His own printing press

[1] *Fortune*, p. 34.
[2] Kolodin, *American Mercury*, XXXV, No. 139, 293, 298.
[3] Swing, p. 56.

produced millions of copies of the weekly sermon to fill mail requests.

Coughlin's correspondents wrote not only to laud his political and economic views but to ask advice for all manner of personal problems. And if the radio shepherd did not have time to attend to all the cares of his flock, he did have efficient assistants to write his replies and pluck checks from the countless envelopes. For the money kept pouring in. In early 1935 Postmaster General Farley sent the President a report on Coughlin's financial affairs in which the Royal Oak post office revealed that in twenty months the cleric had cashed over $4 million in money orders—enough money to allow the Radio League of the Little Flower a handsome surplus which it used not only for contributions to various Michigan charities but for investments in auto stocks and government bonds. While this may have been inconsistent with Coughlin's well-advertised criticisms of interest-bearing bonds and bondholders, it was certainly lucrative.[4]

The priest found the money also to hire outside researchers. He not only put a secret group of Washington correspondents on his payroll, but paid students at Brookings Institute as much as $400 each for papers on economic topics. In addition to the reports regularly provided by his brain trusters, Coughlin also heard frequently from tipsters (called "vigilantes") spread across the country. All this information was carefully collated and added to that which he himself culled, mainly from close scrutiny of the *Congressional Record*. From all sources he collected enough material to fill several filing cases in his own special reference room in the Tower.[5]

Father Coughlin was constantly besieged by visitors to his Shrine. In addition to the faithful, numbering thousands every day in the summer, who came merely to view the building and the man, there were many people who wanted interviews. Sometimes visitors were not entirely certain whom they were visiting; for example, an attaché from a legation in Washington arrived in Royal Oak under the impression that the priest was connected with the government.[6]

But Coughlin's guests, whatever their political persuasion, invariably found themselves liking the charming and effusive man who greeted them at the Shrine. The radio priest seemed to draw his questioners with him into the realm of his most personal concerns. While

[4] William L. Slattery to James A. Farley, March 19, 1935, Roosevelt Papers, OF 306; John L. Spivak, *Shrine of the Silver Dollar* (New York: Modern Age Books, 1940), pp. 88, 159; and Ward, pp. 210–300, 317–40.

[5] Davenport, *Collier's*, XCV, No. 18, 13.

[6] Childs, *New Republic*, LXXVIII, No. 1013, 326.

some visitors found the candor superficial, and observed that this remarkable man was given to role playing even in the intimacy of private
conversation, others saw him as "the builder of the church," and still
others as "the martyr who is being misunderstood." To a few he presented himself simply as a social philosopher. One reporter concluded,
"Perhaps there is no real Father Coughlin."[7]

But there was a real Charles E. Coughlin. He was the man who
worked in the sixth floor office at the top of the Tower, ensconced behind the several locked doors which opened only by means of secret
pressure on a push button. To this room, equipped with bed and stove,
he would retire each week end to write the radio sermon. With several
assistant priests caring for the needs of the congregation, he could devote full time to the political and economic affairs that interested him
most. For unlike other clergymen, he could not be satisfied with the
spiritual leadership of the few; he had to be the political leader of the
masses. The real Father Coughlin was a demagogue.[8]

He was a demagogue not only in the original sense of the word, as he
would have it, but in every sense of the word. He fitted the classic dictionary definition of "one who acquires influence with the populace by
pandering to their prejudices or playing on their ignorance." Certain
that he had discovered the panacea for all the nation's ills, he was willing to use any means to achieve his ends.

He once shocked an interviewer by remarking,

> Do you know how I would live if I renounced religion and was illogical
> enough to disbelieve in a life beyond? Why . . . I would surround myself with
> the most adroit hi-jackers, learn every trick of the highest banking and stock
> manipulations, avail myself of the laws under which to hide my own crimes,
> create a smoke screen to throw into the eyes of men, and believe me, I would
> become the world's champion crook. . . . I would get everything for myself that
> I could lay my hands on in this world.[9]

Coughlin, of course, was not a thief nor was he interested in accumu-
lating wealth for hedonistic purposes. But his unpriestly statement hints
at the lust for power that always seethed beneath the surface. In the
fanatic drive to gain his goals, he was to ignore both the rules of rational
discourse and the norms of democratic politics. This was revealed time
and again; first in his speeches and writings and later in his actions as
political leader.

[7] Swing, pp. 50–52.
[8] *Current Biography* (New York: H. W. Wilson Co., 1940), p. 199.
[9] Quoted in Mugglebee, p. 127.

The radio priest's sermons were flowery, emotional, and misleading. He knew all the tricks of the propagandist, from name calling to glittering generality. A favorite Coughlin technique was the dramatic dichotomy, in which "modern bands of exploitation" were aligned against the "little children, ill-clad mothers, care worn fathers . . . on the bleak, blizzardy countryside." The "widows and orphans and inarticulate farmers" would be at the mercy of the "devouring hordes" of the enemy if not for Charles E. Coughlin, who offered himself as the defender of ". . . servant girls, . . . laborers, (and) children." Indeed the priest never missed an opportunity to tell his followers of the great personal peril, perhaps even physical danger, he was risking by fighting their battles for them. He might, for example, exclaim that he had "sacrificed the right of natural . . . fatherhood to be the spiritual father . . . to thousands of boys . . . on the snow clad dunes of the Dakotas." [10]

Using picture images to manipulate the most incendiary symbols of the time, Coughlin was trying to seduce his followers into a personal allegiance to himself as leader and savior. And he made it clear that for him there could be no middle ground: "You are either with us or against us," he warned; "you can't be indifferent." [11]

As evidence mounted that many thousands of people were not remaining indifferent, but were choosing to join the radio priest in his new crusade, inevitable questions were raised concerning the true Coughlin disciples. The shepherd of Royal Oak thought that the answer was clear enough; he said, "I speak for the little man." In fact, this was no idle boast, for the hard core of his following was found among those industrial workers, farmers and small businessmen particularly hard hit by the Depression. Yet there were many "little men" in America in the thirties and surely not all of them responded to the appeal of Charles E. Coughlin. The more suggestive question, then: Which ones followed the priest, and why? [12]

Almost all ethnic and religious groups were represented in his audience. (Coughlin even claimed that he was helping to break down the prejudice of Protestants against the Catholic Church.) Among Protestant listeners, there was evidence that he had greatest impact in agrarian Scandinavian and German circles. For example, a high percentage of Congressmen petitioning to send the priest to the London Economic

---

[10] Alfred McClung Lee and Elizabeth Briant Lee (eds.), *The Fine Art of Propaganda, A Study of Father Coughlin's Speeches* (New York: Harcourt, Brace and Co., 1939), pp. 23–96; Coughlin, *The New Deal . . .* , pp. 8–9; and Coughlin, *A Series of Lectures . . .* , pp. 173–78.

[11] Coughlin, *Eight Lectures . . .* , p. 99.

[12] Magil, *New Republic*, LXXXVII, No. 1125, 196.

Conference were from Midwestern districts with predominately German or Scandinavian populations.[13]

Yet these were only notable exceptions. For it was clear that Coughlin's strongest appeal was to an urban group—particularly, Irish or German Catholics of lower middle-class origins. Gravely hurt by a Depression which had shattered their expectations of social and economic mobility, these Americans responded by the thousands to the magnetism of the radio priest. It was in areas where they were heavily concentrated that the majority of local units of the National Union for Social Justice were organized; it was over their signatures that most of the pro-Coughlin mail was sent to President Roosevelt and to Father John A. Ryan, an important critic of Coughlin within the Church.[14]

Father Coughlin's Catholic followers saw him as a symbol of their class and an articulate spokesman for their interests. They were not especially religious; indeed, there seemed to be a strong strain of anti-clerical feeling and hatred of the Church hierarchy among them. Yet most were highly sensitive to the discrimination Catholics had experienced in this country and apparently felt that it was sinful for a Catholic to disagree with Father Coughlin, for this divided the group in an hour of crisis.[15]

Most influential American Catholics, however, did disagree with Coughlin's programs and policies. They were, of course, aware of Pope Pius XI's appeal for social justice; in fact, a department of social action had been set up as part of the National Catholic Welfare Conference with Father Ryan as director. But the radio priest's activities went far beyond what many clergy and lay leaders felt to be safe and proper.[16]

[13] Swing, p. 43; and "Ex-Jesuit Insists Radio Priest Is Pope's Envoy," *Newsweek,* V, No. 24 (June 15, 1935), p. 22. *Newsweek* quoted the Methodist-Episcopal weekly, *Michigan Christian Advocate* on how effectively Coughlin was breaking down religious prejudice against Catholics.

[14] Schlesinger, Jr., p. 26; and James P. Shenton, "The Coughlin Movement and the New Deal," *Political Science Quarterly,* LXXXII, No. 3 (September, 1958), 360–66. New York and Massachusetts had four times as many National Union units as did Minnesota and Wisconsin.

[15] Wilfrid Parsons, "Father Coughlin: The Aftermath," *America,* LIII, No. 12 (June 29, 1935), 275–76. Nathan Glazer and Daniel Patrick Moynihan in *Beyond the Melting Pot* (Cambridge, Mass.: The M.I.T. Press, 1963), p. 266, note that a "distinctive quality of the anti-New Deal Irish during the 1930's is that they tended to identify the subversive influences in the nation with the old Protestant establishment." The lower ranks of the New York Irish were especially attracted by Father Coughlin's notions about social justice and Wall Street bankers.

[16] Michael Williams, "The Priest of the Radio," *Today,* I, No. 6 (December 2, 1933), 17. Ryan, a noted economist, made some favorable remarks about the radio priest in late 1933, before Coughlin turned against the President. See Tull, p. 64.

Boston's Cardinal O'Connell was the first to speak out, referring to "this spectacularly-talking man . . . popular in a false cause . . . [who] makes hysterical addresses." Coughlin, never easily intimidated by authority within or without the Church, returned the fire by criticizing the Cardinal's "notorious silence on social justice" and suggesting that "the opposition of a certain cardinal is natural if one will speak publicly the truth against great wealth." [17]

But the Cardinal was not alone. The Chancellor of the New York Archdiocese joined the attack by reprimanding the priest for speaking in that city without asking permission of diocesan authorities. Behind this procedural issue lay the furor Coughlin had stirred up through his accusations that former Governor and leading Catholic layman Al Smith (who had called him a "crackpot") was a lackey of J. P. Morgan. The respected and liberal Catholic journal of opinion, *Commonweal,* and the Protestant weekly, *The Christian Century,* scolded the priest for this outburst, and a Brooklyn cleric called on the authorities to silence the man who "thrived only on the applause of morons and the rabble." [18]

But Coughlin knew that he was virtually safe from censorship. That a priest in America could express his private views free of fear of discipline had been established half a century earlier, when the Vatican intervened directly to restore the rights of an excommunicated priest who had been banished for his radical political views. Only his bishop could officially silence or discipline Coughlin. But the Bishop of Detroit, Michael J. Gallagher, strongly supported the activities of the most famous member of his diocese.

Bishop Gallagher met weekly with Father Coughlin to review the manuscript of the next radio sermon. He stoutly defended his priest against attacks from within the Church and without, praising Coughlin's "sound philosophy" and "keen intellect," stating, "I regard him as a world leader; his arguments cannot be refuted nor can his method be withstood." [19]

While Father Coughlin's supporters in the Church dwindled in direct

---

[17] *Boston Pilot,* April 18, 1932; and Charles E. Coughlin, *A Series of Lectures on Social Justice, 1934–35* (Royal Oak, Michigan: The Radio League of the Little Flower, 1935), p. 70.

[18] "Dangers of Demagogy," *Commonweal,* XIX, No. 6 (December 8, 1933), 144; and "Father Coughlin and Ex-Governor Smith," *The Christian Century,* L, No. 57 (December 13, 1933), 1564.

[19] Ward, p. ix of introduction by Bishop Gallagher; and Father Coughlin's Friends, *An Answer to Father Coughlin's Critics* (Royal Oak, Michigan: The Radio League of the Little Flower, 1940), p. 6.

ratio to his increasingly radical statements, some contemporaries questioned this allegiance of bishop to priest, suggesting that the young, eloquent, and powerful Coughlin was dominating the older man. Others noted Gallagher's own fervent belief in social justice—his strong support for the concept of the priest in politics and his close friendship with the statesman, Monsignor Ignaz Seipel, who had ruled postwar Austria. But whether it was priest or bishop who reigned in Detroit, it was soon obvious that no Church authority would stop Father Coughlin. Leading Catholics might fear and resent his emotional appeal, but he was still free to continue to win converts with it.[20]

Win them he did, through ever more colorful and inflammatory orations. But while his mastery of radio technique was perhaps a necessary condition for his achievement, the real key to Coughlin's success lay in his ingenious exploitation not only of the economic problems his audience confronted but also of the old social and psychological wounds that the Depression had reopened.

For the lower middle classes—small tradesmen, clerks, white collar workers, poor farmers, and skilled laborers—the Depression had been a shocking and humiliating experience. The loss of business, farm, job, or home, the necessity at last to go on a government "dole," had political repercussions both severe and far-reaching.

Some of these Americans had been traditionally conservative in social affairs, emulating the richer middle classes in their attitudes toward capitalism. But the depreciation of property values and their own personal losses during the crisis destroyed their sense of security. It was in this setting that they turned to the radio priest, who advocated some form of property equalization (via his monetary schemes) without a disturbance of basic property relations. Thus could their individualistic ideology, shaken but not destroyed, be reconciled to a changed situation.

Like the followers of a later-day demagogue, these disciples of Coughlin were not right-wing conservatives with substantial power in the business community. Instead, they were often small businessmen who feared and mistrusted concentration and control in government or business. Lacking institutionalized roles on the political scene, they looked in time of crisis to a leader whose boldness and aggressiveness would combat the power and arrogance of the "big shots" and bureau-

---

[20] Franklin, p. 51; and Davis, *Atlantic Monthly*, CLVI, No. 6, 661–64. Bishop Joseph Schrembs of Cleveland and Archbishop Francis Beckman of Dubuque, Iowa, remained loyal Coughlin supporters.

crats while not threatening the capitalist system to which they sub-scribed.[21]

Among other Coughlinites, the political tradition had been strung on a strong thread of liberalism—especially for the German-Americans who could trace their origins back to the 1850 migration of German revolutionaries. These groups too had cause for unhappiness with the performance of the established Democratic and Republican party lead-ers. The reforms of the New Deal failed to satisfy many; the NRA codes, for example, were anathema to the man who was proud that his father had helped form the Milwaukee Socialist organization. Coughlin's radical proposals and dedicated opposition to "the interests" spoke more directly to these Americans.[22]

Whether their persuasion was to the left or the right, the priest's followers found something attractive in his economic panacea. More-over whatever their politics, they felt that Father Coughlin represented their last and best hope in a world that suddenly had started to crumble. Certain sociologists have suggested that when men find their present and future painful to behold, when their belief systems begin to de-teriorate, they may search about for a strong leader. In a situation of acute anomie, they will, under "pressure of anxiety . . . , attempt a solution which sets up the family pattern of political relationships." They will seek succor in a single figure who claims to be able to control the environment. That person will be endowed, in Max Weber's phrase, with "charismatic authority," the belief that he possesses extraordinary, even magical powers which will save them in their hour of greatest need.[23]

The confident and dynamic Charles E. Coughlin, bearing authority

[21] Reinhold Niebuhr, "Pawns for Fascism—Our Lower Middle Classes," *American Scholar*, VI, No. 2 (Spring, 1937), 145–49; and Edward A. Shils, *The Torment of Secrecy* (Glencoe, Illinois: The Free Press, 1956), pp. 92–93, and Martin Trow, "Small Businessmen, Politi-cal Tolerance and Support for McCarthy," in Lewis A. Coser (ed.), *Political Sociology* (New York: Harper & Row, 1967), pp. 188–200.

[22] To some historians, especially those on the "New Left," Coughlin's radical alterna-tive to the "conservative" New Deal was the primary reason for his success. Protest being a rational response to exploitation and inequality, one need only observe the deprivations of the depression to discover the popularity of the radical leaders. See Barton J. Bernstein's essay, "The New Deal: The Conservative Achievements of Liberal Reform," in Barton J. Bernstein (ed.), *Towards a New Past: Dissenting Essays in American History* (New York: Pantheon Books, 1968), pp. 271–72.

[23] Sebastian De Grazia, *The Political Community, A Study of Anomie* (Chicago: The Uni-versity of Chicago Press, 1948), pp. 171–83; and H. H. Gerth and C. Wright Mills (eds.), *From Max Weber: Essays in Sociology* (New York: Oxford University Press, 1958), pp. 52, 246–47, 262–63, 295–96.

as a priest of the Church, seemed to be such a leader. In this limited sense he resembled the *prophetae* of revolutionary messianism in medieval and Reformation Europe, who, Norman Cohn tells us, "set themselves up as divinely appointed leaders" offering followers "not simply a chance to improve their lot and escape pressing anxieties" but also the prospect of carrying out a mission of stupendous importance. To many of his followers Coughlin looked like a millennial saviour and to most he was a father figure. At the convention of his National Union for Social Justice, speakers simply referred to Coughlin as Father: "Father says, . . . Father thinks, . . . Father told us." The woman who nominated him for president of the organization stated, to frantic applause, that "for those of us who haven't a material father, he can be our father and we won't need to feel lonesome." The letters sent to the cleric's critics also dramatically revealed the pitifully personal dependence his followers often felt.[24]

But certainly there were other men who arose during the Depression to serve as personal and political leaders for the masses of scared and confused citizens. Why did Coughlin's followers turn to him rather than to FDR or to other reformers? One explanation would focus on the way in which he offered not only instant salvation in place of liberal evolutionary change, but provided a conflict situation in which the angry members of his mass movement, echoing Georg Simmel, might feel mastery and vitality in confronting their enemies and in overcoming their role as victims of circumstance. The priest's vitriolic style satisfied for his supporters those feelings, heretofore dormant, which had been fomented by the economic crisis. It was, no doubt, the hard cutting edge of hatred that made his rhetoric so popular.[25]

Franz Neumann has suggested that when groups within a society are unsure or threatened in their position, income or very existence, they may, under pressure of great need, convert the real anxiety caused by their discomfort into "neurotic anxiety." Hatred and resentment can then be focused on certain individuals who are denounced as devilish conspirators; anxiety can be overcome by means of identification with a leader.[26]

Coughlin seemed well attuned to this social dynamic. His assault on banker and big businessman, his denunciation of the wealthy, Angli-

[24] Jonathan Mitchell, "Father Coughlin's Children," The New Republic, LXXXVIII, No. 1134 (August, 1936), 73, and Norman Cohn, *The Pursuit of the Millennium* (New York: Harper & Row, 1961), pp. 315–19.

[25] Georg Simmel, *Conflict and The Web of Group Affiliations* (New York: The Free Press, 1954), p. 19.

[26] Franz Neumann, "Anxiety in Politics," *Dissent* (Spring, 1955), II, No. 2, 135, 141.

cized, eastern elite, and his covert anti-Semitism constituted, when juxtaposed with his romantic vision of the small farmer, small business-man, and white and blue collar worker, a skillfully designed appeal to urban Irish and German Catholics and midwestern farmers of the old Populist strain. Rich, well-educated easterners were the real villains: "Congressmen from New York City," the "Wall Street attorney, the erudition of Harvard, of Yale, of Princeton, of Columbia," the bankers with their "grouse hunting estates in Scotland" who never traveled west of Buffalo. For the poorer urban Catholic or impoverished western farmer, this was explosive material; he was often willing to turn his socioeconomic unrest into hostility toward individuals or institutions he was told had caused him suffering and denied him access to a better life.[27]

In Peter Viereck's words,

The stress on revenge for having been humiliated and patronized intel-lectually and socially (and economically) . . . has often been shared by im-migrants in Boston and the East (and, one could add, Midwestern cities) as well as by Populist older stock in the West.[28]

The Catholics who became Coughlin's disciples had long memories. The prejudice against the Catholic Church has been called, by historian Arthur M. Schlesinger, Sr., "the deepest bias in the history of the Ameri-can people." For almost a century American Catholics had been vic-timized by various forms of social and economic discrimination because of their religion and because of the fear and hostility elicited by their membership in Irish, Italian, German, or Polish ethnic groupings. From the Know-Nothings who terrorized Irish immigrants in the 1850's to the Ku Klux Klansmen who rode the old nativist trails again in the 1920's, anti-Catholics posing as "anti-aliens" had soured the lives and poisoned the memories of generations of Catholics.[29]

In the Depression decade, this oppressive heritage became more ap-parent. Social scientists documented what was obvious to the Cough-linites: among Roman Catholics there were more in the lower class and fewer in the upper class than among other groups in the population.

[27] Coughlin, *The New Deal . . .* , pp. 8–9; and Coughlin, *A Series of Lectures . . .* , pp. 173–78. For discussions of the connecting links between urban Catholics and midwestern farmers, see Peter Viereck's essay in Daniel Bell (ed.), *The New American Right* (New York: Criterion Books, 1955), pp. 93–94; Peter Viereck, *The Unadjusted Man* (Boston: The Beacon Press, 1956), p. 205; and Shils, pp. 84–85, 103–04.

[28] Viereck, p. 193.

[29] John Tracy Ellis, *American Catholicism* (Chicago: The University of Chicago Press, 1955), pp. 123–38, 148–52. See p. 149 for quotation from Schlesinger, Sr.

The plight of Coughlin's followers seemed to be exacerbated by the recollections of past wrongs. Startling notes of personal distress in letters written by them were often colored by anguished searchings for scapegoats. As wrote Wilfrid Parsons, editor of an influential Catholic periodical and himself a member of the clergy, after reading the mail which followed his series of critical articles on the radio priest, "The motivation of Father Coughlin's followers is almost entirely one of hatred." [30]

There may even have been also a strain of what Richard Hofstadter has called "pseudo-conservatism" among the Catholic supporters of the messiah from Royal Oak. For although these followers retained a high degree of religious and ethnic identification, they were second, third, or fourth generation Americans who were very much involved in the race for success in a mobile society. Failure in this race carried with it a heavy cost, far beyond the obvious material deprivations. In a culture in which success was not merely a matter of acquisitive instincts rooted in human nature, but, as Robert K. Merton noted, a "patterned expectation regarded as appropriate for everyone," the corollary of the self-made man was the self-unmade man. The failure was more than an unfortunate loser, he was in a sense morally damned, having shown he lacked the capacities and stamina which the American value system demanded of its chosen people. [31]

The status anxieties of such parents would have been inflicted upon the children, and in Hofstadter's words, "an extraordinarily high level of achievement expected of the children in order to relieve the frustrations and redeem the lives of the parents." For these children, the expectations appeared in the form of an exorbitantly demanding authority, "resistance and hostility to which having to be suppressed only to reappear in the form of an internal destructive rage." Thus the pseudoconservative felt himself dominated and imposed upon, and knowing of no other way of interpreting his position, he might imagine that the wealthy and powerful men of the nation, perhaps even his own governors, were engaged in a continuous conspiracy against him. Craving the status and position that he had lacked since boyhood, he might, under pressure of an added economic problem, turn his anger on those

[30] Parsons, *America*, LIII, No. 12, 275–76. For treatments of Catholic economic and social status in the social science literature, see Liston Pope, "Religion and the Class Structure," in Reinhard Bendix and Seymour Martin Lipset (eds.), *Class, Status and Power* (Glencoe, Illinois: The Free Press, 1953), pp. 316–19; and Hadley Cantril, "Educational and Economic Composition of Religious Groups," *American Journal of Sociology*, Vol. 47, No. 5 (March, 1943), p. 576.

[31] See Richard Hofstadter, "The Pseudo-Conservative Revolt," in Bell (ed.), pp. 41–50; and Robert K. Merton, *Social Theory and Social Structure* (Glencoe, Illinois: The Free Press, 1957), pp. 167–68.

objects of authority and social position that he had always envied and feared.[32]

This argument was made, of course, in reference to the supporters of Senator Joseph R. McCarthy in the 1950's. And although some writers, otherwise congenial to this interpretation, would distinguish between status politics in the more affluent fifties and interest politics in the depression thirties, this dichotomy will not do in analyzing the radical movements of the Roosevelt era, whose success was rooted in the problem of life in America, and not only the America of economic disaster.[33]

There were many and complex reasons why Coughlin's urban Catholic followers wanted revenge. The radio priest, in channeling their anger, promoted a kind of inverted nativism. The hunted of the past could now be the hunters. Those who had suffered because, in truth or in their own fantasies, they had been considered unequal by the older and richer groups, could now turn the tables on the oppressors. If, as Coughlin argued, the wealthy Anglo-Saxon Protestant elite of the East Coast were a gang of internationalists and exploiters, then his own followers were at last vindicated. They were more honest, more democratic, and more American than their enemies. And as such they well deserved the brand of social justice offered by Father Coughlin.[34]

[32] *Ibid.* Hofstadter's argument was made in reference to the supporters of Senator Joseph R. McCarthy, but a careful reading of the nature of Coughlinism suggests that, with some changes, it can be usefully applied to a study of the earlier movement.

[33] See Daniel Bell (ed.), *The Radical Right* (Garden City, New York: Doubleday & Company, 1963). Nor is it persuasive to dismiss the status politics argument as manifesting a "suspicion of the people," a fear of radical protest and mass democracy, as do some who celebrate the politics of radical confrontation and reject the analysis of latent and/or irrational forces at work in some mass movements. See, for example, Michael Paul Rogin, *The Intellectuals and McCarthy: The Radical Specter* (Cambridge, Mass.: The M.I.T. Press, 1967), pp. 3, 7, 272, 282.

[34] Nativism has many definitions. Anthropologist Ralph Linton describes it in one of its forms as an effort to "compensate for frustration of society's members . . . to maintain or re-establish self-respect of a group . . . in face of adverse conditions." This would seem to fit the Coughlinites. But where Linton distinguishes between the nativism of dominant and dominated groups within a society, his analysis is less satisfactory. The "dominated" out-groups responding to the radio priest did not fall back on a celebration of their unique and superior group characteristics (as do certain black nationalists today), but identified themselves with "Americanism" and the "dominant" group of wealthy anglicized easterners with the foreign devil. John Higham, one of the most sophisticated contemporary students of American nativism, sees status rivalry among ethnic groups at the core of nativistic movements (focusing primarily on the "defensive nationalism" of the in-group), but perhaps overstates the case against "irrational myths" coloring the "objective conditions" of such status competition. Much of Charles E. Coughlin's rhetoric could be viewed as appealing to the irrational myth of a new chosen people. See Ralph Linton, "Nativistic Movements," *American Anthropologist*, XLV (1943), pp. 230–40; and John Higham, "Another Look at Nativism," *The Catholic Historical Review*, XLIV (July, 1958), pp. 147–58.

Yet the urbanites would not be the only ones to profit. For Charles E. Coughlin couched his arguments in the vocabulary of Populism, and it was not surprising that some western agrarians, Protestant as well as Catholic, responded to his appeal.

There were limits to his attraction for radical farmers. His Roman collar and citified delivery would always cloud the image he tried to project to them. But his exorcising of the old Populist villains often made its mark. For Populism was, in addition to a crusade for economic reforms, a status revolt on the part of agrarians who saw their traditionally high position in American society usurped by urbanite leaders of the new business culture. As with his Catholic supporters in the metropolitan areas, Coughlin offered the western farmers not only money and power, but revenge. The devils for both groups were the same.[35]

In the end, the radio priest was so successful in playing on the fears and resentments buried in certain sectors of the population that some observers, noting a similarity to the hate-filled emotional appeals of contemporary European dictators, expressed the fear that Father Coughlin had the makings of an American fascist.[36]

These observers missed the point. Whereas the priest's career from 1938 to 1944 was influenced by fascism or Nazism, in the years 1932 to 1936, the time of his greatest success, his appeal was rooted not in any foreign ideology, but in his ability to utilize for his own ends social and economic tensions existing in the great, heterogeneous republic. Coughlin's program and technique were not imported. They grew out of the American soil and fed on uniquely American problems.

By late 1934, Charles E. Coughlin's star was rising. "No thinking Democrat could ignore the possibility that [he] might bridge the gulf between the rural Protestants and the urban Irish Catholics, groups

---

[35] Hofstadter, pp. 123–30, describes Populism as being in large part a status revolution. Not all historians agree. For example, in C. Vann Woodward, "The Populist Heritage and the Intellectual," *American Scholar* (Winter, 1959–60), pp. 60–66, there is a discussion of Populism as "agricultural interest politics" in which status worries were negligible factors. Woodward also suggests that Populism had only a marginal appeal in the middle west and that the main thrust of its impact was felt in the South. He denies that there can be any connection between Populism and the demagogues of the 1930's or later. See also Rogin, p. 267.

[36] See, for example, David Carl Colony, "Dictator Coughlin, Fascism Under the Cross," *The Forum*, XCIII (April 1, 1935), 196; Raymond Gram Swing, "Father Coughlin, The Phase of Action," *The Nation*, CXL, No. 3626 (January 2, 1935), 9; and Percy Winner, "Fascism at the Door," *Scribner's Magazine*, XCIX, No. 1 (January, 1936), 35.

whose antagonism had disrupted the party in 1924." No thinking American could do other than look with foreboding if this pied piper of the disaffected decided to stop supporting the policies of the Administration and began to strike out on his own.[37]

[37] Shenton, *Political Science Quarterly,* LXXIII, No. 3, 354.

4

Organizing for
Political Action

Some time between 1933 and 1935, the ominous portent became a reality. Father Coughlin broke with the New Deal and went on to become one of the nation's most powerful and persistent critics of Franklin D. Roosevelt. To understand these developments, one might well consider a parallel and closely related phenomenon: the creation of the National Union for Social Justice.

Coughlin announced the birth of the National Union in a radio sermon on November 11, 1934. Listeners that Sunday afternoon first heard Bishop Gallagher himself deliver an extravagant introduction of his most famous priest. Then the shepherd of Royal Oak took the microphone to tell his followers that their letters had made it clear that "the demand for social justice . . . , like a tidal wave, is sweeping over this nation." His own broadcasts, he declared, had placed him in a unique position to accept the challenge. He alone could mold a great movement, but to do so, his audience must mobilize.[1]

Hitherto you have been merely an audience. Today . . . I call upon you to join this National Union for Social Justice, to rise above the concept of an audience and become a living, vibrant, united and active organization, superior to politics.[2]

In asking his followers to join such an organization, Coughlin was shrewdly appealing to the American desire to be "idealistic," to rise

[1] Coughlin, *A Series of Lectures . . . 1934–35*, pp. 9–16.
[2] *Ibid.*, pp. 16–18.

"above" the sordid level of "politicking." This spurious highmindedness, always an effective device for the demagogue, made politics a simplistic affair and workaday politicians, who had to make compromises to achieve results, objects of contempt.

The priest insisted that his audience would not have to make any compromises with their principles, nor would they have to accept the "regimented poverty of Communism . . . [or] the created poverty of capitalism." The new "articulate organized lobby of the people" could achieve true social justice, and for it Coughlin proclaimed that he would risk everything: "The die has been cast, the word has been spoken, and by it I am prepared to either stand or fall. . . . God wills it! Do you?" [3]

Whether it was God's will or the leader's magnetism, 200,000 people responded by mail within two weeks asking for membership applications. Prospective members were asked to sign a pledge supporting the sixteen basic principles of the National Union for Social Justice:

1. I believe in the right of liberty of conscience and liberty of education, not permitting the state to dictate either my worship to my God or my chosen avocation in life.

2. I believe that every citizen willing to work and capable of working shall receive a just and living annual wage which will enable him to maintain and educate his family according to the standards of American decency.

3. I believe in nationalizing those public necessities which by their very nature are too important to be held in the control of private individuals.

4. I believe in private ownership of all other property.

5. I believe in upholding the right to private property yet of controlling it for the public good.

6. I believe in the abolition of the privately owned Federal Reserve Banking system and the establishing of a government-owned Central Bank.

7. I believe in rescuing from the hands of private owners the right to coin and regulate the value of money which right must be restored to Congress where it belongs.

8. I believe that one of the chief duties of this government-owned Central Bank is to maintain the cost of living on an even keel and the repayment of dollar debts with equal value dollars.

9. I believe in the cost of production plus a fair profit for the farmer.

10. I believe not only in the right of the laboring man to organize in unions but also in the duty of the Government which that laboring man supports, to protect these organizations against the vested interests of wealth and of intellect.

11. I believe in the recall of all non-productive bonds and thereby in the alleviation of taxation.

12. I believe in the abolition of tax-exempt bonds.

[3] *Ibid.*, pp. 18–22.

13. I believe in the broadening of the base of taxation founded upon the ownership of wealth and the capacity to pay.

14. I believe in the simplification of government, and the further lifting of crushing taxation from the slender revenues of the laboring class.

15. I believe in the event of a war and for the defence of our nation and its liberties, if there shall be a conscription of men let there be a conscription of wealth.

16. I believe in preferring the sanctity of human rights to the sanctity of property rights. I believe that the chief concern of government shall be for the poor, because, as is witnessed, the rich have ample means of their own to care for themselves.[4]

The sixteen principles provided for the true believers a catechism of the Coughlin panacea. Mixed in with the vague and pious sentiments, many of which were taken from the reforming platforms of the Minnesota Farmer-Labor and Wisconsin Progressive Parties, were most of the priest's favorite themes. The spirit of Populist thought and of the Papal encyclicals colored the monetary theories which lay at the heart of this program.

Although few Coughlinites questioned the principles, contemporary observers complained that they contained no endorsement of democratic government nor mention of the right of free speech. They also challenged his curious phrase: "vested interests . . . of intellect." But the radio priest denied that he was trying to limit entry into his organization to anyone, even the intellectuals. "All are welcome to join the crusade," he countered; "black and white, Catholic, Protestant and Jew."[5]

But if Coughlin was truly trying to attract a heterogeneous membership, he failed to do so. The movement was weak in the South and West where the Coughlin radio network was thin and the Catholic population meager. When publication began on *Social Justice*, a weekly newspaper originated and controlled by the priest, the editors found it necessary to point out repeatedly that the National Union was "also open" to Protestants and Jews.[6]

Whatever its religious or ethnic composition, the organization was dedicated to political action. To that end, large numbers of subunits, or local political clubs, were formed, with a minimum membership of twenty-five in rural areas and fifty in urban areas. These local groups were in turn members of a larger congressional district unit, and

[4] Coughlin, *A Series of Lectures . . . 1935–1936,* pp. 11–12.

[5] *Ibid.,* p. 13; and Swing, pp. 46, 48. There was one occupational exemption from NUSJ membership: no politicians (people on public payrolls as a result of political affiliation) were accepted.

[6] *Social Justice,* March 13 and April 24, 1936.

through them it was hoped that the "lobby of the people" could put considerable pressure on individual Representatives.[7]

Although officers were elected in each subunit and district unit and some large states had state supervisors as well, there was never any doubt that Father Coughlin was in complete control of the NUSJ. A board of trustees, formed in 1936 and given complete authority in the corporation bylaws, was packed with his employees and sycophants, and the cleric, as board president, made all decisions in regard to policy and property. With all officers subject to his control and all speakers needing his approval before officially addressing even subunits, there could be no question that Charles E. Coughlin was not only the founder but the boss.[8]

With such an authoritarian arrangement, it was not surprising that the National Union failed to attract active minds. The lack of free discussion and independent activity remained a lurking problem for the radio priest. Would it not be easy for the press and the major parties to lure these sleepwalkers back to their traditional allegiances if a showdown came? The leader was depending on the power of his rhetoric to keep the following in line.

That this following would be huge was quickly apparent. By April, 1935, Father Coughlin was claiming that 8.5 million people had expressed support for the sixteen principles. In January of the following year he announced that "at least" 5,267,000 new members had been recruited, noting that the NUSJ was functioning in twenty-six states and represented in 302 of 435 congressional districts, with up to seventy subunits at work in some districts. New York was reported to have almost nine thousand local groups in operation, with over six thousand in Pennsylvania and Ohio, well over three thousand in Illinois, New Jersey and Michigan, and other large groupings in Minnesota, California, Connecticut, Rhode Island and Iowa.[9]

Confusion shrouds the question of how large the National Union actually became. Coughlin seemed to contradict his earlier claims when he remarked in August, 1936, that the movement had enlisted 1.6 million "active" members and 6 million "passive" members. Perhaps he meant that the first figure applied to actual members and the second to

[7] See Craig A. Newton, "Father Coughlin and His National Union for Social Justice," *Southwestern Social Science Quarterly*, XLI, No. 3 (December, 1960), 342, for Coughlin's original plan, soon abandoned, to form units of interest groups such as labor, students, small merchants and even housewives.

[8] *Social Justice*, March 13, 1936.

[9] *New York Times*, April 25, 1935 and January 6, 1936.

the rest of his radio audience; but he was never more explicit. Without the records of the organization, the best estimate is that the NUSJ had well over one million members but never approached the five million mark. The vast radio audience certainly contained additional sympathizers, but just how responsive these "fellow travelers" were to a direct political appeal was unclear.[10]

Whatever its exact membership, the National Union grew to be a major movement requiring large sums of money. Although members were charged no dues, Coughlin's many appeals for contributions brought handsome returns. Individual subunits helped out by selling *Social Justice* and charging admission at countless rallies featuring a speech by the founder. It was reported by July, 1936, that receipts were running ahead of expenditures and that almost $750,000 had been raised.[11]

The money was to be used, of course, to translate the Coughlin program into law. The priest said again and again that he had established no political party, that he had instead organized a gigantic lobby to influence legislation by large-scale mail campaigns aimed at Congress and to elect Congressmen friendly to the sixteen principles.

These objectives were clarified at the Michigan state convention of the National Union in April, 1935. The only one of twelve proposed state meetings to be held, the Michigan gathering was a showcase of the new movement's power and promise. With all fifteen thousand seats of Detroit's Olympia Auditorium filled and with the press gallery overflowing, the priest introduced as "friends of social justice" such speakers as Edward Kennedy, secretary of the National Farmers Union, Representatives William Lemke (R.-N. Dak.) and Martin Sweeney (D.-Ohio), and Senators Elmer Thomas and Gerald Nye.[12]

Father Coughlin told the huge crowd that the NUSJ must devote its energies to supporting four main pieces of legislation: The Frazier-Lemke bill, the Nye-Sweeney bill, the Wagner-Connery bill, and the

---

[10] *Ibid.*, August 17, 1936. Father Coughlin is reported to have burned his papers. The records of the National Union probably have been destroyed.

[11] Coughlin, *A Series of Lectures . . . 1934–1935*, p. 143; *New York Times*, August 16, 1936; and Spivak, pp. 33, 160, 178–79. John L. Spivak, after investigating NUSJ finances, concluded that approximately $100,000 had been transferred into its account from the Radio League of the Little Flower. Since the Radio League was a nonpolitical and nonprofit corporation collecting funds solely to support the priest's broadcasts, Spivak charged that Coughlin's transfer was illegal.

[12] *New York Times*, April 25, 1935. Representatives William P. Connery, Jr. (D.-Mass.) and Thomas O'Malley (D.-Wisc.) were other speakers.

In May, 1935, Father Coughlin told cheering thousands at the Ohio meeting of the National Union for Social Justice, held in Cleveland, that his
organization was "no more a political party than is the American Association of Bankers." With him is Rep. Martin L. Sweeney of Ohio. A year
later, again in Cleveland, speaking before the largest outdoor audience
he had ever addressed, Coughlin outlined plans for a third political party.
Wide World

Wheeler-Rayburn bill. On these issues, he proclaimed, it would stand or fall.

Behind this seemingly innocuous statement gathered ominous storm clouds. Over the preceding months, trouble had been brewing between Coughlin and FDR, and the moment was approaching for the break. The legislative battles which lay ahead would determine how much longer the shepherd of Royal Oak would support his "chief."

Even before the founding of the National Union, there was evidence that the love affair between priest and President was ending. But Coughlin's defection from the Administration camp did not come with one great explosion. As in so many things, the priest was at first inconsistent and equivocal, and it was to be many months between the first hint and the final, irrevocable break.

Of the several factors in play here, no doubt one was that this restless and ambitious man, with a mushrooming popularity of his own, was growing restive in the role of being just another yea-sayer for a celebrated President. Moreover, Coughlin was sensitive to the demands of the radio medium. If he was to continue to capture a vast audience, he must constantly create new issues to argue, new crusades to lead, and new personalities either to vilify or exalt. (This problem was to face all leaders who were to use the mass media; for example, Senator Joseph R. McCarthy in the 1950's.) By mid-1934 Coughlin's sermons had become repetitious. No matter how eloquent the man, he could not use the same speech twice without his listeners knowing it. The priest was running out of material.

But if there were forces pushing Father Coughlin into opposition, there was also a major factor that restrained him. He knew that with praise of the President had come his greatest success; he could not be sure that his popularity would endure an open break with FDR. This doubt caused him to waver a while between commendation and condemnation of the Administration. Thus in early 1934, while he might claim that the National Recovery Act was "borrowed part and parcel from Mussolini," his Sunday audience would still be told that "today I believe in him as much as ever" and "It is 'Roosevelt and Recovery' provided he will strike at the very heart of modern capitalism." [13]

This last statement related directly to the most divisive of the issues separating the two men—the "money problem." Coughlin, disturbed by the New Deal's refusal to remonetize silver and embarrassed by the publicizing of his organization's silver holdings, had increasingly criticized government monetary policies through 1934 and early 1935. First

[13] Coughlin, *A Series of Lectures . . . 1934–1935,* p. 117.

terming the Gold Bill of 1934 "infamous" because it gave control of gold to the hated Federal Reserve bankers, he then equated the Banking Act of 1935 with "Leninism" because it "centralized banking power in the hands of a few individuals." When his appeal for a government-regulated annual "living" wage for labor had fallen on deaf ears at the White House and on Capitol Hill, and when he failed even to get a hearing for his plan to abolish the tax-exempt feature in government bonds (the reason that United States securities had become a "hide-out for great wealth"), the priest began talking of "the President's curious preference for a European system of plutocracy." [14]

Coughlin again clashed with the Administration and lost when he threw his support behind the Patman Plan, a proposal to pay World War I veterans' bonuses by simply printing the money (cost: $2 billion) instead of by the more conventional procedure of a government loan. The plan was rejected despite the cleric's charge that paying interest to bankers was enriching "the greatest organized group of swindlers in the history of barbarism or civilization." [15]

But it was not only the New Deal's refusal to try wild, inflationary gambits that widened the gulf between Washington and Royal Oak. Indeed, one of Coughlin's most publicized and most successful acts of defiance was in the area of foreign policy.

The radio priest, although chiefly concerned with domestic matters during the early Depression years, did occasionally find time to comment on some aspect of international relations. Isolationism and Anglophobia were invariably his twin themes. The spirit of America-First was, of course, very fashionable in this era, but Coughlin pushed his arguments far enough to make even some isolationists squirm. He charged that World War I had been "largely a contest for commercial supremacy in which . . . German thrift and industry threatened England's leadership," and that the war had been won because "a barrage of lying British propaganda" induced President Woodrow Wilson to "betray" the American people and later to allow the British shamefully to mistreat the Central Powers at Versailles. He was even to advance the bizarre theory that the Italian-Ethiopian war was not a case of Italian aggression but of a "camouflaging marauder" (Ethiopia) serving as an agent-state for British imperialism. Describing the League of Nations as the "catspaw of the international bankers of the British Empire," he pleaded with Americans to stay out of "dirty European brawls." [16]

[14] Coughlin, *Money!* . . . , pp. 105–09, 114, 180–81; and Coughlin, *Today*, V, No. 9, 18.
[15] Coughlin, *A Series of Lectures . . . 1935–1936*, pp. 27, 31.
[16] *Ibid.*, pp. 13–25.

When it was proposed that the United States join the World Court, Father Coughlin sprang to the attack. He charged that the "British-run" World Court constituted "an internationalism which is a greater menace to our prosperity than the type advocated by the Soviet Third International." Working with the Hearst newspaper chain (the joint crusade was coincidental—there was no contact between the priest and the newsmen), his colorful and devastating oratory played an important role in the Court proposal's failure to receive the requisite two-thirds majority in the Senate. Both the *New York Times* and the President himself credited Coughlin with a personal victory on this issue. The 200,000 telegrams flooding the Senate, so many that Western Union had to divert part of the record number to Baltimore, were testimony to the power of the radio priest and to his willingness to risk the wrath of the New Deal.[17]

A similar willingness was demonstrated in the struggle over Coughlin's "priority" legislation. The Wagner labor act (insuring the right to collective bargaining) and the Wheeler act (the so-called death sentence for holding companies) were part of the priest's package of essential bills, and he took much of the credit for their passage. With the full power of the White House pushing these bills through Congress, Father Coughlin's claims could be dismissed as grossly inflated. But the priest's efforts on behalf of the Nye-Sweeney and Frazier-Lemke bills could not be dismissed, nor could his anger when they were defeated.

Introduced on March 5, 1935, the Nye-Sweeney bill had been drafted by a committee of the National Monetary Conference, an organization of leading inflationists headed by Robert Owen and including such men as Coughlin advisers Harriss and LeBlanc. The bill called for the establishment of a Bank of the United States and in its provisions incorporated the priest's favorite central banking plans: sole authority to issue currency, complete jurisdiction over other banks, and an elected board of directors. Despite a strenuous campaign in its behalf, Father Coughlin saw his bill buried under a 59–10 vote in the Senate. Franklin D. Roosevelt never even seriously considered dismantling the Federal Reserve System in favor of this extremist alternative. The distraught priest could only turn his energies to a campaign for the agricultural bill.[18]

The Frazier-Lemke Farm Refinance bill was a highly controversial

---

[17] Coughlin, *By the Sweat . . .* , p. 50; *New York Times,* January 30, 1935; and Elliott Roosevelt (ed.), *F.D.R., His Personal Letters, 1928–1945* (New York: Duell, Sloan and Pearce, 1950), I, 451.

[18] Reeve, pp. 88–89.

and very inflationary measure with a $3 billion price tag. Charles E. Coughlin was much enamoured by its solution to the "cruel man-made depression," and argued that it was infinitely more beneficial to the "God-fearing" farmers than the "economic hoaxing" Agricultural Adjustment Act, which had been administered by "inexperienced bureaucrats who live far from the soil." Crying "city worker and farmer, together we stand, divided we fall," the radio messiah warned Congressmen that they had to support this farm refinance program if they ever wished to receive endorsement from the National Union.[19]

He was so anxious to win passage for the bill that his Washington lobbyist (and biographer), Louis B. Ward, was sent to see Presidential Secretary McIntyre, threatening an all-out Coughlin attack on FDR if the New Deal did not drop its opposition. McIntyre made no public statement, privately dismissing Ward as a "blackmailer." But other political figures were not so circumspect. Representative John J. O'Connor (D.-N.Y.), Chairman of the House Rules Committee, infuriated after Coughlin had used his choicest invective in damning the Congressman for blocking the bill in committee, lashed back by calling the priest a "libellous . . . disgrace to the Church" and by threatening to kick him "all the way from Capitol Hill to the White House, clerical garb and all."[20]

In the end, the farm bill went the way of the bank bill, and Father Coughlin called its defeat the "last straw" in his dealings with the President. Indeed the acrimony that accompanied these losing battles capped a period in which the radio priest found himself opposed to more and more Rooseveltian policies, and during which his public statements about the President changed from praise to damnation. Yet the change in tone came slowly as the volatile Coughlin, fearing the outcome of his action, groped his way into opposition.[21]

The period of vacillation lasted through 1935. In March the New Deal was accused of "compromises with the old deal," and in May the President was admonished for seeking "recovery through socialization rather than economics." But on both occasions Coughlin added, "I am always ready to change my mind," and this was certainly true. For in November he was saying, "In this age of transition, I am for the principles of the New Deal," reminding his followers that the party in power "far transcends the activities of the other party in its benefits toward

[19] Coughlin, *A Series of Lectures . . . 1935–1936*, pp. 41–42, 135–38, 170.

[20] Harold L. Ickes, *The Secret Diary of Harold L. Ickes* (New York: Simon and Schuster, 1953), I, 536; and O'Connor to Coughlin, February 16, 1936, Roosevelt Papers, OF 306.

[21] *New York Times*, May 10, 1936; and *Social Justice*, May 29, 1936.

the American people. . . ." This, despite his statement of a few weeks earlier that "both major political parties have long since been seized by the same powerful groups of manipulators."[22]

He scorned the "scientific social workers" in the Administration and warned of an evil conspiracy against organized labor when the National Industrial Recovery Act (with its labor provisions) was declared unconstitutional. With its "army of legal talent," he argued, the government undoubtedly knew the law would be revoked, and thus waged only a "sham battle" on behalf of labor. Yet he came to the defense of President Roosevelt when the American Liberty League charged the President with "Hitlerizing" the nation, remarking, "I honestly believe that Mr. Roosevelt disclaims any desire to be a dictator." But as if not wanting to mar his record for inconsistency, he soon was warning, "Be not too certain that there will be an election in 1940."[23]

As late as January, 1936, Father Coughlin was willing to extol the President's "sound philosophy" and his "resounding" State of the Union address. But this proved to be the last gesture of reconciliation, for the priest now made his break with the New Deal irreparable. When he associated the White House with both of his favorite devils, the Communists and the banker-capitalists, his opposition was finally formalized.[24]

Coughlin charged that the Brain Trust was Communist-infiltrated and that the New Deal was "a government of the bankers, by the bankers, and for the bankers." These bizarre allegations might have provided faculty table humor for economists, but it caused Washington politicians to pause. For when the messiah of the airwaves shouted, "We now have a plutocratic Administration which hypocritically flies the flag of Democracy!" this was important political news.[25]

Charles E. Coughlin finally renounced all earlier support of the President: "Today I humbly stand before the American public to admit that I was in error. Despite all promises, the money changer has not been driven from the temple. . . . The slogan 'Roosevelt or Ruin' must now be altered to read 'Roosevelt and Ruin.' "[26]

These vitriolic attacks on the White House confused and confounded many of the Sunday sermon regulars. Forced to choose between Coughlin and FDR, the vast audience was deeply divided. Many former Na-

---

[22] *Ibid.,* Davenport, *Collier's,* XCV, No. 18, 57; and Coughlin, *A Series of Lectures . . . 1935–1936,* pp. 9, 70, 195.

[23] *Ibid.,* pp. 42–45, 86.

[24] *Ibid.,* p. 111.

[25] *Ibid.,* pp. 29, 61–64.

[26] *Ibid.,* pp. 8, 46.

tional Union supporters chose the President and turned on the priest
with all the anger of apostasy. They wrote adulatory letters to Franklin
D. Roosevelt in which Coughlin was described as a "traitor" and denounced for "stirring up hatred." Some even asked for "an executive
order ruling this dangerous man, greatest menace the country has, off
the air." One disillusioned Coughlinite telegraphed Royal Oak, "You
could talk for the rest of your life . . . and never turn me against our
President." [27]

But the most bitter and unhappy segment of his following stuck by
Father Coughlin. Willingly trailing after their hero, they told the
President that he had "deceived the working man" with his "pagan
methods." One man wrote, "All we need is a leader. We might better be
dead than living as we are; you have failed us." Another said that he
had "personally obtained five hundred members" for Coughlin's anti-
Roosevelt organization. A group in Kentucky sent the Chief Executive
a petition containing seven hundred signatures demanding that the
President cooperate with Coughlin.[28]

The President's friends around the country wrote to warn him of the
priest's growing popularity. An Indianapolis editor implored the White
House not to disregard the strength of the Coughlin movement. A St.
Louis publisher, who had fearfully suppressed editorials attacking the
cleric, wrote of "a power that has arisen in this country greater than
that of the government itself." [29]

Some observers argued that the mounting evidence of Father Coughlin's influence, as well as that of other agitators, forced Franklin D.
Roosevelt into introducing a more liberal program in 1935. According
to this theory, such New Deal legislation as the Social Security Act,
the utilities holding company bill, the Wagner Act, and the "wealth
taxes" were created to steal the rabble-rousers' thunder.

But although their radical alternatives no doubt frightened some
conservative congressmen into voting for the Administration's more
moderate measures, thus easing the passage of some pieces of liberal
legislation, there is no reason to believe that Roosevelt turned left in

[27] See, for example, Adrien Laisy to Roosevelt, September 12, 1934, Joseph D. Murphy
to Roosevelt, December 31, 1934, and Stephen Early to Clara Harman, January 12, 1934,
Roosevelt Papers, OF 306.

[28] See, for example, William M. O'Neill to Roosevelt, March 3, 1935, Claude L. Hagen
to Roosevelt, March 3, 1935, Rep. Brent Spence to Roosevelt, February 25, 1935, and H.
L. Schenedl to Roosevelt, March 25, 1935, ibid.

[29] The Indianapolis editor was Daniel J. Tobin. James A. Farley to Roosevelt, April 26,
1935, ibid. The St. Louis publisher was Elzey Roberts of the St. Louis Star-Times.

the "second" New Deal of 1935 merely because of the messiahs. The Supreme Court's destruction of the NIRA, the President's anger at big business opposition, and the liberal Congress elected in 1934 were much more important factors. One Roosevelt scholar has pointed out that the real trouble with this theory was that it didn't fit the way the President actually behaved. "His reaction to the hurricanes set off by the agitators of discontent was to outmaneuver the leaders and to give way a bit to the blast," not to try to match the demagogues with more liberal policies.[30]

Roosevelt carefully watched Father Coughlin's activities—he had the Postmaster General send him a study of Royal Oak postal receipts and asked the Democratic National Committee to prepare a statistical report on the effect of the demagogues (Long as well as Coughlin) on Democratic and Republican vote potential. The Chief Executive's strategy was to delay a break as long as possible (in September, 1934, he pacified the radio priest by soliciting a Navy Department appointment for one of his friends), and to make the break, when it came, Coughlin's doing.[31]

On May 1, 1935, FDR called a meeting of leading Democratic politicians to discuss the situation. A week earlier Harold Ickes had gone on the air to attack Coughlin, Long and Townsend. The President applauded the comments about two of these leaders, but felt that it had been unwise of Ickes to call Coughlin a "cloistered individual," noting that several irate Catholics had written the White House to complain. Roosevelt disliked such heavy-handed gestures and had devised a much more subtle plan for handling Father Coughlin. He engaged Frank Murphy, a Detroit Catholic who was a personal friend of Coughlin (and who was later to be High Commissioner of the Philippines), to devote his entire time for a month or two to sweetening the volatile cleric. Joseph P. Kennedy, chairman of the Securities and Exchange Commission, was assigned a similar role and saw Coughlin whenever he was in the East. Both men were also to use their influential positions among Catholic laymen in working undercover against the priest.[32]

This unruffled approach to the threat posed by the radical leaders

[30] Burns, p. 224.

[31] The statistical report, prepared by Emil Hurja, revealed a much greater Coughlinite influence on Democratic voting patterns, with Massachusetts the state most affected by the activities of the radio priest. See Roosevelt (ed.), p. 428.

[32] James A. Farley, *Jim Farley's Story* (New York: McGraw-Hill Book Co., 1948), p. 52; *Detroit Evening Times*, February 23, 1935; and Press Conference No. 23 (September 11, 1935), Roosevelt Papers, PPF I-P (Press Conferences).

would be disrupted only once. When General Hugh Johnson, administrator of the dying NRA, decided to attack Coughlin and Long in a radio address in the spring of 1935, he did much more harm than good. His charge that the priest was "Hitler-like" and an advocate of "funny money" only brought a riotous rebuff from Father Coughlin, who astounded a national audience by calling Johnson a "chocolate soldier, . . . a sweet Prince of Bombast, . . . a comic opera cream puff, . . . and a Bourbon with an underslung vocabulary." [33]

In addition to giving Coughlin and Long needless publicity, Johnson erred badly by connecting the two in one speech. To call the priest "Long's little playmate" was, in Raymond Gram Swing's words, to "perform the miracle of combining an excommunication with a public wedding." Some feared that the two leaders might make an alliance, and following the Johnson speech Long did say of Coughlin, "He is a good friend of mine. . . . We are working for practically the same principles." Although there were rumors of a Coughlin-Long coalition at Milo Reno's farm convention in 1935, the priest denied having any formal political ties with the Louisianan. But when Long was assassinated, Coughlin charged that his blood was on the President's hands. Had Long lived, a combination of his movement and Coughlin's would not have been out of the question.[34]

Hugh Johnson's speech, delivered without clearance by the President, was the exception. For the most part, New Dealers were taking their cues from FDR, who was displaying a shrewd and watchful reserve in the presence of the rumblings of the demagogues. Coughlin continued to snipe: "The New Deal has been translated into a raw deal!" and "We can't have a New Deal without a new deck!" But the President kept his head. It was better, Roosevelt wrote Colonel House, to have the "free side show" in 1935 than in 1936, when the "mass performance" would start.[35]

He wrote to Ray Stannard Baker on March 20, 1935:

There is another thought which is involved in continuous leadership. . . . In this country there is a free and sensational press; people tire of seeing the same name day after day in the important headlines of the paper, and the same voice night after night on the radio. For example, if since last November I

[33] Coughlin, *A Series of Lectures . . . 1934–1935*, 230.
[34] Raymond Gram Swing, "The Build-up of Long and Coughlin," *The Nation*, CXL, No. 3637 (March 20, 1935), 325; Joseph F. Thorning, "Senator Long on Father Coughlin," *America*, LIII, No. 1 (April 13, 1935), 8–9; and *New York Times*, September 11, 1935.
[35] For Roosevelt's remarks to Colonel House see Burns, p. 214.

had tried to keep up the pace of 1933 and 1934, the inevitable histrionics of the new actors, Long and Coughlin, would have turned the eyes of the audience away from the main drama itself.[36]

With such a man as an adversary, Father Coughlin must have known that the stakes would be high and his chances slim if he ever attempted to meet Franklin D. Roosevelt on the political battlefield. Yet by the next year he was preparing to do that very thing.

By 1936 the National Union for Social Justice was aligned directly against the Administration. Its record as a pressure group engaged in Congressional lobbying was not auspicious: victorious on a relatively simple and easily exploited issue such as World Court membership, it had been defeated on the farm and banking bills, which were highly complicated and strongly opposed by both major parties. But in April of the election year, Coughlin switched tactics. He announced that the National Union would enter the political arena, with congressional primaries becoming the major test of the movement's strength.

The important contests in Pennsylvania and Ohio became the priority objectives, the priest announcing his organization's disinterest in party labels and willingness to support individuals who endorsed its principles. NUSJ members were directed to prepare and distribute campaign literature and make house-to-house canvasses for the thirty-two chosen candidates in each state.[37]

In Pennsylvania, twenty Democrats and twelve Republicans won endorsement. When twelve of these candidates were victorious, Coughlin took full credit despite the fact that ten of the men were incumbents. Perhaps his most impressive performance came in Philadelphia, where Representative Michael J. Stack, with the priest's help, was renominated despite bitter Kelley machine opposition.[38]

In Ohio, Coughlin personally spearheaded a drive for the seventeen Democratic and fifteen Republican hopefuls he had endorsed by speaking in Toledo and at a huge rally in the Cleveland Municipal Stadium. The highly organized Ohio National Union, numbering 250,000 members in 1936, carefully managed its campaign. It had chosen shrewdly, and at least half a dozen of its selections were at best unlikely to lose. Nevertheless, when fifteen Coughlin-supported candidates won in Ohio, it was widely considered a significant accomplishment. The radio priest was credited with ousting two incumbents and with handing the Cleve-

[36] Roosevelt to Ray Stannard Baker, March 20, 1935, Roosevelt Papers, PPF 2338.
[37] *Social Justice,* April 24, 1936.
[38] *Ibid.,* May 1, 1936.

land Democratic machine a bad beating through the victory of Representative Martin L. Sweeney. The general staffs of both parties were shocked by the influence exercised by the National Union for Social Justice.[39]

The movement also claimed to be instrumental in winning seven other primary contests in Wisconsin, six in Michigan, four in Massachusetts and one in Maine. These were enough to convince Father Coughlin that he had succeeded in molding a political movement which could affect the balance of power. As he said after one primary victory, "Plutocracy has at last come to judgment. . . . A new era in American history has been inaugurated by the National Union." [40]

The priest now turned his attention to the impending general election of November, 1936. He called on his followers to redouble their efforts in every congressional district: "We serve notice that the open hunting season for members of Congress is on." Yet there were growing indications in the spring that the demagogue might not be content with merely affecting the outcome of House and Senate races. Every day more bitter in his denunciations of the Administration, he was finally to proclaim, "The New Deal and the National Union possess principles which are unalterably opposed." [41]

Would his hatred of Franklin D. Roosevelt lead him to contest the presidential election itself? At first he denied that the NUSJ might be transformed into a political party, but late in the spring he began to waver. "I am simply disillusioned," he said. "Democrats and Republicans, a plague on both your houses, a plague on both your political parties." For the first time he suggested that the National Union might endorse "some new party." He told his audience that "the day has come . . . when perhaps it is necessary to establish not a third party, not a fourth party, not a fifth party, but to establish a people's party." [42]

The Reverend Charles E. Coughlin now seemed ready to lead his congregation of despair into its most important struggle. He was willing to risk everything in an effort to defeat President Roosevelt and promote his own radical solutions to the nation's problems.

---

[39] *Ibid.,* May 8, 1936; *Cleveland Plain Dealer,* May 13, 1936; and T.R.B., "Coughlin Calls the Tune," *New Republic,* LXXXVII (June 3, 1936), 100–01. A few months earlier Coughlin had showed his Ohio power by influencing an important Cincinnati City Council election. See Earle Edward Eubank, "Father Coughlin Triumphs in Cincinnati," *Christian Century,* LII, No. 48 (November 17, 1935), 514–16.

[40] *Social Justice,* April 17, 1936.

[41] Coughlin, *A Series of Lectures . . . 1935–1936,* pp. 8, 40–46, 89–90.

[42] *Ibid.,* pp. 50, 95; and *New York Times,* April 6, 1936.

But was his following a real political force or only a devoted fan club for a radio orator? And if it were truly powerful, were there enough other bitter and discontented people in America who would respond to the demagogue's appeal by adding their voices and votes to the National Union in order to change the course of the election? Coughlin had a following and an organization. What he needed in the spring of 1936 were allies, other leaders with other followers who would give his bid for political power a chance at success.

PART II

WILLIAM LEMKE

AND THE NONPARTISAN

LEAGUE

Because he was unorganized, the farmer has been made the financial shock absorber. . . . He fed the nation and he lost his home. —William Lemke, 1936

5

Radical Congressman
from the Northern Plains

If he stands on the outskirts of Grand Forks, North Dakota—where the Red River of the North forms the boundary with Minnesota—and faces west, a man will be looking out at literally hundreds of miles of table-top flatness. This is one of the most level areas on the face of the planet. The few trees stand off the horizon in optical illusion as the terrain stretches out to meet the sky.

The soil is rich and black on these northern plains. But the weather is frivolous, and for the farmers of this vast area, there is always the danger of frost or drought. Nevertheless, in the early 1880's, hundreds of thousands of stolid Scandinavian and German-American immigrants set out in their ox-drawn wagons across the wide expanses, making the Dakotas the locus of one of the last of the great migrations to the agricultural West.

Among these farmer families were the Lemkes, who trekked to the sparsely settled spaces of Towner County in 1883. Fred Lemke had come to the United States from Stettin, in East Prussia, at the age of eight, and his wife, although Wisconsin born, was the daughter of Bavarian immigrants, and her speech and customs very much reflected Germanic traditions. Their decision to head west, though, was in a uniquely American tradition. When the family moved first from Minnesota to Grand Forks, then selling the little hotel they had run in the frontier town in order to try their luck in the spring wheat country across the prairie, they were joining a movement that would raise the population of North Dakota from almost nothing in 1870 to nearly 200,000 in 1890, a movement of people in search of the American dream.[1]

The eldest son of the pioneering family, only five at the time of westward migration, was named William. He was to become one of the most tireless and outspoken workers for farm benefits in modern congressional history, and a political power not only in his state and section but in the nation as well. A true son of the agrarian Middle West, he would spend his adult life fighting to protect that dream which made his parents pioneers.

For the young Lemke, life on the plains was anything but easy. He worked long hours on his father's farm and went to a common school for only two or three months in the summers, studying at home throughout the rest of the year with the assistance of his sisters. Religion was stressed but represented a source of some tension in the family, for he was Lutheran as the result of a compromise between a Catholic mother and a Lutheran father to raise the girls of the family in the mother's faith and the boys in the father's faith.[2]

Not long after their migration, the Lemkes lived through the great drought of 1889, and for several years following that grim period of dry summers and blizzardy winters, hard times stalked all the farmers of the northwest. But Lemke's father rode out the difficult times, and by the mid-nineties had accumulated 2,700 acres of wheat land, enough to be considered a relatively wealthy man.[3]

There was enough money in 1898 to send William to the University of North Dakota, where he was a great success both in the classroom and on the football field. He stayed on at the Grand Forks institution for the first year of law school, going to Washington's Georgetown University for a second year and then for the third and final year to Yale, where his work won the praise of the dean.[4]

The young attorney returned to his home state in 1905 to set up a practice at Fargo, and his clients were mainly farmers and farm organizations. He soon became associated with almost every farm group in

[1] Lemke to August W. Lemke, March 28, 1933, in William Lemke Papers (Orrin G. Libby Historical Manuscripts Collection, University of North Dakota, Grand Forks, North Dakota). Cited hereafter as Lemke Papers.

[2] North Dakota's Bishop Vincent Wehrle tried, as late as 1938, to induce Lemke to become a Catholic, explaining that he had told Lemke's mother that she had erred in allowing the boys to be raised outside the Church. See Bishop Vincent Wehrle to Lemke, July 15, 1938, *ibid.*

[3] Lemke to Cornelius Vanderbilt, Jr., April 22, 1935, *ibid.*

[4] *Ibid.*

the Northwest, including the Farmers' Union and the Cooperative Exchange. It was his work as legal adviser for the Equity Cooperative in its fight against the grain exchange that brought him to the attention of Arthur Townley, founder of the Nonpartisan League.[5]

Organized in North Dakota in 1915, the Nonpartisan League was a movement of agrarian protest against the abuses of the railroads, the financial interests, and the marketing system—and especially the tyranny of the Minneapolis-St. Paul grain elevator operators. After Townley and a few radical cohorts organized the Equity Cooperative Exchange as a device to eliminate profits of elevator companies, grain traders, and futures speculators, they quickly discovered that angry businessmen were refusing them trading rights on the Minneapolis Exchange. They countered with the demand that North Dakota build a state-owned terminal elevator which might be able to store enough wheat to create a truly independent market. When the Republican-controlled legislature refused, an action which seemed to doom wheat growers to dominance by the Twin Cities financial interests, the Nonpartisan League emerged in a drive to build a radical and class-conscious agrarian movement.[6]

The League clearly had its roots in those earlier farm movements, the Grange, the Alliance and Populism. In a sense, Populism came late to North Dakota in the form of the Nonpartisan League, and the rhetoric of that "Sockless Socrates" of an earlier day, Jerry Simpson, would have easily fit the mood and ambitions of the League men.[7]

The major difference between the Nonpartisan League and the Populist revolt was one of technique. The League's emphasis was on absolute solidarity, essentiality of its own press and the use of the direct primary. Unlike its predecessor, it did not seek to start a new political party but attempted to use the primary to force an existing party to express the will of the majority of the voters. The majority of North Dakota's voters were farmers, and there was a motive akin to revenge in many hearts as the League undertook its program to defeat the "interests" and bring the wheat growers a greater return from their crops.[8]

[5] Ibid.

[6] Herbert G. Gaston, The Non-Partisan League (New York: Harcourt, Brace and Co., 1920), p. 59; Paul Fossum, The Agrarian Movement in North Dakota (Baltimore: Johns Hopkins Press, 1925), pp. 85–86; and Andrew D. Bruce, The Non-Partisan League (New York: Macmillan Co., 1921), p. 56.

[7] Theodore Salutos and John D. Hicks, Agricultural Discontent in the Middle West, 1900–1936 (Madison: University of Wisconsin Press, 1951), pp. 149, 185–86.

[8] Robert L. Morlan, Political Prairie Fire (Minneapolis: University of Minnesota Press, 1955), pp. 348, 358.

Lemke joined League organizer Townley in 1916 as an attorney for the movement and very soon was playing an important role in the formation of League policy.

The ambitious young lawyer was ready to devote all his energies to the exciting new venture, for he had just suffered a disastrous setback when his extensive speculation in Mexican lands was virtually wiped out by the effects of the Mexican revolutions. Lemke had put into almost one-half million acres of cheap range land in the Mexican state of Sinaola the proceeds from the sale of most of the North Dakota land he had inherited or homesteaded, along with other money he had raised by subscription or pledges. His investment was safe as long as the Huerta government was in power, but when President Woodrow Wilson refused to extend diplomatic recognition to Huerta and eventually succeeded in overturning him in favor of Venustiano Carranza, Lemke was ruined, for the new revolutionary government confiscated the best holdings of foreigners. The furious Dakotan wrote a bitter anti-Wilson book entitled *Crimes Against Mexico*.[9]

In the new Nonpartisan League, William Lemke's personal troubles were soon eclipsed by a series of smashing successes. As the League quickly grew to a membership of 200,000, spreading across state boundaries to Wisconsin, Minnesota, Iowa, and South Dakota, Lemke was named one of three members of the National Executive Committee. When the League finally gained control of North Dakota's Republican Party, he became chairman of the Republican State Committee as well.[10]

At the state capital in Bismarck, Lemke trained newly elected farmer-legislators in speechmaking, parliamentary procedure and in the Nonpartisan League's legislative program. He was, in fact, author of much of that program, claiming credit for drafting the laws creating the Bank of North Dakota, the Mill and Elevator Association, the industrial commission for the state, and several kinds of state crop insurance.[11]

Although to many this legislation seemed to smack of socialism, Lemke denied it. Arguing that in order to keep free competition alive, the government had to have absolute control of money, banking, natural resources, and the essential few marketing facilities, he explained

---

[9] Walter Davenport, "Mr. Lemke Stops to Think," *Collier's*, XCVIII, No. 18 (October 17, 1936), 25.

[10] Salutos and Hicks, pp. 185–86.

[11] Jonathan Mitchell, "Liberty Bill Lemke," *New Republic*, LXXXVIII, No. 1132 (August 12, 1936), 9.

that the state acted to liberate the farmer from domination by the "interests" in order only to give him a truly free market.[12]

In 1920, William Lemke's star was rising in North Dakota. He was elected attorney general of the state, and many felt that with Townley losing power, this was proof that he had become the unofficial leader of the Nonpartisan League. But the good fortune was not of long duration, for within a year of his election, a scandal rocked the state administration. Spurred on by William Langer, former attorney general and himself a former League member, opponents of the Nonpartisan League charged that Lemke and others had caused the state-owned central bank to deposit public funds in an institution, Fargo's Scandinavian-American Bank, which they knew to be insolvent. Out of these accusations grew indictments, and although the charges were soon quashed, Lemke's reputation was damaged. His problems were compounded when, shortly after the bank affair, he was accused of having had the state Home Building Association erect a house for him using $24,000 of "public money." Although his enemies were unable to provide evidence of personal dishonesty, William Lemke's career was to suffer from the scandals.[13]

In October, 1921, League opponents secured enough support for a recall election of the state administration. Governor Lynn J. Frazier, Lemke's friend and a beneficiary of his influence in League circles, had the dubious distinction of being the first governor in history to be recalled. Down to defeat with him went William Lemke. Ironically, Lemke and his fellow Leaguers had been instrumental in pushing through the very recall act which victimized their government.[14]

The next year, Lemke tried to recoup his losses and vindicate himself by running for governor. He had League support but this time failed to win the Republican nomination, although Frazier became Republican candidate for the Senate. While his friend was sent to Washington, Lemke was beaten soundly by the incumbent governor.[15]

---

[12] Not all Leaguers shared Lemke's antipathy to Socialism. Arthur LeSeur, another legal adviser to Townley, was a self-proclaimed Socialist who recruited Socialist Party members from outside the state to help assist the League's work in North Dakota. This, despite the opposition of doctrinaire leaders within the Socialist Party to the recruitment of farmers. Some of these leaders even accused Townley of being only an opportunist and a hated "reformer." See S. M. Lipset, "The Background of Agrarian Radicalism," in Bendix and Lipset, pp. 562–64.

[13] Dale Kramer, *The Wild Jackasses, The American Farmer in Revolt* (New York: Hastings House, 1956), pp. 187–88.

[14] Morlan, pp. 315, 326.

[15] *Ibid.*, p. 345. The vote was 110,000 for Governor Nestos to 81,000 for Lemke.

Following this defeat, it was a bitter man who retired to private law practice and took no further part in politics for a decade. But William Lemke had been a potent figure in an organization which had a quarter of a million members throughout the Northwest and which wielded immense influence in the political and economic life of the northern plains. He knew that a potentially vast following remained in the farmland, and when the Depression began to cast its dark shadow across the West, he awaited an opportunity to assume its leadership once again.[16]

The opportunity presented itself in the critical election of 1932, when the nation was reeling from the economic crisis and American agriculture was facing problems of unprecedented difficulty. Lemke won the Republican nomination for one of North Dakota's two at-large congressional seats.

Always the maverick, William Lemke was convinced that the Hoover Administration's farm program was a failure. Despite his GOP candidacy, he traveled to Albany, New York, in the early days of the election year to meet with the front-runner for the Democratic presidential nomination, Governor Franklin D. Roosevelt. Lemke was impressed with the future President, telling his wife that FDR, upon hearing his proposals for farm bankruptcy and refinance legislation, had leaned back in his chair and said, "Yes, yes, I am for all that." He claimed that the New York Governor had commissioned him to make the necessary arrangements with the Farmers Union and with the remnants of the Nonpartisan League organization to assure that North Dakota and surrounding states would send delegates to the Democratic national convention pledged to Roosevelt.[17]

During the campaign, FDR's advisers regarded Lemke as the chief strategist of the League, noting with satisfaction that he had traveled in seven states speaking for their candidate and had succeeded in bringing League county leaders in North Dakota to the support of Roosevelt. Lemke achieved this by assuring League and Farmers Union men that Roosevelt would support his proposals and other legislation favorable to farmers.[18]

---

[16] *Ibid.*, p. 277. In 1919, the Nonpartisan League had dues-paying members in 13 states. Biggest representation was in North Dakota, Minnesota, and South Dakota.

[17] Edward C. Blackorby, "Prairie Rebel: The Public Career of William Lemke" (unpublished Ph.D. dissertation, Department of History, University of North Dakota, 1958), pp. 428–29.

[18] *Ibid.*, pp. 429–31. Blackorby quotes Lemke's friend, Cornelius Vanderbilt, Jr., as saying, "Bill was very close to F.D.R. in those early days (1932) before Moley and McIntyre got in there because Louis Howe liked him . . . Farley had no use for him."

But while working hard for the presidential aspirant, William Lemke had also his own congressional race to win. As he campaigned across the state, voters found him, at first glance, a singularly unimpressive man. He was of chunky build, just over five feet six inches tall and weighing 150 pounds. Lantern-jawed and almost completely bald, his face was a maze of freckles and pock marks, the result of a youthful case of small-pox. His eyes had also been disfigured in childhood, and now he wore an artificial left eye and had trouble focusing the right. Yet for all this he was an exceptional campaigner in the farmland. His homely habit of wearing galluses and the plainsman's gray cloth cap, his kindly slouch and wrinkled suits, and his first-hand knowledge of farming conditions all across the Midwest, made him appear truly in and of the soil.[19]

His speaking voice was poor. Touched with a Teutonic accent, it was generally flat and monotonous, though it could become uncomfortably shrill in emphasis. Lemke was never given to oratorical flights of fancy, but he knew the farmer and he knew the law. A shrewd and resourceful advocate for his cause, he left audiences with no doubt that they were hearing a man who could be a forceful farm leader in any legislature. He delighted in quoting statistics of world wheat shipments and in dis-cussing the fine points of the law of marketing cooperatives. He held his large audiences of stolid Scandinavian and German-American farmers spellbound and won his election easily, being credited by many with having carried his state for Roosevelt as well.[20]

On arriving in Washington, Lemke at first threw his support to the New Deal. He termed the inaugural address the "greatest speech ever made by a President" and within a few weeks was promising his consti-tuents that Roosevelt would do all that he could for the farmer. He voted for most of the early Administration bills, including the AAA, the NRA, the 1934 Gold Revenue Act, and the Home Owners Loan Corporation. He even refused an invitation to a proposed meeting of midwestern progressives, noting that "conditions are so improved . . . that the meeting will be a fizzle."[21]

William Lemke was soon to be disillusioned. He had come to the Capitol rather naively expecting to assist the President in making major decisions on agriculture; what he did not realize was that FDR had

[19] Paul W. Ward, "Lemke: Crackpot for President," *The Nation*, CXLIII, No. 2 (July 11, 1936), 36.

[20] *The Kansas Union Farmer*, September 21, 1934.

[21] Undated speech by Lemke entitled "The New America," in Lemke Papers; and letter of William Lemke to Howard Y. Williams, May 26, 1933, in Howard Y. Williams Papers (Minnesota Historical Society, St. Paul, Minnesota). Cited hereafter as Williams Papers.

changed his farm policy since the Albany meeting with the North Dakotan in 1932. The Chief Executive had dropped the idea of dumping agricultural surpluses abroad and stimulating a mild inflation at home. Instead, at the urging of Rexford Guy Tugwell, Raymond Moley, and Henry A. Wallace, he had adopted the Agricultural Adjustment Act concept: crop reductions coupled with parity benefit payments to farmers.[22]

Lemke was willing to support this policy for a while. But he had expected a massive inflationary program to help his farmer-constituents, two-thirds of whom either faced foreclosure or already had suffered from it. He also expected to be close to the seat of power.

In the winter of 1933, when Lemke might have been able to capitalize on the President's indebtedness to him for his work during the campaign, he was busy with state politics at home, and by spring, he discovered that the doors of the White House were closed to him. Those members of Roosevelt's Brain Trust who were advisers on agricultural policy seemed to consider Lemke as he had been stereotyped in the campaign: a prairie rebel, a madman from the sticks. His endorsement earlier in the year of some North Dakota farmers' Councils of Defense, organizations to prevent foreclosures or attempts to dispossess, gave substance to this image. The New Dealers decided that Lemke did not merit the deference accorded those other midwestern progressive farm spokesmen: Gerald Nye, Burton K. Wheeler, and Lynn J. Frazier.[23]

William Lemke was distraught. Instead of being a respected presidential adviser, he found himself just another no-seniority freshman congressman from a minority party—in a bad year for the minority—faced with an inaccessible President and Administration. This was an important factor in turning the North Dakota legislator against Franklin D. Roosevelt; when added to his growing distaste for New Deal policies, it helped make him one of FDR's bitterest enemies only a few years after he worked to elect the President. Like Charles E. Coughlin, Lemke did not at first attack Roosevelt personally. Instead, he directed his anger at the young attorneys of the Department of Agriculture, who had been responsible for rejecting him and drawing up the nefarious farm policies.

He rose in the House of Representatives to attack the Department for releasing figures on the cost of wheat production which, he claimed, were much lower than had been expected by dealers and which were

[22] Blackorby, pp. 438–39.
[23] *Ibid.*, pp. 444–55.

announced after the southern wheat states had harvested their crops at a high price. He accused the unthinking "brainless trust" for the drastically reduced prices of North Dakota wheat in this critical year of 1933. He then told his constituents that "these New York professors do not understand the agricultural problem of the nation." [24]

Although Lemke wrote a friend in early 1934 that "as far as Franklin D. Roosevelt is concerned, I . . . believe he is far more progressive than the reactionary Democratic machine," within a few months he confided that "Roosevelt will have to get rid of the 'brain trust' or he will be in fact as well as in the newspapers a real Kerensky and not a leader of men." His unhappiness mounted with the passing weeks, and by 1935 he was prepared to dismiss the AAA as "a farce," and "the New Deal, as far as the farmers are concerned . . . [as] only a new shuffle with the cards stacked. . . . Nothing has been accomplished and no fundamental changes have been made." [25]

William Lemke's disapproval concerned not only the farm policies of the New Deal, but monetary programs as well. Heir to the Populist tradition of the Nonpartisan League, author of inflationary measures in his home state, and creator of the central Bank of North Dakota, he was prepared to flail any of the old Populist devils he found creeping into the Administration's camp.

He railed against the "Wall Street racketeers" and "international bankers" who were influencing the "coupon-clipper legislation" of the government, specifically denouncing the failure to pass the inflationary Patman bonus bill and the Wheeler bill to remonetize silver. He lamented the creation of the Federal Deposit Insurance Corporation, considering it a futile attempt to shore up the existing system of private banks instead of establishing the infinitely more desirable central bank. He also attacked the Administration for refusing to support the inflationary Thomas omnibus amendment to the Agricultural Adjustment Act, which provided for the issuance of greenbacks, the remonetization of silver, and the alteration of the gold content of the dollar. [26]

Lemke sought to alert midwestern farmers to the disastrous turn of events he was witnessing in Washington. The Farmers Union agreed to sponsor his speaking tour throughout the Northwest, and transcriptions

---

[24] Lemke speech dated January 5, 1934, and Lemke address in House of Representatives, January 16, 1934, copy in Lemke Papers.

[25] Lemke to Covington Hall, February 8, 1934; Lemke to Robert Muir, April 20, 1934; and Lemke to E. J. Hall, March 26, 1935, in *ibid.*

[26] Lemke speech dated January 15, 1934; and Lemke to Vanderbilt, Jr., April 22, 1935, in *ibid.*

of these speeches were mailed to small radio stations all across the plains. But he did more than just talk. Respected by congressional colleagues despite his bucolic ways, he put to use his keen legal mind by drafting legislation designed to save agriculture and help the nation in spite of the New Deal. To this end he wrote several bills which were to stir controversy in the House and affect his own political career.

Congressman Lemke's first legislative venture was a bill to create a Bank of the United States. His experience with central banking on a state level had convinced him that a national bank owned and operated by the government and issuing all currency might solve the nation's depression-bred financial woes. He had collected an extensive library of books and pamphlets on monetary theory and corresponded with William H. "Coin" Harvey and other inflationists, who encouraged him to introduce his bill. But the Lemke central bank proposal, in the hopper in 1933, was buried in the Committee on Banking and Currency by Congressional leaders who opposed this kind of heresy (as the Nye-Sweeney bill advocates were to find out later).[27]

But William Lemke's farm legislation was not as easily disposed of by its New Deal opponents. Writing a constituent that "here in Washington the farmers are being treated like a bunch of suckers and as if they don't know anything and need a guardian," he resolved to change that situation by teaming with his Senate colleague from North Dakota, Lynn J. Frazier, in a series of Frazier-Lemke farm bills.[28]

Frazier, although in Washington much longer than Lemke, still had his whole life focus on agriculture. One observer called him "an old plowhorse who needs a big field to turn around in," and Lemke, with much better legal training, drafted the bills that were to make their names as inseparable as Amos and Andy or Baltimore and Ohio.[29]

The first of these bills, the Frazier-Lemke Farm Bankruptcy Act, was passed in the spring of 1934. It provided for a five-year moratorium on mortgage payments for farmers threatened by foreclosures. It also granted the farmer the right to buy back his land from creditors at a price set by a Federal district court to be "fair and reasonable." Such measures, Lemke explained, were nothing new. They merely extended to farmers "the same rights that the courts have given industry."[30]

But Franklin D. Roosevelt disagreed. During the House debate, the President avowed, "I have never endorsed the Frazier-Lemke bill. . . . If

[27] Lemke to William H. Harvey, May 26, 1934, in *ibid.*
[28] Lemke to Ida Botz, March 6, 1934, in *ibid.*
[29] George Creel, "The Old Homesteader," *Collier's*, XCVIII, No. 14 (October 3, 1936), 22.
[30] Lemke to Fred W. Lewis, June 20, 1934, Lemke Papers.

this type of wild legislation passes, the responsibility for wrecking recovery will be squarely on Congress, and I will not hesitate to say so to the nation in plain language." Yet the Chief Executive did hesitate, for while he tried to have the bill buried in Congress, his fear of alienating farmers caused him to refrain from making a public statement during the legislative battle. And once the fight was lost and the bill passed, he decided that it would be politically unwise to veto it. FDR signed Lemke's bill despite his objections. The North Dakotan had won a battle with the Administration.[31]

The victory made William Lemke an agrarian hero. Letters of thanks from midwestern farmers poured into his office. (One man wrote to say, "For a grisly old fighter, you can't be beat.") In the 1934 Republican congressional primary, he polled a smashing 72 per cent of the total vote, despite the opposition of a representative of the "Rumper Leaguers," a Nonpartisan League dissident group. In the general election, he crushed his Democratic opponent by almost two to one.[32]

But when Lemke returned to Capitol Hill, he discovered that a legal assault on his bankruptcy act was taking its toll. Several federal district courts had declared it unconstitutional, and it was scheduled for appeal to the nation's highest tribunal. The North Dakotan helped argue the case before the Supreme Court, but to no avail, for by unanimous decision, the act was found to "deprive creditors of property without due process of law.[33]

Congressman Lemke growled about the Court's misinterpretation of the "plain language of the Constitution," and then proceeded to rewrite the act to comply with the Court's standards. The revised bankruptcy bill, permitting farmers to retain farms for three years when foreclosure was threatened, was passed in 1935.[34]

Reworking the bankruptcy measure took valuable time from Lemke's primary interest in 1935. He was drafting the Frazier-Lemke Farm Refinance bill, and into this proposal he would put his solution both for the farm problem and for the general problem of depression. It was William Lemke's panacea.

The bill provided for the Farm Credit Administration to supply all cash necessary for farmers to pay off their mortgages or buy back the farms from which they had been dispossessed through foreclosure since

[31] Roosevelt to Stephen Early, April 10, 1934, Roosevelt Papers, OF 1038 (Frazier-Lemke Bill).

[32] See, for example, C. C. Daniels to Lemke, June 19, 1934, Lemke Papers.

[33] The Court's decision came in Louisville Joint Stock Land Bank vs. Radford.

[34] Lemke radio address dated January 6, 1936, in Lemke Papers.

1928. In return, the government would take new mortgages, bearing a low 1–1½ per cent interest amortized over forty-seven years. These mortgages were to be used as security for a federal bond issue bearing 1–1½ per cent interest. The bonds would be offered to the public, but the very low interest rate would almost certainly preclude sales. In this case, the Federal Reserve would be ordered to take the bonds and issue $3 billion of "printing press" money for the farmers, with only the bonds as backing.[35]

When its details were finally revealed, the bill created an immediate furor in Washington. Opponents charged that if enacted, it would be almost impossible to administer since it affected the rights of innocent third parties—holders of property that had gone through foreclosure proceedings. Many considered the $3 billion price tag, to be paid in unbacked currency, as absurdly inflationary, and some questioned the constitutionality of the proposal as well. One Administration spokesman, probably speaking for a New Deal inner circle, simply dismissed the bill as "a pipe dream."[36]

But William Lemke was convinced that he had discovered the way to solve all the economic problems of the land. He wrote that "it would not only relieve the agricultural distress, but the unemployment situation, as it would put in circulation sufficient money to do the nation's business." Not only that, but it would "loosen up frozen assets of insurance companies and other investors" and in this way end the "strike" of investment capital and bring the nation out of the Depression.[37]

Lemke dismissed charges that his bill was inflationary, arguing that inflation is an illusion. In a statement that would have done credit to Charles Edward Coughlin, he insisted that "bank or credit money is imaginary money on which the banks draw interest. . . . We have too much of such money and not enough real money." The refinance bill's billions would, presumably, be "real" money.

Franklin D. Roosevelt disagreed, viewing this third Frazier-Lemke effort as a fantastic scheme which, if implemented, could unbalance or destroy the United States economy. He sought to kill the bill before it could be brought to the House floor, for there a debate would capture the attention of vast numbers of suffering farmers. His specific objective was to tie the bill up in the powerful Rules Committee.

The Administration had tried this tactic with the bankruptcy bill, but that time Lemke countered by securing the requisite 145 signatures

---

[35] Copy of H.R. 2066 in *ibid.*

[36] Blackorby, pp. 477–82.

[37] Lemke to Representative Isabella Greenway, January 1, 1935, Lemke Papers.

William Lemke with his family in 1936. *Wide World*

on a petition to discharge the bill to the House floor. When he undertook to do the same thing for the refinance measure, he faced the new
rules of the Seventy-fourth Congress, which required 218 signatures,
or a majority of the membership, on a discharge petition. This, indeed,
was a challenge.

Throughout the 1935 session, Lemke drove himself relentlessly to
acquire the needed signatures. On two occasions, the total reached 212,
but frantic cloakroom activity by Administration leaders blocked his
efforts on the brink of success. The opposition stood firm throughout
the year and the North Dakotan wrote bitterly of "the gag and schackle

rules used by the reactionary bellwethers" in Congress. But he continued the fight into 1936, and unbelievably, he won the battle. In the winter, the Frazier-Lemke Refinance bill went to the House floor when 218 Representatives defied the President by signing the petition.[38]

Now the New Deal was forced into an open and angry contest with the radical Congressman from the northern plains. President Roosevelt, in an election year, had to formalize his opposition to an attractive plan with wide grass-roots support.

In the ensuing contest, William Lemke used every device at his command. He recruited endorsements from the Farmers' Union, local farm bureaus, and Grange organizations and also received support from Father Coughlin's National Union of Social Justice. On the eve of the vote in the House, he delivered an impassioned radio address over a national network, declaring that "upon the passage of this bill depends the home and security of over 2 million farm families and over 10 million Americans." He envisioned all the evil forces that had combatted agrarian aspirations across the years aligning against him, noting darkly, "You may be sure when this bill comes up on the floor there will be plenty of telegrams from dead men in Pennsylvania. . . . Multimillionaires will again be registering under assumed names in Washington hotels." In the end, however, it was not the wealth from Wall Street that broke the back of his refinance bill, but the president of the American Federation of Labor. William Green sent a letter read by the Speaker of the House just before the vote was taken, in which he claimed that "labor would suffer" because the bill could lead to a "reduction in living standards, reduced buying power and a more acute unemployment problem." This, coupled with a strenuous New Deal counterattack which featured a detailed memorandum sent by the Farm Credit Administration to every representative blasting the proposal, resulted in a crushing 235–142 rejection of the bill.[39]

The defeat shattered William Lemke. He might have defiantly claimed, "We won, because there will be eliminations in the November elections," but after eight months of ceaseless activity in a lost cause, these words had a hollow sound. Accusing William Green of "selling out" to the Administration in return for promises of more labor legislation, he had acid words for the fifty-eight "double-crossers" who

[38] Lemke to Vanderbilt, Jr., April 22, 1935, in *ibid.;* and *New York Times,* May 1, 1936.
[39] Copies of Lemke addresses dated February 22 and May 5, 1936, in Lemke Papers; and U.S., *Congressional Record,* 74th Cong., 2d Sess., 1936, LXXX, Part 7, 7167, 7210, 7229.

signed the discharge petition but voted against the bill. But acrimony could neither change the result nor help him decide what to do now.[40]

Undoubtedly the most important result of the refinance bill's defeat was its effect on Lemke's attitudes toward both the New Deal and its extremist enemies. His unhappiness with the President had turned to hatred, and hatred led to thoughts of revenge. Soured and frustrated, he would now not hesitate to join FDR's worst enemies in an anti-New Deal crusade.

[40] Lemke to H. A. Bane, May 21, 1936, Lemke Papers.

6

Neopopulism and the
Political Gamble

In the spring of 1936, a bitter William Lemke cried, "Truth is on the scaffold, wrong is on the throne. . . . The little coteries of bureaucrats in Washington representing the money changers are trying to destroy the farmer." Pointing his finger at "the other end of Pennsylvania Avenue," he said, "They have declared open war upon agriculture in this nation. . . . We accept this challenge, and from now on the enemy will know where we are. . . . This battle will continue, if necessary, until the November election when we are confident of a complete victory."[1]

Lemke, unlike Charles E. Coughlin, was not cut from demagogic cloth. Instead, he was ordinarily a sincere and dedicated servant of the state and sectional interests in his agricultural homeland. Nonetheless, Lemke's German-Lutheran background presented interesting similarities with the Irish-Catholicism of Father Coughlin. Both men were pietists, and being members of social and economic out-groups, they suffered the political trauma endemic to the polyglot American culture: the desire to overcome the obstacles that confronted them and to "get even" with the people who had put them at a socioeconomic disadvantage. When he found unhappy conditions piling one upon the other in the dreary years of the midthirties, William Lemke, almost against his will, would be changed into something more than just a stolid farmers' spokesman. He would become a demagogue for a season, as it were,

---

[1] Lemke addresses, dated February 14 and February 22, 1936, copies in *ibid.*

in a desperate effort to change the dismal circumstances which plagued him and his followers.

The circumstances driving this neopopulist to take the political gamble were clear enough. Midwestern farmers had been cut off from the mainstream of American political and intellectual life for several decades. Discontented with their social and economic lot in "normal" times, they had never really recovered from the serious recession which followed America's participation in World War I. The Depression was the final straw, compounding poverty with humiliation. The loss of farms through foreclosure, the necessary reliance on government aid, and the knowledge that city men were being paid for "boondoggling" on such projects as leaf-raking under the Civil Works Administration, were bitter pills indeed.[2]

Even the most prosperous farmers sought solutions in violence. The proud dairymen of Iowa, working under the auspices of the Farm Holiday Association, unsuccessfully tried to raise prices by setting up milk "blockades" of nearby towns in 1932. And less fortunate farmers, understandably, were even more desperate.

In the northern plains, 1936 was the year of the great drought. Whole towns were blacked out from morning to night by dark wind-driven clouds which swept away the precious topsoil that meant money and a livelihood to hundreds of thousands of people. Secretary of Agriculture Wallace called it "the worst period in history, especially in North Dakota." Residents of that state had to agree, one old wheat raiser exclaiming, "I've been here 27 years and have never seen anything like this—it's a catastrophe!" Farmers everywhere might have been agitated over low prices, but in the widening dust bowl of the Northwest it was not certain that the cash crop could be harvested at all.[3]

The region had witnessed the growth of the Farmers' Alliance, the Populist Party, and the Nonpartisan League in an earlier period. The lingering distress that had expressed itself in such ventures was converted by the natural and economic disasters of the Depression into abysmal fear and hatred. Many northwestern farmers were ready for a radical movement, and William Lemke, whose personal political for-

[2] In his influential study, *Virgin Land: The American West as Symbol and Myth* (New York: Vintage Books, 1950), Henry Nash Smith describes the myth of the nineteenth century agrarian west as a garden of the world, peopled by "heroic, idealized, frontier farmers" who distrusted urbanization and industrialization. But the myth of the garden allowed for little pessimism and its believers were peculiarly vulnerable to economic disaster. See pp. 138, 218.

[3] *New York Times,* June 28, 1936.

tunes were in eclipse at this very time, was just the man to lead them.[4]

Lemke fervently believed in the Populist myth of the natural superiority of farmers. Rooted deep in American history, the image of the idealized agrarian — virtuous, liberated from the tyranny of the market, living a life of true fulfillment free of the subservience of his urban brother — had great influence throughout the rural west. The western farmer thought of himself, in Henry Nash Smith's words, not as a peasant "but as a peer of the realm. . . . His contribution to society was basic, all other derivative and even parasitic" in comparison. "The farmer is more of an individualist, thinking more deeply on fundamental subjects than his brothers in the cities," Lemke explained, "His time is not so occupied with social functions and with more or less frivolous and passing issues of the day." And like the Populists, Lemke was certain that the evil financial and governmental conspirators of the East were driving his beloved agrarians into servitude: "We are fast approaching a feudal system, with farmers as the feudal serfs."[5]

But the Dakotan managed to contradict himself in a number of ways in his approach to the agricultural problem. He disliked businessmen and lamented the farmer's loss of primacy in American life to them, but in a real sense he was an agricultural businessman himself. Unlike the European peasants of an earlier age, farmers in the United States did not simply love the soil, but the rewards of the soil, and William Lemke was both a lawyer and a land speculator.

Lemke also hated bigness, state centralization, and the growth of impersonal bureaucracies, yet he advocated programs which would build even stronger governments and larger bureaucracies. He was emotionally dead to the social service side of the New Deal for his frontier origins and frugal German ancestry, his strict Lutheran fundamentalist upbringing and childhood of hard farm labor led him to believe that this intrusion of government into personal life was not only unnecessary but immoral. "We must," he implored, "turn away from the dole and hand-me-a-sandwich idea and back to giving each person an opportunity for self-expression," and we must "turn backward to the true democracy of Jefferson, to a nation not under too much centralization."

[4] Glenn Lowell Brudvig, "The Farmers' Alliance and Populist Movement in North Dakota" (unpublished Master's Thesis, Department of History, University of North Dakota, 1956), pp. 201–06.

[5] Henry Nash Smith, p. 224; Leo Marx's illuminating *The Machine in the Garden: Technology and the Pastoral Ideal in America* (New York: Oxford University Press, 1964), pp. 126–28; and Lemke addresses dated May 26, 1934, and February 22, 1936, copies in Lemke Papers.

But in this promotion of Jeffersonian goals, he was being caught in an old ideological trap. The industrial revolution had turned the liberalism of that earlier period upside down, for the creation of enormous wealth and power in the hands of a few private citizens, the entrepreneurs of this new age, had changed the liberals' view of the state. No longer was government considered the individual's greatest enemy; instead, modern progressives saw government as the protector of the "small man" in the battle against domination by the powerful few. Lemke, deeply committed by background and training to the nineteenth century philosophy, was forced by circumstances to propose the most radical solutions of twentieth century liberalism. Hating government handouts, he essentially called for a huge government handout to save his own supporters. Like those other North Dakota radical-conservatives who could at once be Republicans and Nonpartisan Leaguers, he used the vocabulary of Jefferson's agrarian democracy, but nowhere would the state be more centralized than in his legislative program.[6]

He supported the Townsend Plan, a proposal requiring a vast bureaucracy to administer a gigantic government investment designed to save the aged (who, like the farmers, were being "exploited by the interests"). He looked with favor upon Senator Huey Long's "valiant battles" for the Share-Our-Wealth scheme, which also called for unprecedented federal power and control, and wanted government ownership of the railroads and the regulation of interstate commerce. His own central bank and farm refinance bills, despite arguments to the contrary, demanded more massive government intervention. While he tried to overcome the contradictions through fervor and rhetoric, Lemke was the perfect neopopulist, trying to save and preserve the old agrarian America by building a new America with a strong and centralized government, a new America in many ways alien to the convictions he held most deeply.[7]

There are, of course, those who feel that William Lemke personified and led not a farmers' movement but one of German-American, ethnic isolationists. Samuel Lubell, noting the Germanic composition of his following at the time of the darkening international scene of the midthirties, argues that he "represented the most belligerently isolationist voters in the country."[8]

[6] Lemke to Covington Hall, June 8, 1935, *ibid.*

[7] Lemke to Harvey, May 26, 1934; Lemke to Hall, August 2, 1935; and Lemke to B. W. Lemke, May 25, 1936, *ibid.*

[8] Samuel Lubell, *The Future of American Politics* (Garden City, N.Y.: Doubleday Anchor Books, 1956), p. 152.

But this thesis is unconvincing. Lubell declares that by 1936 Franklin D. Roosevelt and Adolph Hitler were locked in an "epic duel," yet this critical date was one full year before FDR's "quarantine the aggressors" speech, almost two years before Munich and three years before the rape of Poland and the outbreak of war. Hitler was one of Europe's menacing figures in 1936, but with its army and air force still abuilding his Third Reich still lacked the strength of other great powers. In that year President Roosevelt continued to play a relatively quiet role in international affairs, for the Nye Committee hearings which led to the Neutrality Act of 1935 had fostered a strong feeling in Congress against American participation in European quarrels. Indeed, many of the leading isolationist congressmen were active New Dealers in domestic affairs, and the President took pains not to alienate them.[9]

Even more persuasive than the facts of foreign policy is the nature of William Lemke's world view. To emphasize the ethnic strain in Lemke's background is to misunderstand the man; the motherland for him was not some dimly remembered nation across the Atlantic but the majestic and open prairie of the Midwest. He was in and of the American soil — from early career to death, he was a spokesman for the western farmer.

It is true that Lemke hated war and disapproved of U.S. involvement in 1917. But, typically, he attacked American participation in World War I because the farmer suffered through price ceilings during the conflict and lost markets when it was over. It is not true either that Lemke was a complete isolationist or that he supported Hitler's Germany. He favored military preparedness and feared that the United States might have to defend itself against aggression in the near future. Rejecting the racist policies of the Reich, and being free from the bigotry which had marked some earlier agrarian leaders, he endorsed the Zionist movement and was later to offer his name as a sponsor of the American Jewish Congress.[10]

But Lemke's international concerns were always marginal, his main interest being the state of American agriculture. By 1936 he was frantically searching about for a way to fight the hated New Deal. With the Republican Party in the control of conservatives, there was nowhere for him to turn but to a new party.

William Lemke had always equivocated about a national third party.

[9] *Ibid.,* pp. 147–53.

[10] Copies of Lemke addresses dated February 4 and August 16, 1936; Lemke to Major C. S. Farnsworth, January 26, 1934; Lemke to Kitty Thomas, December 23, 1938; and Lemke to Rabbi Stephen S. Wise, December 20, 1939, in Lemke Papers.

He had once declared that "when the liberals are ready to unite, I will go with them anywhere," but on most occasions he had advocated working within the framework of established political organizations to make desired changes. Indeed, the genius of the Nonpartisan League had been its ability to capture regular party organizations for its own ends.[11]

Yet in the critical presidential election year, several factors combined to push Lemke toward his greatest political gamble. An element of romanticism—the craving to undertake grand projects—runs through his career like a silver cord. His adventure with the League, his gubernatorial race as an independent in 1922 and his support for Senator Robert La Follette's third party presidential bid in 1924 all suggest that he was willing to work against the odds in politics. In 1936 he was beginning to believe that a national third party might bring not only revenge against Roosevelt and personal fame and power, but the beginning of a national farmer-labor organization. He always had been sensitive to the possibility of creating such a "new force" in American life and pointed with pride to his role as drafter of the first platform of the Minnesota Farmer-Labor party in 1918. He had been the recipient of extravagant praise and vows of support by farm leaders in the past, and E. W. Everson, President of the National Farmers Union, had written him that "I want you to know I am for William Lemke for the next President and I don't give a whoop which ticket he is on." [12]

In this setting, it is easy to see how Lemke could convince himself that a third party presidential campaign might capture enough electoral votes to throw a close contest into the House of Representatives, an event which would give him great prestige and enormous bargaining power. And even if not this successful, he felt that a strong showing at the head of a third party ticket in 1936 could put him in a position to lead a true Farmer-Labor coalition in 1940, when a fading New Deal could surely be beaten at the polls.

But Lemke realized that he could not organize and lead such a party alone. He needed the help of other discontented political figures, particularly those with national movements that could serve as a base of power for a new party. The obvious choice was that most spectacular political dissident: the Reverend Charles E. Coughlin.

By May, 1936, Lemke's friend Edward E. Kennedy, a power in the Farmers' Union and a Roman Catholic, was urging the North Dakotan

[11] Lemke to Williams, July 16, 1934, Williams Papers; and Lemke to Ray McKaig, December 19, 1934, Lemke Papers.

[12] Blackorby, pp. 501–05; and E. W. Everson to Lemke, June 12, 1935, Lemke Papers.

to make an alliance with the radio priest of Royal Oak. Not much urging was required. Lemke had made contact with Coughlin in the previous months and had found in the priest one of the most persuasive
and articulate supporters of his farm legislation. Regarding the refinance bill, Father Coughlin had told the members of his National
Union that "no member of Congress is worthy of our support at any
time unless he signifies his intention of supporting the Frazier-Lemke
Bill for the farmers." He had attempted to persuade several congressmen and even the President to push the bill through and had filled several of his national broadcasts with praise for Frazier and Lemke.[13]

In return for this support, Lemke had appeared several times on the
platform at NUSJ rallies. Friends, growing concerned, had advised him
to steer clear of men like Father Coughlin and Huey Long, but Lemke
replied that while he did not "accept all of their ideas and ideals," he
admired much of what they were trying to do. The Congressman and
priest exchanged praise-filled letters, Coughlin referring to Lemke as
a "valiant worker in the cause of social justice," and Lemke writing
Coughlin of his admiration for the cleric's efforts "on behalf of all of
humanity." In a nationwide radio broadcast, the farm leader called
Coughlin "that doughty champion of the people's rights."[14]

The radio priest must have seen William Lemke as an attractive ally
in a third party effort. A practicing politician and proven vote getter
in the farm belt, he had gained national repute through his agrarian
crusades in Congress. Lemke's political and economic ideas dovetailed
with Coughlin's at many points. With other leading inflationists, such as
Senators Elmer Thomas of Oklahoma and Gerald Nye of North Dakota,
finding it advisable to support Franklin D. Roosevelt in 1936, Lemke
seemed to be the most "available" man for Coughlin's political purposes.

To Lemke, an alliance with Father Coughlin in the creation of a new
third party must have seemed to be the opportunity of a lifetime. He
was aware that grave problems had haunted previous efforts to unite
an agrarian movement—created under the symbols of rural virtue and
independence—with a city-centered, primarily Catholic, working class
movement. He remembered the difficulties confronting the Knights of
Labor in the 1880's as well as the Bryan-led Democratic party in the

---

[13] Coughlin, *A Series of Lectures . . . 1935–1936*, pp. 135, 138; *New York Times*, May 1 and
May 10, 1936; and Louis B. Ward to Roosevelt, January 25, 1936, Roosevelt Papers,
OF 306.

[14] Covington Hall to Lemke, July 16, 1935; Lemke to Hall, July 20, 1935; Charles E.
Coughlin to Lemke, May 11, 1935; Lemke to Coughlin, May 18, 1935; Lemke address
dated February 22, 1936, in Lemke Papers.

Lemke speaking at the National Union for Social Justice convention in
Cleveland, August 16, 1936. *Wide World*

1890's, and he recalled the particularly unhappy squabbles among Socialists and Nonpartisan Leaguers. He knew too that in the midthirties,
deep religious and ideological differences would divide his followers
from Coughlin's. But he believed that the commonality of political and
economic programs would somehow bridge the gap between the two
groups. William Lemke felt that a successful alliance with the famous
and powerful radio priest represented perhaps his last opportunity to
bid for great fame and influence, strike back at the hated Roosevelt,
and publicize the plight of his beloved farmers.

Strengthened in his resolve by a lifelong association with causes
that initially had demanded sacrifice, Lemke thus found himself on the
brink of a risky new adventure in the spring of 1936. If this leader
and prophet of thousands of western farmers and farm tenants could
find a few more discontented national leaders to aid Coughlin and himself in building a third party, he would willingly throw himself into
the struggle. William Lemke was an unlikely prospect for a presidential candidacy in normal times, but to this farmer-turned-legislator,
1936 seemed to be anything but normal. The neopopulist was ready to
take the political gamble.

PART III

GERALD L. K. SMITH

AND THE SHARE-OUR-WEALTH

SOCIETY

Let me tell you a little about my philosophy.
. . . You've got to be in a state of crisis to
do things. That means you've got to look
over men and events, convince yourself
that there is a crisis. Then you've got the
mentality of a soldier in a trench. Nothing
stops you. You're ruthless. When you're
right and know you're right, you should
now be ruthless. — Gerald L. K. Smith, 1936.

7

The Training of a Mass Leader

It was a scene that repeated itself in a hundred sleepy crossroads towns across the deep South in the early Depression years of 1933–35. A sound truck would drive up and stop at the village square. A tall, powerful man in his early thirties would step out, climb atop the vehicle and adjust the loudspeaker. He was handsome, with flashing blue eyes and with thick sandy hair topping a bronzed, high cheekboned face. His large, strong mouth was almost always set in a winning smile. He would look out at the virtually deserted streets, knowing that with his opening words, a crowd would immediately gather. For his voice was his most important asset. Warm and embracing, deep and rich-timbered, it enabled him to be both loud and mellow, both terrifying and reassuring. It made him, in Senator Huey Pierce Long's words, "next to me the greatest rabble rouser in the country." And it made him, in H. L. Mencken's words, "a rhetorician who was even greater than Bryan."[1]

His name was Gerald L. K. Smith, and in these years he had become first lieutenant to Huey Long, the virtual dictator of the state of Louisiana. He had been appointed chief organizer of Long's Share-Our-Wealth movement, the instrument with which the southern demagogue hoped to capture the White House itself. It was in the service of this movement that Smith was touring the countryside. He would begin each speech by referring to the members of his audience as "brethren," who would then be asked, "How many of you have five suits? Hold up your hands." When no hands would be raised, he would repeat the ques-

[1] H. L. Mencken in Crane (ed.), pp. 192–93.

113

tion again and again, each time lowering the number of suits. When finally he shouted, "How many got just one pair of pants?" hundreds of hands would shoot up and hundreds of voices roar with indignation. This was the cue for Smith to burst into his thundering Share-Our-Wealth sermon, with which he harangued more than two million persons in Dixie in an eighteen month period in the midthirties.[2]

Gerald Smith could turn the crossroads rallies into old-fashioned revival meetings, with himself as the minister and showman, and the Share-Our-Wealth organization spread rapidly across a desperate and poverty-stricken land. By the autumn of 1935, Smith bragged to a reporter that with success in the South, it might be possible to sweep the nation and thus "to duplicate the feat of Adolph Hitler in Germany."[3]

Smith's dreams of glory proved to be outrageously inflated. But unlike some other would-be dictators of the Depression, whose actions were both futile and foolish, this man and his mentor and friend, Huey Long, could not be easily dismissed. Like Father Coughlin, they were indigenous American political extremists who organized a movement which proved to be formidable while it lasted. Smith would be an important factor when the demagogues made their bid for power in the Depression decade.

Indeed Gerald L. K. Smith was one of the most colorful demagogues of modern American history. He parlayed a golden voice and an insatiable lust for power into a national reputation while still a relatively young man. His ambition was boundless: he wanted to rule all America.

Gerald Lyman Kenneth Smith was trained to be a leader. He came by his religio-rhetorical bent honestly, for he was a product of the midwestern Protestant fundamentalist tradition. Born in Pardeeville, Wisconsin, in 1898, he was the son of a circuit-riding third generation minister of the Church of the Disciples of Christ, one of the rural "hell-fire and brimstone" preachers of the late nineteenth century.[4]

The younger Smith had to ride fourteen miles on horseback to attend high school, where he won a reputation of being, like his father, a fine orator. Soon known as the best debater in the county, he won elocution contests with, fittingly, Bryan's Cross of Gold speech. Indeed, there was

[2] Carlton Beals, *The Story of Huey P. Long* (Philadelphia: J. B. Lippincott Co., 1935), p. 291.

[3] *New York Times*, September 22, 1935.

[4] U.S., Congress, House, Committee on Un-American Activities, *Hearings, Investigation of Un-American Propaganda Activities in the United States (Gerald L. K. Smith)*, 79th Cong., 2d Sess., 1946, p. 7.

a strong strain of Populism in his rural boyhood training—he admitted to having been "brought up" on *La Follette's Weekly.*[5]

Smith went to Indiana for college training where he studied literature, Biblical history, and dramatics at Valpariso University, graduating after two and one-half years at the age of nineteen. He then moved to Butler University in Indianapolis to engage, briefly, in postgraduate work.[6]

But the pastor's son was destined for the ministry. Ordained in the Christian Church at eighteen, he had assisted at various pulpits throughout the remaining months in college. His first legitimate "call" was to the farming community of Deep River, where his Billy Sunday-like evangelism brought thirty-eight new converts and baptisms within a month. After a rousing performance as guest preacher in St. Louis, he moved to more prestigious pulpits in Indianapolis, serving first at the Seventh Christian Church and then at the bigger Butler University Church.[7]

Gerald L. K. Smith's ministerial record in Indiana was a curious and inconsistent one. Early in his career at Butler, he was known to be one of the more important members of the booming Indiana Ku Klux Klan, but he was liked by the congregation because he was eloquent, interested in social work, and, as always, a superb money raiser. He might have stayed permanently at this church if his wife had not suffered a serious illness in 1928 which required a move to the South. He chose Louisiana, becoming minister of the Kings Highway Christian Church in Shreveport, largest of his denomination in the state. The move to Louisiana was to change his career and his life.[8]

At Shreveport, Smith revitalized the congregation, broadening its rolls and making his dynamic presence felt by joining businessmen's clubs, sponsoring athletic teams and inaugurating his own radio program over a chain of southern stations. Always the compelling speaker, he turned social reformer on the air and launched attacks on working conditions in mines and farms throughout Louisiana and southwestern Tennessee. His microphone audiences responded in the same way as did Coughlin's. Mail response increased rapidly enough to convince Gerald Smith that exposure of injustices was the road to fame and fortune. He became a full time harvester of the grapes of discontent, at-

[5] *Ibid.*

[6] *Ibid.*

[7] Herbert Harris, "That Third Party," *Current History,* XLV, No. 1 (October, 1936), 84–85.

[8] House Committee on Un-American Activities, *Gerald L. K. Smith Hearings,* 1946, p. 7.

tacking public utilities companies and exposing sweat shop conditions (even becoming a union organizer on the side).[9]

Taking over the directorship of the local community chest, he demanded that the 218 men and corporations owning 72 per cent of the property in town contribute a similar percentage to the $200,000 chest fund. This irritated his more affluent congregants, who were already grumbling over the minister's accusation that one of their number had been engaged in shady oil dealings in Texas. When Smith accepted an invitation to be a representative to the 1932 Olympic games in Los Angeles, and then overstayed his leave by making a series of eastern trips before returning home, he had so exacerbated relations with the church's membership that his ministerial career at Shreveport was in serious jeopardy.[10]

It was his contacts with that most famous of all Louisianians, Huey Pierce Long, that ended one career and led to another. Smith had first met Long when, upon discovering that local businessmen were about to foreclose on a million dollars worth of Shreveport homes before final passage of the Home Owners Loan Corporation Act, he helped persuade the Governor to sponsor state legislation blocking the realty sharks. When the southern strong man went to the Senate, the minister became a close associate, traveling to Washington for several meetings and even being identified in the caption of a Washington newspaper picture as a Long bodyguard. Understandably perplexed, church elders questioned Smith about this curious behavior. The preacher's impolitic answer soon had the congregation split wide open on the question of whether to ask him to leave. A truculent Smith resisted pressure but at last was forced out.[11]

Smith did not really seem to care. Perhaps it was his close contact with great power that made the church feel too restricting, for now he appeared to be looking about for a more imposing forum. Briefly flirting with William Dudley Pelley's fascistic Silver Shirt Legion of America, he gave lectures in late 1933 on such topics as "Some Day 100 Million Americans Will Hide Behind the Silver Shirt For Protection," and "Why I Left the Conventional Pulpit to Join The Christian Militia of the Silver Shirts." But the Pelley movement was too weak to hold a man like Gerald Smith, and Huey Long, impressed by the preacher's

    [9] "News and Comment From the Nation's Capital," *Literary Digest*, CXIX, No. 11 (March 16, 1935), 12.
    [10] *Ibid.*
    [11] Harnett T. Kane, *Louisiana Hayride* (New York: William Morrow & Company, 1941), pp. 150–51.

magnetic personality and taken by the idea of having an ordained minister in his entourage to add lustre to a tarred organization, offered Smith a better position.[12]

Smith's job was to be a twofold one. He would be both a speechmaker for the Senator and the national organizer for a network of Share-Our-Wealth clubs which Huey Long proposed to establish throughout America. So now Gerald L. K. Smith could turn his considerable persuasive talents to a new crusade. Once again he was to be ostensibly a social reformer, setting out to argue for an equitable distribution of the nation's wealth. But just as in his earlier periods, the liberalism was only a surface sheen. For this man seemed to have no political or ethical principles. He had been not at all troubled earlier in his career in hopping from the social gospel to the racist-nationalist fanaticism of the Klan or the Silver Shirts. Nor was he troubled in 1934 as he moved to Huey Long's side.

Smith was the complete opportunist. This was the driving force in his life, and he was frank about it. Later, when he was famous enough to have reporters cluster about him, he would grin as he was kidded about the tricks of the trade of mass leadership. "Oh I'm a rabble rouser," he once told a journalist. "Put that down, a rabble rouser. God made me a rabble rouser of and for the right. Better spell that word right with a capital R." [13]

Hungry for success and power, Gerald L. K. Smith was certain that he could win nationwide fame and influence in the new Share-Our-Wealth movement. Shortly after coming on the job he boasted, "We're getting 20,000 new members a day. When we have enough millions, we'll make ourselves heard. We'll change things in this country!" [14]

---

[12] Ralph Lord Roy, *Apostles of Discord* (Boston: The Beacon Press, 1953), p. 60.

[13] Walter Davenport, "The Mysterious Gerald Smith," *Collier's*, CXIII, No. 10 (March 4, 1944), 15.

[14] Herman B. Deutsch, "Huey Long, The Last Phase," *Saturday Evening Post*, CCVIII, No. 15 (October 12, 1935), 27.

8

The Share-Our-Wealth Movement

Gerald L. K. Smith once wrote that "in order to succeed, a mass movement must be superficial for quick appeal, fundamental for permanence and dogmatic for certainty." The Share-Our-Wealth movement certainly fulfilled these criteria. But Smith also knew that any successful movement had to be built around a strong, magnetic, and even ruthless leader. Huey Long, the minister believed, was a man unique in all America. "Long's thinking is a correct representation of the mass mind," he marveled. "Huey is the greatest political strategist alive. . . . He is a superman."[1]

Smith's superman was forty-one years old in 1934. Born and raised in Winfield, Louisiana, Huey Long had spent his boyhood among the hill folk of the upper parishes who grubbed out a living on marginal land and who hated the plantation owners and business hierarchy in New Orleans. Winn Parish had been a center of Populist discontent in the 1890's and had elected a Socialist to local office in 1908. The young Long was profoundly influenced by this environment of political and social ferment.[2]

At school he, like Smith, excelled at elocution, and was continuously committing to memory passages from the Bible, practicing his evangelistic style at summer camp meetings. After studying briefly at the University of Oklahoma and Tulane Law School, Long was admitted to the

[1] Gerald L. K. Smith, "How Come Huey Long? (2. Or Superman)," *New Republic,* LXXXII, No. 1054 (February 13, 1935), 15.

[2] T. Harry Williams, "The Gentleman from Louisiana: Demagogue or Democrat," *The Journal of Southern History,* XXVI, No. 1 (February, 1960), pp. 6–7.

Louisiana bar at twenty-two and within three years won election as a Railroad and Public Service Commissioner. Two stormy terms in this office brought him statewide fame as an enemy of big corporations. Capitalizing on his popularity among the Cajun, redneck, and hillbilly voters, he campaigned across the state with religious fervor to win election as Governor in 1928.[3]

Governor Huey Long effected changes that benefited the rural poor and middle class. He increased state social services by building roads, schools, public housing, bridges and reclamation projects, as well as improving education and health programs. He shrewdly manipulated the support which these efforts brought his administration, creating a political machine so powerful that within a matter of years he could run the state legislature as if it were his own private fiefdom. Intimidating rival leaders and carefully brandishing patronage, he became not only the most powerful state executive in the nation but one of the most autocratic leaders in high office in American history. A brilliant campaigner—some called him the best stump speaker in America— Long made himself the personification of the aspirations and prejudices of the underdog southern farmer and villager. Playing on the country folks' deep-seated hatred and jealousy of downstate big city people, he utilized the symbols of the old Populist crusaders to become both the reformer and the reactionary, who took from the rich to give to the poor but who also punished those who denied the old line American farmer his place in the sun. He did for the poor-white Anglo-Saxon Protestant agrarians of the South what Coughlin was doing for the Irish and German Catholics of the urban north: providing an outlet for frustrations, a way of both redressing economic and political wrongs and closing old social and psychological wounds. But unlike Coughlin and some other mass leaders, Long produced real reforms which brightened the lives of his followers and his early success was due more to his record than his tactics or latent appeals.[4]

Huey Long was a political genius, and by 1930, having solidly established himself as ruler of Louisiana, he turned his attention to the national scene and easily won election to the United States Senate. In Washington, Long soon made his presence felt. Clad in incredible suits and shirts which cried out for color photography, he packed the galler-

[3] Reinhard H. Luthin, *American Demagogues* (Boston: The Beacon Press, 1954), pp. 237–43.

[4] *Ibid.*, pp. 246–51; Ferkiss, p. 156; and Swing, p. 88; and Williams, *The Journal of Southern History*, XXVI, No. 1, pp. 13–18.

ies and infuriated his colleagues by delivering long and bizarre speeches filled with Biblical quotations and vituperative personal attacks on fellow legislators. If the Senate be a citadel, if it be the most exclusive of clubs, then Huey broke all the rules and loved it. Like Father Coughlin, he too at first was a supporter of President Roosevelt. But this lone wolf proved an unreliable friend of the New Deal in Congress. More interested in winning national repute for himself than in aiding the Administration's legislative program, the Louisianian refused to be subordinate to anyone, including the President. Inevitably a break came between the Long machine and the Administration — the specific issue being a squabble over control of federal patronage in the southern state — and the Kingfish declared war on FDR.[5]

Long's instrument for conducting this war was the Share-Our-Wealth movement. For many years he had toyed with various schemes for an enforced equitable distribution of the wealth of the United States, and in the spring of 1933 he went so far as to introduce a Senate resolution to confiscate incomes over $1 million and inheritances over $5 million. But it was not until after his split with Roosevelt that Long, in January, 1934, set up a national organization, without dues of any sort, known as the Share-Our-Wealth Society.[6]

In a radio address announcing its formation, the Senator traced the origins of his wealth-sharing scheme from King Solomon to Socrates to Pope Pius XI, and from the Pilgrim Fathers to Theodore Roosevelt and finally to himself. Actually, he owed more to the attitudes of the Winn Parish petty capitalists and poor farmers of his boyhood and their hatred of men of wealth.[7]

Radical was indeed the word for Long's movement. Those who joined it were asked to endorse an eight point program:

1. Limitation of poverty by providing every family at least $5,000 debt free;
2. Homes, automobiles and radios provided for every family needing them;
3. "Adequate" old age pensions;
4. Limitation of hours of work to balance production with consumption;

[5] Stan Opotowsky, *The Longs of Louisiana* (New York: E. P. Dutton & Company, 1960), p. 75.

[6] Deutsch, *Saturday Evening Post,* CCVIII, No. 15, 90.

[7] Forest Davis, *Huey Long, A Candid Biography* (New York: Dodge Publishing Company, 1935), 275, 283. One prominent southern historian, a student of Long's career, has suggested that the idea for Share-Our-Wealth came not only from the populism and socialism of Long's youthful home, but Huey Long's knowledge of Reconstruction history and the Freedmen's Bureau's experiment with forty acres and a mule. See Williams, *The Journal of Southern History,* XXVI, No. 1, p. 8.

5. Agricultural surpluses to be purchased by the federal government;

6. Immediate cash payments of veterans bonuses;

7. Universal free college education to all qualified by I.Q. examinations;

8. Community redevelopment, highway construction and industrial dispersal to be undertaken throughout the country.[8]

To pay for this program, and especially to assure the equal division of wealth, Long proposed a financial census of the nation's population and taxation or capital levy used to seize all savings above a certain figure, set first at $10 million and later lowered to $5 million and finally $1.7 million. Huey wrote a book with the engaging title, *My First Days in the White House,* to explain the details of the scheme. Published posthumously in 1935 and written in narrative fashion as if Long had been elected President in 1936, it was partly satire (he wrote, for example, that FDR had been appointed Secretary of the Navy and Al Smith Director of the Budget), and partly a vehicle for his grandiose proposals for reform of almost everything from the penal code to railroad ownership. But it contained also significant statements revealing Long's attitude toward contemporary panaceas and their proponents. He enthusiastically endorsed Father Coughlin's plan for a national bank and warmly embraced the idea of the old age pension advocated by Dr. Townsend. The main burden of the volume, however, was to demonstrate that wealth-sharing would work. Long convinced few economists.[9]

In point of fact, Long's plan was only a wild dream. In computing the national wealth to be divided among the people, he included purely latent resources. Only by some miracle could he hope to convert forests and mines, highways and schools, oil wells and transportation systems, factories and battleships into house and bank account for every family. The Senator had no training in economics, and his knowledge of economic relationships was skimpy at best. In the end, economists dismissed Share-Our-Wealth as a hoax, one critic calling it "a monstrous and tragic joke . . . based upon either demagogic hypocrisy or else ignorance so abysmal as to inspire awe." Far from being able to provide every family a minimum of $5,000, Long, in 1933, would have had to confiscate all incomes over $4,000 to assure a paltry $1,400 to the needy.[10]

[8] Davis, pp. 276–78.

[9] Huey Pierce Long, *My First Days in the White House* (Harrisburg, Pennsylvania: The Telegraph Press, 1935), pp. 3–6, 26–88, 112–13, 143–50.

[10] Beals, pp. 311–12; and *The Statistical History of the United States* (Stamford, Conn.: Fairfield Publishers, 1965), pp. 163–66.

If he had believed in socialism, Huey's plan would have at least had the virtue of consistency. However, he defended the theory of capitalism and argued that he wanted not to destroy private management but merely to break up monopoly control. This, despite his scheme for a federal share-our-wealth corporation which would confiscate existing large business and his curious response to the charge that this might destroy individual initiative: "If America for its greatness must depend on exciting super-greed for the sake of modern development, we have set a bad example to selfless science and political heroes past and future." [11]

Huey Long denied that he was a demagogue. "I would describe a demagogue as a politician who don't keep his promises. On that basis, I'm the first man to have power in Louisiana who ain't a demagogue because I kept every promise I ever made!" And it was true that in his own state Long had, in his words, only fought "fire with fire," using ruthless and autocratic tactics to fight a corrupt and oligarchical machine—the "Old Regulars"—which had protected privilege and turned its back on the poor. Still, whether it was the burden of southern history or his own lust for power which led to repressive and vengeful actions along with reform, it is not enough to accept his apologia that social and economic progress justified all. (Nor can even that defense be used in reference to the unrealistic Share-Our-Wealth scheme.) Long himself questioned his methods but insisted that "the people" were on his side. His close friends and supporters went further, acknowledging and sometimes celebrating his one-man rule. Gerald Smith explained, "It is the dictatorship of the surgical theatre. . . . The man is in charge because he knows." [12]

Huey Long was also a cynic. Never attempting to share the wealth in Louisiana, in the years in which he controlled the state, income and inheritance taxes remained low (although corporate taxes were raised)

[11] Long, *My First Days* . . . , pp. 95–111.

[12] Quoted in Swing, p. 73; and Kane, p. 140; and Williams, *The Journal of Southern History*, XXVI, No. 1, pp. 8–12, 15–21. T. Harry Williams, in an important paper utilizing interviews with a number of Long and anti-Long leaders, deplores the use of the "much abused" word "demagogue," prefering Eric Hoffer's term "mass leader." While acknowledging Long's faults, Williams suggests that Huey Long's iron will, capacity for hatred and audacity made him the ideal enemy of a destructive old order and the instrument for bringing long overdue change to his state. Yet was there, in Williams' words, an "essential respect for the democratic system" in Long's Louisiana? And in devising Share-Our-Wealth, was not Huey Long, whatever his "faith in humanity," attempting "to use the frustrations of men to build a brave new theoretical world," the one thing a good mass leader will always avoid?

and many of the thirty-five new taxes levied were ungraduated and directed at the consumer. Indeed, he was accused of personally attempting to share in the state's wealth, for the U.S. Secret Service was investigating over $100,000 of his unreported income on graft. When confronted with such charges, the Kingfish was reported to have leered and said, "There may be smarter guys than Huey Long, but they ain't in the state of Louisiana." [13]

But although many Americans were frightened by such a man and such a plan, although they recoiled at the radical nature of the scheme and the hypnotic power of its creator, and although some even expressed fears that another native fascist movement was under way in the United States, contemporary European events do not seem particularly relevant to this discussion. For, as a British student of fascism has pointed out, the Share-Our-Wealth appeal was "based on the very notion which fascism scorns more than anything else — that it is the function of the state to take care of all the individuals in it." [14]

The southern strong man denied the charges of fascism. He once remarked, "Just say I'm *sui generis* and let it go at that." In an effort to analyze the origins and nature of Share-Our-Wealth, however, one cannot simply "let it go at that." For Long's organization was not unique — but it was uniquely American. [15]

Like Coughlin's National Union, the Share-Our-Wealth scheme owed much to the Populist tradition in the United States. The desire to pro-

[13] Davis, p. 276; Luthin, pp. 243–45, 250; and Opotowsky, pp. 73–74. Williams suggests that Louisianians' concept of corruption, perhaps based on "Latin realism" as opposed to Anglo-Saxon "sanctimoniousness," is different than that of other Americans: "They admire a deal" if it is "executed with skill and a flourish." But he quotes Long's associates in denying charges of graft against the Long machine. While road builders and others winning large state contracts might be "called on for regular contributions" and the many state employees assessed dues for the war chest, the Long deputies defended their system as more moral than that of the opposition and so effective that Huey Long "did not have to graft." See Williams, *The Journal of Southern History*, XXVI, No. 1, pp. 4, 14.

[14] Ferkiss, pp. 133, 151; and E. B. Ashton, *The Fascist: His State and His Mind* (New York: William Morrow & Company, 1937), p. 280.

[15] Davis, pp. 34, 37; and Kane, p. 140. Gerald L. K. Smith, in an address thirty years after the death of Long, claimed that "we were represented to the world as fascists . . . because we dared to fight the barons." He recalled that Long "refused to receive any representative of the German Nazi regime." See Gerald L. K. Smith's essay, "The Huey Long Movement," in Rita James Simon (ed.), *As We Saw the Thirties* (Urbana, Illinois: University of Illinois Press, 1967), pp. 61–62. Williams notes that Long fought the Klan, and when Dr. Hiram Evans denounced him as un-American, he declared that "that imperial bastard will never set foot in Louisiana." Indeed, in state and national politics he rejected both religious and racial prejudice. See Williams, *The Journal of Southern History*, XXVI, No. 1, pp. 13–16, 21.

tect the small entrepreneur from the abuses suffered at the hands of monopolists and bankers was the heritage of Populism. The very slogan of the movement, "Every Man A King," was taken from a campaign speech of William Jennings Bryan in 1900; in fact, most of the public statements of Long and his protégé Smith were couched in the vocabulary of that earlier crusade.[16]

The Louisiana Kingfish lectured Congress on the "Doom of America's Dream" and hinted darkly that the "hoarders of wealth . . . (would) destroy humanity by the millions." When a bond issue in his state failed, the Wall Street banking houses were accused of being "out to get" the common man's leader, and when a national magazine printed a critical article about Share-Our-Wealth, the "Wall Street controlled press" was to blame. *The American Progress,* spokesman for the S-O-W organization, featured stories describing J. P. Morgan's increasing wealth, the record sales of "millionaires' yachts," and an alleged "Standard Oil plot to kill Huey Long." Sometimes all the enemies of Populism would be lumped into one story: "High-brow Brain Trusters, brutish . . . low-brow eastern politicians, [and] top-hatted . . . cigar-smoking Wall Streeters" who combine with evil Europeans to cheat and defraud the common citizen.[17]

That the Share-Our-Wealth movement appealed chiefly to lower-class, rural, southern whites was reflected partly in the massive flow of mail received by its founder. Ninety per cent of the correspondence directed to Huey Long in 1934 consisted of poorly written, ungrammatical letters in pencil on lined note paper. The indigent and uneducated country folk, suffering severely in the Depression, turned in large numbers to the men who offered themselves as saviors. As Gerald L. K. Smith wrote, "We did not create a state of mind; we merely discovered and recognized a state of mind that had been created by conditions."[18]

Indeed, it was Gerald Smith, shrewdly exploiting this "state of mind," who was playing an ever more powerful role in the Share-Our-Wealth movement by 1935. While some observers still found the minister "as

[16] Ferkiss, pp. 323–24; and Huey P. Long, *Every Man A King* (New Orleans: National Book Company, Inc., 1933), p. 297. Long wrote a symbolic poem, using the Share-Our-Wealth slogan: "Every Man a King, Every Man a King; For you can be a millionaire; There's Something belonging to others; There's enough for all people to share." But Long made it clear that he was to be the leader, even in an organization of "kings." He affected the title of "Kingfish" (taken from the name of a character in the radio program "Amos and Andy").

[17] *Ibid.*, pp. 316–19; and *American Progress*, January 4, February 1, and May 4, 1935.

[18] Franklin, pp. 21–22; and Smith, *New Republic*, LXXXII, No. 1054, 15.

meek as Moses when Huey is around," Smith seemed to sense that his position in the organization was ever improving. Arguing that "this movement is already bigger than Huey," he began to use the collective "we" in discussing the formation of policy: "We decided Huey should take this stand. . . . We decided to make some money." [19]

Smith roamed across Dixie in search of new converts, making the most of his role as national organizer of the Share-Our-Wealth movement. In one brief barnstorming tour of South Carolina in March, 1935, he enrolled forty thousand new members after a series of performances which mixed Barnum with Billy Sunday. Any platform trick was good enough if it elicited results: one of Smith's favorites was to stand with arms outstretched as though pinned to a cross while telling his listeners, "If I'm not speaking the truth, shoot me while I stand here helpless." (But of course his sound truck was surrounded by vigilant state police.) So it went with the man Mencken once called "the gustiest and goriest, loudest and lustiest, the deadliest and damndest orator ever heard on this or any other earth . . . , the champion boob-bumper of all epochs." [20]

But just how large did Long and Smith's Share-Our-Wealth movement grow? In January, 1935, *The American Progress*, whose monthly circulation had risen quickly to 150,000, claimed that the society "now voices the demands of 12 million people." A few weeks later, Huey Long's headquarters boasted that it had on file the records of 27,431 S-O-W clubs located in over eight thousand cities, towns and villages. Yet contemporary observers viewed these figures with caution, noting the arbitrary manner in which the organization's leaders manipulated numbers. For example, in February, 1935, one such leader claimed 7.6 million members and another mentioned "three million plus," the earlier and more grandiose figures having been quickly forgotten. [21]

But if the dimensions of the movement were open to dispute, the geographical area in which its appeal was strongest seemed clear enough. Most powerful in the South, its greatest number of supporters were from Louisiana, Arkansas, Oklahoma, Mississippi, Alabama, Georgia, South

[19] F. Raymond Daniell in Hanson W. Baldwin and Shepard Stone (eds.), *We Saw It Happen* (New York: The World Publishing Company, 1941), p. 96; and Heywood Broun, "Broun's Page," *The Nation*, CXLIII, No. 8 (August 22, 1936), 213.

[20] Hodding Carter, "How Come Huey Long?" (I. Bogeyman), *New Republic*, LXXXII, No. 1054 (February 13, 1935), 13; and William Bradford Huie, "Gerald Smith's Bid For Power," *American Mercury*, LV, No. 224 (August, 1942), 147.

[21] Smith, *New Republic*, LXXXII, No. 1054, 15; *American Progress*, January 4, 1935; and Francis Chase, Jr., *Sound and Fury* (New York: Harper and Brothers Publishers, 1942), p. 85.

Carolina, and East Texas. Yet there were followers in all sections of the country and even Ontario, Canada, had seventeen Share-Our-Wealth clubs.[22]

These local clubs were the backbone of the organization, and the key to their success was simplicity. Any two persons could form a Share-Our-Wealth club, whose only function was to distribute the plan's literature throughout the community. They met in living rooms and were unencumbered by fund raising efforts, Long facetiously saying "most organizations are broken up by the treasurer running away with the money."[23] The proliferation of these local units kept Huey Long's clerical staff busy around the clock. Twenty-one secretaries worked the day shift in his Washington office and fourteen were employed nightly. If a person wrote to the Senator on any subject, he would receive in return a circular from the Share-Our-Wealth movement containing a coupon with spaces for names and addresses of officers for a local club. Once this form was completed, the individual would become president of a local club and would be called on then merely to send in from time to time names of newly recruited members. Smith and Long wanted the units to remain small, arguing that if "the opposition" infiltrated one or two of them in a town through offers of bribes or federal patronage to key members, the national effort would be unharmed if there were a dozen still functioning. Club presidents were well supplied with copies of recent Long speeches and other literature, for the Kingfish made full use of his congressional franking privileges.[24]

The nature of these organizing tactics raised the question of how seriously this movement should be taken. Were its local units anything more than fan clubs for colorful orators who promised to share the wealth in a time of scarcity? Was its national organization anything more than a glorified mailing list? Events were soon to suggest that although the Share-Our-Wealth movement's strength in 1935 was somewhat nebulous, it contained within it the raw material for significant political action. One man who believed this was the chief strategist of the Democratic Party, James A. Farley.

Farley, who had learned to respect Huey Long's campaigning ability in 1932, saw the Louisianian as a "formidable political figure" who was

---

[22] Wallace S. Sayre, "Political Groundswell," *Current History*, XLIV, No. 3 (June, 1936), 57.

[23] Gerald L. K. Smith in Simon (ed.), pp. 64–65. Smith claimed that there were "at least a hundred thousand" little Share-Our-Wealth societies operating at the time of Long's assassination.

[24] *Ibid.*; Opotowsky, p. 73; and Franklin, pp. 23–24.

undoubtedly planning the formation of a third party for 1936. Noting private reports that wealthy men were prepared to finance such a venture "in a substantial way," Farley asked National Democratic Committee statistician Emil Hurja to make a secret poll of the Kingfish's strength. The results indicated that on a third party ticket, Long could poll three to four million votes and that his following was strong in the North as well as in the South, in industrial as well as in farming areas. Other leading Administration men echoed these fears—Louis Howe told the President that White House mail indicated how wide a currency the Share-Our-Wealth idea was gaining (even a bank president wrote that he preferred Huey Long to FDR), and Colonel House warned the Chief Executive that there was talk that Long could do to him what Theodore Roosevelt did to Taft in 1912.[25]

It seemed incomprehensible to some observers that a man of Long's political plasticity would lead a quixotic Share-Our-Wealth crusade against President Roosevelt in 1936. They speculated that Huey might set up a third party but not head its ticket himself, a tactic designed possibly to force the Democrats to grant him concessions, or, if particularly fortunate, to throw a close election to the Republicans. There were rumors that Long was really preparing for 1940—"1940 will be my real year," he had told one friend. And although he made boastful statements about his 1936 presidential plans, he also indicated that he would run for either the governorship or the Senate in that year. But those who feared a Long bid for the presidency in 1936 noticed that Huey had made sure that the date of the congressional primary in Louisiana was shifted from September back to January to coincide with the state office primary in order to permit him to run for President without forfeiting his Senate reelection.[26]

It is more than likely that the Kingfish himself had not decided what role to play in 1936. Obviously, his ultimate aim was the Presidency. (When he rebuilt the governor's mansion in Baton Rouge, he made it a replica of the White House, "so I'll be used to living in it.") He told New Orleans Mayor T. Semmes Walmsley, "There's going to be a revolution in this country and I'm going to lead it." When and how the revo-

[25] James A. Farley, *Behind the Ballots* (New York: Harcourt, Brace and Company, 1938), pp. 171, 249–50; Raymond Moley, *After Seven Years* (New York: Harper and Brothers Publishers, 1939), p. 305; Farley, *Jim Farley's Story*, p. 51; Ickes, I, p. 423; W. E. Warren to Roosevelt, February 14, 1935, Roosevelt Papers, Official File 1403 (Huey P. Long); and Emil Hurja's report on "Huey Long's impact on those voting in 1932 and 1935" in Elliott Roosevelt (ed.), p. 428.
[26] Allan P. Sindler, *Huey Long's Louisiana* (Baltimore: The Johns Hopkins Press, 1956), pp. 85–86; Davis, pp. 213, 273–74; Kane, p. 126; and Beals, p. 298.

lution would come remained unclear. But its inevitability was a certainty to him: Huey Pierce Long was on record as insisting that "we ain't depending on anybody else or any political party. . . . We're building up an organization in the country like we did in Louisiana. . . . There positively will be a Share-Our-Wealth ticket in the field in the 1936 campaign, there's no doubt about that." Pointing to his political base of strength in the South, he declared, "I already have Louisiana, Mississippi and Arkansas and I'll take Alabama when I get ready." [27]

Long launched a series of smashing attacks on the New Deal early in 1935. Dismissing the relief legislation as a "half-starvation dole," he called the pension plan of the Administration "a fake" and termed the NRA "fascistic." FDR was portrayed as an unprincipled, corrupt, venal politician, and New Dealers James A. Farley, Hugh Johnson and Henry Wallace were accused of dealing in graft. He carried this message to many states, campaigning with Gerald L. K. Smith throughout the South and ranging as far north as Des Moines, Iowa, where he addressed the National Farm Holiday Association meeting in April. He boasted to *New York Times* correspondent Arthur Krock, "I can take this Roosevelt. . . . He's scared of me. . . . I can outpromise him and he knows it." [28]

The President heard this threat and struck back vigorously at Huey Long. He asked Senator Theodore Bilbo to counterattack Share-Our-Wealth forces in certain southern states, a tactic which bore fruit when a friend of the Administration won an important primary election in Mississippi in August. While the Federal Bureau of Investigation and the Treasury Department were urged to accelerate their investigations of the Long machine in Louisiana, Public Works Administration projects were halted in that state. At the same time patronage was dispensed lavishly to Long's foes throughout Dixie. [29]

The battle between Franklin D. Roosevelt and Huey P. Long was still building to its climax when the Kingfish fell victim to an assassin's bullet on September 8, 1935. The sudden loss of its leader destroyed the Share-Our-Wealth movement's chances of sweeping northward in 1936. And the sudden death of Long moved Gerald L. K. Smith to the center of the Share-Our-Wealth stage.

The demagogic minister lost no time in asserting his leadership. With

[27] Opotowsky, pp. 71, 82; and Davis, pp. 41, 259.

[28] "Our Blundering Generation," speech delivered by Huey P. Long over radio network NBC on March 7, 1935, copy in Franklin D. Roosevelt Library; Robert Morss Lovett, "Huey Long Invades the Middle West," *New Republic,* LXXXVIII, No. 1067 (May 15, 1935), 10–11; and Oral History Research Project, Reminiscences of Arthur Krock, No. 54.

[29] Burns, p. 214; Luthin, pp. 265–67; and Davis, pp. 244–45.

Huey P. Long's funeral at the State House in Baton Rouge, Louisiana, September, 1935, drew a crowd of 125,000, who heard Gerald L. K. Smith eulogize the fallen leader. *Wide World*

a single stroke the central pivot had been removed from the organization, but Gerald Smith, billing himself as "the head of the Share-Our-Wealth Society of America, with ten million members," sought to make Long's death his opportunity. In an angry telegram to the President, he asked federal aid in "bringing to justice the perpetrators of the assassination." Preaching to 125,000 mourners at Huey Long's funeral, the Reverend Mr. Smith deified the fallen leader and called for renewed Share-Our-Wealth activity in Long's name. Describing Long as a "statesman . . . , a tender father . . . [and] a musical heart that loved the songs of the common people," he asked that "the blood which dropped upon this soil . . . seal our hearts together," and he implored his listeners to "take up the torch [and] complete the task." Shouting his peroration, Smith cried, "This untimely death makes restless the souls of we who adored him. . . . The ideals which he planted in our hearts have created a gnawing hunger for a new order. This hunger . . . can only be satisfied by the completion of that victory toward which he led us." [30]

In the days following the funeral, the minister kept his name before the public by hinting that the assassination was the result of a "dastardly plot" involving several federal employees. But Gerald Smith soon discovered that the time for oratory and publicity-seeking was over in Louisiana; he found that attempts to implicate the Roosevelt Administration in Long's death fell on deaf ears as Huey's heirs prepared for the battle which would decide the future course of Louisiana politics.[31]

Although Smith announced that "as organizer for the Share-Our-Wealth movement," he intended "to carry out the work of our leader . . . supporting only those I think Huey would support and that does not include any political lineup," it soon became obvious that there was no avoiding alignment with one of the two political blocs which "lined up" within the Louisiana machine shortly after Long's death. The machine politicians had never really liked the bombastic Smith; they felt that he was little more than a hired hand who had never been involved in the inner councils of the Long organization. But for a brief period in the autumn of 1935, the minister was in a strategic position. As the best known of Long's heirs, his name was familiar to mil-

[30] Smith to Roosevelt, September 16, 1935, OF 1403, Roosevelt Papers; and Luthin, p. 270. Long's assassin was Dr. Carl Austin Weiss, a 30-year-old physician who was the son-in-law of Judge Benjamin F. Parz, a political enemy who Long was planning to gerrymander out of office. Weiss was shot and killed by Long's bodyguards moments after firing the fatal bullet.

[31] Smith to Roosevelt, September 9, 1935, Roosevelt Papers. Later, Smith became more explicit in his accusations concerning Long's murder. "The Roosevelt Gang . . . conspired with those who effected his assassination," he wrote in *The Cross and the Flag*, September, 1952.

lions throughout the South and many Louisianians were sure that he controlled the Share-Our-Wealth movement. Thus he could prove a valuable asset to a group engaged in the struggle for mastery of the state party.[32]

Smith joined a coalition that included Earle Christenberry, formerly Long's executive secretary, and James A. Noe, lieutenant governor and former president pro tempore of the State Senate. On the other side was a group of hard party professionals led by the speaker of the State House of Representatives, Allen J. Ellender, and including such powerful politicians as Seymour Weiss, treasurer of the Long machine, Jules Fischer, leader in the State Senate, John Fournet, chief justice of the State Supreme Court, Robert Maestri, Abe Sushan, and Huey's brother, Earl Long.[33]

At four o'clock one morning shortly after Long's funeral, the press was called to a Baton Rouge hotel room where the Smith group issued copies of the "Long ticket" for the coming elections. The nominees were James A. Noe for Governor and Wade Martin for the United States Senate. Smith announced that he would accompany Martin to Washington and become the new Senator's secretary—continuing the leadership of the Share-Our-Wealth society with the aid of Congressional franking privileges. The minister pointed out that both Earl Long and Governor Oscar K. Allen had endorsed the Noe-Martin ticket.[34]

Maestri, Weiss, and the other members of their group were appalled. They knew that Long and Allen had not committed themselves to Noe's candidacy. Allen was such an issue-straddling mediocrity that he had refused to cast his lot with either side; indeed, it was rumored that Huey Long had once remarked that if a leaf flew through the window while Allen was signing legislative bills, "OK" would sign the leaf as well. And as for Earl Long, the Maestri-Weiss group wanted him on their Democratic slate, for his name was magic among the followers of the late Huey. Furious at what they considered a baseless, publicity-seeking piece of trickery on the part of the Noe-Smith cabal, they quickly called another press conference. The real Long ticket, Maestri and Weiss declared, would be headed by gubernatorial candidate Richard Webster Leche, a District Judge who was considered a political lightweight—a man who knew how to take orders. Earl Long was named the nominee for lieutenant governor and Allen Ellender and Governor

[32] Kane, p. 150.

[33] Thomas Martin, *Dynasty: The Longs of Louisiana* (New York: G. P. Putnam's Sons, 1960), pp. 152–53.

[34] *Ibid.*, pp. 154–55; and Kane, p. 153.

Allen were listed as the senatorial choices, Allen to fill the one year remaining from Huey Long's original term. The battle lines had been drawn.[35]

It was at this point that Gerald L. K. Smith wilted under fire and changed sides. Always an undependable political ally, he caved in once again after a heated meeting with Robert Maestri and declared that he was switching his support to the Leche-Long ticket. Predictably, this enraged James A. Noe, for it doomed any chance he might have had of securing the nomination. Noe bitterly accused Gerald Smith of being a "double-crosser" who had changed sides only because "Boss Maestri" had threatened to shut off his pay checks from the Share-Our-Wealth organization, which reportedly had reached over $600 weekly. Noe charged that Smith had even tried to blackmail him, promising to stay on the side of the Noe-Martin slate only if he be given a "$10,000 consolation fund." Noe boasted that he had told Smith "to go to hell," adding, "I told him I'd beat him to a pulp if he ever showed up in my parish." Gerald Smith not only refused to deny the charges, but brazenly invaded his earstwhile ally's home town and attempted to turn a Noe rally to Maestri. The demagogic minister was given five minutes to get out of the town "in one piece" and he promptly left the scene.[36]

But this time Huey's pupil had erred. Once Leche secured the nomination, Smith was allowed only a small role in the ensuing campaign. The few inflammatory speeches he delivered (one notable theme being "The Martyr's Blood Is the Seed of Victory") only whetted his appetite for more, and he privately complained of being "kept under wraps." Yet the worst was still to come, for when Leche was returned an easy winner on election day, the politicians had no more reason to camouflage their personal distaste for this self-styled successor to Huey Long.[37]

Seymour Weiss harbored a special hatred towards Smith. He had heard the fiery orator make anti-Semitic remarks in the past, and shortly before Long's assassination he had squashed Smith's plan for a Share-Our-Wealth campaign against rich Jewish merchants in New Orleans. Anti-Semitism was not, in fact, an important element in the minister's work until relatively late in his career, but these early rum-

[35] Sindler, p. 118.

[36] *Ibid.*, pp. 155–56; Martin, p. 155; and "Gerald Lyman Kenneth Smith," *Current Biography,* 1943, p. 708.

[37] Kane, pp. 156–59.

blings were enough to make a powerful Louisiana politician a personal enemy.[38]

For all of this, Smith might have been allowed to continue his work in the South had not the leaders of the Long machine decided that the Share-Our-Wealth movement had outlived its usefulness. This decision was taken as part of a larger deal with the Roosevelt administration, which had been harassing Weiss, Sushan, Fischer and other party wheelhorses for possible income-tax evasion. With Huey Long dead and their one measure of protection in Washington thus removed, the machine men feared impending jail sentences. Moreover, they were interested in winning back the federal patronage which had been denied the organization during Long's days of maverick behavior. A rapprochement with the New Deal seemed attractive, and the Roosevelt Administration, for its part, was eager to have the Louisiana Democracy support the President at the 1936 party convention (Long had vowed it would not), to have the anti-Federal relief laws passed in Louisiana repealed, and to have the potentially dangerous Share-Our-Wealth movement discredited and destroyed forever.[39]

The deal which came to be known as the "Second Louisiana Purchase" was sealed. The federal government dropped its criminal cases against the members of the Long machine, being satisfied with the collection of $2 million in back taxes. On the other hand, Louisiana not only endorsed FDR at the nominating convention in 1936, but its leaders feted him during a New Orleans visit and its legislature traveled to Texas for that state's centennial for the sole purpose of cheering the President. Finally, the Share-Our-Wealth movement, while never officially abolished, was effectively killed in Louisiana.[40]

Gerald L. K. Smith had called the Leche-led slate "the real Share-Our-Wealth ticket in 1935." But during the campaign, not even lip service was paid to the movement by those candidates who claimed to be the heirs of Huey Long. When the dimensions of his mistake finally became clear in late autumn of the year, Smith was beside himself with

[38] Broun, *The Nation*, CXLIII, No. 8, p. 213; and Ferkiss, pp. 162, 308.

[39] Sindler, p. 122; Davis, p. 245; and Martin, p. 154.

[40] Kane, pp. 153, 183. Westbrook Pegler coined the term "Second Louisiana Purchase" but it soon gained wide currency, with North Dakota Senator Usher Burdick and others picking it up. See *Times Picayune* (New Orleans), June 21, 1936. James A. Farley, however, denied that there was any deal made by the New Deal with the Long leaders. "Louisiana was sure to be a Democratic state in 1936—what was there to purchase?" he asked. See Farley, *Behind . . .* , p. 252.

anger. If he was to be duped, if the Share-Our-Wealth society was to be liquidated, he demanded at least some financial consolation—he insisted on being "taken care of." But the party leaders were unimpressed. They told him to "get out of Louisiana under your own power or be carried out." Defiantly, Smith purchased radio time across the state for a speech describing the "sellout," only to be arrested and jailed by New Orleans police following the address. Gerald L. K. Smith was literally forced to flee the state. He was now a leader in search of a movement.[41]

[41] Opotowsky, p. 115; and Smith in Simon (ed.), p. 72. Smith in later years denied that he had demanded any compensation for the destruction of his movement, recalling that at a climactic meeting of Long's heirs, "I rose and told [them] there was nothing they had that I wanted."

9

A Leader In Search
of a Movement

Before formalizing his break with the Long machine, Gerald Smith desperately searched for the mailing lists of the Share-Our-Wealth organization. In a movement so loosely constructed, these lists were the only tangible evidence of a large following. The would-be mass leader had to have them.

Mystery shrouded their whereabouts. Smith knew that Earle J. Christenberry, as Huey Long's executive secretary, had gained possession of the lists shortly after the assassination. But what had he done with them? Christenberry had made a brief appearance in October, 1935, at the national convention of Dr. Townsend's Old Age Pension Plan movement in Chicago, and there were rumors that the all-important lists had been left with Townsend. Other sources indicated that Christenberry had given them for safekeeping to Mrs. Rose Long, Huey's widow.[1]

Playing a hunch that Mrs. Long had the lists, Gerald Smith grandly named the widow "titular head of the Share-Our-Wealth society," proclaiming further that "I, as national organizer, shall continue the work of recruiting the masses for the great cause and . . . am instructing organizers all over America to that effect." In any event, Smith made the right choice, for Christenberry had given not only the coveted

[1] Kane, p. 190. Christenberry denied any ties between Share-Our-Wealth and the Townsend movement, stating that he had attended the Townsend meeting only as an adviser on convention organization.

lists to Mrs. Long but also patents and copyrights covering every detail of the movement. These he had taken out in his own name for possible future use if the moribund society was ever to be revived by the Louisiana party.[2]

It was at this critical time that Rose Long was suddenly thrust into the political limelight. When Governor O. K. Allen, elected to fill the remaining year of Huey Long's Senate term, died suddenly in Baton Rouge, the new Governor named Mrs. Long to fill the seat. Smith, eying both her mailing lists and her congressional franking privileges, moved to become her secretary. But it was his mortal enemy, James Noe, who had been elevated to the state house. Governor Noe and his ally Earle Christenberry quickly moved to block any liaison between the minister and Mrs. Long. Christenberry himself, it was announced, would go to Washington to serve the new Senator as he had her husband. Smith had been frozen out again.[3]

Frustrated and defeated, Gerald L. K. Smith was finally forced to leave Louisiana. Traveling north to New York, he issued a series of biting attacks upon his former coworkers, denouncing the Leche Administration as an "ungodly betrayal of Huey Long" and calling upon his followers throughout Dixie to oppose the state government which had made an alliance with FDR, "Huey's worst enemy." But the Long machine returned the fire with devastating effect. Christenberry released a story accusing Smith of approaching him on the morning of Huey Long's funeral with a plan to make a small fortune through misuse of the Share-Our-Wealth files. (The alleged proposition concerned dues of ten cents per month for the movement's eight million members, an arrangement which could net the conspirators $800,000 monthly.) Smith quickly denied the charges, but his name had been badly tarred and a deadly seed of doubt planted in the minds of his followers: was he just another racketeer interested only in sharing other people's wealth?[4]

With his position as Share-Our-Wealth leader shaken, a rebellion soon broke out in the ranks. In Connecticut, a self-styled "New England Organizer" of the society named Lester Barlow announced to newsmen that Smith had "no right to lift the hammer from the dead hand of Senator Long" and nominated a puzzled Senator Lynn Frazier of North Dakota as permanent head of the movement. Nothing came

[2] *Ibid.*
[3] *Ibid.*, pp. 191–92.
[4] *Ibid.*, pp. 196–97; and *Michigan Democrat*, July, 1940.

of this insurrection, but it was symptomatic of the problems faced by
Gerald L. K. Smith in the months following his expulsion from Louisiana. Without the mailing lists, he was the leader of a movement, but
had no idea who or where his followers were; without access to his
home state, he was cut off from the all-important personal contact with
his strongest supporters; without the monthly stipend he had been paid
as the Share-Our-Wealth organizer, he was even without an income.[5]

But Gerald Smith was far from ready to bow out. He knew that somewhere there were "eight or nine million people who subscribe to my
ideas." Acutely aware of his own extraordinary talent on the political
platform and certain that the Depression would continue to fuel the
fires of discontent, he wanted only to keep his name in the news and to
keep his following aware of his presence, until the time came to strike
for power. And so when he told reporters in late January, 1936, that
"we will go into the Democratic Convention in Philadelphia with five
states pledged against Roosevelt," he knew the words were nonsense,
but they made the front pages and to this extent served his purpose.
He regaled reporters daily with such ringing statements as "the ghost
of Huey Long is haunting all his foes in the South"; "we will support
Al Smith in his opposition to Roosevelt"; and the most curious and baseless of all: "I control 110,000 votes in Georgia."[6]

Yet this last remark was the clue to Smith's next move. Soon he was
pledging support to Georgia Governor Eugene Talmadge's unofficial
Presidential boom: "I'm the balance of power in Georgia between Roosevelt and Talmadge and I am going to support Talmadge." Pleased to
have this robust rabble-rouser winning headlines for him, the Georgia
Governor invited Smith to come south to Macon for the convention of
"The Southern Committee to Uphold the Constitution," a meeting
dreamed up by Talmadge for the purpose of publicizing his name across
the nation.[7]

Better known as the "Talmadge Grass Roots Convention," the 31,000
Georgians and 150 outsiders who met in Macon liked to think of themselves as "Jeffersonian Democrats," and indeed they were bitterly
opposed to all the interventionist state activities of the New Deal.
They even proposed the elimination of the graduated income tax, a
stand which won them the moral support of the Liberty League and the
Hearst Press. That Gerald L. K. Smith, the great proponent of wealth

---

[5] Kane, p. 189.
[6] Huie, *American Mercury*, LV, No. 224, 147; and *New York Times*, January 27, 1936.
[7] *Ibid.*, January 27 and 29, 1936.

confiscation and income sharing, should make an appearance before such a group of fiscal reactionaries was new evidence that the man was no stickler for logic. Smith was never particularly concerned about ideological consistency, and at this juncture in his career he would have done anything for a forum. He found one in Georgia.

His address was filled with his characteristic oratorical fireworks. Hatred of FDR was the theme for the day: it was the one area in which he could find agreement with the Talmadge supporters. "Roosevelt is rapidly becoming the most despised President in the history of the country," he shouted. "This man gave us the Russian primer and cursed the Bible!" As the speech progressed, the words grew fouler, the images more poisonous. In a grotesque peroration, Smith roared, "We're going to turn that cripple out of the White House. . . . He and his gang are in the death rattle. We have only to put the cloth of the ballot over his dead mouth." [8]

Gerald Smith's performance had the crowd cheering wildly—too wildly. Eugene Talmadge did not like the idea of anyone stealing the show at "his" convention. In an exchange of angry words, Talmadge made sure that the minister understood that his services and presence were no longer desired in Georgia. And so Gerald L. K. Smith was forced out of yet another southern state, another area in which he could find support.[9]

Still the leader in search of a movement, Smith decided to resume the quest for the Share-Our-Wealth mailing lists, without which he felt like a general with no roster of his army. Thwarted in his efforts to make contact with Mrs. Long, he had no choice but to pursue that other rumor concerning the whereabouts of the elusive lists: that they were in the hands of Dr. Francis E. Townsend.[10]

The decision to approach Dr. Townsend came at a fortuitous moment for Gerald Smith. The leader of the crusade for an old age pension was experiencing hard times. His organization was under heavy attack by the Administration, and he had been called to Washington to testify before a congressional committee investigating its financial affairs. The elderly physician, feeling the pressures of political controversy and harassed by hostile legislators, was ready to respond with enthusiasm to anyone who held out a helping hand. And this is literally what Gerald L. K. Smith did.

[8] "Goober Democrats," *Time*, XXVII, No. 6 (February 10, 1936), 17.

[9] Broun, *The Nation*, CXLIII, No. 8, 213.

[10] Harry Thornton Moore, "Just Folks in Utopia," *New Republic*, LXXXV, No. 1093 (November 13, 1935), 10.

Smith was among the spectators in the hearing room when Townsend, after three days of grueling questioning, decided he had had enough of the committee. Suddenly saying, "Good day, gentlemen," the doctor stood up and walked toward the door. The Congressmen were flabbergasted, but Representative Clare Hoffman (D.-Mich.) recovered in time to shout, "Stop that man!" The frail oldster was having trouble pushing through the crowd when Gerald Smith leaped to his feet and came to the doctor's side. Seizing Townsend's arm, the powerful minister elbowed his way through the throng to the corridor and safety. After gasping, "I'd rather march to jail than go back to that investigation," the physician asked Smith to accompany him to the Baltimore headquarters of the Old Age Revolving Pension Plan. A new friendship had been made.[11]

Smith lost no time in cementing his ties with Townsend. At a press conference held later in the day in Baltimore, he dominated the scene: "I am the national head of the Share-Our-Wealth Society. I am the successor of Huey Long. . . . The program of persecution is the thing that has drawn me to Dr. Townsend. Isn't that right, Doctor?" "That's right," said Townsend. "We symbolize the following of one leader who was shot and another who is being persecuted. How's that, Doctor?" "That's all right," Townsend replied once again. The following day Smith grandly told the newsmen that "we here and now join hands in what shall result in a nationwide protest against this Communistic dictatorship in Washington."[12]

Dr. Townsend seemed dazzled by the powerful personality of his new ally. Ironically, his own newspaper, *The Townsend National Weekly,* had remarked upon the occasion of Huey Long's death a few months before that "his [Long's] crusade was personal. . . . That was his triumph and his tragedy. No strong character shared his influence who was able to seize the torch of the fallen leader." But now the old doctor's response to Smith's hypnotic charm was so intense that his subordinates in the pension movement soon were fearing that he might find himself playing Trilby to Gerald Smith's Svengali. They cautioned him against

[11] "Townsend: Congress Poises Axe," *Newsweek,* VII, No. 22 (May 30, 1936), 11. Townsend never forgot his "rescue by Smith." Writing years later in his autobiography, the physician recalled the minister at the congressional hearing as "a big hombre who did not fear the devil or any of his cohorts." See Francis E. Townsend, *New Horizons, An Autobiography* (Chicago: J. L. Stewart Publishing Company, 1943), p. 204.

[12] "Dictators' Unite: A Doctor and a Divine," *Newsweek,* VII, No. 24 (June 13, 1936), 9. Smith recalled that he and Townsend first visited the home of their common friend, H. L. Mencken, when they reached Baltimore, Mencken, he acknowledged, was not "ideologically in agreement with us, but he was hungry for drama, individuality, and the guts of resistance." See Smith in Simon (ed.), p. 74.

Gerald L. K. Smith speaking at the second session of the Townsend convention at Cleveland, August, 1936. Dr. Townsend is visible in the background. *Wide World*

any partnership with the minister, and at their urging Townsend told reporters that "the Reverend Mr. Smith simply made a friendly gesture. . . . There will be no amalgamation of the Townsend movement with any other." But Smith, having sensed the possibilities of a new alliance, could not be put off that easily. In early June he persuaded the physician to join him on a speech-making tour of eastern Pennsylvania, and there he reasserted his influence on the old man. In a dramatic climax to the trip, he took Townsend to Valley Forge, where, as he told the press, "Dr. Townsend and I stood under the historic arch and vowed to take over the government." By this time parroting his articulate young companion, the doctor agreed, saying, "We are presenting a common front against the dictatorship in Washington."[13]

Gerald Smith had discovered that Dr. Townsend did not have his coveted mailing lists. In this regard he remained, as he put it, "like a bridegroom still trying to catch up with my bride." But he had discov-

[13] *Newsweek*, VII, No. 24, 9; and *The Townsend National Weekly*, September 7, 1935.

ered in the pension organization something almost as good. For here was a new following on which to work his demagogic ways: he could now dream of combining the Townsendites with whatever elements of the Share-Our-Wealth following he might still control into an instrument with which to wield great influence.[14]

Smith suddenly became a great advocate of old age pensions. As in the past, the new-found zeal was overlaid with cynicism. Only a year before, when he was the mouthpiece for Share-Our-Wealth, he had written, "We originally promised a $30 a month pension, but we discovered we were running afoul of the $40 pension advocates and the Townsend $200 per month advocates, so we decided to use the word 'adequate' and let every man name his own figure. This attracted a lot of Townsendites to us." Indeed, the Share-Our-Wealth movement had paid only lip service to the pension concept, and Long's Louisiana regime was notably cool toward old-age benefits, weakening the mother's pension law during the Depression. But no matter, Smith was now the self-styled expert on the harsh financial problems confronting the aged. Of course he exhibited vast ignorance of the economic facts of the plan, as when he told interviewers that "one-fourth of the population is over sixty and one-fourth of the population should have one-fourth of the income." In reality, only one out of eight Americans was over sixty, and if the Townsend Plan were to be implemented, it was conservatively estimated that this fraction of the population would be receiving one-half the nation's income.[15]

But Dr. Townsend overlooked these factual errors. He was too fascinated by the ingenious way in which Smith could couch the pension appeal in emotional terms. "Doesn't a boy always put his mother first?" the minister would ask. "We do it socially, why not economically? You take your hat off to her when she gets out of the elevator, but you let her starve when she gets old." The doctor admired the style. Smith had the ability, as Harnett Kane noted, to "play the organ notes of a shouting crowd as though his fingers caressed and pounded a keyboard controlling their throats and tongues." His inflammatory language electrified the listeners when he bellowed, "I'm going to show that there is something solid behind your enthusiasm, I'm going to show what is behind all this—the hunger of millions of poor people." [16]

---

[14] Baldwin and Stone, p. 98.
[15] Sindler, p. 105; Beals, p. 314; and Frank, *The Nation*, CXLIII, No. 8, 93.
[16] *Ibid.;* "Four Preachers In Political Arena," *Literary Digest*, CXXII, No. 5 (August 1, 1936), 6; and Kane, p. 197.

In this way, Gerald L. K. Smith became "the tough guy" of the Townsend movement. One contemporary journalist wrote:

He's dynamite. When he speaks he hitches his trousers, rubs his nose, dries the palms of his hands on his blue shirtfront, gulps water direct from the water pitcher. He has the gift of a homely simile. "We walked out of the hearing room," he would say, speaking of the Townsend investigation, "our arms linked together like an old steer and a young one galloping across the Texas prairies." He is ruthless and proud of his ruthlessness. The prevailing attitude of the Townsend leaders toward him is fear.[17]

Townsend's cohorts in the movement were unable to handle Smith. His tremendous personal appeal, his cunning, his ruthlessness overwhelmed them. By using the tactics and vocabulary he had sharpened in the Share-Our-Wealth crusade, Gerald L. K. Smith created a new niche for himself in the Townsend Plan. By wedding his old organization to the new one, the leader at last found a movement.[18]

Smith contributed few new ideas to his new movement. At his urging, efforts were made to broaden its appeal by changing the name from Old Age Revolving Pensions, Ltd. to The Townsend Recovery Plan. He also pushed for the establishment of a series of nationwide "youth battalions" to complement the established Townsend clubs, whose membership was dominated by the elderly. That little came of these gestures did not dismay Smith, for his real concern was not for the problems or the programs of the organization. What he was interested in—what he had an insatiable thirst for—was power. He once stated:

I'm not a teacher, I'm a symbol—a symbol of a state of mind. When the politicians overplay their hand, certain nerve centers of the population will begin to twitch. The people will start fomenting and fermenting, and then a fellow like myself, someone with courage enough to capture the people, will get on the radio, make three or four speeches, and have them in his hand. I'll teach 'em how to hate. The people are beginning to trust true leadership.[19]

In the spring of 1936, Smith felt that the time was ripe to assert his "true" leadership. Calling himself the head of one national social movement, and securely ensconced as a top leader of another, he turned his ambitions to the political arena. The national elections, looming ahead in November, became his prime objective.

[17] Frank, *The Nation,* CXLIII, No. 8, 93.
[18] In late June, Dr. Townsend—speaking of Smith—stated that "he and I stand for the same principles. There is no formal association of the Townsendites and the Share-Our-Wealth crowd, but we think alike." See *New York Times,* June 19, 1936.
[19] Quoted in Harris, *Current History,* XLV, No. 1, 83.

Smith never believed that he could take over the government in 1936. Oratorical outbursts notwithstanding, he simply wasn't that unrealistic. But he did believe that social and economic conditions across the country provided the perfect setting for a mass leader offering a panacea to the distressed. If he could lay the groundwork in 1936, true power might be his in the future. As he told an interviewer at this time, "You know what my ambition is? I think chaos is inevitable. I want to get as many people as I can now, so that when chaos comes, I'll be a leader. I lead some of them now." [20]

Political action in 1936 would also give him the chance to launch a free-swinging attack on the President. The record showed that Gerald L. K. Smith had been insincere and unprincipled in almost all the adventures undertaken in his short but spectacular career: in the pulpit, on the platform, and in the executive offices of the organizations he had led, expediency had ruled his every action. But his hatred of FDR was real enough. It was the New Deal that had harried the Long machine and blocked Huey's expansionist drive across the South; it was the New Deal that had made the "Second Louisiana Purchase" and doomed Smith's dream of building Share-Our-Wealth into a great national power; it was Franklin Roosevelt who stood for everything he despised. And so when Smith called the President's Administration "a contemptible and damnable dictatorship with a fake liberal foreground and a Communist background," he was speaking, for once, from conviction. "Communism" was a word Smith could not clearly define; to him it was merely a term of derision to hurl at the opponent, and President Roosevelt, surely, was his greatest opponent.[21]

The problem of how to organize for effective political action haunted the minister throughout May and June. He had puzzled over the question in preceding months, stating as early as January that "we [the Share-Our-Wealth membership] are friends of all the foes of Roosevelt. . . . The recent great reform movements opposed to Roosevelt are the National Union for Social Justice, the Old Age Revolving Pension organization, and the Share-Our-Wealth society." It must now have become obvious that a coalition of the mass movements provided the best chance of building a powerful anti-New Deal political machine.[22]

Smith's meteoric rise in the Townsend movement was the first significant step in the making of such a coalition. At the old doctor's insistence, he had been made a member of the Townsend Board of Directors, and

[20] Frank, *The Nation*, CXLIII, No, 8, 93.

[21] Duncan Aikman, "Lemke's New Party, and Three Key Men," *New York Times Magazine*, July 26, 1936, 18.

[22] *New York Times*, January 27, 1936.

by virtue of his own proclamation, he had become "director in charge of political policy" for the plan. It was relatively easy at this point for Smith to persuade Townsend to make a political move against Franklin D. Roosevelt. The old man's own bitterness toward the President having been capped by the ignominies of the committee hearings, he was now amenable to his young colleague's suggestion that they seek revenge on the New Deal.[23]

With Townsend in tow, Gerald Smith could turn his energies to building a bridge between the groups he represented and the one headed by Father Charles E. Coughlin. Smith had known Coughlin since February, 1935, when the radio priest had held a series of meetings with Huey Long. It had been rumored at that time that Coughlin had pledged his support for Long's proposed 1936 presidential bid, and when Long was killed, the priest had called the assassination "the most regrettable thing in modern history." [24]

Father Coughlin's own feud with Roosevelt, of course, had made him eager to join a political alliance aimed against the Administration. The priest's association with agrarian leader William Lemke made the potential support for such an alliance appear to be wide and powerful. Smith was not only pleased at the prospect of working with Coughlin, such an old admirer of Huey Long, but also approved of Lemke for he knew that the North Dakotan had also endorsed many of the Kingfish's programs. Indeed Lemke had written to a friend in April, 1935, that "Long has consistently supported legislation for the betterment of 130 million Americans, and his record is 1,000% against Wall Street." [25]

Smith took steps to tie the mass movements closer together when he announced in late May that he, Coughlin, and Townsend were about to "congeal under a leadership with guts." One week later he spoke of a "bloodless revolution to be expressed with ballots in the Fall" as the only way to stop "this damnable tyranny set up by the Farley-Roosevelt regime." Soon he was asserting that "more than 20 million votes" could be controlled by a Smith-Townsend-Coughlin-Lemke axis. A loose working agreement among the four leaders was about to be made.[26]

With this new coalition, Gerald L. K. Smith began the most ambitious adventure of an ambition-filled career. Now this professional leader of the masses would be able to operate in the national arena. This, he felt, could be the beginning of his bid for power.

[23] *Ibid.*, June 23, 1936.
[24] Colony, *The Forum*, XCIII, No. 4, 201.
[25] Lemke to Vanderbilt, Jr., April 22, 1935, Lemke Papers.
[26] *New York Times*, May 23, May 29, and June 17, 1936.

PART IV

DR. TOWNSEND AND

THE OLD AGE RETIREMENT

PLAN

Elderly people, trained and experienced by life's activities, can be made the greatest asset humanity possesses if they are liberated from the slavery of poverty and are permitted to exercise their talents as circulators of money. — Francis E. Townsend, 1935

10

An Old Man's Dream

To the casual observer, everything seemed normal outside Chicago's huge Stevens Hotel during those late September days in 1935. But inside, it appeared as if all the clocks had been set ahead and the whole population had aged by a generation. For thousands of white-maned old folks coursed through the lobbies and filled the meeting halls. The elderly had taken over the building.

This was not a conference on geriatrics, nor had the owners turned their hostelry into a nursing home. The fervor and excitement that radiated from the crowds, the intensity of feeling in the assembly halls, made it abundantly clear that there were vital social, economic, and political issues driving these like-minded people together.

The object of their hopes was the Townsend Old Age Revolving Pension Plan. The man of the hour was the founder of the plan, Dr. Francis E. Townsend, that stern but kindly old physician whose picture was everywhere in evidence, and whose deification shocked the unbelievers. The first national convention of the Old Age Revolving Pension organization was neither as large nor as important as its successor in Cleveland would be in the following year. But the Chicago meeting gave America its first good look at one of the most curious but potentially formidable mass movements in the nation's history.[1]

The events which led to Chicago had begun some two years before in Long Beach, California. It was there that Francis E. Townsend had seen his great vision.

---

[1] Neuberger and Loe, p. 204; and Moore, *New Republic*, LXXV, No. 1093, 10.

Dr. Francis E. Townsend personified the frustrations and the aspirations
of older Americans whose lives had been blighted by the Depression.
Wide World

In 1933, Townsend was almost sixty-seven—a quiet, country-bred
physician, who had come to the retirement community of Long Beach
a few years earlier to spend his old age in the sun after decades of
service in the Middle West. Most men spend the years after sixty-five
in the twilight of their careers, but in Dr. Townsend's case, all the years
that went before seemed to serve only as a prelude for the great work to
be undertaken in later life. Yet there was nothing in this man's earlier
career to suggest that he might ever become so prominent.

Francis E. Townsend was born near Fairbury, Illinois, in 1867, one of seven children in a poor but deeply religious family. A regular participant at summer and fall camp meetings, the young Townsend grew up with a deep belief in a God who looked after the destinies of individuals and nations. This belief helped him overcome the disappointments which inevitably accompanied the hard farm life of the post-Civil War era. The Townsend's land was particularly unproductive, and the family moved west to Nebraska in search of more fertile soil. Later Francis took one of his brothers to southern California in a brief but abortive effort to cash in on the first of the Los Angeles area land booms.[2]

When Townsend's western adventure ended in failure, he returned to the midwestern plains, filing on a homestead in Kansas and teaching at a district school to raise money for improvements on his land. Always somewhat more inquisitive than his fellow farmers, he enrolled in an obscure college in Kansas, where he was tutored by an inspired teacher who encouraged him to read volumes on science and medicine. This was enough to convince Townsend that homesteading was both unprofitable and uninteresting, and he left his farm for Colorado, where frugal saving during two years of odd jobs in the city provided a nest egg of $100 with which to start a career in medicine.[3]

Francis Townsend entered Omaha Medical School at the age of twenty-six. He worked his way through school covering newspaper routes and selling stereopticon viewers, and when he received his degree four years later, he was the oldest member of his class. The proud new doctor went directly to Bear Lodge, South Dakota, a small Black Hills town, where his practice was to include cowhands and miners, professional gamblers and adventurers who lived throughout the rough frontier area. He often had to travel many miles into Wyoming and the Dakotas to reach some of them.[4]

Townsend spent twenty years in the Black Hills. But the demanding life of a physician in that difficult territory affected his health, and when the advent of the First World War brought enlistment in the Army Medical Corps, the ties to South Dakota were broken. After the Armistice, the now aging doctor decided to take his family to California. He settled in Long Beach in 1920.[5]

---

[2] Neuberger and Loe, p. 38.
[3] *Ibid.*, pp. 38–40.
[4] Richard Milne, *That Man Townsend* (Los Angeles: Prosperity Publishing Co., 1935), p. 5.
[5] Neuberger and Loe, pp. 41–47; Swing, p. 125; and Franklin, p. 77.

The golden West proved for a second time that it was anything but his promised land. Aggressive young doctors and established older ones limited his practice, and soon he was struggling to earn money for the necessities of life. He even tried to supplement his income by selling building lots for a shrewd and enterprising young real estate broker named Robert Earl Clements, but the elderly physician was no salesman. When the Depression struck California, most of his savings were wiped out and the Townsends' financial situation became serious.[6]

Good fortune smiled briefly on the old man when a medical school classmate was named director of the Long Beach health program and Dr. Townsend was appointed assistant director of the City Health Office. The job carried him through the difficult early period of the economic crisis and also afforded him the opportunity to see just how cruelly the Depression had ravaged the old people of America, whose small fixed incomes had withered with the stock market decline and whose age and health made it impossible to find work in a land where unemployment rolls grew longer every day. The spectacle sickened Francis E. Townsend. Years later he recalled, "I stepped into such distress, pain and horror as to shake me even today with its memory. . . . They were good men and women, they had done all they could, had played the game as they had been taught to play it, and suddenly, when there was no chance to start over again, they were let down."[7]

When the doctor suddenly lost his job through a local political upheaval, he found himself once again in grave financial straits, remembering in his autobiography that "day after day went by without a cent coming in," and that "while there was still some wreckage to get along on for a while and we were not dead broke . . . , with our bank accounts being paid out, we were worried." This personal crisis seemed only to intensify a growing feeling that something had to be done to help the old people of America, so many of whom were much worse off than Townsend in that haven of the aged and retired, southern California. It was in this setting that the doctor conceived the idea for the plan that was to make him famous.[8]

The story he later enjoyed recounting about the experience which finally moved him to action may have been apocryphal—for Townsend did not mention the episode in his earliest discussions of the plan's origins, "remembering" the experience over a year after it was sup-

---

[6] The Committee on Old Age Security of the Twentieth Century Fund, *The Townsend Crusade* (New York: The Twentieth Century Fund, Inc., 1936), pp. 5–6.

[7] Townsend, *New Horizons . . .* , p. 131.

[8] *Ibid.*, pp. 135–36.

posed to have happened. But as Townsend told it, he was looking out the rear window of his home one evening in late 1933 when he saw three old women searching through his garbage, hoping to find something to eat. The doctor was at first saddened, but then he became angry. "A torrent of invectives tore out of me, the big blast of all the bitterness that had been building in me for years," he was to recall. He resolved to do something about the misery and suffering which lay heavy upon the land, and which haunted the old people in particular. When his wife tried to quiet him, he roared, "I want all the neighbors to hear me! I want God Almighty to hear me! I'm going to shout until the whole country hears!" [9]

Francis E. Townsend was an old man when he decided to arouse the nation. Gaunt and white-haired, with a lantern jaw and the smudge of a mustache, his deep-sunken eyes were set off by the high stiff starched collar that he always wore above his threadbare clothes. He was old and he was poor but he had seen a vision, and now he was to become a committed man.

Townsend's vision was of the American old age population permanently freed from the evil effects of economic privation. The method of liberating the elderly would be a substantial pension, dispersed monthly by the Federal government, to every citizen of sixty and over. The government could raise the huge sums of money needed for the pension plan through a small "turnover tax" to be levied on every business transaction made in the nation.

The doctor had read somewhere that in 1929 the gross business done in the United States amounted to $935 billion. He deduced that it would be possible, by tapping this enormous business transaction with a sales tax, to produce $20 billion per year, enough to give $200 a month to everyone over sixty.[10]

Townsend did not devise the rather intricate details of his plan at one stroke; it took him several months to work out the specific provisions. He finally settled for the $200 figure because it was high enough to compel attention and because, as the founder pointed out, "with our figure so high we could feel reasonably sure that no one would bring out a plan with a higher amount." He at last rejected a 10 per cent retail sales tax in favor of the 2 per cent tariff on all transactions—wholesale as well as retail—because this would presumably place the burden

[9] Milne, p. 2; and Abraham Holtzman, "The Townsend Movement: A Study in Old Age Pressure Politics," unpublished Ph.D. dissertation, Department of Government, Harvard University, 1952, pp. 66–67.

[10] Franklin, p. 79.

less heavily on the consumer. Nor did Townsend develop the idea without outside assistance. He was almost certainly influenced by another old age pension plan that had been created by Stuart McCord of Seattle, and by yet another "plan" which Bruce Barton had toyed with in a humorous article entitled "How To Fix Everything," published in *Vanity Fair* in August, 1931. He might also have been influenced by Major C. H. Douglas' social credit plan, advanced in Great Britain in 1921.[11]

But the physician denied that his scheme was a mere copy of any other. And, as the months rolled by, he gradually began to advertise his pension program as a panacea not only for the aged, but for the rest of the population as well. He decided that spending the $200 within thirty days should be made mandatory. Thus he began to stress the revolving aspect of his proposal—that the $20 billion paid to the elderly every year would tend to stimulate the entire economy as the old people spent their money on food, clothing, shelter, and all manner of consumer goods. He now spoke in terms of the "velocity of money," pointing out, for example, that the dollar spent by an old man for food would be used by his grocer to pay the wholesaler, and so on down the line. In this way, the pension money would "revolve" and would multiply—the pension checks coursing through the economy would revitalize every aspect of American enterprise. The "velocity effect" of the pension money would sweep away the Depression.[12]

And Townsend began to make even more grandiose claims for his plan. Millions of new jobs, he promised, would be created by withdrawing the aged from the employment rolls. State and local governments would save the $18 billion lost yearly on crime and crime prevention as the pension panacea eliminated poverty and privation—the sole cause of criminal activity, in the old doctor's opinion. Federal, state, and local governments, as well as religious and fraternal societies, would save $20 billion every year on charity. The plan, the doctor fi-

---

[11] Holtzman, pp. 72–74; and Neuberger and Loe, pp. 35–53. Townsend indignantly refused to discuss the possibility of his being influenced by the Barton article. But there is a striking similarity between his plan and the one announced in *Vanity Fair.* Barton got his idea from an unknown New York reporter who suggested, in a story written on a "dead news" day, that apple sellers of the depression sell bananas. The slippery peels, it was speculated, would cause falls leading to employment of doctors, medicine makers, tailors (for soiled clothes), etc. Barton built on this story, facetiously recommending that everyone 45 and over be paid one-half his earning power of the preceding five years just to be idle and to spend, thus putting all who were under 45 to work. "Let the young do the work and the old men loaf," said Barton. "Age for leisure; youth for work," urged the Townsend supporters.

[12] Milne, p. 28; and Holtzman, pp. 87, 94–95.

nally concluded, would do so much good in so many areas that the people would actually enjoy paying the transaction tax that would make it possible.[13]

Dr. Townsend was sure that he could solve it all. Like many another cracker-barrel Utopian, he was certain that he had discovered the single formula that would resolve all the tragic and obstinate dissonances of the economic struggle and forever banish human hardship from the nation. As in his favorite book, Bellamy's *Looking Backward,* the America of the Townsend Plan would become the perfect society men had been striving to build for generations.[14]

Thus did the doctor describe his dream to the aged, and it did not seem too far-fetched. To most Americans, the Depression was a grotesquely atypical phenomenon. The economy of abundance of the 1920's had provided the ideological framework for these people; the "permanent boom cycle" was, in fact, a phrase made famous by Calvin Coolidge. The Townsendites played upon these memories of prosperity and added to it their own thesis. To a generation who had largely escaped economics in school and even college, their economic arguments seemed virtually unassailable.

So it was not surprising that when Francis E. Townsend—old man and amateur economist though he was—first proposed his plan in late 1933, it almost immediately spread with a consuming flame across America.

The initial public appearance of the plan was in the form of a letter written by Townsend for the People's Forum column of the local Long Beach newspaper in late September. When the doctor advertised for canvassers to obtain signatures of endorsement, he was overwhelmed by replies. Within a matter of days he had received completed petitions containing the names of two thousand supporters of the proposal.[15]

Townsend now searched about for what he called a "super-salesman," a person to help him set up the organization with which the Townsend Plan could be transformed into law. He turned to his former employer, Earl Clements, whose realty firm had foundered with the Depression and who had been searching around for some new venture. The young and driving businessman was impressed by the flood of letters endorsing the plan and agreed to spend some time in the local library "re-

[13] Morgan J. Dorman, *Age Before Booty: An Explanation of the Townsend Plan* (New York: G. P. Putnam's Sons, 1936), pp. 16–18, 57; and *Age of Plenty* (Minneapolis, Minnesota), October 25, 1935.

[14] Francis E. Townsend and Nicholas Roosevelt, "Townsend Pensions: Sense or Nonsense," *Forum,* XCV, No. 5 (May, 1936), 282.

[15] Townsend, *New Horizons . . . ,* pp. 137–42.

searching" the idea, although he had no training in economics and it was unclear just what he would investigate. In any case, he emerged from his studies announcing that "the plan is wonderful and it is sound. It will work." [16]

Clements helped Dr. Townsend draw up an official description of the pension proposal and persuaded a local printer to make up leaflets and pledge blanks on credit. The two men then opened in Long Beach the first headquarters for the plan, moving into a sparsely furnished room in a dreary concrete block building on New Year's Day, 1934. The articles of incorporation for the nonprofit organization to be known as the Old Age Revolving Pensions, Ltd., were officially filed a few days later —the sole directors of the corporation being Dr. Townsend, Earl Clements, and the physician's brother, Walter L. Townsend, a Los Angeles hotel porter. The Townsend movement was under way.[17]

Townsend and Clements began sending out literature—to friends, neighbors, former clients, anyone whose name they could pick up. After five weeks, an average of one hundred replies a day were pouring into the office along with demands for the twenty-five cent leaflets they had written, 1,500 a week being purchased within two months of the incorporation. Area physicians and ministers were induced to become spokesmen for the plan, and a newspaper, *The Townsend National Weekly*, was started. Excitement began to spread across southern California, and Townsend was forced to abandon his original headquarters and move to larger offices in Los Angeles. A staff of ninety-five was hired to handle the mounting flow of mail, and by September, 1934, one year from the time the old man conceived his great idea, the letters were averaging two thousand per day.[18]

As the movement continued to grow, local "Townsend Clubs" were beginning to form; by January the leaders proudly announced that more than three thousand local units were operating with a total membership approaching one-half million. Voluntary and paid organizers soon were at work all around the country setting up the clubs, which had a minimum membership of one hundred and a maximum of one thousand. With the twenty-five-cent dues imposed on each new member supplementing the income from sales of leaflets and collections made at

[16] Neuberger and Loe, pp. 54–57.

[17] Herbert Harris, "Dr. Townsend's Marching Soldiers," *Current History*, XLIII, No. 2 (February, 1936), 456.

[18] *Ibid.*, 455–56; and Neuberger and Loe, pp. 60–65. *The Townsend National Weekly* was not the first publication devoted to the pension proposal. *The Modern Crusader*, edited by C. J. MacDonald, one of Townsend's earliest disciples, preceded it.

public meetings, Townsend and Clements found that they had accumulated in the last eleven months of 1934 almost $90,000 with which to finance an even greater expansion. In Ohio, Indiana, Michigan, Massachusetts, and New York, new Townsendites were enlisted into the old folks' crusade. Emulating the tactics of the National Union for Social Justice, the Townsend Plan leaders decided to organize their clubs by Congressional districts in order to maximize the political pressure they hoped to bring to bear on the House of Representatives. Soon they announced that several districts had eight or ten clubs in which two thousand voters endorsed the plan. A central office was opened in Washington, D.C. Almost overnight, the Townsend movement had become a force to be reckoned with in America.[19]

San Diego, California, was, perhaps, the best example of a city that responded to the Townsend appeal. One of the nation's largest retirement centers, 35,000 of its 180,000 people were aged sixty or over in 1935. By early 1935, there were thirty thousand dues-paying Townsendites in San Diego, an incredible one-sixth of the entire population. When the movement's local organizers circulated a Congressional petition endorsing the plan, 105,000 signatures were obtained.[20]

The skilful advertisement of the pension scheme affected even the immediate expectation levels of area residents—gullible oldsters tried to buy food, clothing, and other items on the promise of money they expected to have when the plan became law. When merchants refused to sell on promises, abuse was heaped upon them. Hysterical intolerance prevailed throughout the city. A modest physician's simple idea had taken hold of an entire community, and San Diego was only the most striking example of what was becoming a nationwide phenomenon.[21]

Francis E. Townsend was rather stunned by it all. Unaccustomed to success, he was speaking from the heart when he said, "You know, when this thing began to go over, nobody was more surprised than I was." But perhaps the old doctor should not have been so surprised. For in devising his plan, he had given the country a new and attractive panacea in an era in which many men were searching for total solutions. The question, in fact, was not whether the panacea would prove popular. It was, instead, would it work?[22]

[19] Harris, *Current History*, XLIII, No. 2, 455; Committee on Old Age Security of the Twentieth Century Fund, p. 7; and Stuart N. Lake, "If Money," *Saturday Evening Post*, CCVII, No. 45 (May 11, 1935), 12, 121–22.

[20] *Ibid.*

[21] *Ibid.*

[22] Quoted in Russell Owen, "Townsend Talks of His Plan and Hopes," *New York Times Magazine* (December 29, 1935), p. 15.

11

The Old Age Revolving Pension Plan

Dr. Townsend's critics derogated his plan, but they could not fault him for lack of ambition. The old age revolving pension scheme was actually two plans in one: it was not only a method of bringing economic relief to the aged but a means of generally stimulating the American economy and lifting the nation out of the Depression. These may have been considerable undertakings, but the conditions of the times cried out for imaginative and even radical solutions.

So bleak were the prospects for the elderly in the thirties that one student of the period called the doctor "a water carrier in a drought area." In 1934, only twenty-eight of the forty-eight states had any pension plan at all, and the ones which did exist were woefully inadequate, ranging from Montana's payment of $7.28 to Maryland's stipend of less than $30 monthly. Almost three-quarters of a million Americans of sixty-five and over were on some form of federal relief, while less than 60 per cent of those in this same age group were gainfully employed. And the situation appeared to be getting worse, not better. For while the aged were quietly but relentlessly being displaced in the job market, they were steadily increasing both in absolute numbers and in percentage of the total population. In 1935, seven and one-half million Americans (or 6 per cent of all citizens) were sixty-five and over. These millions were living in a land locked in the grip of history's worst depression, a land in which even the young and strong could not find work, a land in which two-thirds of all families had an income well below the minimum figure of $2,000 that both the economists of the Brookings Institute and the American public, in the polls conducted by the American Institute of

Public Opinion, agreed was necessary for living in health and relative comfort.[1]

To deal with this grim situation, to solve the problems of both the aged and the rest of the population, Dr. Townsend advanced a plan which had the merits of concreteness and apparent simplicity. The Townsend plan shared the assumptions which underlay the monetary schemes of the National Union for Social Justice, the Share-Our-Wealth Society, and the Lemke farm relief bills: the belief that free issuance, wide distribution, and rapid circulation of money would automatically assure prosperity and security.

In another sense, the pension plan represented a hyperexpression of the consumption theory of the academic economists and the New Deal planners, for the Townsendites felt that the Depression was the result of the inherent capacity and persistent tendency of modern industry to produce more goods and services than could be consumed, and that failure to consume was due both to labor displacement by machinery and to the improper distribution of the national income. Indeed, the Townsend theoreticians often used the term"pump priming" to describe their plan, arguing that the Roosevelt Administration had started in the right direction but had ultimately become an "economic failure" because it poured enough money into the economy only to prevent starvation and not enough to effect real recovery.[2]

But although some big business spokesmen were only too happy to implicate the New Deal in their attack on the economics of the Townsendites, calling the plan "only a logical extension of the assumption upon which U.S. policy is based," there existed only a coincidental connection between the pension scheme and Keynesian economics. Townsend went far beyond the wildest dreams of the New Deal spenders. In proposing that $200 pensions be given monthly to all who were sixty or over in the United States, his only conditions were that the recipients be citizens who had never been convicted of a crime or institutionalized in a mental hospital and who did not already earn as much as the proposed pension, those agreeing to take part giving up all other sources of income and spending the pension within a month. It was estimated that between eight and ten million of the 11.4 million Americans in the

---

[1] Holtzman, pp. 8–11, 26–38; and Hadley Cantril, *The Psychology of Social Movements* (New York: John Wiley & Sons, Inc., 1941), pp. 173–76.

[2] Dorman, pp. 16–18, 57; and Vaso Trivanovitch, *The Townsend Scheme* (New York: National Industrial Conference Board, Inc., 1936), pp. v–vii (introduction).

specified age bracket would qualify. The cost of the plan would range from $20 to $24 billion per year.[3]

The Townsend following recognized that the controversial 2 per cent transaction tax would raise the cost of living throughout the country, but they claimed that the $2 billion injected into the economy each month by the aged would create such a rosy glow of new prosperity that the rising prices would soon be overlooked. For each dollar that the pensioner "distributed," Townsendites argued, a chain of transactions equaling ten or more dollars would be initiated. Some even boasted that this velocity effect allowed their plan to follow the principle of "pay as you go," through which the national debt could be "wiped out in ten years."[4]

Most of these ardent supporters of the old doctor were committed to the capitalist system; they did not share the socialist predilections of the Technocrats or the followers of the End Poverty in California movement. Like the Coughlinites and the Share-Our-Wealthers, they wanted to rescue the free enterprise system from the "fearful profit-keepers," whose bungling had caused the Depression. They fervently attacked bankers and other "financial middle men" who refused to circulate money rapidly enough to keep capitalism viable. They scornfully dismissed the New Deal as a failure and indignantly rejected the Administration's Social Security Act as a "miserable dole," an "insult to elderly Americans," and a "mere bid for political support."[5]

Scoffing at the idea that their plan might be ruled unconstitutional if ever put into practice, the Townsendites pointed out that the Supreme Court, in striking down the Agricultural Adjustment Act and National Recovery Act, had not disturbed the federal government's taxing power. Indeed, they launched vitriolic counterattacks on any nay-sayer, saving their greatest anger for those economists who had the temerity to question the validity of their assumptions or the accuracy of their statistics. The politicians should "stop listening to academic economists," one

[3] *Ibid.;* George E. West, *The Spotlight of Truth on the Townsend Plan* (Chicago: P. W. Treloar, 1936), pp. 6–7; and Francis E. Townsend, *Old Age Revolving Pensions* (Long Beach, California: Old Age Revolving Pensions, Ltd., 1934), p. 4. Insurance statistics revealed that of 100 persons reaching the age of 60, only 8 had been fortunate enough to retire on savings, 78 of 100 were wholly or partially dependent upon earnings and 14 were entirely dependent upon public or private charity.

[4] Francis E. Townsend and Robert E. Clements, *The Townsend Plan* (Los Angeles: Old Age Revolving Pensions, Ltd., 1935), p. 10; and *The Modern Crusader* (Long Beach, California), November 17, 1934.

[5] Seymour J. Milliken, "$200 A Month At Sixty," *Forum,* XCII, No. 5 (November, 1934), 326–28; and Dorman, pp. 30, 66–67, 74–75, 85–87.

supporter urged, for they are but "husk-dry pedants who rely upon books, formal rules and abstract theories. . . . They are outraged by the plan probably because they never thought of it." Other spokesmen for the movement bitterly assailed "brain trust professors . . . who don't care a tinker's damn how the old folks live or die." Dr. Townsend himself was in the forefront of the anti-intellectual assault, exclaiming on more than one occasion: "God deliver us from the professional economists." [6]

But virulent attacks and prayers to the Almighty could not prevent economists from investigating the plan and pointing out its enormous loopholes.

Merely reviewing the price of implementing the plan stunned economists. The yearly costs would equal one and one-half times the amount spent on all government—federal, state and local—in 1932, almost one-half the total national income for 1934, and over three-quarters of the amount of all retail sales in the country in 1933.[7]

The transaction tax, they decided, would almost certainly fail to produce the requisite income. A number of factors would render it inadequate. First, the Townsendites based their estimates of income on the gross national product of the last of the predepression years, 1929. But their taxing program would have to take place in a far less prosperous America, the estimated national income for 1934 being some 40 per cent less than that for the year upon which the tax base was figured. Secondly, the argument concerning the velocity of money was mythical—a dollar would not "turn over" ten times within a month, for in the boom years of the 1920's the average turnover amounted to less than three times monthly. Indeed, as one critical economist pointed out, the velocity of turnover is not a cause of business prosperity but merely a reflection of it; production of goods and services is the key. And although Townsend's supporters looked for economic wonders through money distribution, the promised goods and services simply could not be produced because of the limitations on plant capacity. The nation was told that under the plan the national income would multiply five-fold within a year—but this would mean the utilization of two and one-half times the plant capacity available in the United States.[8]

The transaction tax had many other defects. Essentially, it was an

[6] *Ibid.,* pp. 24, 94–96, 98–99; and Harris, *Current History,* XLV, No. 1, 87.

[7] Trivanovitch, p. 42.

[8] Stuart A. Rice, "Is The Townsend Plan Practical?" *Vital Speeches of the Day* (January 27, 1936), p. 254; and Committee On Old Age Security of the Twentieth Century Fund, pp. 48–49.

incredibly high sales tax and as such, it was ungraduated. Professor Paul H. Douglas estimated that retail prices on many items would have increased by as much as 75 per cent, and the real income of most workers would have been reduced by about one-half. The burden would have fallen upon those who were least able to afford it; as Douglas put it, the Townsend plan constituted "merely a transfer of purchasing power from one distressed sector of the population to another," from younger jobholders to the aged. Moreover, the tax would have been doomed to almost certain failure if ever levied. Considering the French and German experiences with transaction taxes, it was estimated that a 2 per cent tax would yield perhaps $50 to $75 per month for the aged, instead of the much ballyhooed $200. In fact, it would have taken, in some experts' opinion, an impossible 26 per cent levy to produce the promised pension, and this would have only meant that a new privileged class had been established with fiat money. As Nicholas Roosevelt put it, in selling the idea of the transaction tax, Dr. Townsend had "taught people to believe in Santa Claus again." [9]

Another problem in the plan was the enormous administrative costs it surely would have entailed. The keystone of the revolving pension idea was the expenditure of the monthly payments made to the elderly. But frugal oldsters, unaccustomed to such a sizeable income, might well have attempted to save part of their monthly checks as a hedge against the day when the golden faucet would be turned off. If they were inclined to hoard, the possibilities of collusion were innumerable. In order to enforce the spending provision, the government would have had to employ a veritable army of spies at a cost of perhaps one-half a billion dollars a year. The total administrative costs, which would also have included the collection of the tax and eligibility investigations of prospective pensioners, could have reached $1 billion yearly. [10]

As if this were not damning enough, it was noted further that securities exchanges would literally have been driven out of the country because the 2 per cent tax to be levied on every sale would have been higher than the margin on which many transactions were made. The loss of the markets would have paralyzed the financing of both government and private enterprise. But more important, the omnipresent transaction tax would almost certainly have changed the nature of the

[9] *Ibid.*, p. 38; Harry D. Gideonse (ed.), *The Economic Meaning of the Townsend Plan* (Chicago: The University of Chicago Press, 1936), pp. 14–23; Paul H. Douglas, *Social Security in the United States* (New York: McGraw-Hill Book Co., Inc., 1936), pp. 71–72; and Townsend and Roosevelt, *Forum*, XCV, No. 5, 286.

[10] Mabel L. Walker, *The Townsend Plan Analyzed* (New York: Tax Policy League, 1936), pp. 17; and Trivanovitch, pp. 14–15, 32–33.

Dr. Townsend expounds his pension plan to Rep. Joseph Hendricks and
Senator Claude Pepper. *Wide World*

nation's economic system, for great vertical monopolies would have
grown up in many industries as the only alternative to the payment of a
crushing 2 per cent on every wholesale turnover. Chain stores and mail
order houses, in fact large corporations of every kind, would have had a
tremendous advantage over smaller competitors. The Townsend Plan
would have altered the nature of American capitalism.[11]

When all of its deficiencies had been uncovered, almost every respectable economist dismissed it as utterly impractical and unworkable.
Donald Richberg termed the plan "a cruel hoax which will kill not cure
the American economy"; Stuart A. Rice, acting chairman of the United
States Central Statistical Board suggested that "what the Townsendites
are really demanding is a revision of the science of arithmetic by law."[12]

Townsend and his supporters tried to meet these attacks with denial
or derision, one publicist for the movement even picturing the old

[11] Professor Edwin E. Witte to Merrill G. Murray, December 11, 1935, Roosevelt Papers,
Official File 1542 (Dr. Francis E. Townsend); and The Committee on Old Age Security of
the Twentieth Century Fund, pp. 32–38.

[12] Donald Richberg, "The Townsend Delusion," *Review of Reviews*, XCIII, No. 2 (February, 1936), 27; and Rice, *Vital Speeches of the Day*, January 27, 1936, 264.

doctor himself as something of an expert on the economy. "The physician," he wrote, "understanding physiology, may be especially qualified to feel, by the process of intuitive analogy, the most fundamental economic principles." But this, obviously, was not good enough. In mid-1935, the leaders of the organization were forced to make some slight alterations in the plan itself, the occasion for the change being the revision of the congressional bill providing for its implementation. Townsend announced the addition of three new taxes to his proposal: on gifts, inheritances and supplementary income. He also tampered with the cherished $200 pension figure after Dr. Robert R. Doane, director of research of American Business Surveys and the only notable economist who even partially supported the plan, had testified that he did not believe a pension of that amount to be feasible. Townsendites were now told to speak in terms of "a pension of not more than $200." [13]

But the changes did not silence the criticism. Experts rejected the new taxes as totally inadequate, and the leaders of the movement consciously neglected to stress the change made in the value of the pension after some members reacted negatively to the proposed reduction.[14]

The plan remained an economist's nightmare. It became the butt of jokes. Dr. Lewis Haney of New York University humorously suggested that Townsend had not gone far enough, that $200 should be given to everyone every week. If the government can afford $24 billion, Haney said, it can afford $2,400 billion. In Battle Creek, Michigan, a "rival" to the OARP was announced. The "Retire at Birth Plan" proposed that every newborn child receive $20,000 payable with interest at age 20.[15]

Like Charles E. Coughlin, William Lemke, Huey Long, and Gerald L. K. Smith, Dr. Townsend was a thinker in the long tradition of a peculiarly American idealism. The monetary panacea had been at the heart of American radicalism throughout the history of the nation. But like his contemporaries in the Depression decade, Francis E. Townsend's single solution was bold but completely unfeasible. Winston Churchill, who was traveling through the United States during these years, put it best: "The Townsend Plan is an attempt to mint the moonlight into silver and coin the sunshine into gold." [16]

---

[13] Dorman, p. 20. By 1941, Townsend was actively denying his advocacy of a $200 pension, exclaiming that "the notion that our plan provides $200 a month is wholly and completely false." See Dr. Francis E. Townsend, *The Townsend National Recovery Plan* (Chicago: Townsend National Recovery Inc., 1941), p. 6.

[14] Witte to Murray, December 11, 1935, Roosevelt Papers, OF 1542.

[15] Neuberger and Loe, pp. 175–76; and "Pensions Progress," *Time*, XXVII, No. 52 (December 30, 1935), 6.

[16] Winston Churchill, "Soapbox Messiahs," *Collier's*, XCVII, No. 25 (June 20, 1936), 46.

12

The Social-Psychology of Townsendism

While competent economists were busy dismantling his arguments, Dr. Townsend was busy recruiting new supporters. The apparent incongruity of the movement's growth in the face of a devastating assault on its very reason for being could be explained in part by the intellectual naïvete and economic illiteracy of the membership, people driven to desperation by the crushing economic crisis. But there was something else at work. The fanaticism with which Townsend's growing thousands of followers promoted his plan at first astounded and finally frightened journalists, politicians, and social critics throughout the nation. There were ugly rumors that newly organized Townsend clubs in the Pacific Northwest were threatening merchants and newspapermen with an economic boycott if they refused to support the plan. There were rumblings in Washington when Congressional offices were flooded by petitions and letters imploring — and in some cases threatening — senators and representatives to back the pension scheme. The emotional pitch among the followers ran so high that the observer was forced to look beyond the obvious economic bases for the growth of the movement to the more subtle social and psychological factors driving millions of old folks into the OARP. Dr. Townsend had struck into a subsoil of fear and discontent that went far deeper than that related to the material privations of the depression.[1]

The Townsend leaders played upon the old people's confusion and

---

[1] Thomas L. Stokes, *Chip Off My Shoulder* (Princeton, N.J.: Princeton University Press, 1940), p. 412.

unhappiness concerning their place in a rapidly changing society. Most Townsendites had grown to adulthood believing they were heirs to a tradition of self-reliance and rugged individualism. They recalled the America of their youth as a land in which opportunity abounded, a land in which a man's failure was the result only of his own inadequacy, and a land in which the thrifty could count on security in old age. It was also a land of close family ties, a place where age was respected and where father and son often worked together and could always depend upon each other in time of crisis.

But in the 1930's, these ideas were only memories. Now the old people lived in a nation where industrialization and urbanization had taken root, a nation of social and physical mobility. A man was less independent in this new America: the factory system robbed him of his individualism and the economics of industrial capitalism subjected him to the vagaries of the business cycle, the uncontrolled and uncontrollable movement from prosperity to depression and back again. A man was also less secure in the new America. Family ties were all too often broken as children moved far from their parental homes. Even old age seemed to lose its dignity; the highest premium in the land now seemed to be on youth. Feted in novels and advertisements, prized by corporations and institutions, the young man was now in the spotlight; the old man had been pushed into the shadows. It was little wonder that many elderly people were bewildered and disturbed by these changes.[2]

Dr. Townsend appeared on the scene to soothe and comfort the aged. Exposed and defenseless as were the men and women who responded to earlier millenarian movements, they nonetheless had learned in childhood the myth of America as a special and superior land, a Garden of Eden where a man's success was a measure of his salvation and utter poverty a mark of moral lassitude. Townsend responded to this critical problem. Their sorry plight in the Depression was not their fault, he told them again and again. Industrial society was the culprit. In a certain sense he was an early visionary of an America of complete automation and abundant leisure, for he told his followers that in some rosy future not only the elderly, but all men, young as well as old, would

---

[2] Dorman, p. 6; and Cantril, p. 208. While the distinguishing feature of America vis-à-vis Europe always had been its mobility, with diminished authority of church, state, family and class and weakened attachments to village or countryside, the twentieth century had accelerated movement in every sector and the results were staggering for old people. On American mobility, see George W. Pierson, "Mobility," in C. Vann Woodward (ed.), *The Comparative Approach to American History* (New York: Basic Books, Inc., 1968), p. 115.

be displaced by labor-saving machinery but would be able to live a respectable life of constructive leisure. He warned, however, that before that day could arrive, the crisis of the thirties would have to be met and conquered. And in describing how this could be done, the doctor preyed upon the fears and emotional needs of his supporters.[3]

He appealed to the hurt pride of the old folks in arguing that a comfortable pension was well deserved after a lifetime of sacrifice and to their sense of self-esteem in defining an important part for the elderly to play in the America of the Townsend plan. Explaining that "people over 60 were selected to be the circulators of large sums of money because they have more buying experience than those of fewer years," he called old people "Civil Veterans of the Republic" and told them they could become a "research, educational and corrective force in both a material and spiritual way in the United States."[4]

Thus were the aged offered the best of all possible worlds. They might live in great comfort but they would not be forced to work. But in this very Utopia lay a socioeconomic problem more subtle and perhaps more devastating than the ones Dr. Townsend was hoping to solve. For what exactly would enforced retirement mean to men and women reared in the tradition of the "Protestant Ethic?" How would these people, completely untrained in the use of leisure time, find satisfying activities to fill their days?

Townsend skirted the issue by assigning his old folks the "vital role" of "circulators of money." But the words were magic, and no one bothered to look beneath the surface. It seemed so clear that they would be able to have their cake and eat it too: the life of affluent leisure with a *raison d'être* as a bonus. Dr. Townsend had solved it all.

Yet in solving it all, in producing a panacea for not only the economic but the social and psychological problems besetting a large part of the population, Dr. Townsend did not force his followers to choose between his plan and basic American values. There could be no doubt that the plan was wholesomely patriotic. As one member put it, "The plan stands for everything a nice person ought to favor." One could be a Townsendite without the risk of being called a foreigner, a "red," or an atheist. Club meetings were opened with the salute to the flag and the singing of patriotic songs. The leaders proclaimed their faith in the

---

[3] Townsend and Clements, pp. 6–7; and Townsend and Roosevelt, *Forum*, XCV, No. 5, 282–83; Cohn, p. 315; and Charles Sanford, *The Quest for Paradise* (Urbana, Illinois: The University of Illinois Press, 1961), pp. 27, 123–24.

[4] *Age of Plenty*, October 25, 1934; and West, p. 19.

political and economic system of the nation, and capitalism was celebrated continuously, as in Clements and Townsend's statement that
"we believe the profit system is the very mainspring of civilized progress." The Townsend solution was clearly a radical one, but it was presented in conservative terms. It offered to preserve the "American way
of life." "The Townsend Plan," one publicist went so far as to say,
"will save America from Radicalism." Thus did it become for its followers, in the words of a contemporary observer, "simply the means of re-
deeming the promises of the little red school house."[5]

Along with this patriotic tone was the movement's religious content.
The aura of the evangelist's camp meeting surrounded Townsendism.
The leadership included many clergymen; the spokesmen described
their causes as being "God-given" and "ordained by the Lord"; well-
known religious songs became the anthems of the movement; and Bible
reading was part of most Townsend gatherings. "The Townsend Plan
is religion in action" — the member usually saw these words plastered on
the walls of the meeting halls. Francis E. Townsend himself rarely forgot to remind the faithful that "I was raised in a Methodist family."[6]

This peculiar combination of religiosity and patriotism fascinated
and impressed those nonmembers from the press and public life who
flocked to the local Townsend club meetings to observe this striking
new movement.

They found the auditorium usually packed and overflowing with old
folks, the occasional shiny bald pate or black head seeming like a reef
in an ocean of the white-haired. The elderly men with hearing problems
sat in the front rows, bending over their ear trumpets. Sitting along-
side them were often five or six Civil War veterans, attired in their GAR
hats. Spread throughout the hall were cardboard pictures and plaster-
of-Paris busts of the lean old man with horn-rimmed spectacles who
had founded the organization.[7]

The ceremonies commenced with the offering of a prayer by a min-

---

[5] Holtzman, p. 102; Cantril, p. 207; and Duncan Aikman, "Townsendism: Old Time
Religion," *New York Times Magazine* (March 8, 1936), 25. The Townsend Plan, rejecting
Socialism or "radicalism" and celebrating the "Americanist ethos," is an example of
what Louis Hartz described as the ideologic force of the "national irrational liberalism,"
which sought to expand state power while retaining Lockian principles. The most bizarre
socio-economic and political panaceas were offered as part of the American consensus.
See Louis Hartz, *The Liberal Tradition in America* (New York: Harcourt, Brace & World,
1955), pp. 259, 279.

[6] Aikman, *New York Times Magazine*, p. 5; and Neuberger and Loe, p. 63.

[7] The description of a typical Townsend Club meeting is based on reports of such
gatherings found in *ibid.;* Frederick A. Delano to Roosevelt, November 25, 1935, and Dr.
Stanley High to Roosevelt, August 29, 1935, Roosevelt Papers, OF 1542.

ister. Next came the perfunctory message from Townsend and Clements read by the local unit's president. Little more than an appeal for dues payment, it was usually prefaced by such an exhortation as "All members must be loyal and steadfast; Right and God are on our side."[8]

The evening's speaker was always the feature attraction. A man who had been certified by organization headquarters to perform these duties, he invariably began with a few jokes of pre-1890 vintage and then made some affectionate remarks which tended to unify the throng. He might begin, "You dear old folks," or "You good old people," and the elderly men would beam and their ladies smile shyly. The address itself was always a paean of praise to the plan, the speaker perhaps explaining that Dr. Townsend's scheme would not only set the abundance in the United States flowing but also would "make jobs for young people and take them out of their cigarette-smoking, whisky-drinking, road-side-petting hell of idleness." With the oldsters now sitting very straight, looking fiercely proud and happy, the peroration would picture Francis Townsend as a David fighting Goliath, a Jesus battling the Pharisees. Dark hints were dropped about "entrenched interests," and "money changers," and "wicked, selfish, rich men" who opposed the plan. The crowd might be urged at the end to "take up the cross of this crusade."[9]

The members left the auditorium happier for having been there. Their fellows were congenial, the themes stirring, and the hope held out for the future heartening. This was all the more significant when one remembered the loss of friends and relatives in the depression-torn land, and the subordination in the twilight of old age to a younger and more aggressive generation. Little wonder that more than one wife described herself as "a Townsend widow" because she spent most of her evenings "working on club business."[10] The social disorder which accompanied rapid change and mobility in America, heightened to an intolerable pitch by economic crisis, made the quest for what one historian termed "reintegration" an imperative for the aged. The Townsend Plan offered its members not only financial salvation, but involvement, commitment and identification. In the movement they could compensate for what Simmel called "that isolation of the personality" which resulted from the breakdown of those tightly knit primary groups found in their old communities.

[8] Neuberger and Loe, pp. 21–23.

[9] Aikman, *New York Times Magazine,* March 8, 1936, 5; Delano to Roosevelt, November 25, 1935, Roosevelt Papers; and Cantril, p. 206.

[10] Cantril, pp. 199, 206–07.

Thus did the OARP work its magic. As Dr. Stanley High explained in a letter to the White House, "The more I see of it the more I am impressed with its power. . . . These particular people, when they've got going, are not the sort to quit."[11]

But what kind of people were these Townsendites? One member said that they were "just folks . . . just Methodist picnic people." Most of them were of old American stock, Protestants of British origin, who could trace their families far back into American history. Sociologists would place the majority in the middle class, for they were farmers or small businessmen, clerks or skilled independent workers, many already retired. There were virtually no wealthy businessmen in the movement and only a handful of professional men on the one extreme and un-skilled factory workers on the other.[12]

Each local club had a small enrollment of the middle-aged, men and women drawn to the plan perhaps because they had some prevision of their own possible fate. In addition, there were always a few landlords, clergymen, boarding-house proprietors and physicians—individuals who might benefit from a more affluent elderly population. And, of course, there were the handful of aspiring political or financial pro-moters, those who hoped to manipulate the old folks to their own advantage. But the younger members were a tiny minority. The Town-send movement was an old peoples' crusade. Most of its members were traditionally conservative registered Republicans, hardly surprising in view of their socioeconomic status. Dr. Townsend's stance—the revolu-tionary as conservative—had won them away from their traditional allegiances.[13]

Many were of midwestern origin. When the first clubs were organized in California in 1934, the membership represented a new wave of migra-tion to the West, men and women who had left their homes in Iowa and Kansas, Illinois and Indiana ten or fifteen years earlier. Buoyed by the

[11] Rowland Berthoff, "The American Social Order: A Conservative Hypothesis," *The American Historical Review*, LXV, No. 3 (April, 1960), 504–05, 507–09; Yonina Talman, "Pursuit of the Millenium: The Relation Between Religion and Social Change" in William A. Lessa and Evan Z. Vogt (eds.), *Reader in Comparative Religion: An Anthropological Ap-proach* (New York: Harper & Row, 1965), pp. 529–32; Simmel, p. 163; and High to Roose-velt, November 3, 1935, Roosevelt Papers, OF 1542.

[12] Holtzman, p. 264; and Cantril, p. 192.

[13] Reports from across America sent by local party chiefs to Democratic National Chairman James A. Farley during the 1936 campaign provide convincing evidence of the Townsendites' political affiliations. See, for example, Mark E. Maghan to James A. Far-ley, September 14, 1936, in Democratic National Campaign Committee Correspondence, 1936, Roosevelt Papers.

interest of these expatriates, the movement flourished throughout the western states, and California—fertile ground for the growth of Technocracy, EPIC, the Utopian Society, Thirty Dollars Every Thursday and so many other panaceas—was naturally the state with the most enthusiastic following. But the local Townsend clubs were soon a nationwide phenomenon, and by mid-1936 they were even more numerous in the East and Midwest than in the West.[14]

As the Townsend movement itself grew stronger, so too did the control of the leaders of the organization. And although the followers were told that "the movement is all yours, my friends; it belongs to you," in reality, the movement was very much the property of Francis E. Townsend and the few leaders who surrounded him. They held the power, and they made all the decisions.[15]

Moreover, the old physician began to be affected by his meteoric rise to fame. The speech making, the plane trips, the cheering throngs made him feel, as he confessed to one interviewer, that "he had been chosen by God to accomplish this mission." The plan's newspaper had begun to compare him to the great men of the past—Washington and Lincoln, Columbus and Copernicus, Franklin and Luther and even to Christ. He reveled in the praise and began to speak of himself as one of the great inspirational leaders of his time. "Yes, I suppose you might call me the Hammer of Thor," he told one newsman.[16]

But he did not change his speaking style. His soft, warm voice was not fitted for oratory, and even after delivering dozens of addresses, the old man still seemed ill at ease on the speaker's platform. Yet this very ineptitude proved an asset, for the old folks in the Townsend crusade did not want their leader to be articulate and dynamic; they wanted him to be like themselves. And this the doctor knew. His conversation was punctuated with homely phrases such as "dang" and "by gum." He wore suspenders and even occasionally received reporters in slippers. His publicists pictured him as the folksy older American who had

---

[14] *The Townsend National Weekly,* November 2 and December 21, 1936 claimed 1,200 clubs in California and some 2,400 in the three west coast states combined. It listed almost 2,500 in seven large eastern and mid-western states, with 500 in Ohio and more than 400 in New York and Michigan. Pennsylvania, Illinois, Indiana and Massachusetts were other Townsendite strongholds.

[15] Quoted in Cantril, p. 186.

[16] *The Townsend National Weekly,* July 8, 1935; and "Messiah On The March," *Time,* (XXVII, No. 22 (June 1, 1936), 10. As with Father Coughlin, the deification and self-deification of Townsend sometimes recalled the medieval prophets who "claimed to be charged with the unique mission of bringing history to its pre-ordained consummation." See Cohn, p. 518.

triumphed over adversity and who now was helping all America over-come its troubles as well.

Thus the man was converted into the symbol. Dr. Townsend, who never before had been a demagogue, could begin to play the role of the messiah people told him he was and could begin to act in the megalo-maniacal tradition of the uglier demagogues of his era.

But this messiah was not an organizer. Townsend needed a cadre of sleek and efficient proselyters, men who were accustomed to talking for their living, men who were willing to serve as salesmen of Utopia. He needed men like Robert E. Clements. Clements (who insisted on being addressed as the "cofounder" of the Townsend Plan) was the manager and fund raiser of the organization. It was he who devised the authoritarian system of centralized control under which the OARP organization was run, and it was he who ruthlessly disposed of those dissidents who rebelled against official policy.

The constitution drafted by Clements, although ostensibly democratic, covered the activities of every local club and gave national headquarters a tight rein on everything from the collection of dues to the selection of speakers. No local autonomy was allowed: under article XII, the state manager, appointed by Clements and responsible to him, had the real power in each state. This manager, who was given a sizeable commission on membership fees and other fund-raising schemes, had the right to approve all local delegates elected to the state area board and had the authority to force any local unit to surrender its charter, records, and funds if national headquarters so desired. As Clements later admitted to a congressional investigating committee, he and Townsend had never intended to allow local clubs any voice in the operation of the national organization.[17]

This system of centralized control naturally led to resentment in the ranks, the first revolt taking place in Oregon, where liberal Townsend-ites objected to Clements' assault on two popular state senators who had criticized some aspects of the plan. The offending local clubs were promptly dubbed "red" by the state leaders and their charters removed. So thorough was the purge of these liberal elements that progressives in the Pacific Northwest soon were referring to the OARP as "Only Ardent Reactionaries Permitted."[18]

A more serious rebellion began in Colorado. When the founders

---

[17] The Committee On Old Age Security of the Twentieth Century Fund, p. 12; and Townsend and Clements, p. 32.

[18] Richard L. Neuberger, "The Townsend Plan Exposed," *The Nation*, CXLI, No. 3669 (October 30, 1935), 506.

deposed Frank Peterson as editor of *The Townsend National Weekly*, Peterson moved to Denver and joined forces with unhappy Colorado Townsendites in setting up the Citizens Retirement Annuity League, an organization which supported the Townsend Plan but opposed the methods of its leaders. A new publication, *The People*, lambasted Townsend and Clements and sparked the growth of other rump groups in the West and Midwest. At a meeting of the dissident elements in Minneapolis in July, 1935, the founding of a National Annuity League was announced. Meanwhile, *The Townsend National Weekly* ran banner headlines announcing that "The Modern Deliverer Is Sold Out," and "A Judas Is Revealed," and Clements soon crushed the revolt by banning all discussion of the advisability of any part of the plan during club meetings, by licensing speakers for only thirty days with a warning to toe the national line or else, and by freely revoking local charters and expelling dissenters and noncontributors.[19]

Clements left few stones unturned in his drive to build up the movement's finances. He arranged card parties and quilting bees, raffles and box suppers. He wrote a manual for OARP speakers which one reader described as "the last word in high-pressure salesmanship applied to an economic idea." His organizational booklet containing suggestions for money raising ventures so fascinated Harry Hopkins that he sent excerpts from it to President Roosevelt.[20]

Clements made the promotion of the Townsend Plan into a big business. He marketed Townsend license plates, tire covers, radiator emblems, pictures, pamphlets, songs, buttons, badges, and banners, all of which were sold at a handsome profit for the national headquarters. He set up a society known as the Townsend National Legion of Honor, with which he promised to make those old folks who could afford more than regular dues "special Townsendites." For $12 per year, membership was offered in the "National Legion's program of Proxy . . . , a personification which substitutes the purse for the self." He explained that "thousands of the world's best people do not possess the qualifications for leadership in our cause, yet they can partake by letting their money become proxy for them in the Legion." Within months, ten thousand gullible oldsters had joined.[21]

[19] *Ibid.*, 505; and Neuberger and Loe, pp. 134, 143–57.

[20] Harry L. Hopkins to Stephen Early, December 26, 1934, Roosevelt Papers, Official File 494-A (Old Age Pensions). Among the excerpts quoted by Hopkins: "The speakers should urge every interested person to give A DOLLAR or AS MANY DOLLARS AS POSSIBLE (the dollar idea should be put into the minds of the people)."

[21] *The Townsend National Weekly,* July 22, and September 9, 1935.

But of all the lucrative schemes devised by Clements, none was so profitable as *The Townsend National Weekly*. The newspaper's circulation rose steadily to over 300,000 and was soon returning a profit of $200,000 yearly to Townsend and Clements. The bulk of the income from the *Weekly* came through advertisements and no potential advertiser was turned away. Many preyed on the fears and anxieties of old people, filling pages with testimonials to the magical qualities of bladder tablets and gland stimulants, kidney pills and all manner of patent medicine panaceas for the aged, with names like Kum-Bak and New World and Electron-O-Meter. National headquarters even made editorial appeals for the support of these products, for the leaders had been promised a percentage "cut" on all such merchandise sold. In yet another way, then, did Townsend and Clements manipulate the discontents and frustrations of the aged in order to add to the power of their organization. In yet another way were the social and psychological appeals of the Townsend Plan at work alongside its economic arguments to make this one of the Depression's most successful mass movements.[22]

[22] Neuberger and Loe, pp. 26, 111–17; and Townsend, *New Horizons* . . . , p. 182.

13

Politics and the Plan

The intensive campaign to build the Townsend organization was paying rich dividends by late 1935. Headquarters announced that in the first fifteen months, total receipts approached three-quarters of a million dollars, and seven thousand clubs were in operation with a total membership of 2.2 million. Less than a year later, the leaders of the movement were to claim that more than three and a half million Americans had joined the Townsend Crusade. There were many who agreed with Abraham Epstein of the American Association for Social Security when he told a Congressional committee that "the Townsend Plan is the finest promotional job that has ever been done in American history." [1]

But in order to justify the growth of their movement, the Townsend leaders had to exert political pressure toward the goal of legislative adoption of the plan. Dr. Townsend, every day more certain that he had discovered the golden road out of the Depression, eagerly awaited the hour when the whole nation would hail his achievement.

The first attempt to influence political events came on the state and local level. When Upton Sinclair lost to Frank F. Merriam in the 1934 gubernatorial election in California, he attributed his defeat to strong Townsend movement support for his opponent. A few months later, California pension promoters were to strike again when Ralph W. Wallace, a young and dynamic state assemblyman and a frequent critic of

[1] U.S., Congress, House, *Hearings on H.R. 443,* 74th Cong., 3d Sess., 1934, I, 288; Wecter, p. 204; and *New York Times,* April 5, 1936.

the plan, fell victim to a recall campaign initiated by angry constituents in San Diego County.[2]

The Townsendites entered the national political arena with the election of John Steven McGroarty as a first-term Democratic Congressman from southern California. A seventy-two-year-old dramatist and
former poet laureate of his state, McGroarty was an ardent anti-New
Dealer and a great believer in the Townsend plan, and his election was
due in large part to the strong campaign waged in his behalf by local
OARP organizers. Once in Congress, McGroarty was happy to become
a spokesman for the pension scheme and introduced a bill to implement
the plan in January of 1935. Responding to the movement's pressure,
city councils in Los Angeles and Minneapolis and state legislatures in
Arizona, California, Nevada and North Dakota sent to Congress memorials urging quick passage of the McGroarty bill. A sad and ironic note
in the voting on these memorials was that many conservative state legislators preferred to go on record as favoring an enormous federal
pension if by so doing they could both win the affection of elderly voters and destroy the chances of any proposed state old-age pension,
while many liberal legislators who considered Townsend's plan a pie-
in-the-sky dream and who had worked for passage of realistic if modest
state pensions, were threatened with recall and defeat if they opposed
the memorial statements.[3]

The Townsend plan leaders also undertook a letter-writing and peti-
tion-signing campaign. Within a period of three months, members of
the movement secured the signatures of over twenty million Americans
(an incredible one-fifth of the adult population of the nation) on
petitions urging congressional approval of the plan. This was an exhi-
bition of public support unmatched in history. As one observer put it,
the mail campaigns regarding the soldiers' bonus or the entry into the
World Court were "mere rivulets compared with this torrent."[4]

But the massive pressure was not sufficient to insure passage of Mc-
Groarty's bill. Even when the Townsendites revised their bill, providing for a pension "up to" $200 per month, there was no chance of

---

[2] Lake, *Saturday Evening Post*, CCVII, No. 45, 127. Merriam, although a conservative,
promised support of the plan.

[3] Chester T. Crowell, "The Townsend Plan: A Challenge to Congress," *American Mercury*, XXXIV, No. 136 (April, 1935), 457; and Bruce Bonner Mason, "American Political Protest, 1932–1936" (unpublished Ph.D. dissertation, Department of Political Science,
University of Texas, 1953), p. 125.

[4] H. E. Hunter to Roosevelt, January 6, 1935, Roosevelt Papers, OF 1542; Swing, p. 132;
and Neuberger and Loe, p. 79.

Dr. Townsend giving his opening address at the first national convention
of the OARP in Chicago, October, 1935. *Wide World*

winning a majority. On a vote to have a roll call on the measure, the
plan lost by almost four to one. Yet Dr. Townsend and his followers
were not at first discouraged. The loss of the bill was considered merely
a tactical setback; the war was still to be won. When Verner W. Main, a
Republican from Michigan's Third Congressional District, won both a
primary and a by-election in the spring of 1935 and attributed his victory to strong backing from the OARP organization, the Townsendites
were elated. "As Main goes, so goes the nation," became the battle cry
as the movement assembled in Chicago for its first national convention.[5]

They were "WCTU types," one newsman observed of the Chicago
delegates. "They were anti-sex, anti-liquor and anti-tobacco people."
The convention's first order of business was a resolution prohibiting
smoking in the auditorium. But while a fervor of puritanical and religious zeal surged through the followers on the floor, the leaders on the

---

[5] *Ibid.*, pp. 106, 259. Main, of course, had strong GOP backing after the primary and
Senator Arthur Vandenberg campaigned with him.

rostrum used the meeting as a showcase for their power. And Townsend and Clements were not the only celebrities in the house. There was the articulate Reverend Clinton Wunder, who gave the invocations and helped chair the proceedings. There was the doctor's attorney, Sheridan Downey, a smooth politician who had switched sides after running for lieutenant governor of California on Upton Sinclair's ill-fated ticket. There was the Oklahoman, Gomer Smith, whose rousing anti-Roosevelt harangue harked back to the style of Huey Long.[6]

But if Clements and the others were able to share the spotlight at the beginning, it was Dr. Townsend who dominated the scene by the convention's close. In a remarkable concluding address carried on a nationwide radio network, Francis E. Townsend told the cheering thousands:

> We dare not fail. Our plan is the sole and only hope of a confused and distracted nation. . . . We have become an avalanche of political power that no derision, no ridicule, no conspiracy of silence can stem. . . . Where Christianity numbered its hundreds in its beginning years, our cause numbers its millions. And without sacrilege we can say that we believe that the effects of our movement will make as deep and mighty changes in civilization as did Christianity itself.[7]

Now the old doctor was sure that he had power as well as purpose. He was ready to use this power to turn his plan into law. In late 1935, he prepared for a new and greater effort in the political arena.

Early in December, the Townsend plan high command asked all congressmen if they would vote for the Townsend plan bill in the next session of Congress. Only sixty replies were received from the 531 letters. Only thirty-nine were affirmative. Of the nationally known politicians, only Senator William Borah of Idaho would go so far as to say a few kind words about the movement, and even he refused to endorse the pension plan.[8]

Dr. Townsend was angry. At first he could not understand the rebuff from Washington. All across the country there was new evidence of the movement's strength, and in early January, an American Institute of Public Opinion poll revealed that over one-fourth of all eligible voters in Oregon and one-eighth of all Californians favored the $200 pension. During this same period, dispatches appeared in newspapers

---

[6] Moore, *New Republic*, LXXV, No. 1093, 10; and Stokes, p. 18.

[7] Quoted in "For Mothers and Fathers," *Time*, XXVI, No. 19 (November 4, 1935), 20.

[8] Harris, *Current History*, XLIII, No. 2, 461; and *New York Times*, January 29, 1936.

almost every day testifying to the strength of the plan. Clements was undoubtedly exaggerating when he bragged that Townsend could elect 80 per cent of the Congressmen in eleven western states and many more in the Midwest, but the movement was certainly stronger than indicated by the reaction in Congress.[9]

Townsend decided that the New Deal was inspiring the Congressional "conspiracy" against his plan. Although the Administration had carefully avoided making a public statement on the proposal, the old physician had been finding more and more reason to resent President Roosevelt.

One major cause of Townsend's irritation was that FDR had once refused to see him, an incident that *The Townsend National Weekly* referred to as "an insult that the masses of people should resent." Another and more important factor was the Social Security Act. The doctor considered the old age insurance provision of $30 monthly for people seventy and over to be not only insignificant but pernicious, merely token display on the part of Roosevelt to take the public spotlight off the Townsend plan. There was a grain of truth to the old man's charge: for although the Social Security Act was part of the more liberal "second New Deal" program of the midthirties and would have become law if Townsend had never come on the scene, there is little doubt that the existence of the OARP organization did speed passage of the measure. As FDR said to Frances Perkins, Secretary of Labor: "We have to have it. . . . The Congress can't stand the pressure of the Townsend Plan unless we have a real old-age insurance system." [10]

A final reason for Dr. Townsend's displeasure with the Administration related to the humiliating experience he had undergone in testifying before the House Ways and Means and Senate Finance Committees in the February 1935 hearings on the first McGroarty bill. Even with the aid of several advisers, he had become confused and befuddled in explaining the intricacies of his plan to the highly critical Congressmen.[11]

Townsend was justified in feeling that the New Deal was his enemy. Convinced by economists that the pension plan was a dangerous and

---

[9] *Ibid.,* January 9 and 12, 1936; and Owen, *New York Times Magazine,* December 29, 1935, 14.

[10] *The Townsend National Weekly,* February 3, 1935; Marvin McIntyre to Townsend, December 18, 1934, Roosevelt Papers, OF 1542; and Frances Perkins, *The Roosevelt I Knew* (New York: The Viking Press, 1946), pp. 278–79, 294.

[11] U.S., Congress, House, Committee on Ways and Means, *Hearings, Economic Security Bill,* 74th Cong., 2d Sess., 1935, p. 677.

impossible dream, President Roosevelt, in early 1936, instigated a new series of attacks on the Townsend movement by Democratic congressmen.

Representative Maury Maverick of Texas opened the assault by charging that the plan was "only a way of avoiding discussion of the real issues." Other congressmen, hoping to discredit Townsend and thus pacify unhappy constituents, joined in. Representative Phillip Ferguson of Oklahoma termed the plan, "a racket," Senator Kenneth McKellar of Tennessee argued that it was nothing more than a "fantastic . . . devastating . . . wild-eyed scheme for looting the treasury of the United States," and Representative Thomas L. Blanton filled nine pages of the Congressional record with an address entitled, "Dr. Townsend Bleeding the Aged of Their Life's Blood to Enrich Himself." New Dealers Harry Hopkins and Frances Perkins strengthened the attack by issuing skeptical statements concerning the feasibility of both the pension and the tax.[12]

Francis E. Townsend, now certain that the New Dealers in particular and all politicians in general were his enemies, was ready to fight back. He accused the New Deal of being "a misdeal . . . where political appointees experiment in human misery." He labeled certain actions of the Administration, "nothing more than Mussolini Fascism." He said of President Roosevelt's attitude toward old age pensions: "One marvels at the indecision . . . by one in that position, 2,000 years after the Death on the Cross." He issued threats, and noting the opposition of conservative Republicans and Liberty Leaguers, used the GOP as well as the Democratic Party as a target. The man who had once written that "all politicians are cowards" now hinted at the formation of a new political party.[13] Addressing himself to the nation, he proclaimed:

> Fellow Americans, let us not put our trust in either of the old political parties. Both of them are owned and controlled by the same set of men. Self-interest is their God and their guide in every political move that they make. . . . Let us never again be such fools as to permit them to deceive us.[14]

Townsend had declared war on Congress and on the Administration, and congressmen, with New Dealers in the lead, fought back. Their weapon was a new congressional investigation of the plan in the spring of 1936. Chosen to head the subcommittee which held the hearings was

---

[12] Neuberger and Loe, pp. 181, 264, 267–69.
[13] *The Townsend National Weekly,* July 1, 1935; and Dorman, pp. 7, 90–91, 96.
[14] Quoted in Harris, *Current History,* XLIII, No. 2, 462.

Representative C. Jasper Bell, Democrat of Missouri, who was named for the job perhaps because he was known to be a lieutenant of Boss Tom Pendergast of Kansas City and, as such, thought to be safe from reprisals by the OARP forces.[15]

The Bell Committee's purpose was almost wholly political in nature; its objective was the discrediting of the movement and the humiliation of its leader. It aimed to destroy the Townsend organization's effectiveness as a political force in the 1936 elections.

A parade of hostile witnesses, including disgruntled ex-members and certain critical economists, was called to testify along with the leaders of the plan. Chairman Bell and his committee counsel, James R. Sullivan, an aggressive little man who was formerly a Kansas City police prosecutor, missed no opportunity to denounce violently the OARP. They accused the leaders of being "quacks and charlatans, false prophets of social reform . . . making vast sums of unholy profits." [16]

The financial aspects of the Townsend operation were carefully examined. It was revealed that some state area managers had made enormous commissions, California's Edward J. Margett averaging $2,000 monthly. Townsend and Clements' profits were shown to be far greater than the small salaries they listed, each receiving over $35,000 from the newspaper alone. The congressmen heard how the movement's leaders spent money with reckless abandon—for example, over $20,000 was raised to pay a team of Washington lobbyists for only a few months of unsuccessful efforts. Finally, it was charged that these leaders were hopelessly inept administrators of the dollars collected from thousands of poor old people who had been convinced that their contributions would bring them undreamed of wealth in a short time. A famous accounting firm testified that the movement's books were so incomplete and muddled as to make a reasonable audit impossible.[17]

Counsel Sullivan summed up the case against the leaders of the Townsend organization by reading a letter from Dr. Townsend to Clements in which the old physician had written, "You and I have the world by the tail, Earl, if we work it right." The committee members thus accused Townsend himself of having started his plan only for personal aggrandizement.[18]

---

[15] T.R.B., "Representative Bell Stalks Fame and Townsend," *New Republic*, LXXXVII, No. 1123 (June 10, 1936), 128.

[16] Neuberger and Loe, pp. 271–77, 285, 293; and "Men, Money and Methods," *Time*, XXVII, No. 15 (April 13, 1936), 16.

[17] "Townsend Plan: Rift and Inquiry," *Literary Digest*, CXXI, No. 14 (April 4, 1936), 6.

[18] "Messiah On The March," *Time*, XXVII, No. 22 (June 1, 1936), 10.

With such damaging evidence in the record, the subcommittee concluded its weeks of hearings by calling Francis E. Townsend as its final witness. The doctor was disturbed by the harsh questions, and finally he began to crack under the pressure. "You can't argue this idea away with just figures," he pleaded. Pressed to explain his proposed transaction tax, he said, "People have to buy or die. . . . If we can catch every person and tax him when he buys, the taxing would be harmless." His incredible naïvete was revealed time and again. As E. B. White put it, "When forced to deal with the fundamental problems, he quietly came apart, like an inexpensive toy." [19]

For Townsend, the Bell Committee hearings represented a disaster. Not only was he personally defamed and humiliated, but leading members of his movement began to defect under the pressure.

In April, the doctor had a sudden and bitter quarrel with Representative McGroarty. Townsend accused his old friend of attempting to use the movement for his own "private political ambitions," and McGroarty fired back that the founder "seems to have abandoned his original plan and is talking just like a fool." The two men stopped speaking and the congressman dissociated himself from the OARP organization. But more serious than McGroarty's departure was the resignation of Robert Earl Clements, the "cofounder" and chief organizer of the movement. Relations between Clements and Townsend had cooled perceptibly in the weeks before the Bell Committee investigation. The younger man had always been less than liberal and had become irritated with certain changes that the doctor was planning for the movement. He opposed Dr. Townsend's scheme for plowing back much of the profits from the *Weekly* into the OARP in the form of "Townsend Centers" for the jobless and indigent aged, and the physician's program for democratizing the plan by a town-meeting system of government for clubs in California. He particularly objected to the old man's occasional threats to start a third political party, believing as he did that pressure politics within the established parties was the only hope of getting the plan adopted, and fearing that a third party might effectively kill the golden cow that he was milking.[20]

Clements resigned from the OARP the day after he was summoned to appear at the hearings. And once he faced the congressional investigators, he proved willing to give damaging anti-Townsend testimony.

---

[19] Holtzman, pp. 442–43; and Aikman, *New York Times Magazine,* July 26, 1936, 7.
[20] "Townsend Plan's Change of Drivers," *Literary Digest,* CXXI, No. 15 (April 11, 1936), 5; and Neuberger and Loe, pp. 251–52, 280.

Robert E. Clements and his wife with Dr. Townsend shortly before Clements resigned from the movement under pressure of a congressional investigation. *Wide World*

He revealed that he had made $75,000 during his brief tenure in the plan and provided detailed information concerning the authoritarian nature of the movement's leadership.[21]

Dr. Townsend was in trouble. The pitiless harassment of the Committee and the defections of his fellow leaders led some observers to conclude that his organization was crumbling and would soon break apart. But they underestimated the old man, who was already preparing a counterattack, first moving to meet the criticism concerning centralized control by democratizing the plan through the creation of a National Advisory Committee. Then he lashed out at the Bell hearings, calling them a "hoax" and an "inquisition." He pointed out that as head of a national organization, he had been quizzed about the affairs of local clubs. Did FDR, he asked, know all about the activities of local Democratic bodies, such as the Kansas City political machine? Bell and

[21] U.S., Congress, House, Select Committee Investigating Old Age Pension Organizations, *Testimony of Robert E. Clements*, 74th Cong., 3d Sess., 1936, I, 55, 84–92, 211–33.

Sullivan had gone too far; instead of exposing a charlatan they had made a martyr, and Townsend shrewdly played the part of the innocent victim of slander. His newspaper headlined, "Moses Before Pharoah." [22]

Dr. Townsend's followers rallied to their leader. Many members traveled to Washington to provide him moral support, some bearing petitions with hundreds of thousands of signatures attesting that Townsendites had "donated the money to be used as the leader saw fit." Angry letters poured into the White House, calling the Bell Committee "the worst disgrace ever brought upon the American people," the "besmirching of one who was sent to us from on high," and the "crucifixtion [sic] of the greatest emancipator since Christ." [23]

Heartened by the growing evidence of widespread support, Townsend decided to defy the committee and the New Deal. After several days of grueling questioning, the old physician, with the aid of Gerald L. K. Smith, staged his spectacular walkout, exclaiming, "I refuse to go back . . . I'll show them how much contempt I have . . . I predict this administration has committed political suicide with this unjust and unfair hearing." Townsend rightly predicted that the Committee, fearful of alienating voters in an election year, would hesitate before acting on his refusal to testify. "They will weakly evade the issue," he said; "They will put this unhappy baby in the lap of the district court and the case will not come to trial before the election." Dr. Townsend was not cited for contempt of Congress until 1937.[24]

Safe at last from the investigators, the pension messiah went on his tour of the Northeast with Gerald Smith. For Smith, the timing was perfect. The sudden departure of Robert Earl Clements had left a power vacuum in the movement; Dr. Townsend was lonely and craved advice and direction. Smith, like Clements, was an articulate and dynamic young organizer, just the type of man the doctor needed. It was not surprising, then, that the old man so eagerly attached himself to the newcomer and readily allowed him to assert great authority.

Gerald L. K. Smith's major contribution to the Townsend organization was his insistence on the formation of a third political party. But Dr. Townsend's mounting hatred of Franklin D. Roosevelt had already made him amenable to such a plan. Smith only had to sharpen the anger and channel the thinking. Following the hearings, Townsend referred

[22] *New York Times*, May 5, 1936; and Neuberger and Loe, pp. 91, 289–90, 301.

[23] *Ibid.*, 297, 302; and C. N. Walters to Roosevelt, May 24, 1936, Mrs. H. H. Hall to Roosevelt, May 22, 1936, and W. V. Milliken to Roosevelt, May 22, 1936, Roosevelt Papers, OF 1542.

[24] *New York Times*, May 23 and May 29, 1936.

to the New Deal as a "deliberate Machiavellian, planned attempt to discredit and wreck America."[25] Including Republicans in his vitriolic attack on all politicians, he told his followers:

The way for us to lick the stuffing out of the old parties is to become militant and go after them hammer and tongs for being totally incompetent. . . . We should begin to talk about the Townsend Party and not wait in the foolish hope that one of the old groups will adopt us. If they do, they will treat us like poor adopted trash. To hell with them.[26]

Townsend had growing confidence that a new political party could make an excellent showing in the election. He was aware of the newspaper reports indicating that Townsendites were in practical control of at least eight and probably ten states. He began to boast that "we have strength enough to elect a candidate. We have at least 30 million votes." He believed in Gerald Smith's simple but startling arithmetic: six million Townsend Planners plus four million Share-Our-Wealth members equals ten million votes "to start with."[27]

At first, Dr. Townsend was not sure who should head the third party ticket. He denied having any personal presidential ambitions, claiming to possess "neither the mental nor the physical equipment for the job." But he did evidence some interest in being "the power behind the throne." Throughout late May he equivocated: at one juncture he suggested Senator Borah; another time he told reporters, "I'd like to see it go to some young man, like Gerald Smith."[28]

Smith, however, had his own plans, and they did not include running for President in 1936. Now hoping to make the grand coalition between the Townsendites and the forces of Father Coughlin and William Lemke, he began to push a reluctant Dr. Townsend inexorably toward this alliance.

Certain unhappy questions were raised in the effort to tie Townsend to Coughlin and Lemke. The old doctor was aware that the radio priest had considered the Townsend Plan impractical, and once had even termed it "economic insanity." For his part, Dr. Townsend had criticized the sixteen-point program of the National Union for Social Justice, calling it "14 points too many" and had even irritably complained

[25] Quoted in Holtzman, p. 452.
[26] *New York Times*, May 20, 1936.
[27] *Ibid.*, January 12 and June 1, 1936.
[28] *Ibid.*, May 28, 1936.

of the priest: "He's stealing our stuff anyway, organizing in Congressional districts."[29]

As for Lemke, Townsend's position vis-à-vis the problems of the farmer was not conducive to a congenial relationship with the agrarian leader. In response to a question about agricultural issues, the doctor had replied, "Oh, they don't matter. . . . Every party thinks alike on those things." The author of the Frazier-Lemke bills could not have disagreed more.[30]

Despite these points of conflict, Coughlin and Lemke moved closer to Townsend in the spring of 1936. Spurred on by Smith and sensing what a prize might be theirs in an alliance with the millions of pension supporters, both men sought to make themselves more acceptable to Francis E. Townsend. The radio priest strongly defended Townsend during the Bell Committee hearings, and even "endorsed the principle of social security which the Townsend philosophy advocates." Lemke, who had always supported the plan, rallied to the old man's side during his time of troubles in April and May, delivering a forceful radio address and writing enthusiastic letters to his constituents.[31]

The setting was made for the Townsend plan to join the coalition of the radical movements of the Depression. Old Dr. Townsend, emboldened by his meteoric rise to fame and angered by his brush with "the politicians," was now almost ready to bring his army of the aged into the joint battle against the New Deal. And with the addition of this powerful force, the birth of a new and strange party was imminent.

[29] Cantril, pp. 184–85; Townsend, *New Horizons* . . . , p. 171; and Owen, *New York Times Magazine*, December 29, 1935, 15.

[30] *Ibid.*

[31] *New York Times*, March 30, 1936; Charles E. Coughlin, *The Townsend Plan* (Royal Oak, Michigan: The Shrine of the Little Flower, 1935), pp. 1–2; radio speech entitled "Old Age Pensions," delivered by William Lemke on April 23, 1936, copy in Lemke Papers; and Lemke to B. W. Lemke, May 25, 1936, Lemke to O. S. Gunderson, June 3, 1936, and Lemke to Covington Hall, June 10, 1936, Lemke Papers.

BOOK TWO

THE ACTIVITIES OF THE PARTY: THE ELECTION CAMPAIGN OF 1936

My friends, there is a way out, a way to freedom! There is an escape from the dole standard of Roosevelt, the gold standard of Landon. No longer need you be the targets in no-man's land for the financial cross-fire of the sham-battlers. . . . A new party is now in the field. — Charles E. Coughlin, 1936

PART V

A NEW PARTY IS BORN

I foresee no third party. I see no need.
What would it be? A gathering of political malcontents with personal grudges to
air! Have we ever had a dearth of such?
... As for myself, I have no political
fences to maintain, no job to defend. And
I seek none. — Charles E. Coughlin, May,
1935

14

The Making of the Alliance

Charles E. Coughlin's penchant for contradiction haunted him throughout the spring of 1936. Only a year earlier he had told a reporter that
he could foresee no third party and had no personal interest in one,
that such an organization would be merely "a gathering of malcontents
with personal grudges to bear." But events had moved quickly as the
presidential election campaign approached. By May, Father Coughlin's
growing hatred of Franklin D. Roosevelt was matched only by his growing confidence in the political strength of his National Union for
Social Justice. As he looked around the nation, it seemed obvious that
forceful and willing allies were available in the persons of those other
malcontents, Lemke, Smith, and Townsend. What better time to strike
for power and glory?

Yet even in the climactic month of May, when rumblings about an
anti-New Deal crusade could be heard in each of the radical leader's
camps, confusion and tentativeness continued to hamper efforts to make
the grand alliance. As late as May 27, Coughlin could tell the *New York
Times* that the only hope of saving America lay in a "renovated Republican Party," adding only that if the GOP front-runner, Governor Alfred
E. Landon of Kansas, won the nomination, even that hope would be lost
and that the NUSJ would be forced to "concentrate activities in Congress
and wait until 1940 before trying to influence the presidential election."
The radio priest, always the equivocator, was on the fence once again.[1]

But the setting for the bid for power proved too enticing. Within two

[1] *New York Times*, May 28, 1936.

weeks of his disclaimer, Father Coughlin was hinting at the formation of a "third political force," and it was only a matter of days before his hints materialized. This decision to go ahead seemed a kind of spur of the moment affair: the dearth of correspondence between Coughlin and Lemke in the preceding weeks provides mute testimony on the point. In fact, none of the participants had expected to act so quickly or so decisively. But the radio priest had suddenly become a man of impulse; when he decided to move the others soon followed.[2]

In the planning of the new organization, Charles Coughlin was clearly the strong man, the driving force, without whom there would have been no alliance. During the first week of June, after making his decision, he boastfully announced, in a letter to Lemke, the birth of a new political party, naming his friend its North Dakota state chairman. The congressman was pleased but still rather confused; two days later he would write to an old acquaintance: "I think the new alignment will take place shortly after the two conventions are over." But of course Coughlin had no intention of waiting that long. On June 17, he proclaimed from New York the creation of a "united front" of the supporters of the National Union for Social Justice, the Townsend Plan, the Share-Our-Wealth Society, and the Lemke "farm bloc." At the same time he allowed Gerald L. K. Smith to announce in Chicago that a "loose working agreement" had been made between the "Smith-Townsend" and "Lemke-Coughlin" forces.[3]

The priest refused to tell reporters anything about the presidential candidate of his proposed "third force," except to warn that "if this man runs, Landon will run a poor third." Yet there could be only one choice from among the four radical leaders. Coughlin himself was ruled out because of his unwillingness to give up the priesthood, something a political candidate would have to do. Townsend was admittedly too old to run. Smith was more interested—at least at this time—in being a backstage manipulator and platform orator than a nominee; in any case, Coughlin considered him undependable. William Lemke alone was "available."[4]

As late as June 8 the radio priest had written the North Dakotan only that "in due time, I will send you the name of our presidential candidate." But after a flurry of telephone calls between the two men, that name was soon established as Lemke's own. For he was, after all, the only

[2] *Social Justice*, June 9, 1936.
    [3] *Ibid.; New York Times*, June 17, 1936; Charles E. Coughlin to Lemke, June 8, 1936. and Lemke to Covington Hall, June 10, 1936, Lemke Papers.
    [4] *New York Times*, June 17, 1936.

Gerald Smith and Dr. Townsend visit Rep. Lemke in Washington on
June 23, 1936, to discuss plans for the formation of a third party. *United
Press International*

practicing politician of the four, the only member of Congress. He was
the only one who had had experience as a winning candidate on a third
party ticket. Moreover, he was a Republican officeholder who was dependent on neither the Republican nor the Democratic Party. And William Lemke certainly was interested in running. The hundreds of letters
from around the nation urging him to continue his fight for various
monetary reform bills had convinced him that wide support could be
expected for a party advocating enactment of the Coughlin, Townsend
and Smith proposals, as well as his personal farm refinance plan. When
Father Coughlin predicted that "a third party would engage the attention of 25 million voters," and when Smith spoke of the "20 million
Americans" who would respond to a united appeal by the leaders of the
mass movements, Lemke was convinced. He agreed to make the race.[5]

[5] *Ibid;* and *Detroit News,* June 17, 1936.

On June 20, William Lemke formally announced the birth of the party. "I have accepted the challenge of the reactionary elements of both old parties," he told newsmen. "I will run for the Presidency of the United States as the candidate of the Union Party, which I am instrumental in establishing officially." Speculating that a national convention of all interested persons would probably be held in Cleveland some time in August, he promised: "It will be a mass convention, similar to the one at which Lincoln launched his party." But reporters remained skeptical concerning both Lemke's role in the creation of the party and the popular support it might generate. They joked that his nominating convention had really been held in a telephone booth, with Father Coughlin on the other end of the line. They asked why the name "Union" was chosen. Lemke replied, "Each group within the party will keep its identity but will work together for legislative victories. We don't accept each other's ideas in their entirety. . . . That's why we call it the Union Party." But few were persuaded that this was the whole story, for the name "Union" smacked of the National Union for Social Justice, Father Coughlin's own movement, and the radio priest had wanted it that way. Only six hours after Congressman Lemke's initial announcement, Coughlin was on a national radio network delivering the first formal speech in promotion of the new organization.[6]

It was not "morally possible," said Coughlin, to support either of the two major parties in 1936. Lamenting the lost promise of FDR, who had spoken "golden words of hope" in the inaugural address only to implement a program that "multiplied the profits of the monopolists and threw back God's best gifts in His face, while stealing from wives and children," the priest exclaimed, "It is not pleasant for one who coined the phrase, 'Roosevelt or Ruin,' to be constrained to admit that in reality it is 'Roosevelt and Ruin.'" Yet it was not possible to "return to the Landons and the Hoovers," those "Old Deal exploiters who honestly defended the dishonest system of gold standardism and rugged individualism." Alas, those "moribund New Deal critics . . . , the Punch and Judy Republicans," were as dominated by "the ventriloquists of Wall Street" as were the objects of their scorn, the "sham battling Democrats."[7]

Reaching his peroration, Coughlin's mellow voice rose as he spoke the words of promise. Now there was an alternative, the huge audience

[6] New York Times, June 20, 21, and 28, 1936; Basil Rauch, The History of the New Deal (New York: Creative Age Press, Inc., 1944), p. 243; and Charles E. Coughlin, "A Third Party," Vital Speeches of the Day, II, No. 20 (July 1, 1936), 613–14.

[7] Ibid., 614–15.

was told; now in the field was a new party that presented a program "in harmony substantially with the principles of social justice." The presidential candidate of this party had "already carved for himself a niche of fame in the industrial and agricultural temple of America." He was a man who had made promises but had kept them, one who had fought for the right things and fought hard, an American and not an internationalist, "a liberty lover and not a slave trader," a battler who was prepared to "fight for financial freedom as did his prototype Lincoln, who waged war for physical freedom." William Lemke, said Coughlin, "has taken the step and has officially asked the National Union for Social Justice for its support and we declare him, on the strength of his splendid record and his platform, eligible for indorsation." [8]

This Union Party platform would command the attention of many students of American politics in the months that lay ahead. It was strikingly unlike the platforms of the major parties—it was in no way the result of an effort to compromise the clashing interests of the nation which are usually represented within the great parties. Instead, it was a potpourri of the monetary panaceas of the time. The only clashing interests compromised here were those of the radical movements themselves.

The basis of the platform obviously was the sixteen-point program of the National Union for Social Justice. But it included also a plank urging security for the farmers in the manner of the Lemke refinance bills, a plank demanding help for the aged—clearly a gesture toward the Townsend supporters—and several planks which were reminiscent of the program of the Share-Our-Wealth Society. There were fifteen planks in all:

1. America shall be self-contained and self-sustained: no foreign entanglements, be they political, economic, financial or military.
2. Congress and Congress alone shall coin, issue and regulate all the money and credit in the United States through a central bank of issue.
3. Immediately following the establishment of the central bank of issue, Congress shall provide for the retirement of all tax-exempt, interest-bearing bonds and certificates of indebtedness of the Federal Government, and shall refinance all the present agricultural mortgage indebtedness for the farmer and all the home mortgage indebtedness for the city owner by the use of its money and credit which it now gives to the control of private bankers.
4. Congress shall legislate that there will be an assurance of a living annual wage for all laborers capable of working and willing to work.
5. Congress shall legislate that there will be assurance of production at a profit for the farmer.

[8] *Ibid.*, 615–16.

6. Congress shall legislate that there will be an assurance of reasonable and decent security for the aged, who, through no fault of their own, have been victimized and exploited by an unjust economic system which has so concentrated wealth in the hands of a few that it has impoverished great masses of our people.

7. Congress shall legislate that American agricultural, industrial, and commercial markets will be protected from manipulation of foreign moneys and from all raw material and processed goods produced abroad at less than a living wage.

8. Congress shall establish an adequate and perfect defense for our country from foreign aggression either by air, by land or by sea, but with the understanding that our naval, air and military forces must not be used under any consideration in foreign fields or in foreign waters either alone or in conjunction with any foreign power. If there must be conscription, there shall be conscription of wealth as well as a conscription of men.

9. Congress shall so legislate that all federal offices and positions of every nature shall be distributed through civil service qualifications and not through a system of party spoils and corrupt patronage.

10. Congress shall restore representative government to the people of the United States to preserve the sovereignty of the individual States of the United States by the ruthless eradication of bureaucracies.

11. Congress shall organize and institute federal works for the conservation of public lands, waters and forests, thereby creating billions of dollars of wealth, millions of jobs at the prevailing wages, and thousands of homes.

12. Congress shall protect small industry and private enterprise by controlling and decentralizing the economic domination of monopolies, to the end that these small industries and enterprises may not only survive and prosper but that they may be multiplied.

13. Congress shall protect private property from confiscation through unnecessary taxation with the understanding that the human rights of the masses take precedence over the financial rights of the classes.

14. Congress shall set a limitation upon the net income of any individual in any one year and a limitation on the amount that such an individual may receive as a gift or as an inheritance, which limitation shall be executed through taxation.

15. Congress shall re-establish conditions so that the youths of the nation as they emerge from schools and colleges may have the opportunity to earn a decent living while in the process of perfecting themselves in a trade or profession.[9]

Much of this platform, as one critic soon pointed out, represented a "complete economic hallucination," which could "bring almost certain and unmitigated disaster if ever put into practice." But forceful it was, and the Union Party organizers expected that its broad promise of fed-

[9] Reprinted in *The Union Party: On To Victory* (Chicago: Union Party, 1936), p. 7.

eral aid coupled with the spectacular sendoff candidate Lemke had received from Father Coughlin would dominate the headlines. To their dismay, many newspapers featured instead the upset knockout of America's heavyweight boxing contender, Joe Louis, at the hands of Germany's Max Schmeling; others chose to headline a new tax bill. Desperately seeking national publicity, William Lemke set off on a speaking tour.[10]

On June 21, the North Dakotan spoke at a press conference: "This is the first time the people ever have had a presidential candidate who believes it good political strategy only to tell the truth and keep his word." Within a few days it became clear what he meant by "the truth," and how bitter was his hatred of those who scoffed at his version of it. "The only overproduction we are suffering from is an overproduction of ignorance in Washington!" he shouted. "We no longer have a representative government. We have instead laws written by a brainless trust, and steamrollered through a bunch of 'representatives of the people' who don't know as much about the issues as the page boys in Congress." [11]

Assailing the "international bankers" and "money changers in the temple" in the style of Father Coughlin, Lemke defended the radical programs of the Union Party leaders as America's sole hope. "Both parties are one and the same," the candidate told the nation. "Now I'm giving you a choice." And he, like Coughlin, grandiloquently compared his new party to the Republican Party of 1860:

Some three-quarters of a century ago this nation was at the crossroads. The issue was human slavery. . . . Today we are again at the crossroads and the issue again is slavery—economic slavery. Today we are in the midst of another war—a war against a man-made depression. It has reduced our nation to the lowest economic state in its history, leaving a trail of suffering, starvation and want in the land of plenty. As in those earlier times, the major parties have failed to solve the problems confronting the nation. The only solution is through the victory of our new party.[12]

Lemke used all the devices of the underdog politician. He appealed to local xenophobia, as in Des Moines in late June, when he told a crowd of two thousand, "Henry Wallace, your distinguished former citizen with a foreign complex, imported 43 million bushels of corn in 1935. How

[10] "Union Party Economics," *Saturday Evening Post*, CCIX, No. 9 (August 22, 1936), 22; *Chicago Daily Tribune*, June 20, 1936; and *New York Times*, June 20, 1936.

[11] *Ibid.*, June 21, 29, 1936.

[12] Press release by William Lemke, July 1, 1936, copy in Lemke Papers.

do you Iowa farmers like that?" And he even issued the standard challenge to both major party candidates to meet him in a series of debates.[13]

Yet with his fears mounting that he lacked the magnetic qualities to capture many new supporters in the short campaign which lay ahead, the bucolic candidate more and more referred to the following which his allies could deliver to him on election day. He heaped lavish praise on Coughlin, Townsend, Smith, and the late Huey Long, and revealed that Father Coughlin had predicted that 85 per cent of the five million members of the National Union for Social Justice would vote the Union ticket in the fall. In an effort to ingratiate himself further with the radio priest, Lemke even managed great enthusiasm in naming a Coughlin man as his running mate: Thomas Charles O'Brien of Boston, Massachusetts.[14]

There was little reason for such enthusiasm. A heavy-set, bespectacled, slow-spoken man of forty-nine, O'Brien was an attorney who had been both a Democratic and Republican officeholder in the past. He had worked as a railroad brakeman to pay his way through Harvard University and Harvard Law School, and upon graduation had become a counsel for the Brotherhood of Railroad Trainmen. A successful career in labor law had led to appointment as Deputy Director of the Massachusetts Prison Department and then to election, as a Republican district attorney of Suffolk County. Switching back to the Democratic camp, he had unsuccessfully bid for that party's senatorial nomination in 1930. His public career had not been uneventful, but it was hardly the distinguished record of one who would aspire to a place on a national ticket. And although William Lemke lauded O'Brien for being a "rousing good orator," there was little in his public utterances to substantiate even this claim.[15]

In reality, Lemke hardly knew his running mate; his first contact with him had come only a few days before the birth of the party. But O'Brien, a fervent supporter of the Social Justice movement in Massachusetts, was clearly Coughlin's choice, and the North Dakotan would embrace him on that basis alone.[16]

---

[13] *New York Times*, July 12, 1936; and Louis A. Pareth to Williams, September 15, 1936, Williams Papers.

[14] *New York Times*, June 26 and 29, 1936.

[15] *Ibid.*, June 24, 1936; *Social Justice*, July 13, 1936; Roger Shaw, "Third Parties of 1936," *Review of Reviews*, XCIV, No. 2 (August, 1936), 30; and *Chicago Daily Tribune*, June 20, 1936.

[16] Lemke to Thomas C. O'Brien, June 16, 1936, Lemke Papers.

The priest obviously felt that as an easterner and an Irish Catholic, O'Brien would balance the Union Party ticket. "Lemke and Yale, Agriculture and Republican, O'Brien and Harvard, Labor and Democrat!" Coughlin shouted in one speech. "East and West, Protestant and Catholic, possessing one program of driving the money changers from the temple, permitting the wealth of America to flow freely into every home." Some observers found it curious that Charles E. Coughlin, the man who scorned the "brain trusters" and the "so-called Eastern intelligentsia," would tie his national ticket to the hated Ivy League. Perhaps the third party organizer was merely groping for anything that might add stature to the uninspiring presidential aspirant and his little-known running mate. And perhaps this is why he not infrequently said of Lemke, who spent one year at Yale Law School, that "he has made his mark for erudition on the halls of Yale." [17]

In less hectic times, an embarrassed William Lemke might have objected to being portrayed as a Yale man, hardly a winning image among northern plains agrarians. But the candidate was too busy campaigning and organizing the headquarters of the new Union Party. For whereas Coughlin was the central figure in the birth of the party, the maverick congressman was the experienced politician who could name trusted lieutenants as the party's key workers. From Chicago, he announced the appointment of Representative Usher L. Burdick of North Dakota as national chairman, John Nystul, another North Dakotan, as campaign manager for 1936, and Richard W. Wolfe, an assistant to Robert M. La Follette, Sr., in the 1924 Progressive Party, as treasurer of the Union Party. A national office was opened in the 188 West Randolph Street Tower in downtown Chicago.[18]

The organizational charts in the new headquarters, the much ballyhooed speaking tours, and the boastful statements of the leaders created the illusion of progress in party building. But Lemke and Coughlin knew that their new venture was in trouble only days after they had launched it, for they saw that Dr. Townsend was hesitating before committing his movement to the third party cause. With OARP support vital to Union success, this was a potentially disastrous development.

On his first day as candidate, Lemke had told reporters, "We are assured that all these groups—the Coughlin followers, the supporters of

[17] Coughlin, *Vital Speeches of the Day*, II, No. 20, 615.

[18] *New York Times,* July 12, 1936; and Louis A. Pareth to Williams, September 15, 1936, Williams Papers.

Dr. Townsend, and the members of the Share-Our-Wealth movement
—welcome the opportunity to unite under the banner of this party."
But the fact was that on this date Dr. Townsend still vacillated on his
future course of action.[19]

On June 15, the old physician said, "I have no wish that the Townsend movement shall become the sole factor in creating this new party
alignment." Three days later he brushed off all discussion of a Town-
send-Coughlin alliance as "the bunk," adding that "if Father Coughlin wants to support us, all well and good, but we're not endorsing anybody at this time—why should we, haven't we got the strength which is
growing every day?"[20]

Yet Gerald L. K. Smith demurred. This would-be messiah's political
ambitions seemed to grow with every passing day of the election year,
and he bragged, "We have the balance of power. . . . This is the most
phenomenal political year in the history of America and anything can
happen."[21] He urged his old friend to join the crusade:

> We are convinced that a presidential candidate who will permit the Rever-
> end Charles E. Coughlin to define his money plank, Dr. Townsend to define
> his old-age security plank, Gerald Smith to define his plank on labor, education
> and homesteads, and the Farmers' Union to define their plank in agriculture—
> this man will be the next President of the United States. . . . We believe we have
> the combined strength to win. My greatest strength is south of the Mason-
> Dixon line, Dr. Townsend's is west of the Mississippi, and Father Coughlin's
> is in the remaining areas, but we are all strong in all of these areas.[22]

Smith joined Townsend for an OARP rally before 3,500 supporters
in Syracuse, New York, and persuaded the old man to reconsider the
third party coalition. The doctor now told the press, "It's all right with
me if they [Townsend Plan members] back Lemke at the [Townsend]
Convention.[23]

Lemke and Coughlin moved quickly to bring Francis E. Townsend
closer to their new party. On June 21, Townsend and Smith visited
Washington, D.C., where they conferred first with Elmer O'Hara, a
former Michigan state democratic chairman who was a Coughlin spokesman, and then with candidate Lemke himself. But the results of this
meeting proved inconclusive. Townsend insisted on holding back, and

[19] *New York Times,* June 21, 1936.
[20] *The Townsend National Weekly,* June 15, 1936; and *New York Times,* June 18, 1936.
[21] *Ibid.,* June 19, 20, 1936.
[22] Quoted in "Third Party Threat," *Literary Digest,* CXXI, No. 26 (June 27, 1936), 5.
[23] *New York Times,* June 21, 1936.

Gerald Smith reluctantly went along, seeming to sense that even he could not push the old man too far or too fast at this critical juncture.[24]

Dr. Townsend was hesitating for several reasons. His suspicion of rival mass leaders and desire to reassert his own independence as a leader after the humiliations of the Bell Committee hearings made him wary of giving total support to any new party organized by others. In addition, he obviously was concerned about the autocratic image of the Townsend organization created by the congressional hearings, and he wanted to emphasize the democratic nature of the movement by insisting that "any decision on the third party must await the convention in July." He also hoped to elicit an unequivocal statement of support for the Townsend Plan from Lemke and Coughlin, explaining, after his meeting with the congressman, "Lemke never has endorsed our plan fully; he thinks some revisions should be made, but he should know that he has to be 100% for it, as 99% won't do." [25]

For several weeks the leader of the aged equivocated. One day he would announce that "no merger of any kind is proposed," and on the next he would report, "We may consider cooperation for the time being . . . but we won't lose our identity as a separate organization." For once Smith trailed meekly behind his old colleague, following his lead and alternating snideness in his remarks about Lemke's chances — "Huey was a practical politician, he liked not only to run but to win" — with the hope that "we might have an expression of our strength this year." [26]

But ambivalence could not be maintained for long. Before mid-July Townsend and Smith made their decision. The desire to advertise themselves and their movements in the national spotlight of the coming campaign seemed to increase with the rising fever of political activity around the country. Their desire to destroy Franklin D. Roosevelt had not abated; their unhappiness with the Republican candidate could not have been greater. As Townsend said, "I saw Landon about a year ago, and he thought we were on the lunatic fringe." And so, to the great relief of Coughlin and his candidate, the pension messiahs finally decided to cast their lot with the Union Party. "Lemke," said Townsend, "does after all represent my kind of people . . . and he is the only one of the three candidates who is not our enemy, but our friend; we must therefore do all we can to help him." [27]

---

[24] *Ibid.,* June 22, 1936; and Gerald L. K. Smith to Lemke, June 22, 1936, Lemke Papers.
[25] *Chicago Daily Tribune,* June 22, 1936; and *New York Times,* June 22 and July 13, 1936.
[26] *Ibid.,* June 24 and 29, 1936; and *The Townsend National Weekly,* June 28, 1936.
[27] Harris, *Current History,* XLV, No. 1, 88; and *New York Times,* June 22 and July 4, 1936.

Smith and Townsend would join the coalition. Yet they stopped a step short of complete commitment, deciding that if they wished to avoid the stigma of officially backing a losing horse, it would be a tactical error to have their movements formally endorse Lemke. But they proclaimed their personal endorsement of the Union candidates, pledged to campaign across the land for the new party until election day, and revealed that Lemke and Coughlin would be invited to address the great Townsend convention. Indeed, this meeting would be turned into a gigantic Union Party rally. They would only hold back on an official convention vote of endorsement for the new party.[28]

Lemke and Coughlin were elated. The failure to win formal OARP endorsement was a trifle compared to the fact that their Union speakers would have access to Townsend Plan meetings and activities undertaken by Share-Our-Wealth Clubs. With Townsend and Smith backing their ticket, Lemke and Coughlin could rest easier by mid-July of 1936. The radical alliance had now been made.[29]

[28] *Ibid.*, July 15, 1936.
[29] See Lemke to D. S. Walters, July 21, 1936, Lemke Papers. The Congressman was confident of having won Townsend support and wrote, "Townsend and Smith have publicly stated that they will vote for me and I feel that 90% of the Townsend People will do the same."

15

Prospects and Problems

Announcing the formation of a new political party—even one based upon a coalition of several strong-willed leaders—was one thing; influencing the outcome of a presidential election was quite another. Could the new Union alliance, created less than five months before the crucial test at the polls, make an impact on the 1936 campaign? Rarely has the birth of a new party given rise to such a flurry of political speculation across America. As Duncan Aikman of the *New York Times* put it, "Not for a dozen years has a movement outside the major parties aroused such curiosity among voters, or stimulated such fear and hope among the political professionals."[1]

A large majority of the nation's journalists were sure that the radical coalition would change the strategy if not the results of the presidential race. The conservative press gleefully hinted that New Dealers would suffer when the Unionites rolled into gear: an editorial in the *Los Angeles Times* predicted that "Lemke's third party may defeat Roosevelt"; and the editors of the *Literary Digest* concurred, noting strong Union backing in the Northwest. Liberal journals reflected more a feeling of foreboding, the *New Republic* editorializing that "this party is far more formidable than Al Smith's Liberty League. . . . It is a much greater danger to F.D.R. and ought to give the President serious concern. . . . It might prove that the New Deal has not been radical enough to satisfy popular discontent."[2]

---

[1] Aikman, *New York Times Magazine*, July 26, 1936, p. 6.

[2] *Los Angeles Times,* June 20, 1936; "Political X," *Literary Digest,* CXXII, No. 1 (July 4, 1936), 6; and "Al Smith to Right of Them, Coughlin to Left of Them," *New Republic,* LXXXVII, No. 1126 (July 1, 1936), 226.

In areas where the radical leaders had shown particular strength, newsmen looked for dramatic changes in voting patterns. The *Minneapolis Journal* suggested that the Democratic cause would be badly hurt all across the midlands by the new force; the *Minneapolis Tribune* headlined, "Lemke Candidacy Makes F.D.R. Farm State Vote Doubtful." On the West Coast, a survey in the *New York Times* revealed that strong Townsendite support for the Union cause could change the traditional Democratic and Republican votes in Oregon and Washington as well as California.[3]

Even in Europe, the new party received respectful attention. The *London Daily Telegraph* concluded that "it may possibly poll enough votes to let Landon in."[4]

But while the journalists were openly impressed, political professionals reacted in predictably guarded and partisan terms. Democratic National Chairman James A. Farley denied that the Unionites would be responsible for any change in his party's platform or tactics: "We are not a bit disturbed about a third party and how it will affect our nominee." Vice-President John N. Garner agreed, "I don't think the Lemke ticket will cut into our vote any more than it will the Republicans." Senator Tom Connally (D.-Texas) and New Dealer Hugh Johnson went even further, Connally caustically remarking, "There's no place for a third party in the United States," and Johnson suggesting that only Huey Long could have hurt the President with a third party. W. W. Hawes, Democratic national committeeman from South Dakota and manager of FDR's campaign in the critical northern plains states in 1932, proclaimed that "no one can set up a political organization in four and one-half months. . . . Even Teddy Roosevelt failed. . . . Lemke does not bother us at all."[5]

Newsmen refused to believe that the Democrats were really that unruffled. "They are badly, badly worried," one reporter wrote. "Philadelphia's convention-filled hotel lobbies on this eve of the Democratic convention echo to reports of last minute changes to be made in the party platforms to woo prospective Lemkeites," another stated. Many rumored revisions in the platform's agricultural plank to keep unhappy farmers from being drawn to the candidacy of their congressional champion. There was also talk of the Administration's fears of heavy

[3] *Minneapolis Journal*, June 21, 1936; *Minneapolis Tribune*, June 21, 1936; and *New York Times*, June 28, 1936.

[4] "How Europe Views Our Candidates," *Literary Digest*, CXXII, No. 3 (July 18, 1936), 8.

[5] *New York Times*, June 20, June 21, and July 14, 1936; *Washington Post*, June 20, 1936; and *Time*, XXVII, No. 26, 10–11.

losses in urban Catholic areas where Coughlin was strong. And some suggested that President Roosevelt himself was hastily conferring with party lieutenants about methods of combating the threat of the third party.[6]

In the Republican camp, too, was the confident facade shadowed by latent fears. But GOP leaders had better reason for mixed feelings. They could profess honest delight at the appearance of any new ally in the coming battle against the New Deal, as did Governor Landon in welcoming "all parties to the great debate," and vice-presidential hopeful Frank Knox in speculating on the dangers Lemke posed "to Democrats in the Midwest and on the west coast." National Chairman John D. M. Hamilton even claimed that Unionites would help the Republicans "materially" in the Mississippi Valley where they would take six Democratic votes for every GOP vote. But sources close to the party leadership noted anxiety in many traditionally Republican farm states and in sections where many faithful Republicans had turned to Townsend. The Lemke candidacy could hurt as well as help the Landon cause.[7]

For both major parties, then, the advent of the new political force would be a confusing and unsettling element in the campaign about to begin. The only certainty was that very few national political figures were defecting to the new party. Only Senator Lynn J. Frazier, the longtime friend and associate of Lemke in North Dakota, along with Utah's Senator Elbert Thomas and Ohio's Congressman Martin L. Sweeney, supporters of Father Coughlin and his program, announced their approval. Senator William Borah said that he agreed with the money and wage planks of the Union platform but refused to give any personal endorsement of the party.[8]

The major party leaders remained, then, guarded and ambivalent, but the spokesmen for the minor political factions were clearly and unhesitatingly angry.

Norman Thomas, perennial presidential candidate on the Socialist ticket, termed the Union Party "two and a half rival messiahs plus one ambitious politician plus some neopopulists plus a platform which reminds me of the early efforts of Hitler." Referring to Gerald L. K. Smith as a "great and sinister influence" with dictatorial aspirations, he dismissed the entire party as "fascistic" and angrily denied that it was radical in any "liberal" sense. He feared that the Unionites might "help

---

[6] *Minneapolis Tribune,* June 21, 1936; *New York Times,* June 21, 1936; and *Newsweek,* VII, No. 26, 7.

[7] *New York Times,* June 23, June 24, and July 1, 1936.

[8] *Social Justice,* June 20, 1936.

the Republicans win in 1936," and, lumping their efforts with those of the Liberty League and the Hearst press, he declared that they "threatened with destruction during gestation" the development of a "real farmer-labor party" in America. Communist Party chief Earl Browder, speaking for an organization now well into its Popular Front period of support for moderate reform and repudiation of revolutionary tactics, agreed with Thomas, depicting the new party as an "evil conspiracy" out to destroy the social reforms of the New Deal.[9]

The Union leaders were unmoved by the barrage of criticism from the far left. But they were vitally concerned about the reaction of those powerful, liberal political parties of the Midwest, the Wisconsin Progressives and the Minnesota Farmer-Laborites. There had been a chance that these two organizations would take the lead in the creation of a farmer-labor party in the spring of 1936, but when Minnesota Governor Floyd Olson instructed his party to boycott the Chicago convention held in May to set up the machinery for the proposed party, the possibility had vanished. Now the Unionites wondered if they might not be the beneficiaries of the midwestern enthusiasm for a "third political force."[10]

William Lemke made the first step in the direction of these progressive elements by winning over a small group on their periphery. After having met spirited opposition, he persuaded the leaders of the small Iowa Farmer-Labor Party to back his candidacy. Soon some influential members of the larger Minnesota party also were expressing interest in the Union cause. Alfred Bingham and Howard Y. Williams, disappointed that their dream of a true farmer-labor party could not be realized in 1936, briefly discussed "making some effort to win concessions from this setup . . . , making it dependent on a democratically organized convention to give us a chance to influence it greatly in the future." Williams, facing a difficult congressional election campaign in St. Paul and fearful of alienating the large Coughlin following in his district, assured the local National Union for Social Justice leader that he had personally prevented the issuance of any anti-Union statement at the August meeting of the leaders of both the Minnesota and Wisconsin parties. But Bingham and Williams were soon appalled by the demagogic outbursts of Smith and Coughlin and disenchanted with Lemke's "inadequate" economic philosophy. Concluding that the Union Party

---

[9] Norman Thomas, *After The New Deal, What?* (New York: The Macmillan Company, 1936), pp. 2, 5–6, 143, 203; *New York Times*, June 21, 1936; and McCoy, pp. 145–46.
[10] *Ibid.*, pp. 104–12, 154.

was, in reality, a "tragedy" for the farmer-labor cause, they resolved to give no aid to the new organization.[11]

The death blow to Lemke's hopes of winning support among midwestern progressives was delivered by the leaders of the two minor parties. In Wisconsin, veteran Progressive Thomas Amlie decided that the Union coalition represented "just another cheap money third party," and in late June the Wisconsin Farmer-Labor Progressive Federation overwhelmingly voted against a resolution pledging support for the Union ticket. Candidate Lemke's later effort to convince Wisconsinites that his party was "founded on the true principles of old Bob La Follette" fell on deaf ears; Governor Philip La Follette and his brother, Senator Robert "Young Bob" La Follette, Jr., ignored the North Dakotan, throwing their support to FDR and voicing opposition to the new venture. In Minnesota it was Governor Olson who turned his back upon the Unionites. Dying of cancer in a Rochester, Minnesota hospital, he wrote Senator La Follette that "even though I have the utmost respect for the Union ticket and for Father Coughlin, whose program of monetary reform is sound, I think the defeat of Landon is of the utmost importance . . . , and if we liberals, by splitting our votes, place Landon in office, we will have performed an act for which we will never be forgiven." [12]

With this rebuff by the midwestern progressives, the Union leaders' efforts to expand their base of support ended in failure. The only encouraging note had been the endorsement of their ticket by President Edward Everson and Secretary Edward Kennedy of the Farmers Union — these old friends of William Lemke promising to do "all in their power" to prevail on their membership to vote Union in 1936. But even among the militant agrarian groups, Lemke had failed to win complete support; when his friend Milo Reno, leader of the National Farm Holiday Association, died in the spring of 1935, Lemke lost his influence in that organization. It was true that "General" Jacob S. Coxey — a radical figure whose moment of glory was forty years in the

[11] George F. Buresh to Williams, June 22, 1936, Helen Olson to Minnie Duvall, July 6, 1936, Williams to Charles E. Coughlin, July 6, 1936, Alfred M. Bingham to Williams, June 22, 1936, Williams to Bingham, June 24, 1936, Williams to Winifred Proctor, June 26, 1936, and Williams to John D. Sullivan, August 20, 1936, Williams Papers.

[12] *New York Times,* June 22 and 29, 1936; Thomas R. Amlie to Wallace M. Short, July 9, 1936, Williams Papers; *Minneapolis Journal,* August 19, 1936; and George H. Mayer, *The Political Career of Floyd B. Olson* (Minneapolis: The University of Minnesota Press, 1951), p. 297.

past—withdrew his independent candidacy and asked his followers (if any) to vote for Lemke; but this announcement elicited only wry smiles in the Union headquarters. The radical leaders, it was clear at last, would have to stand alone in their bid for power. And although journalists predicted that even alone they might be strong enough to make a vital difference, and politicians of all stripes feared this strength, the Unionites themselves had to ask some critical questions: Could the alliance of the radicals produce the votes and could it hold together throughout a long and arduous election race? What were its chances of success in light of the history of third parties in America? What were the problems a new political party had to face in this country? [13]

Coughlin and Smith bragged about the ingenious nature of their party's political appeal: with the radio priest powerful in the East, the pension movement strongest on the West Coast, the Lemke following centered in the Midwest and the Share-Our-Wealth support in the South, the entire country was bracketed. Voter response, they insisted, would have to reflect the power of this "natural" alliance.

But how "natural" was the alliance? There were, of course, several factors tying the radical movements together. Most important, perhaps, was the Unionites' mutual hatred of Franklin D. Roosevelt. In every case, it had been the President who had thwarted the personal political ambitions of the messianic leaders and had prevented their panaceas from becoming law. Now, together, they planned revenge. The nature of their social and economic programs was another unifying force. Each of the allies looked to "cheap money" as the way out of the great Depression, and they all owed something to the Populist tradition in America—agreeing that manipulation of the currency and/or the banking system could work miracles by allowing the highly complicated operations of the economic machinery to be by-passed.

Yet in another sense, their very panaceas comprised the first of the divisive factors that would haunt the Union coalition. For the leaders were not uniformly happy with each other's programs. Father Coughlin considered the Townsend Plan rather simplistic: it did not account for the changes in "modern capitalism" which he felt must be made before any old age pension scheme could work. The priest was also critical of the Share-Our-Wealth plan, suspecting that it lacked an economic theory, without which it could never live up to its name. Dr. Townsend, in turn, was unimpressed by the sixteen points of the National Union for Social Justice, suggesting that they were overcomplicated and wholly

[13] *New York Times*, June 21 and 28, 1936; and Ward, *The Nation*, CXLIII, No. 2, 35.

unnecessary because, in fact, he claimed to have cured all the nation's ills with just one point. The old physician was also uninterested in the Lemke farm refinance plans; indeed, the problems of agriculture had not concerned him for many years. Gerald L. K. Smith's wealth-sharing scheme was so open-ended that he could avoid serious conflicts with his allies, but the minister always had been less interested in reform than in power, and he found Coughlin's central banking fetish rather tiresome and Lemke's agricultural policies uninteresting. Of all the leaders, William Lemke was by far the least critical of his colleagues' dreams. But even the pliant Lemke was in constant trouble over his position on the Townsend Plan, finally being forced to state, "I am 100% for the Townsend old-age revolving pension. . . . As President . . . my first message to Congress will recommend such a revolving pension fund." Yet even this did not satisfy Francis E. Townsend, for the North Dakotan had added, "The amount of the pension will depend upon the amount Congress provides for that specific purpose." Thus did the members of the Union coalition clash on a number of critical ideological issues; thus were the seeds of discord sown at the very beginning of the new party's life.[14]

Another divisive element was that very broad base of support which Coughlin and Smith celebrated as the genius of the Union political appeal. All sections of the nation were represented in the several movements which had joined in the new coalition, but there were perils as well as promise in this arrangement. Father Coughlin's greatest following was among the Catholic populations of the great urban areas of the Northeast and Midwest. If the voluble priest pitched his campaign speeches to these old friends, he might please the populistic Lemkeites but alienate the Townsendites. Dr. Townsend's aged, middle-class disciples, despite their devotion to the pension plan, were conservative folk: Republican in politics, British in origin, and puritanical in their social attitudes. They might easily be frightened by Coughlin's violent demands for changes in cherished American institutions. Some Coughlinites, conversely, could take offense at the innuendos that marked Gerald Smith's campaigning style, for the poor-white rural voters of the South often enjoyed derogatory references about immigrants and Easterners. Similarly, candidate Lemke's appeal, if directed only to his farmer followers of the northern plains, would disturb both the Townsendites and the Coughlin urbanites, for these groups did not be-

[14] Lemke to B. W. Lemke, May 25, 1936, and Lemke press statement, issued July 1, 1936, copy in Lemke Papers.

lieve that agriculture was at the center of American life. Townsend's speeches, on the other hand, would have little meaning for any following but his own. And so the possibilities of tension among the various movements were almost innumerable.

But not only among the members of these movements: the personal ambitions of each of the leaders represented a final divisive factor within the party. Charles E. Coughlin, for example, was riding a wave of great personal popularity in 1936. Widely respected as the founder of one powerful mass movement, he considered himself the creator of the Union Party. He had refused to stand in any man's shadow in the past—even that of Franklin Roosevelt. Was it likely that he would brook opposition for the leadership of "his" new party? But party candidate William Lemke was not one to submit meekly. A veteran of many political battles on the state and national levels, he had constantly surprised colleagues in North Dakota and Washington with his tenacity and ability. As titular head of the new organization, it was unlikely that he would now eschew a policy-making and leadership role. As for Gerald L. K. Smith, the notion of being a team player in a joint endeavor had no meaning for him. Only once before had Smith served under another leader, but that leader was Huey Long—Huey had given the minister his start and, in any case, Huey was unique. Now Gerald Smith considered himself the leader supreme. For this man of consummate political ambition, activity in the Union Party had to bring power to himself, or at the very least, a free hand to go his own way in promoting the interests of Gerald Smith.

Dr. Francis E. Townsend also loomed as a figure of growing independence as the campaign got under way. Once an elderly and retiring country doctor, the adulation of his disciples had convinced him that he could do no wrong. His angry reaction to congressional harassment and his refusal to join the new alliance without being courted first, suggested that he, too, would reject a secondary role.

When all of the uniting and divisive factors had been examined, it was clear that the Union coalition was a rather unstable one at best. Only by grasping the larger hope was it conceivable that this fragile alliance would survive a difficult campaign. Yet even if it did, what were its prospects when viewed against the record of other third parties in America?

Father Coughlin liked to boast that "a third party elected Jackson to abolish the hated private Bank of the United States . . . , a third party elected Lincoln to abolish slavery . . . , and we can repeat these deeds this year." But the priest's reading of United States history, as usual, was spotty. The fact was that third parties had not fared well in the past. As John D. Hicks put it, "Like the decalogue or the practice of monogamy, or the right of the Supreme Court to declare a law of Congress unconstitutional, American citizens have thought of the two-party system as peculiarly sacred." [15]

The pressures on a new political movement in America are enormous. A new party cannot take time to build slowly and "educate" the voters; it must simultaneously educate, recruit members, seek office, and exercise power wherever and whenever possible. These pressures had simply overwhelmed those third party organizers who had preceded the Unionites down that difficult trail.[16]

In the half century prior to 1936, only three minor parties had polled as much as 8 per cent of the vote in a presidential election, hardly an encouraging record and yet one which was actually bleaker than the figures suggest because of the extenuating circumstances around each of these performances.

In 1892, with a new age of reform on the horizon and with neither major party responsive to the demands of many groups suffering as a result of the rapid industrialization marking the post-Civil War era, the People's (Populist) Party successfully appealed to unhappy agrarians of the West and South who felt that their problems had been unattended by the weak and business-oriented Administrations in Washington. Yet the candidate of this single-interest party still received only 8.5 per cent of the popular vote. In 1912, the Progressive (Bull Moose) Party did considerably better, its standard-bearer running well ahead of the Republican incumbent and winning over 27 per cent of votes cast. But of course the Bull Moose candidate had been Theodore Roosevelt, one of history's great and colorful campaigner's and not only the best known public figure of his day but a man who already had been a remarkably successful President for seven years. Teddy Roosevelt brought with him into his new party large elements of the Republican Party—men and women responsive only to his dynamic leadership. The Progressive Party of 1924, likewise, had a strong and famous leader. Robert La Follette, Sr., boasted a large liberal following when he ran for the highest office in a year when both major parties offered conservative candidates and

[15] *Social Justice*, July 6, 1936; and John D. Hicks, "The Third Party Tradition in American Politics," *Mississippi Valley Historical Review*, XX, No. 1 (June, 1933), 3.

[16] William B. Hesseltine, *The Rise and Fall of Third Parties* (Washington, D.C.: Public Affairs Press, 1948), p. 9.

platforms. He captured over 16 per cent of the vote, but this was more of a monument to his own reforming record and the lack of alternatives offered discontented liberals than it was to the power of his new party.[17]

In the face of this sorry history of third party failure, could the Union leaders really feel that they had a chance in the coming election?

Lemke told reporters that he was sure of victory: "I see the Union Party on top and I'm not concerned with who will be next." He predicted a sweep of all New England states, Ohio, Michigan, Pennsylvania, Illinois, most of the Middle West and the Far West. He modestly admitted that "Indiana will be nip and tuck." Coughlin was also sanguine in public statements. "Lemke is three to one to win the Presidency," he announced.[18]

In their private conversations, the party leaders showed that they had no illusions about winning the White House in 1936. But they insisted that there was a good chance of making a respectable showing, and they noted that the senior La Follette had polled almost five million votes in 1924 after starting his party as late in the election year as they had in creating the Union Party.[19]

At best, the Union leaders dreamed of capturing enough electoral votes in a close presidential race to throw the election into the House of Representatives. This would give them a powerful bargaining position, enhance their prestige, and make possible the continued growth of their new party with the prospect of an even better showing in 1940.[20]

Short of deadlocking the Electoral College, they hoped to poll a sizeable popular vote for the Presidency while electing a number of Congressmen. Aware that one traditional function of the third party had been to press Democrats or Republicans into adopting certain reforms, they sought to frighten lethargic or timid politicians into voting their favorite panaceas into law.[21]

But if all else failed they hoped, at the very least, that Lemke would take enough votes away from Franklin D. Roosevelt to defeat this hated enemy. Although they knew that some political analysts were saying that they were more likely to hurt Landon than FDR, that in this election the only votes a protest party could draw were anti-Roosevelt votes, which inevitably would go to the Republicans if no third force

---

[17] Louis H. Bean, *How to Predict Elections* (New York: Alfred A. Knopf, 1948), p. 71.

[18] *New York Times*, June 26 and July 11, 1936; and *New York Herald Tribune*, June 26, 1936.

[19] *Social Justice*, June 20, 1936; Ward, *The Nation*, CXLIII, No. 2, 36; and *New York Times*, June 28, 1936.

[20] Blackorby, pp. 503, 509–12; and Mitchell, *New Republic*, LXXXVIII, No. 1132, 10.

[21] Hesseltine, pp. 29–30.

had been created, they remained convinced that traditionally Democratic Coughlinites living in urban-industrial areas and followers of
the other leaders who had voted Democratic in 1932 would defect in
large enough numbers to destroy the President's bid for reelection.[22]

If they had any reason for high hopes as the campaign got under way,
however, the Unionites were aware of the difficult organizational problems confronting the builders of any new party in the United States.

Would they be able to finance their new venture? In the beginning,
William Lemke had belittled the question of fund raising: "I am not
concerned about finances; money is considered important only when
deals are to be made and the sovereignty of the people bargained away
before an election." But within weeks, this brave rhetoric was forgotten in the rush of unpaid bills that plagued the Union men. Now
Lemke recalled that William E. Borah, when approached to head a third
party movement in 1924, had said that a minimum of $3 million was
needed to start a new party on a sound basis. Resources of this size
would never be at his disposal, and the candidate sadly remarked in
July, "All I can say is that the National Union for Social Justice has
its treasury and the Townsend Plan has its treasury. . . . The Union
Party has something less than $20,000 so far, but it's somewhat early."
This open appeal to the two rich movements backing his party suggested
more desperation than confidence; the financial problem was to prove
troublesome throughout the long campaign.[23]

The difficulties involved in building state and local organizations
capable of nominating candidates for Congress and other offices was
also to haunt the party. At first the Union leaders equivocated on these
pivotal questions. Lemke said, "As far as Congressional elections are
concerned, the Union Party will be nonpartisan . . . , supporting those
members of Congress who voted for progressive legislation regardless
of party affiliation." Coughlin announced that "only in those congressional districts where neither Democrat nor Republican is acceptable to the National Union because of their refusal to accept its principles, will there be a candidate on the Union Party ticket." But soon
the priest was demanding that congressional candidates — whatever their
party membership — actively campaign for William Lemke if they desired NUSJ support. Candidate Lemke also began to talk in terms of
"electing a majority in the next Congress," telling newsmen in early
July that "we plan now to concentrate on the election of Congressmen

---

[22] *Minneapolis Tribune,* June 21, 1936; and *New York Times,* July 12, 1936.
[23] Blackorby, p. 499; and Davenport, *Collier's,* XCVIII, No. 16, 26.

favorable to our cause." Even vice-presidential candidate O'Brien joined the new chorus, stating that he would tour the country to help form state and local party committees which would nominate slates of candidates for all offices. The initial indecisiveness, however, was to prove more important than the grandiose plans which followed. Grass roots organization was a continuing dilemma.[24]

The same could be said of the more immediate problem of winning a place on the ballot. Most state laws made it very hard for any new party to receive official recognition; indeed, only in Iowa, Michigan, and Montana were there no regulations concerning the requisite number of voters who must endorse a new party. In a few states, the total signatures required on a ballot petition was low: North Dakota asking only three hundred, Rhode Island and Delaware five hundred. Other states were less lenient. Illinois demanded the names of 25,000 qualified voters, including two hundred from each of fifty counties. New York asked for twelve thousand signatures, including fifty from every county, and the minimum acceptable in Ohio amounted to 15 per cent of the total vote for governor in the previous election. Some smaller states were proportionately difficult, with North Carolina requiring ten thousand endorsements and Oklahoma five thousand.[25]

Obtaining the needed signatures to win that cherished place on the ballot was a Herculean task, leading only to total frustration in some states. The due date for completed petitions in Kansas, for example, was noon, June 20—only eighteen hours after the party had been presented to the public! In Oklahoma, the filing deadline was May 2, and in West Virginia it was May 12, weeks before the radical leaders had even decided to make their political alliance.[26]

In other states, the new party found that it could get on the ballot but could not use the name Union. In Michigan, Union candidates had to run under the bland heading of "The Third Party," for their local organizers failed to meet the deadline for registering a party title. In Pennsylvania, state Democratic Chairman David L. Lawrence preempted the name Union by telegraphing his county chairman on June 21 to file that name throughout the state. Thus in the Quaker State, and in Ohio as well, Unionites had to settle for the "Royal Oak Party"

[24] *New York Times,* June 24, 1936; Statement by William Lemke, July 1, 1936, copy in Lemke Papers; and *Social Justice,* July 6, 1936.

[25] Morton S. Goldstein, "The New Party and the Ballot," *The New Republic,* LXXXVII, No. 1122 (June 3, 1936), 99–100; and *New York Times,* June 21, and July 14, 1936.

[26] *Ibid.,* June 21, June 23, and July 11, 1936.

(after the site of Father Coughlin's church) under which to list their candidates.[27]

The ballot problem, like the other thorny organizational problems, would plague the party leaders time and again in the months ahead. But in the first flush of optimism attending the birth of their party, Union men were thinking less of problems than of the dream of success. The great Cleveland conventions of the Townsend and Coughlin movements served not only to cement the radical alliance but to fuel the fires of hope. With the close of the NUSJ convention, the partners in the strange new political marriage were armed with enthusiasm as they set out on the campaign trail.

[27] *Ibid.,* June 28, September 1, and September 14, 1936.

PART VI

THE CAMPAIGN

There is no question that it is all a dangerous situation, but when it comes to showdown, these fellows cannot all lie in the same bed and will fight among themselves with almost absolute certainty. — Franklin D. Roosevelt, 1936

16

The Major Parties Forge Ahead

Despite the oratorical fireworks at the Townsend and Coughlin conventions, despite grandiose predictions by the four radical leaders and frantic enthusiasm by their thousands of followers, Unionites still glumly noted that the major parties continued to monopolize the news as the campaign got under way.

The Democrats, of course, were clearly in the lead from the very start and, the notoriously inaccurate *Literary Digest* poll notwithstanding, their strength seemed to grow with every passing day. The party which had swept to power in 1932 had in the New Deal a strong and successful program with which the electorate was familiar. More important, it had Franklin D. Roosevelt, an incumbent President who was the incomparable master politician and showman of his time. For in this election year, FDR was giving a performance that would be remembered as long as there were histories of democratic politics.

It began with his stirring acceptance speech at the Philadelphia convention in which he flailed the "royalists of the economic order" and aroused a huge audience with the memorable words: "There is a mysterious cycle in human events. To some generations much is given. Of other generations much is expected. This generation of Americans has a rendezvous with destiny." And it ended at that gigantic rally in New York's Madison Square Garden on the last day of October, when he told a roaring crowd that "in my second Administration . . . I should like to have it said that the forces of selfishness and lust for power will have met their master." Franklin D. Roosevelt throughout spoke and acted with consummate political skill. His themes were simple

217

enough: the contrast between conditions in the spring of 1933 and in the fall of 1936; the role played by the New Deal in overcoming the Depression; and the interdependence of the American people—of business and labor, of agrarians and urbanites, of state and national governments. As he toured the nation, it was obvious that he was winning converts—and that he was having a grand time in the process.[1]

In contrast to the President, Republican candidate Landon seemed hesitant and unpersuasive. Uncertain of the direction in which lay the road to victory, he tried both appeals to traditional Republican conservatism and "me too" promises to liberals who had been charmed by the New Deal. Veering recklessly from left to right as he traveled across the land, he would lecture one audience on the necessity for fiscal responsibility and budget-balancing and entice another with Roosevelt-like relief programs. As his arguments became increasingly inconsistent, even such prominent Republicans as Charles Taft and Frank Kellogg became disgusted. And Landon's colorless personality and uninspired platform style left crowds unenthused and uninterested. The GOP bandwagon was soon creaking to a standstill.[2]

Noting the ineptness of his Republican opponent, FDR was increasingly confident that he could handle the major party challenge with relative ease. Moreover, reasoned Roosevelt, if Landon could not make the race close, the potentially crucial role of the third party would lose its meaning. The President had gradually accepted the view that Unionites could at best only share the protest vote with the GOP. "Curiously enough," he wrote to Vice-President Garner, "I don't think the Lemke ticket will cut into our vote any more than it will into the Republican vote." The man who supported Lemke, he pointed out, probably would cast his ballot for Landon if no third party were in the field. As he told Raymond Moley, "There's only one issue in this campaign—it's myself—and people must be either for me or against me." [3]

Roosevelt and his Democratic cohorts quickly realized that the heart of the Union appeal lay in the demand for increased government action to arrest the suffering caused by the Depression. But while the New Dealers admitted that they could never match the extravagant promises of the radicals, they were certain that the successful record of interventionist activities of the first Roosevelt Administration would retain most potential dissidents in the Democratic camp—men and women who

[1] Burns, pp. 275, 280, 283; and Schlesinger, Jr., p. 632.
[2] *Ibid.*, pp. 610–15.
[3] Roosevelt to John Nance Garner, July 19, 1936, Roosevelt Papers, President's Personal File 1416 (John N. Garner); and Burns, p. 271.

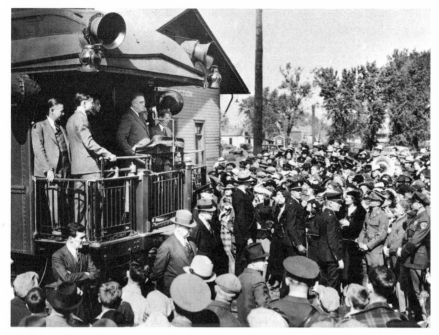

Franklin D. Roosevelt makes a whistle-stop speech at Pacific Junction, Iowa, October 11, 1936, while en route to Omaha, where he made the first major address of his 5,000-mile tour of the West. *Wide World*

would clearly prefer Lemke to a conservative like Landon. Indeed, they had the ultimate weapon with which to keep these malcontents in line: the ancient call that major party politicians had always used against the newcomers, "Don't throw your vote away," and over and over again the New Dealers issued that call. The Unionites, they explained to voters, could not possibly win the election. Thus a vote for William Lemke would be at best merely wasteful but at worst truly damaging to the hopes of those who desired more government action, for it might help Alfred Landon defeat Franklin Roosevelt. An editorialist for the *Cleveland Plain Dealer,* a newspaper which had endorsed the President, asked, "Whom, then, do the Townsendites, the Coughlinites and the remnants of the Huey Long forces prefer for President during the next quadrennial: Mr. Roosevelt, who has gone farther along the path of social justice than anyone else who ever held the office, or Governor Landon?" Using this approach, Democrats were sure that they could hold most of the radical vote.[4]

As the campaign proceeded, FDR grew even more certain. The vote of confidence he received from the midwestern progressives, together

---

[4] *Cleveland Plain Dealer,* July 17, 1936.

with the reluctance of farm leaders to back the new party was convincing evidence that he would win his share of the votes in those northern plains agrarian areas of Lemke strength. The reviving economy
plus the strenuous efforts on his behalf by labor's Nonpartisan League
reassured him that most of the urban industrial workers who had joined
Coughlin's National Union also would return to the Democratic fold
in November. Even many of the Townsendites, attracted by the new
Social Security Act, might be expected to back him on election day.
Lemke might be denied the support of all, then, but a few incorrigible
fanatics.[5]

The New Deal high command decided against a frontal assault on
the Union leaders, fearing that such an attack might only serve to
alienate voters who were personally devoted but not politically tied to
one or another of the leaders. Secretary of the Interior Ickes' few
speeches denouncing Father Coughlin were only exceptions to the rule;
the Democrats chose to ignore the Union Party in most official statements and to dismiss it with the "wasted vote" argument whenever the
subject was broached by reporters. But their growing confidence never
led these shrewd politicians to turn their backs upon the third party
threat. Democratic National Chairman James A. Farley was an adroit
and sensitive manager, who overlooked few possibilities in this critical
year.[6]

Farley kept in close touch with Union activities through his massive
correspondence with party workers, friends, and post office employees
around the country. Indeed, the Postmaster General's built-in network
of local political pulse-takers made him the best informed party organizer in the land.

For the most part, Jim Farley's reporters sent encouraging news. In
the crucial state of New York, local Democrats noted that Union supporters were "not as numerous as had been thought" in upstate cities,
and that "the Lemke vote will be confined to irreconcilable and, in a way,
irresponsible Coughlinites," for "more and more of those who were for
Lemke . . . are realizing it is a vote thrown away and they are coming to
Roosevelt." [7]

[5] McCoy, p. 52; and *New York Times*, October 18, 1936.

[6] *Ibid.*, October 10, 1936; and "Conning the News," *New Masses*, XXI, No. 4 (October
20, 1936), 9.

[7] William O. Dapping (Auburn, N.Y.) to James A. Farley, September 8, 1936, Cornelius
J. Nugent (Syracuse, N.Y.) to Farley, September 9, 1936, and George H. Kennedy (Buffalo, N.Y.) to Farley, October 7, 1936, in Democratic National Campaign Committee,
1936: Correspondence of James A. Farley, Chairman (Franklin D. Roosevelt Library,
Hyde Park, N.Y.). Cited hereafter as National Committee Correspondence.

In areas where the Unionites had been feared most, reports were particularly heartening. From Lemke's home state of North Dakota came word that "the Lemke campaign has resulted in nothing like the popular reaction it was hoped to have"; and that Father Coughlin was making a "distinctly unfavorable impression" among the Scandinavian people, many of whom "are intolerant and bitterly resent these clerical appearances." Even as early as August agents disclosed that "the Lemke boom has slowed down a lot, and it's being said that Lemke has no hope of winning." [8]

From California, the hotbed of Townsendism, came similar reports. State Chairman Culbert L. Olson told Washington that "many of our dependable Democrats have recently become members and officers of Townsend Clubs to hold them in line for the party." George Creel sent assurances from San Francisco that "Townsend will not hurt us out here," and other party workers wrote of the "disillusionment of many Townsendites who have discovered that Dr. Townsend has clay feet" and of the "confusion" in the minds of other pension supporters who could not understand their hero's alliance with Lemke, Coughlin, and Smith. Senator William Gibbs McAdoo (D.-Cal.), drawing on his own sources of information, suggested that Lemke's appeal was waning in the West, and that "California . . . appears to me to be the strongest Roosevelt state in the union." [9]

In heavily Catholic Rhode Island, fears of Coughlin strength were allayed by reports that FDR should carry the state by 150,000 votes, with Lemke drawing less than one-quarter of that plurality. From the northern plains state of South Dakota, the word came that Lemkeites represented "the radical element here which almost always votes against the Administration regardless of what party is in power. . . . They would probably be for Landon if a third ticket were not present." [10]

Many state reports flooding into Farley's office did not even mention the Union Party; others dismissed it as a totally insignificant factor. Only in a handful of states did local Democrats confess that the new

[8] Thomas H. Moodie (Bismarck, N. Dak.) to Farley, July 21, 1936, Nellie Dougherty (Minot, N. Dak.) to Farley, August 7, 1936, and John C. Eaton (Fargo, N. Dak.) to Farley, August 12, 1936, *ibid.*

[9] Culbert L. Olson to Farley, July 28, 1936, George Creel to Farley, July 23, 1936, and Henry R. Briggs to Farley, July 21, 1936, *ibid.;* and William Gibbs McAdoo to Mrs. Lewis Lawlor, October 6, 1936, in William Gibbs McAdoo Papers (Library of Congress, Washington, D.C.). Cited hereafter as McAdoo Papers.

[10] Francis B. Condon to William J. Bray (Central Falls, R.I.), September 10, 1936, and F. W. Bicknell (Webster, S. Dak.) to Farley, August 17, 1936, in National Committee Correspondence.

force was causing them anxious moments. But these were strategic states.[11]

In Massachusetts, Representative John W. McCormack voiced alarm about the results of a primary contest, in which "forty thousand Coughlin followers placed stickers on the ballots for his candidate for Senator." Thomas C. O'Brien, Union vice-presidential nominee, was also the senatorial aspirant in question, and while he actually ran a poor third to Governor James M. Curley, the fact that a Unionite could capture 10 per cent of the vote in a Democratic primary without having his name on the ballot disquieted state party leaders. McCormack told FDR that the Coughlinites were "sullen, discontented and bitter, . . . and determined, using any argument that they think will appeal to the hearer." Governor Curley remarked sourly to Farley that Lemke would show "noticeable strength" in the industrial areas. State Senator David I. Walsh went even further, predicting that the Union candidate would "carry up to 200,000 votes in November." James Roosevelt concluded that "Coughlin is probably stronger in Massachusetts than in any other state."[12]

National Chairman Farley acknowledged Massachusetts as a Coughlin stronghold, but he disagreed with the President's son. Said Farley: "It is quite apparent to me that the Coughlin influence is greater in Ohio than in any other state." Almost daily, Democratic headquarters received reports like the following: "The greatest menace that threatens the party [in Cleveland] is Coughlin." Party workers bitterly complained about the priest's tremendous influence in German and Irish Catholic areas. A precinct captain explained, "I am not anti-Catholic, . . . but go into any Catholic settlement in Northwestern Ohio and you will find a lot of strong Lemke sentiment and following." Things became so bad in one county that Democratic organizers mailed letters addressed "To Lemke Voters," warning that "Lemke has no chance to win. . . . A vote for Lemke is a vote for Landon!"[13]

Considerable Union Party sentiment was also reported in Michigan, where Frank Murphy's private political poll revealed that Lemke, with

[11] E. T. Taylor (Greenwood Springs, Colo.) to Farley, August 12, 1936, *ibid.*

[12] John W. McCormack to Roosevelt, September 26, 1936, Roosevelt Papers, PPF 4057; James M. Curley to Farley, September 10, 1936, David I. Walsh to Farley, August 24, 1936, and James Roosevelt to Farley, September 17, 1936, National Committee Correspondence; and Tull, p. 204.

[13] Farley to William R. Thom, August 24, 1936, John L. Mikelich to Farley, September 10, 1936, H. R. Loomis to Farley, September 8, 1936, and J. F. Trump to Farley, October 5, 1936, in National Committee Correspondence.

almost 10 per cent of the presidential vote, held the balance of power in the state. Representative John Lesinski warned Farley that "Coughlin has quite an urban following here," and a prominent government attorney in Detroit predicted that Unionites would defeat Roosevelt. Other Michigan observers disagreed, but the national chairman had sufficient evidence to put the radio priest's home state on the list of those in which third party activity had to be monitored and neutralized.[14]

On balance, Democrats felt that the Unionites were being kept well in check, but they were causing difficulties in a few strategic areas. And while Lemke, Townsend, and Smith all were making some impact, it seemed clear to headquarters that Father Coughlin's appeal to Catholic voters represented the greatest danger. Thus the efforts of lay and clerical supporters of the President to wean fellow Catholics away from the Union camp constituted the major, albeit unofficial, New Deal counterattack on the third party.

FDR became aware of the massive Catholic opposition to Coughlin after receiving many letters from distressed Catholics who felt they must personally apologize for the priest's Townsend convention tirade, when the President had been called a "liar" and "double-crosser." Roosevelt noted with approval that prominent Catholic laymen in his party were moving to meet the Coughlin threat. Former Congressman Joseph A. Corry of Boston helped establish an anti-Coughlin group, dedicated to opposing those who "aroused class discontent and fanned flames of religious bigotry." Distinguished attorney Charlton Ogburn told FDR that he was using contacts in Rome to inform the Vatican of "the harm which Coughlin is doing to the Church in America by attacking you." [15]

Even more effective were the actions of the President's supporters among the clergy. As the campaign gained momentum, many pro-New Deal Catholics became convinced that the radio priest had to be confronted by other clergymen. Even Catholics in Roosevelt's own personal circle, including secretary Margaret Le Hand and Bronx County leader Ed Flynn, had reputedly threatened to leave the Church if Coughlin's attacks were not countered in this way. Two prominent members of

[14] Frank Murphy to M. H. McIntyre, September 11, 1936, Roosevelt Papers, OF 300 (Democratic National Committee); and John Lesinski to Farley, August 21, 1936, John C. Lehr (Detroit, Mich.) to Farley, September 17, 1936, and John J. McGinty (Bay City, Mich.) to Farley, September 14, 1936, in National Committee Correspondence.

[15] Joe O'Connor to Roosevelt, July 17, 1936, Roosevelt Papers, OF 306; *New York Times*, August 14, 1936; and Charlton Ogburn to Roosevelt, September 10, 1936, Roosevelt Papers, President's Personal File 3794 (Charlton Ogburn).

the faculty of The Catholic University of America, the Reverend Maurice S. Sheehy and Monsignor John A. Ryan, were soon to lead this counterattack.[16]

Father Sheehy told Roosevelt in mid-July that "your friends are not ignoring the calumnies of Father Coughlin. . . . At a meeting in New York, four bishops, three monsignori, another priest and I, discussed for four hours the attacks on you by Father Coughlin. . . . We decided how this matter might be handled most effectively and we have taken action." Sheehy kept the White House informed of anti-Coughlin activity by Catholic clergymen throughout America, especially noting the strong statements of Cardinal Mundelein and Bishop Bernard J. Sheil of Chicago. By late September he could point to "the number of Bishops who are writing to the President to affirm their faith in him in view of the charges that have been made of his Communistic sympathy." [17] And in October he wrote,

I made a trip through the west recently at the suggestion of Senator O'Mahoney. Among the people I visited, which included four Bishops and several score of priests, President Roosevelt is stronger than ever before. There is a feeling now prevalent among the priests that the priesthood, through Father Coughlin, has betrayed the President, and some extraordinary things are being attempted to offset this betrayal.[18]

Monsignor Ryan was ready to perform one of these "extraordinary" acts. Judging that Coughlin was doing a disservice to his church and his country, and fearing that Roosevelt's great work might be ended through the efforts of a Catholic priest—with all American Catholics suffering as a result—Ryan struck out at Father Coughlin in a national radio address in early October.[19]

Ryan told his listeners that he was answering the radio priest because "I love truth and hate lies," and that Coughlin's attacks on the President had been "false and despicable assertions . . . ugly, cowardly and flagrant calumnies." He charged that Coughlin's "explanation of our economic maladies is at least 50% wrong and his monetary remedies

[16] Ickes, p. 687.

[17] Maurice S. Sheehy to Roosevelt, July 18, 1936, Steven Early to Roosevelt, September 30, 1936, Roosevelt Papers, OF 306; Sheehy to Early, September 29, 1936, *ibid.*, PPF 3960. For the efforts of other Catholic clergy on Roosevelt's behalf, see Bishop James H. Ryan (Omaha) to Roosevelt, September 25, 1936, and Bishop Bernard J. Mahoney (Sioux Falls, S. Dak.) to Sheehy, September 26, 1936, *ibid.*, OF 306 and PPF 3960.

[18] Sheehy to Margaret Le Hand, October 5, 1936, *ibid.*

[19] John A. Ryan and James J. Carberry, "The Ryan-Coughlin Controversy," *Commonweal*, XXV, No. 2 (November 6, 1936), 44–45.

at least 90% wrong," and that the priest's whole program "opposes the spirit of the encyclicals to which he so often makes references." The peroration was a call for votes for Roosevelt: "In this critical hour, I urge you to use all effort at your command among your relatives, friends, and acquaintances in support of Franklin D. Roosevelt." [20]

A few Catholics objected to the Ryan speech, and Father Coughlin denounced the efforts of "the Right Reverend New Dealer." But influential Catholic publications, including *Commonweal*, backed the monsignor. Ryan, acknowledging that after the speech he had received over one thousand letters from devoted Coughlinites, most of them couched in "abusive and insulting language conveying hate . . . prejudice . . . and a strong strain of anti-clericalism," later termed his address "one of the most beneficial and effective acts that I have ever performed in the interests of my religion and my country." [21]

The manner in which President Roosevelt's Catholic friends rallied to his defense gave Democratic headquarters added assurance that the most dangerous element in the Union Party could be effectively contained. Confidently, the major party forged ahead with its own campaign.

[20] *New York Times,* October 9, 1936; and "Father Coughlin Denounced By Father Ryan," *The Nation,* CXLIII, No. 16 (October 17, 1936), 434.

[21] Coughlin, *An Answer to . . . ,* p. 44; and "Ryan-Coughlin Controversy," *Commonweal,* XXIV, No. 26 (October 23, 1936), 597–98.

17

Unionites on the Hustings

While Franklin D. Roosevelt was charming voters and Jim Farley subtly counteracting efforts of New Deal opponents, the leaders of the Union Party were out toiling on the hustings, desperately trying to deny victory to the hated "Roosevelt-Farley clique." But something had gone wrong with the radical party's campaign almost from the very start. The reports of diminishing Union sentiment filtering into the Democratic chairman's office could not be explained solely in terms of the President's personal popularity or the shrewd moves of his political lieutenants. The four self-styled messiahs were proving far less effective in an election race than as organizers of social movements. They were working hard enough, but their movements were not coordinated, their arguments were not complementary, and their perspective and tempers began to crack under the pressure of a strenuous campaign.

Each of the leaders operated, for the most part, on his own. Charles E. Coughlin, perhaps the most effective and flamboyant, made a few joint personal appearances with candidate Lemke, but these were exceptions. As the radio priest said, "I must operate independently of the others. . . . They have different organizations and different principles."[1]

After Coughlin suspended radio broadcasting for the summer— which was his usual practice—he set off on a series of speaking tours for the party. Local units of his National Union for Social Justice arranged rallies in large eastern and midwestern cities, and in certain farming centers scattered across the plains states. These were areas in which the priest's broadcasts had attracted millions of listeners, and he sought to turn this audience into a political force. His newspaper, *Social Justice*,

---

[1] *Detroit News*, August 13, 1936.

beat publicity drums for meetings several weeks in advance, and local National Union members worked hard to bring out big crowds.[2]

Coughlin's speeches grew more vicious and defamatory with the passing weeks. At first he was content to damn Democrats and Republicans with equal vigor: "Neither is worth a nickel or a plugged one at that . . . , they represent the left and right wings of the common bird of prey, the banker." If the New Deal's evil ways seemed more obvious, it was only because Democrats were in power, for Roosevelt was only trying to "out Hoover Hoover by forcing one out of every four Americans to work for J. P. Morgan or Bernard Baruch." The radio priest warned FDR that his "government by high commissions of prostituted patronage" would not work. "You can't be a dictator any more; anyone who tries to play the part of God will stumble." But his own self-deification apparently did not embarrass him, for in denying that his opposition to the major parties made him an extremist, Coughlin remarked, "Christ would advocate what I am advocating; if I am a radical Christ is a radical."[3]

Later in the summer, the emotional tone of the priest's oratory rose to new heights and his denunciation of the President became more lurid. Addressing fifteen thousand farmers at the fairgrounds in Hankinson, North Dakota, he made his first appeal for violence:

> If Lemke is not elected, there is only one thing to do—repudiate your debts and if anybody tries to enforce them, repudiate them also. . . . Go back and tell your friends that if either Roosevelt or Landon is installed in the White House, there will be no election in 1940. Fascism will be here and Communism will be making a bid for power.[4]

Coughlin's North Dakota audience did not respond well to the call to arms. Chagrined, the political priest was soon denying that he had urged forceful repudiation, claiming instead that he really only meant that farmers would be "forced" to repudiate if conditions worsened. But the return to moderation was only momentary; soon he was headed east, and his vitriol was stronger than ever.[5]

Throughout upstate New York and across New England, Father Coughlin denounced his bitter enemy, the President. The term "double-cross" found its way back into his vocabulary, but now it was lost in a torrent of uglier phrases. FDR was called "a scab President" leading a "scab army" of reliefers. The New Deal was "surrounded by atheists . . . , surrounded by red and pink Communists and by 'frankfurters' of de-

[2] *Social Justice*, July 6, 13, 20, 27, and August 3, 1936.

[3] *New York Times*, June 15, July 5, 11, and 26, 1936.

[4] Quoted in *St. Paul Pioneer Press*, July 27, 1936.

[5] Nellie Daugherty to Farley, August 7, 1936, National Committee Correspondence; and "Strategy Behind Coughlin's Campaign," *Business Week*, I, No. 361 (August 1, 1936), 41.

struction." In Providence, R.I., 25,000 sat in stunned silence while he roared that if Roosevelt were elected, there would be "more bullet holes in the White House than you could count with an adding machine." In New Bedford, Mass., twelve thousand heard him vow, "As I was instrumental in removing Herbert Hoover from the White House, so help me God, I will be instrumental in taking a Communist from the chair once occupied by Washington." [6]

Now there was no limit to his invective. "Well, we all know whom we're voting for if we vote for Mr. Roosevelt," the priest cried. "We are voting for the Communists, the socialists, the Russian lovers, the Mexican lovers, and the kick-me-downers." Traveling to Chicago to address an enormous throng of 100,000 at Riverview Park, he exposed the "Commies" who had been given sensitive positions in the Administration: "Rexie Tugwell . . . hand-shaker of Russia, plow-me-down Wallace, . . . Josephus Daniels—the man who applauds the slaughter of priests and nuns in Mexico." After a long harangue on evil-doings in Washington, he asked, "How many of you 100,000 children of toil are not going to vote for William Lemke for President?" Not a voice was raised. Then he bellowed, "Well then, how many here will pledge themselves not only to vote for Bill Lemke, but will promise to deliver five additional votes to him next November?" An ear-splitting shout arose from the vast crowd, hands shot into the air, and hats and flags appeared above the heads of the demonstrators. [7]

The wild enthusiasm of Chicagoans bouyed the spirits of the radio priest. A few weeks earlier he had been so heartened by a similar reception in Rhode Island that he had wagered a local industrialist $25,000 (he later withdrew) that Lemke would beat Landon in the state. The message of the crowds in both places seemed the same: the new and virulent assault on the White House was successful and could win new converts to the Union Party. Coughlin pushed ahead with the theme. "The revolution is coming," he told newsmen, "as surely as God is in his heaven—unless we can drive the money changers out this year." More than forty thousand midwestern members of the National Union assembled at West Allis, Wisconsin, to hear their leader speak his words of hatred. [8]

But now the pace of the campaign was accelerating. Once more the priest flew east, to tell a gathering of 22,000 in Brooklyn's Ebbets Field

[6] *New York Times*, August 3 and 6, 1936.

[7] *Ibid.*, September 7, 1936; and *Chicago Herald & Examiner*, September 7, 1936.

[8] *New York Times*, August 3, 5, and 15, 1936; and *The Leader* (North Dakota Nonpartisan League), September 10, 1936.

that the election represented a battle "between the basic principles of Christianity and the old doctrines of paganism . . . , a struggle for the preservation of Americanism." Here Coughlin reached the nadir of his crusade against the Administration, his derogations including the physical features of various New Dealers. It was really open season now on almost all Roosevelt appointees. Earlier in the summer, the priest at least had found favorable things to say about Joseph P. Kennedy, "a shining star among the dim knights" of the New Deal. But even Kennedy had turned on him; there were no friends in Washington now.[9]

In mid-September, Father Coughlin resumed radio broadcasting with a series of Saturday night "discourses" on national affairs. The old master of the microphone was returning to his favorite haunt, but the incessant pressure to keep up with speaking engagements limited his effectiveness. The radio addresses were journeys over well-trod paths: charges that the Democrats—with their "Stalinistic relief"—were the real inflationists, and warnings that "unless this flirting with Communistic tendencies is halted, the red flag of Communism will be reared in this country by 1940."[10]

In late September, the priest temporarily interrupted his all-out attack on the New Deal. It was a shocking reversal. Whereas only a few weeks before he had told reporters that "if Lemke loses, the country would be better off, temporarily, under the leadership of Landon," he soon began to pay tribute to the President's "poetic voice and artistic prose," suggesting that "Roosevelt has not done the things he has done maliciously, but has been a great victim of those who have surrounded him." Coughlin continued to chide FDR for "whipping Congress and crucifying the Supreme Court," but he stopped calling the Chief Executive a "Communist," substituting the tepid charge that "we are being led into socialistic and semi-communistic fields." The radio priest, responding to pressure from his superiors and from other clerics of the Catholic Church, obviously had decided to modify his position.[11]

But moderation was to prove unsuccessful. In New Jersey and in Massachusetts, crowds which were well below expectation greeted him at rallies. And Coughlin now was beset suddenly with a host of problems. While in Rhode Island, he concluded an angry meeting with the National Union state board by firing the director and deputy director. Hounded by newsmen, he lost his temper and had to be restrained from

[9] *New York Times*, September 12 and 13, 1936; *Social Justice*, July 3, 1936; and Tull, p. 213.

[10] *The Leader*, September 20, 1936; and *New York Times*, September 13, 16, and 17, 1936.

[11] *Ibid.*, September 20, 1936; and *Social Justice*, September 26, 1936.

assaulting a *Boston Globe* reporter, shouting as he was dragged away, "If I ever see that fellow again, I'll tear him to pieces." Such unpriestly behavior led Governor Curley of Massachusetts to predict that "the Coughlin movement is in a state of collapse throughout New England," and journalists began to write that the radio messiah was "losing his grip." [12]

Goaded by self-doubts and perhaps by the fear that both his movement and party were losing popularity, Charles E. Coughlin decided to resume his denunciations of the New Deal in the campaign's remaining few weeks. For despite the dangers involved in an all-out attack on the President, this might be the only way of avoiding a humiliating personal defeat in the coming election.

The last, furious offensive against FDR was unleashed during a midwestern tour. At Cincinnati, the priest told an NUSJ mass meeting that "when any upstart dictator in the United States succeeds in making this a one party form of government, when the ballot is useless, I shall have the courage to stand up and advocate the use of bullets. . . . Mr. Roosevelt is a radical. . . . He is an anti-God and a radical." This blatant call to the barricades catapulted Coughlin back into the headlines, and the theme of "Communism in Washington" was repeated time and again as the priest criss-crossed the country in October.[13]

Everywhere he pleaded with voters to support the Union Party. "Put us in a position to bargain," he cried. "All Lemke needs is 6% of the electoral vote to throw the election into the House of Representatives." Threatening that if Lemke were not successful, "the flower of American youth will perish in a war to defend international bankers that Roosevelt will surely have us involved in by 1937 or 1938 through his policy of extending money and credit to England and France," Coughlin damned the whole New Deal as "a broken down Colossus straddling the harbor of Rhodes, its left leg standing on ancient Capitalism and its right mired in the red mud of communism." [14]

Just before election day, his disposition became even uglier, his drive for power even more violent. If the Unionites were victorious, he told one crowd, "We will ride rough-shod over the press of this country," for it was only another tool of the "international bankers." In response to one reporter's question, he snapped, "We are at the crossroads. One

---

[12] *New York Times,* September 27, and October 14, 1936.

[13] "Coughlin's Bullets," *Time,* XXVIII, No. 14 (October 5, 1936), 33; and *New York Times,* October 13, 1936.

[14] *Ibid.,* September 20, October 25, 30, 1936.

Father Coughlin, speaking in Cleveland, October 27, 1936, termed FDR a "scab President," and WPA a "great scab army." *Wide World*

road leads toward fascism, the other toward Communism. I take the road to fascism." [15]

Thus Father Coughlin's campaign turned the full circle. And at its end, the priest was tired. He had worked hard for his party, and certainly it was his keen sense of drama and florid oratory that gave the Union cause a much-needed emotional charge. But Coughlin's inconsistency— his vacillation between militancy and moderation—confused many of his followers. And the recklessness of his attacks on the President not only repelled many other voters, but led them to suspect his capacity to perform in a politically responsible manner.

Worst of all, the colorful nature of the Coughlin campaign tended to overshadow the efforts of candidate Lemke. Lemke worked as energetically at carrying the party's message to the people as did the priest; in-

[15] *Ibid.;* "Conning the News," *New Masses,* XXI, No. 2 (October 6, 1936), 10; and Kramer, *Harper's Magazine,* 181, No. 9, 390.

deed, he probably gave more speeches and surely visited more states on speaking tours. But the North Dakota congressman could never match Coughlin's flamboyant style or his ability to hold the attention of both press and public.

Yet William Lemke was not easily discouraged. Although some newsmen disparagingly called him "little more than Coughlin's Washington agent," the agrarian leader actually took orders from no one. He met only occasionally with the radio priest, had even rarer contact with Smith or Townsend, and almost never communicated with his running mate, Thomas O'Brien, who seemed much more interested in his senatorial contest than in supporting the Union presidential ticket. Lemke worked only with his personal advisors, and with them he worked with feverish energy and enthusiasm. But in the end, both his personality and program failed to excite voters, and he was never able to project the image of a real presidential candidate.[16]

From the very outset of the campaign, William Lemke exposed his extraordinarily bad judgment about political publicity. For while he had no fondness for the name, he allowed Coughlin's weekly, *Social Justice*, to saddle him with the title, "Liberty Bell Bill." Wisecracking reporters immediately pointed out that the Liberty Bell was also cracked. And so even before he had an opportunity to carry his case to the people, he was being dismissed once again as a madman from the sticks.[17]

In the past, Lemke had never played the demagogue on the speakers' rostrum. Earnest but unpersuasive, he had preferred to argue all night to win one hundred listeners by the power of conviction rather than coax a cheer from a crowd of ten thousand by a platform trick. In the Union campaign, he finally resorted to making the extravagant promises and wild claims his critics expected of him, but still the cheers did not come.

The North Dakotan was an unimpressive figure on the rostrum. He presented a factual exposition in a high-pitched voice tinged with a slight Teutonic accent, and the only oratorical gesture he could muster was slapping his hands sharply on both legs for emphasis. A balding, slouching man, who sometimes did not find time to shave, he was often clad in a wrinkled gray suit, dusty black shoes and a blue shirt, and looked so little like a presidential candidate that he arrived in many cities without attracting the notice of the reception committee and had to drive to the Union Party rally alone. Newsmen mercilessly derided

---

[16] T.R.B., "Father Coughlin's Union Party," *New Republic*, LXXXVII, No. 1127 (July 8, 1936), 266; and Lemke to O'Brien, July 22, 1936, Lemke Papers.
[17] Harris, *Current History*, XLV, No. 1, 91.

his appearance, Drew Pearson writing of his "bald, egg-shaped head, . . . his dour bucolic look, . . . his weirdly incongruous, frozen, chorus-girl smile," and asserting that "the one sure way to lick him is to have him appear regularly in the newsreels." [18]

Lemke tried to capitalize on the disadvantage, telling audiences that "there are more of us dirt farmers and good, honest common people in this nation than there are Wall Street coupon clippers," and suggesting that "American Presidents put on too much dog. . . . When I'm in the White House, the common man will be able to see me." But while this approach might have been successful for election to Congress from an agrarian area, it simply was bad politics in a national campaign.[19]

Almost as serious was William Lemke's failure to develop any new and compelling political arguments. He tried to take advantage of what Secretary of Agriculture Henry A. Wallace called "one of the worst droughts in history," by proposing the creation of thousands of artificial lakes for the western regions between the Mississippi and the Rockies, a combination reclamation, conservation, and flood-control project which would "restore moisture to the western air" and prevent the spread of the dust bowl in the plains. But if this plan pleased midlands farmers, it received little notice in the rest of the country. Even when he tried an appeal to isolationists, he could not resist riding his old hobby horse, for he promised "an embargo on imports of all farm products that can be produced in the United States at a profit." [20]

But it would be unfair to consider Lemke a single-interest candidate of the farming region. His passionate concern for agriculture colored all of his actions, but he had picked up many inflationist notions from Coughlin and the other monetary radicals. Once again, however, the arguments were old and tired.

Lemke promised to put $6 billion of unbacked currency in circulation if elected. Taking his cues from the radio priest, he explained that this paper money would be issued after all government bonds and Federal Reserve notes had been retired. Leveling the standard charge against "international bankers," he promised the creation of a national Bank of the United States.

The Union standard bearer angrily denied that his party was "out to get anybody," insisting that "we are out to stop both Roosevelt and Landon." Nonetheless, the North Dakotan spent much more time attacking FDR than his GOP rival. "Roosevelt is a bewildered Kerensky

[18] *Ibid.*, 92; and *Boston Evening Transcript,* August 1, 1936.

[19] *Minneapolis Star,* July 27, 1936; and *New York Times,* June 30, 1936.

[20] *Ibid.*, June 26, and July 12, 1936; and *The Leader,* July 2, 1936.

of a provisional government," he cried. "The public is looking for a real statesman yet to come."[21]

In his effort to demonstrate that he was the "real statesman" of the future. William Lemke traveled over thirty thousand miles, most of them by air, and visited thirty-three states in his futile quest for the White House. Few third party candidates had ever made such an effort.[22]

Lemke began the speechmaking in the Midwest in July and August. He made the traditional opening address in his home state, where supporters distributed broadsides urging voters to "remember, this is the first time that a North Dakota man has ever reached national prominence to a point where the presidency is at stake — do not fail him now." Moving to Iowa, he told a group of farmers that the Administration's agricultural experts were "curly headed bright boys from Boston who wouldn't know the front end of a pig from the hind end." He predicted that the Republican and Democratic parties would merge and the Union Party would become the "liberal party of the country." This kind of talk worried local Farmer-Labor leaders in Minneapolis, where Lemke attracted 35,000 to a political picnic sponsored by the National Union for Social Justice. The candidate also drew encouraging crowds in Greeley, Colorado, where he challenged FDR to debate money and banking issues; in Norway, Michigan, where he promised to serve only one term as President, because "I'll do the job so well anyone can do it after that"; and in Cleveland, where he accused the Administration of being staffed by "dilapidated old line politicians and bureaucrats who believe in economic slavery and regimentation."[23]

For a brief period in mid-August, it appeared as if the Lemke campaign were picking up momentum. A straw vote in the magazine *Farm Journal* showed him making significant gains in the preceding three weeks and polling up to 25 per cent of the votes in certain midwestern states. On the heels of the poll came a successful visit at a Farmers Union meeting in Davenport, Iowa, where the Unionite drew loud applause for shouting, "We should have an end to this business of making false gods of humans, as with the present incumbent of the White House." He now told newsmen, "I think I am going to be the next President," and he seemed to believe it. But then William Lemke set out

[21] Davenport, *Collier's*, 98, No. 16, 26; and radio address by Lemke, July 28, 1936, copy in Lemke Papers.

[22] "Hopper," *Time*, XXVIII, No. 18 (November 2, 1936), 10.

[23] *The Leader*, July 2, 1936; *Minneapolis Journal*, August 6, 1936; *New York Times*, August 3, 6, 1936; and address by Lemke delivered August 16, 1936, entitled "America for Americans," and leaflet entitled "Lemke Is The Man," copies in Lemke Papers.

on a coast-to-coast trip, at the end of which he would have a much more realistic view of his political strength.[24]

First, he invaded New England. This was Coughlin territory, and he obligingly confined his remarks at Worcester, Massachusetts, to one of the priest's favorite subjects: the evils of interest-bearing, tax-exempt bonds. But at neighboring Somerville, he could not resist a discussion of the sorry plight of the midwestern farmer, and the crowd in this eastern industrial area sat on its hands. He found a similar reaction on the West Coast. In Los Angeles, his blast at William Green of the A. F. of L. for "selling out" farmers on the Frazier-Lemke bill drew only scattered applause. Only when he advocated a "return of the oldsters to colleges, where they could teach the brainless trusters something practical," did he get a real cheer. In San Francisco, Lemke pictured his party as "the most conservative of any on the money question. . . . We stand for the stable dollar"; in Portland, shouting ineffectually through a dead microphone, he railed about "the Harvard and Yale boys sent to teach our pigs birth control." Everywhere he traveled in the West his audiences were mainly composed of Townsendites; everywhere he spoke the crowds were smaller than anticipated.[25]

Returning East, the candidate stopped off at Omaha for a Coughlin-like diatribe against "an Administration which clings to the dying shadows of past civilizations." Touring a series of Indiana county fairs, he termed the New Deal "our country's greatest enemy of freedom." In Peoria, Illinois, he tried to meet the "wasted vote" argument by dismissing both major parties as "backed by the same international gangsters," crying to an unresponsive crowd, "You people have no business to vote your children into slavery because you were born a Democrat or a Republican." [26]

In Delphos, Ohio, he was encouraged for a few hours after appearing at a local fair, riding atop a float portraying a Lincoln-like image of himself. But flying on to the eastern seaboard, Lemke once again encountered disappointing audiences. In New York, where he contradicted Coughlin by calling Roosevelt "no Communist, just a coupon clipper, a capitalist like the rest of them," and in Philadelphia, where he tried to ring some changes on the isolationist theme by decrying the reciprocal trade agreements as a "manifestation of this Administration's foreign

[24] *Davenport Democrat* (Davenport, Iowa), August 19, 1936; and *New York Times,* August 17, 1936.
[25] *Ibid.,* August 28, September 1, 7, 1936; *Los Angeles Examiner,* September 12, 1936; *San Francisco Examiner,* September 13, 1936; and *Portland Oregonian,* September 14, 1936.
[26] *New York Times,* September 18, 20, 22, 1936.

Speaking before 100,000 people at a Coughlin rally in Riverview Park, Chicago, in September, 1936, Lemke promised that if elected President he would "tell Congress to go home and make an honest living instead of riding on the backs of the taxpayers." *Wide World*

inferiority complex," it became clear that his campaigning efforts were failing to make a dent in the electorate.[27]

Yet he persevered. Back in the Midwest at the beginning of October, he squabbled with the Minnesota Democratic party manager, who accused him of being "a tool of the Hearsts, Duponts and Morgans," after Lemke had charged that "75% of the Congressional liberals backing F.D.R. are on Jim Farley's payroll." Undaunted, the candidate toured his home state of North Dakota, blasting the "insane" policies of the Agriculture Department, and telling grim-faced wheat farmers that Farley and Roosevelt were "trying to Tammanize the country by putting labor and farm leaders on the payrolls of 75 different alphabetical agencies."[28]

[27] *Ibid.*, September 24, 27, 1936; and Ferguson to Farley, September 25, 1936, National Committee Correspondence.

[28] *Minneapolis Tribune*, October 2, 1936; *The Fargo Forum* (Fargo, N. Dak.), October 4, 1936; and radio address over a state-wide (N. Dak.) network, delivered October 5, 1936, copy in Lemke Papers.

In the remaining three weeks of the campaign, William Lemke somehow managed to accelerate his already exhausting pace. From October
14 to election day, he visited forty cities in every section of the country
but the deep South. Clambering in and out of a rickety Ford trimotored
aircraft, he journeyed from St. Louis to Dallas, stopped at several southwestern points and then arrived once more in Los Angeles. Speeding
across the West, he visited a host of Rocky Mountain communities from
Denver to Spokane before returning to tour farming centers in the
plains states and industrial centers in the Great Lakes area. A final swing
through Middle Atlantic and New England cities preceded the whirl-
wind election-eve finale in his homeland of Minnesota and the Dakotas.

In this last, desperate effort to reach the voters, the agrarian radical
returned to his favorite campaign themes. There were the traditional
attacks on the New Deal for its "regimentation . . . , dictatorial beyond
reason." There was the ritual denunciation of "the international banker
domination of this Administration." And always, there were the explosive, hate-filled assaults on Rooseveltian agricultural policy, laments
for the death of his cherished Frazier-Lemke bills, and the "unGodly"
destruction of crops under the AAA. But endless repetition had blunted
the cutting edge of his rhetoric until what was meant to be sensational
sounded merely banal. The gallant but outmatched Lemke was a weary
man at the end. Still, he was proud of his effort, and speaking at home
near the end of his journeys, the pugnacious congressman concluded,
"My coat may be wrinkled, but my record is not." He had done all that
he could.[29]

The same could not be said of Gerald L. K. Smith and Francis E.
Townsend. Smith's efforts were particularly inconsistent. For a few
weeks he would be on the road, strenuously working in behalf of his
party. But then he would remain silent for days. And when he did campaign, his curious tactics were unlike those of any other political organizers for major or minor parties, for Smith operated very much alone.
After joining Townsend for a few appearances before pension supporters in early summer, he took leave of his allies and began to travel
without aides, entering towns where he had no organized support. He
tried to adapt to a national political campaign those methods he had
employed so effectively in backwoods southern towns when he was
drumbeater for the Share-Our-Wealth Society.

In July and August, Smith journeyed through the East and Midwest.
In Newark, he predicted that Lemke could lose only if the electorate

[29] *New York Times*, October 25, 29, and November 2, 1936; and *The Leader,* October 15,
1936.

was "bribed." In Columbus, Ohio, he told a crowd of six thousand that Roosevelt was "planning to enroll the United States in World War in support of Russia." In Washington, D.C., he informed the National Press Club, in his best Louisiana bayou vernacular, that Lemke was "my man," while the President was merely "a soft, vacillating politician being used by Tugwell and the other Reds," and that Landon was a "weakling . . . , putty in the hands of the Wall Streeters." Responding to questions by baiting newsmen, he denied that the Share-Our-Wealth program led to socialism and in the process reached new heights of economic confusion: "Public ownership? We don't want it in any-thing . . . even the police and fire departments. I mean it, we don't want it anywhere." [30]

In late August, Gerald L. K. Smith began a unique speaking tour. The technique, he told one interviewer, was to be "just religion and patriotism. I'll keep going on that. It's the only way you can get them really het up." [31]

In mid-September, a reporter met him in Birmingham, Alabama. As usual, the minister was going around introducing himself to strangers in coffee shops and on street corners, working without an organization, with no hired auditorium in which to speak, with no help of any kind. "I'm Gerald Smith," he would say. "I'm here to make a speech against the vermin that are trying to destroy America. I want you to come out and hear me tonight." There would be no other publicity; he simply would hire a loudspeaker truck and go to a centrally located park. With no one to introduce him and no crowd on hand, he would begin to speak to the handful of park sitters.[32]

Now the showman took over. Soon an audience of one hundred or more would drift in off the streets to hear what all the shouting was about. After two hours, perhaps one thousand or fifteen hundred would be enjoying his histrionics. Wet with perspiration, his shirt front open, waving his arms and pounding his fists, he would shout: "Oh you feudal lords! You hired tools! You lying newspapers! You damnable hypo-crites! Burn your bridges! Burn our ballots! We will meet you with Jefferson and Lincoln! We will meet you with Father Coughlin and William Lemke! We will meet you with Dr. Townsend and the spirit of Huey Long!" [33]

[30] *New York Times,* July 26, August 8 and 24, 1936; and "Messiahs," *Newsweek,* VIII, No. 5 (August 1, 1936), 10.

[31] Harris, *Current History,* XLV, No. 1, 84.

[32] Huie, *American Mercury,* LV, No. 224, 148.

[33] *Ibid.,* 149.

When the florid performer sensed that the crowd was with him, responding to the cries about "money changers and sons-of-Beelzebub enthroned in Washington," he would turn to a favorite demagogic device for enlarging an audience: calling a twenty-minute intermission "to change clothes," and asking his listeners not only to wait but to call friends to join them. Upon his return, the throng often had doubled. "You who toil are nailed to the cross tonight," he would tell them, "but remember, the resurrection follows the crucifixion." [34]

These park-side and street-corner perorations were classic examples of Smith's religiopolitical style. Taking out the ever-present Bible, he would shout, "Let's have everybody that's happy stand up. Now everybody that's mad." Then, to a standing crowd, he would cry:

> They tell me I mustn't refer to our sacred flag. That would make me a rabble-rouser. They say I must not speak of our glorious Constitution. That would be rabble-rousing. They tell me that I cannot quote from my beloved Bible, which I hold here in my hand. Let me tell you, my friends, that if it is rabble-rousing to praise the flag and the constitution and to love and revere the Holy Bible, then I pray to God that He in His wisdom will make me the greatest rabble-rouser in the land and fit to follow in the footsteps of Huey Long, who chose me as his great disciple.[35]

Were these colorful harangues winning any new voters to the Union cause? If this was the intention, most of his speeches in the solid Democratic South certainly were wasted. But it became obvious that Smith was at least as interested in advertising himself as in promoting the party. If his speeches made the newspapers, that was good enough.

Later in the campaign, Smith's statements for the press began to take on a paranoid tone. Often in the past he had darkly hinted of conspiracies to shoot or stab or even hang him; now he talked of a Communist plot to kill him. Suddenly revealing "definite information" that FDR had plans to seize power forcibly, he then announced a scheme to "recruit one million patriotic young men who will see to it that our ballots are cast in the daytime and counted at night . . . , young men who will prevent strong arm tactics by Roosevelt's CCC storm troops." [36]

As Smith's public utterances grew increasingly bizarre, increasingly antidemocratic and fascistic, his fellow party leaders could no longer remain silent. If the demagogic minister was losing interest in their

[34] *Ibid.*, 148–49.
[35] Quoted in Broun, *The Nation*, CXLIII, No. 8, 213.
[36] *New York Times*, August 16, 1936; and "Conning the News," *New Masses*, XX, No. 13 (September 22, 1936), 9–10.

joint venture and was planning to form a new vigilante group of his own, strong measures would have to be taken. Even in the loosely constructed Union alliance, there were limits on individual action.

Yet it was a measure of the lack of coordination among the party organizers that while Smith was shouting until he turned even his comrades against him, and Coughlin and Lemke were relentlessly touring the nation, Dr. Francis E. Townsend could conduct a much more placid campaign in support of Union candidates.

July and August were the pension leader's most active and outspoken months on the campaign trail. He repeatedly called for Lemke's election and in Lincoln, Nebraska, charged the New Deal with "constituting the most gigantic bribery in the world. . . . The morale of the great mass of the people has been destroyed; fear has us by the throats." Townsend told his followers to "turn out the Washington gang—it is no better than the gang that preceded them." [37]

But after exertions at the conventions of his own movement and of the National Union for Social Justice, the seventy-year-old physician fell ill with what his doctors described as "physical exhaustion." And in the following weeks his activities were restricted to a speech at a Topeka, Kansas, rally where he damned both Roosevelt and Landon, the publication of a few pamphlets explaining his endorsement of Lemke, and Union Party publicity in the *Townsend National Weekly*.[38]

When his health improved enough to allow the resumption of active campaigning, it quickly became clear that the postconvention lull had taken a toll on the old man's interest as well as his energy. For now he proved to be an inconsistent champion of William Lemke. One day he would extravagantly praise the North Dakotan, but the next day he might qualify his endorsement with the words, "Of course, I am speaking only for myself." He even remarked petulantly to a reporter, "It is a lamentable thing that we did not organize our own Townsend Plan party for these national elections." [39]

Late in the campaign, when it seemed likely that Lemke's name would not appear on the ballots of several states, Townsend strayed even farther from the third party alliance. Like Gerald Smith, whose wild accusations and ugly postelection plans frightened off many potential supporters, Townsend's failure to commit himself fully to the Union cause only hurt the new party.

[37] *New York Times,* July 12, 1936.
[38] *Ibid.,* August 18, 1936; *Literary Digest,* CXXII, No. 7, 4; and Townsend, *Dr. Townsend Tells Why . . . ,* pp. 2–10.
[39] *New York Times,* September 4, and October 26, 1936.

In the end, the performance of the four radical leaders on the hustings was anything but impressive. Hampered by their inability to work together, these self-styled messiahs expended enormous energy to little effect. For the Union Party, this failure of its spokesman to advertise creatively both program and candidates proved a crushing blow. For it had little beyond the rhetoric of its leaders on which to depend. As the campaign progressed, Unionites were finding it increasingly difficult to overcome problems of organization.

18

The Hard Facts of Political Life

As Lemke and Coughlin relentlessly toured the country and Smith and Townsend campaigned in their own fashion, the less dramatic but even more essential business of building a "grass roots" political organization, providing adequate financing, and winning a place on the printed ballot continued to confound Union Party leaders and workers.

The failure to create an effective political structure was especially damaging. Put to the test, national headquarters in Chicago proved weak and indecisive, particularly after National Chairman Usher Burdick resigned in midcampaign to conduct his own congressional reelection battle. Burdick's replacement, Campaign Manager John Nystul, was a man whose previous experience had been limited to North Dakota politics. Under Nystul, party headquarters did little more than issue reports on the speech-making schedules of various leaders (received with disdain by a hostile or indifferent press) and publish a few pamphlets describing the party's platform and candidates. Some of these publications, such as *Why "Waste" Your Vote On Lemke*, were well-reasoned arguments for supporting a third party. Most, however, were wildly misleading attacks on the opposition, filled with gross errors and specious "revelations." Sales figures were not released, but there is no evidence that they were widely circulated.[1]

---

[1] T.R.B., "The Old Folks Crusade," *New Republic*, LXXXVIII, No. 1133 (August 19, 1936), 46; *New York Times,* July 16, 1936; S. O. Sanderson, *Why "Waste" Your Vote On Lemke* (Rochester, Minn.: The Union Party, 1936), pp. 1–2; Richard W. Wolfe, *Lemke or Stalin—Which?* (Chicago: The Union Party, 1936), pp. 2–7; and *The Union Party Will Win With Lincoln Legal Tender Money* (Spokane, Washington: The Union Party, 1936), pp. 1–4.

But as ineffective as was the national office, it seemed a tower of strength next to the Union state and local organizations. If the party was to nominate full slates of candidates and project a regional appeal, "grass roots" units had to be established. Yet the melancholy fact was that in many areas, especially in western and southern states, Unionites could not even find contact men around which to start building political machines. In states where chairmen were appointed, there was almost total failure in the crash program to recruit a disciplined army of party workers, precinct captains and committeemen.[2]

In the absence of a functioning party structure, the Union chiefs turned to the local chapters of their own individual movements. Here, too, the results were disappointing.

Lemke's Nonpartisan League was operating only in North Dakota by 1936, and even there, the congressman was not its sole leader.

Smith's Share-Our-Wealth organization—little more than a paper tiger even in the heyday of Huey Long—had disintegrated in the month's following the founder's assassination. By the start of the campaign summer of 1936, most Share-Our-Wealth clubs had disbanded, and with Smith lacking even the mailing lists of the original membership, his claim of a following of "six million" was a baseless boast. When the chips were down, Unionites discovered that they certainly could not look to local units of the Lemke or Smith movements for organizing purposes.

The Townsend movement, of course, had thousands of active local clubs. But they had been established as vehicles for bringing pressure to bear on congressmen on specific issues and as social centers for the aged. Useful for circulating petitions and conducting letter-writing operations, they were never meant to serve as components of a political party. The old folks simply lacked the experience, and in many cases the energy, to identify and enlist potential third party voters. And with their beloved Dr. Townsend refusing to insist that local clubs endorse Union candidates, many lacked interest as well. Townsendites did provide forums for Union speakers, but they did virtually nothing more.

Local units of Coughlin's National Union for Social Justice played a larger role. NUSJ clubs organized rallies for the radio priest and other Union speakers and canvassed for Lemke. But Father Coughlin never attempted to overextend his groups. He had forced his movement at its convention to endorse only candidate Lemke—not the whole new

[2] H. F. Swett (Director of Organization of The Union Party) to William Skeels, July 30, 1936, Lemke Papers.

party. Some members even had rebelled at this; several local clubs dissociated themselves from Coughlin during the campaign or disbanded entirely because of the Lemke endorsement. Fearing the effects of tying his successful movement too closely to his faltering party, the priest was unwilling to push his local chapters into grass roots political service.[3]

For the radical leaders, this organizational failure meant that their arguments would not be translated into significant local terms and that on election day, they could not get out the vote. Moreover, it meant that slates of candidates for state and local offices—which could balance the national ticket and give it regional appeal—would be missing in most areas.

In the end, the Unionites could offer nominees for positions other than the presidency and vice-presidency in less than ten states. And while Coughlin and Lemke had hoped to name large numbers of congressional candidates, this hope would go largely unfulfilled.

In Pennsylvania and Ohio, where the NUSJ had mounted its most impressive effort in primary contests, the party did field a respectable number of congressional aspirants, eleven in the Keystone State alone. The picture in Michigan, another Coughlinite stronghold, was less rosy. There the "Third Party" nominated but five candidates for lower offices, the most notable being the priest's lieutenant, Louis B. Ward, who ran for the United States Senate seat under the new party label only after failing to win the Democratic nomination by less than eight thousand votes out of a total of almost 240,000 cast.[4]

Massachusetts was the home of the most powerful Social Justice forces in the East, but there the congressional hopefuls who supported Father Coughlin did not run specifically on the Union Party ticket. John McLaren filed in the Tenth District as a "Townsend-Coughlin-Laborite," Albert P. McCulloch in the Eleventh as a "Father Coughlin's Principles Republican," and John Henry McNeece as a "Social Justice-Townsend" candidate. Frank Bushold ran for governor as a "Union-Coughlin-Townsendite." In addition, incumbent Democratic Representatives John P. Higgins, Arthur D. Healey, and Joseph Carey agreed to abandon their support of FDR and back Lemke, thereby securing NUSJ endorsement.[5]

In the upper Midwest the situation was truly dismal. The only name

[3] *New York Times*, August 8, 1936.

[4] Masters, pp. 218–20; *Pennsylvania Blue Book*, 1937; *New York Times*, September 17 and 24, 1936; and Coughlin to Lemke, October 4, 1936, Lemke Papers.

[5] *Massachusetts Blue Book*, 1937; and *New York Times*, October 13, 1936.

appearing on the ballot with Lemke and O'Brien in Wisconsin, for example, was the gubernatorial candidate, Joseph H. Walsh. And in North Dakota, home base of standard-bearer William Lemke, no one, not even Lemke himself, ran for a lower office under the Union aegis.[6]

The farmer's champion was wearing two hats in this campaign, running for reelection to the House of Representatives as well as for the presidency. To protect his party from the charge that even its titular head had no faith in victory, presidential aspirant Lemke explained, "I am running for Congress because I want to be there when this election is thrown into the House; I want to look after the interests of the common people and help elect a President who will carry out the Union Party platform." But congressional candidate Lemke preferred to defend his seat on the Republican ticket with Nonpartisan League endorsement rather than to risk the race as a Unionite. For Lemke had discovered that the Union name carried no magic in North Dakota. Powerful state politicians had opposed his presidential plans, and he had lost Nonpartisan League endorsement for his White House campaign. Both gubernatorial candidates, William Langer and Walter Welford, had announced for Landon, and influential Senator Gerald Nye, casting a cautious eye to the reelection race he faced within two years, referred to himself simply as "a conservative" who would stay out of all contests. Only Senator Lynn J. Frazier and Representative Burdick backed Lemke, and Frazier's support amounted to little more than a verbal acknowledgment of past political debts.[7]

Curiously, only in Illinois did Unionites field anything like a full slate of candidates. Running under the name Union Progressive, the party offered nominees for senator, governor, a host of lesser state offices, and five congressional seats. The senatorial candidate was Newton Jenkins, a Chicago attorney who had polled over 150,000 votes as a third party aspirant in 1930. The gubernatorial choice was bombastic William Hale "Big Bill" Thompson, xenophobic former mayor of Chicago. The presence of these perennial soreheads on the Union ticket pointed up the problem faced by any new party that tries to contest elections before doing adequate preliminary organization: it can become a home for all manner of political pariahs. For while Thompson tried to tie himself to the four radical leaders in announcing that "Lemkeites, Townsendites, Coughlinites, Huey Longites, and Thomp-

---

[6] *The Wisconsin Blue Book,* 1937; and *The North Dakota Blue Book,* 1937.

[7] Radio address by Lemke, October 5, 1936, Lemke Papers; *New York Times,* October 14, 1936; and *The Leader,* October 15, 1936.

Lemke appearing at a rally held at a Chicago amusement park under the sponsorship of the former mayor, "Big Bill" Thompson (right). Thompson was candidate for governor of Illinois on the Lemke ticket. *Wide World*

sonites are going down the pike together with the American people in November," he soon went off on his own crusades.[8]

Despite a famous name and a colorful personality, Thompson's campaign made little headway. The ex-mayor promised "to find out whether this country is a tail to England's kite," and to enact legislation "which will outlaw all taxation on homes with incomes of $3,000 and less." When Illinoisians turned a deaf ear and newspapers brushed him off as a mere ghost from a best-forgotten past, "Big Bill" tried to recoup prestige by distributing one million free tickets for a gigantic rally featuring candidate Lemke at Riverview Park. But he could attract only eight thousand supporters—only a few days after Coughlin had drawn 100,000 to the same site—and it was clear that the editorialists were right.[9]

By late summer, Thompson's reckless actions were hurting the party more than helping it and creating a bad image throughout the Midwest. In a desperate search for a following, he attended the annual picnic of the Chicago Nazi Clubs, where he was escorted to the platform by swastika-decorated "troopers," and won thunderous cheers

---

[8] *Illinois Blue Book*, 1937–38; *Chicago Herald and Examiner*, August 7, 1936; and *New York Times*, July 1 and 26, September 28, 1936.

[9] *Ibid.*, September 9, 1936; and *Detroit News*, June 20, 1936.

by denouncing "Reds and Jewish bankers." Such performances could not have helped the Union presidential campaign, and Lemke, hearing after the election of this fascistic activity, was appalled.[10]

While certain elements of the lunatic fringe were working their divisive ways in one state, extremists of a different stripe were operating in another. In pivotal California, where Unionites were having trouble winning a place on the ballot, the wild charges and bizarre pronouncements of a small group of fanatically committed Lemkeites won wide currency but little support among the general public, for here too, those who supplied the manpower for the campaign were to offset their hard work by the ill will they engendered.

Ellis O. Jones and Robert Noble were the party's dedicated organizers in California. Remarkably energetic in promoting Lemke's candidacy, they published a weekly newspaper called the *Lemke Leader* and wrote and distributed numerous pamphlets and leaflets.[11]

But they were erratic and unsubtle in the extreme. Not only did Jones and Noble fill their publications with preposterous stories, such as one describing Lemke as a "big, virile, vital man . . . with a bronzed, carved face," they also used them as vehicles for personal vendettas against rival leaders, particularly the Townsend Plan's state chairman, Edward J. Margett. Noble was especially unstable; his career had been a repetitive story of commitment and disillusionment in many radical groups — including EPIC, the Utopian movement, and Share-Our-Wealth — and his allegiance to quasi-fascist clubs would land him in a federal penitentiary during World War II.[12]

Such men could only frighten away conservative Townsendites, and so in California too did the third party's efforts to build grass-roots support end in ignominious failure. The Union leaders' effort to handle yet another pressing problem, that of obtaining adequate campaign funds, met with hardly more success.

Unionites needed money desperately for research and clerical help, travel expenses, purchase of radio and newspaper advertisements, and printing of campaign posters and pamphlets. Candidate Lemke's initial optimism about finances — perhaps rooted in a successful Nonpartisan League experience which might have suggested that any third party

[10] *New Masses*, XX, No. 13, 10; and Lemke to Myrtle Ellsworth, October 4, 1936.

[11] *Lemke Leader* (Los Angeles, California), September 5, 12, 21, 28, October 5, 12, 26, November 2, 1936; Robert Noble, *How Lemke Can Be Elected* (Los Angeles: Robert Noble, 1936), pp. 6–15; Robert Noble, *Lemke And The Union Party* (Los Angeles: Robert Noble, 1936), pp. 2–8; and Ellis O. Jones, *Lemke's The Man For President* (Los Angeles: Ellis O. Jones, 1936), pp. 3–28.

[12] *Lemke Leader*, September 12, 21, and 28, 1936; and Jones, p. 6.

could be started on a shoe-string—dissipated in direct relation to the mounting pile of unpaid bills in headquarters.

At the outset of the campaign, Coughlin called for contributions for "William Lemke, the impoverished leader of the impoverished party." The priest felt that his "Dollars for the Poor Man's Party" drive had to net $500,000 to be successful, but it fell far short of that goal. Few were interested in "charter membership certificates" at one dollar apiece, and only the large contributions of a few generous individuals saved the national office the embarrassment of a completely bare cupboard. According to reports of receipts and expenditures made to the House of Representatives (a mandatory procedure for all parties), Unionites raised less than $60,000 between June 1 and election day.[13]

Among those listed as large contributors in the early stages of the race were names well known to party leaders: William Hale Thompson gave $5,000, John Nystul, $2,000, and Phillip Johnson and Alan Blackburn, $5,000. Johnson and Blackburn were the wealthy young Harvard graduates who appeared at the Coughlin convention, ostensibly representing the "Youth Division of the NUSJ." Although inactive in Union affairs, they were fascinated by radical politics and their financial aid gave them access to party organizers. Later, they were to form the quasi-fascistic National Party. None of larger contributors late in the campaign had such ambitions; indeed D. H. Wilson of Bethlehem, Pennsylvania, and William Seigel and E. H. Byrne of Chicago were newcomers to party circles.[14]

Clearly, the total Union election expenses far outstripped the paltry sum reportedly raised. And Charles E. Coughlin alone saved the party from a complete financial debacle, for Dr. Townsend contributed little aside from that money spent on his own speechmaking trips, and Gerald Smith was in no position to help because of a personal financial squeeze. The radio priest reported that his movement's disbursements from June through August were $190,000, and he told Congress that NUSJ total campaign expenditures were $575,000, some $16,000 less than receipts.[15]

But Father Coughlin spent most of the National Union money on his own campaign: covering costs of the Cleveland convention, the many

[13] *New York Times,* July 12, September 12, 13, and October 27, 1936; *Social Justice,* June 27, 1936; and Blackorby, pp. 512–22.

[14] *New York Times,* September 12, October 27, 1936; and Newton, *Southwestern Social Science Quarterly,* XXLI, No. 3, 346. Lemke noted that he received "on his own behalf," $5,321 by late October. See *New York Times,* October 22, 1936.

[15] *Ibid.,* September 15, October 27, 1936. Assets for Coughlin's Radio League of the Little Flower for 1936 were over $205,000. See Spivak, p. 160.

NUSJ rallies held across the country, the purchase of radio time, and the extensive travel bills for himself and his entourage. Little was left for contributions to Union Party national headquarters and candidate Lemke. Indeed, William Lemke invested $7,000 of his own money in the campaign for which he was never reimbursed, and several workers in the Chicago office dipped into their own savings. Almost three years after the election, there were still unpaid bills at headquarters dating from 1936, and former National Chairman Nystul reported that he was "broke."[16]

But still other problems haunted the new party throughout the summer and fall, such as that of getting the Union name on the ballot of several states.

After the initial shock of discovering that filing deadlines in a few states precluded even an attempt to put the party on the ballot, Lemke announced, "We will be on the ballots of all 48 states despite the election laws . . . by using slates which other groups have already filed in states we are barred from." But little headway was made in this effort: in Iowa and Michigan, where negotiations were under way with local Farmer-Labor parties, arguments between area Unionites and managers of the older splinter groups wrecked any chance of using alternate labels.[17]

As the months passed, the situation became increasingly serious. In some cases, workers simply could not obtain the requisite signatures on filing petitions by due date; in other cases—particularly in sparsely populated Western states and in the deep South—no competent personnel were found to head the drives. Most frustrating were the instances in which the party mounted a tremendous effort only to fall just short of producing the necessary endorsements. In California, Unionites barely missed the required 118,040 signatures; in New York, the party's petition was voided only because it lacked 50 valid signatures in a handful of remote upstate counties. The loss of these great and populous states was irreparable. The massive Townsend strength in southern California and the vast Coughlin following in the Empire State would not now be registered at the polls.[18]

---

[16] John Nystul to Lemke, November 3, 1938; Nystul to Lemke, March 3, 1939, Lemke to Nystul, March 8, 1939, and Lemke to Covington Hall, May 2, 1939, in Lemke Papers.

[17] L. S. Hill to Farley (Des Moines, Iowa), September 12, 1936, National Committee Correspondence; Coughlin to Lemke, October 4, 1936, Lemke Papers; and *New York Times*, June 28, and October 8, 1936.

[18] *Ibid.*, June 21, October 22, 1936; Goldstein, *The New Republic*, LXXXVII, No. 1122, 100; George W. Baker, Jr. to Farley, October 6, 1936, McAdoo Papers; and "Report on the Union Filing Situation," August 7, 1936, Lemke Papers.

In the face of a growing disaster in the battle for the ballot, the Union leaders at first tried to organize write-in campaigns in certain strategic areas. In Kansas, precious funds were spent printing 100,000 circulars containing the names of presidential electors for Lemke. But realists in the Chicago headquarters privately acknowledged that a write-in had no hope of success. As election day neared, it became clear that the new party would be on the ballot of only thirty-four states, and in eight of these, under names other than Union.[19]

In the fourteen states where the party was denied a line on the ballot, there lived not only a sizeable percentage of the nation's population with a huge bloc of electoral votes, but thousands of potential Union supporters. The failure to win access to these voters, like the failure to master problems of organization and financing, was due not only to the institutionalized advantages favoring the two major parties in the American political system but also to the inexperience of the political amateurs running the Union enterprise. Coughlin, Townsend, and Smith were not, after all, professional politicians. Instead, they were self-proclaimed messiahs, hoping to make revolutionary changes in the economic and social arrangements of the nation despite the hard facts of political life in a huge democracy. And as the new party's troubles multiplied, so too did tensions among these leaders. Just as President Roosevelt had predicted, severe strains started to weaken the radical alliance.

[19] *New York Times*, October 13, 17, and 23, 1936.

19

Strains in the Alliance

The leaders of the Union Party were never really comfortable with one another. The natural jealousies that strong and ambitious men would feel toward each other were compounded by the stresses of a major political campaign. Even in early summer, these ambivalent allies were grumbling about their partners.

Father Coughlin, for example, displeased by the overshadowing platform pyrotechnics of Gerald L. K. Smith at the two Cleveland conventions, was soon voicing concern about the anti-Catholic, Klan background of the Louisiana minister. Dr. Townsend, conversely, was unhappy with Coughlin and candidate Lemke for their continual equivocation about his pension plan in campaign speeches. When the priest endorsed the plan "in principle," only to add that in its present form it was "mathematically impossible," and when William Lemke remarked that "we must help the old people. . . . I don't care whether that means $50 a month or $200 or $20,000," the old man angrily complained about departures from the "100% endorsement" that he had demanded.[1]

Even Lemke and Coughlin found fault with each other. The radio priest wondered about a remark by the candidate's friend, Usher Burdick, to the National Farm Holiday Association, that "six weeks after election as President, Lemke will be making conservative speeches." And Congressman Lemke resented the minor billing given him on

[1] *Ibid.*, August 3, September 11, 1936; Davenport, *Collier's*, XCVIII, No. 16, 26; *The Nation*, CXLIII, No. 8, 201–02; *Literary Digest*, CXXII, No. 7, 4; and Ferkiss, pp. 310–11.

posters and pamphlets announcing joint speaking appearances with Coughlin.[2]

But during the campaign's early stages, the Union leaders still were able to work together. As the summer turned to fall, however, three crises caused a rupture in the relationships among the curious allies.

The first of these was Gerald L. K. Smith's erratic behavior and subsequent expulsion from the party. From the very start, the flamboyant minister had seemed more intent on promoting private interests than party matters. As early as July he had proposed formation of "Townsend Recovery Youth Groups," composed of "twelve young men in every community . . . , picked young men 16 to 25 years old of physical fitness, sacrificial aims, alertness and loyalty to government." This youth corps was to train at a Commonwealth University that Smith planned to establish.[3]

Other Unionites considered such statements innocent enough, merely Smith's idle dreams. They even ignored his antidemocratic outbursts to reporters, such as "Politics is prostitution. . . . What I really want is an organization of 1,000 eloquent men to go up and down the country preaching true Americanism," or "The democratic method . . . is a lot of baloney; it doesn't really mean anything. We can tell what they're thinking without taking a vote."[4]

But when Gerald L. K. Smith announced, in late October, that he was proceeding immediately with the formation of a new, quasi-fascistic organization, he could be ignored no longer. Smith described the new movement at a press conference in New York's Hotel Warwick on October 19. It would be "a nationalist organization," he disclosed, "combining the best features of the Townsend Plan, the National Union for Social Justice, and the Share-Our-Wealth Society." Its aim: "ultimately to seize the government of the United States." To that end he would recruit a following of "10 million patriots who will risk their lives to save the U.S.A. from the internationalists' plot to collectivize it."[5]

Smith claimed that "1,000 politically potent leaders in various parts of the country" awaited his orders. Bragging about "400 businessmen in 22 cities" who had "pledged 1% of their 1936 incomes" to enable him to wage "the crusade for private property . . . , the crusade to make America a vigorously nationalistic country," he spoke assuredly of a

---

[2] Ward, *The Nation*, CXLIII, No. 2, 36; and Blackorby, p. 512.
[3] *New York Times*, July 21, 1936; and Harris, *Current History*, XLV, No. 1, 83.
[4] *Ibid.;* and Strack, *New Masses*, XX, No. 5, 7.
[5] *New York Times*, October 18, 19, 20.

"war chest of at least $1,500,000" (adding jauntily that forty of his backers were "wealthy New Yorkers, one of whom has a $280,000 yearly income").[6]

And so now the man who had roasted the rich in the Share-Our-Wealth Society would pander to his former enemy in a new movement to save capitalism from the scourge of collectivism. The "Nationalist Front Against Communism," or, as it was soon to be renamed, The Committee of One Million, was born at Smith's self-styled "mass meeting of New York and New Jersey patriotic societies." Despite the ballyhoo, fewer than six hundred people were attracted to New York City's massive Hippodrome to hear him shout for more than an hour about "The New Deal's Contribution to World Communism." After the speech, the press was informed that the idea for this new organization came from Gerald Smith's eleven-week tour of the country. When asked by a reporter if this tour were not part of his Union Party campaign, Smith replied, "I joined the Union Party only for a forum. What I am really interested in is forming this new force against Communism."[7]

The minister's Union Party allies reacted quickly, Coughlin, Lemke and Townsend each issuing statements disavowing any connection with Gerald L. K. Smith's new group, and in effect reading Smith out of the Union Party. Francis E. Townsend, particularly distraught by the action of a man he had befriended and taken into the councils of the pension movement, announced, "If the press reports concerning the fascist action of Gerald L. K. Smith are true, then I hereby disavow any connection that I may have had with Mr. Smith. . . . I am against fascism; it is un-American and smacks of dictator-like policies. . . . The Townsend Plan wants no part of a fascistic organization; there is no room for fascism in the traditions and heritage which we of America hold so dear."[8]

Thus ended Gerald L. K. Smith's adventure in Union Party politics. "No great movement has ever succeeded," he had once said, "unless it has deified some one man." And for Smith, any movement that he joined must deify none other than himself. With no thought for his fellow Unionites, he had struck off on his own, hoping to find success in a new venture that need not be shared with any rival leader. But the

[6] *Ibid.*

[7] *Ibid.;* and "Conning the News," *New Masses*, XXI, No. 5 (October 27, 1936), 9.

[8] *New York Times*, October 20, 21, November 1, 1936; *Current Biography*, 1943, pp. 708–09; "Conning the News," *New Masses*, XXI, No. 6 (November 3, 1936), 9; and "Last-Minute Squabbles Weaken Coalition of Messiahs," *Newsweek*, VIII, No. 18 (October 31, 1936), 9.

new organization was to prove a disappointment, and Smith was to make the news columns only once more in 1936. That was a brief item just before election day, reporting that the former Louisianan, returning to New Orleans to make a speech despite warnings by the Long machine, had been attacked and beaten by three men and had ended up in jail.[9]

Gerald L. K. Smith's bizarre activities were, of course, damaging to the Union cause. But at least the flare-up resulting in his expulsion from the party dissipated in a matter of days. In the case of Father Coughlin's problems with his superiors in the Catholic Church, the trouble lasted for weeks and was a continuing source of tension among party workers and Coughlin followers.

The radio priest's struggles with pro-Roosevelt clergy reflected but one aspect of the controversy within the Church over his campaign activities. Many Catholic clerics, quite unconcerned about the President's reelection prospects, were vitally concerned about Coughlin's effect on the image of the Church in America. They were aware that a growing number of Protestants, including a faculty member at the Concordia Lutheran Theological Seminary, were asserting publicly that "the voice behind that radio priest is the voice of his church," and aware that certain liberal publications, among them the *New Republic*, were suggesting that "the Union Party marks the deliberate entrance of the Roman Catholic Church into national politics. . . . The Vatican, leaning heavily for financial support on wealthy American Catholic families . . . is backing Coughlin because influential and wealthy Americans, such as Al Smith and John J. Raskob, think he can help them defeat Roosevelt." These alarmed clergy were convinced that something must be done about the Reverend Charles E. Coughlin.[10]

The first sign of pressures to muzzle Father Coughlin came in late July after his outburst at the Townsend convention. The priest's ecclesiastical superior, Bishop Gallagher, told newsmen, "I do not approve of the language Father Coughlin has used in expressing himself on the President. . . . He should have more respect. . . . I do not consider the President a Communist and it is not wise to call a man a liar because he may not agree with you." Within a week, Coughlin published "An Open Letter to The President" in *Social Justice,* meekly stating, "In the heat of civic interest . . . , in righteous anger . . . I used the word 'liar.' I now offer the President my sincerest apology."[11]

[9] Deutsch, *Saturday Evening Post,* CCVIII, No. 15, 27; and *New York Times,* October 24, 1936.
[10] *Ibid.,* August 2, 1936; and *New Republic,* LXXXVII, No. 1127, 265–66.
[11] *New York Times,* July 19, 21, 1936; and *Social Justice,* July 27, 1936.

In early August, Bishop Gallagher was in Rome, and the newspapers were full of rumors that he had been called to the Vatican to explain the radio priest's campaign antics. The Detroit Bishop and his traveling companion, Cleveland's Bishop Joseph Schrembs, denied the charges and even endorsed "Father Coughlin's fight for the preservation of the American democracy." Quickly making use of this new vote of confidence, the priest gleefully told a Massachusetts audience, "You see, despite the rumors, my Roman collar will not be consigned to the moth balls." But the jocularity was short-lived. Gallagher soon admitted that he had, indeed, discussed Coughlin with prelates in the Vatican, including Monsignor Giuseppe Pizzard, the Pope's closest political adviser. He pointedly remarked, "I, personally, would favor Mr. Roosevelt more than any other candidate at present," and revealed that "Bishop Schrembs and I . . . have been advised to cease talking about Father Coughlin." [12]

Any lingering doubts about the Vatican position on Coughlin were erased by an article in *L'Osservatore Romano* on September 2, 1936. The Vatican newspaper severely criticized the priest's political activities and his attacks on the President. When the former scoffed at "this one newspaper's opinion," the Vatican sent a note directly to all press organizations, reiterating in unusually sharp language the criticism of Coughlin and emphasizing that *L'Osservatore Romano* represented the official Vatican opinion on this issue. Many non-Catholics who had questioned the Church's policy toward Father Coughlin applauded this official reprimand. [13]

The volatile priest at first professed unconcern. He boarded the Italian liner *Rex* to greet Bishop Gallagher on his return from Rome. Perhaps the smooth-talking Coughlin was able to prevail on his superior to give him support; in any case, at a dockside interview, the Bishop told newsmen that "everything is hunky-dory in the Vatican. . . . Father Coughlin is an outstanding churchman and his voice . . . is the voice of God." Coughlin proceeded to Chicago, where he told a rally audience, "Don't let them deceive you by fake propaganda originating from Rome or anywhere else that the Vatican has cracked down on Bishop

[12] *New York Times*, August 2, 1936; *Minneapolis Star*, July 27, 1936; and *Time*, XXVIII, No. 7, 28–30.

[13] *New York Times*, September 3, 10, 1936; *New York Herald-Tribune*, September 10, 1936; and T.R.B., "Coughlin in the Papal Doghouse," *New Republic*, LXXXVIII, No. 1138 (September 23, 1936), 182–83. Another possible reason for Vatican action: angry reaction by Jews to Coughlin's late August remark about "Jewish traffickers in gold." The priest did not deal in anti-Semitism in the Union campaign, except for this one remark, in a Cleveland Speech. See *Newsweek*, VIII, No. 8, 12.

Gallagher or Father Coughlin. That's a lie! If they had cracked down, I wouldn't be here today."[14]

But the Bishop had got the message from Rome. Rapidly recovering from his confrontation with the persuasive Coughlin, within hours he was making an address filled with hostility for his famous subordinate. The Union Party, he pointed out, was in no way a Catholic party. The Union platform contained "dangerous" planks, particularly on Coughlin's favorite "money" question. Hitting harder, Bishop Gallagher termed FDR "much better prepared to work out problems than William Lemke," adding, "I am sure Father Coughlin thinks that if Lemke gets in he can control Lemke. Well, he couldn't control Roosevelt." In response to this slashing attack by his direct superior, Father Coughlin almost immediately softened his campaign against Roosevelt and the New Deal. Late September became the radio priest's time of indecision and inconsistency. The entire thrust of the Union Party attack was temporarily blunted, and Lemke was deeply disturbed.[15]

In October, as Coughlin grew bolder and renewed his reckless offensive against the Administration, the very fact that it had been possible even temporarily to silence him seemed the cue for clergymen, Catholic and non-Catholic, to assail him from all sides. The President's friends, such as Monsignor Ryan, were joined by other antagonists. Cincinnati's Archbishop John Timothy McNicholas, incensed over the priest's call to violence during a visit to his midwestern city, announced, "As the public and responsible teacher of morality in this community . . . , I cannot let pass the advocacy of the use of bullets and I condemn such remarks." South Dakota's Bishop Mahoney and Coughlin's old adversary, Boston's Cardinal O'Connell, joined the attack, Mahoney publicly calling him a "cultural vulgarian." The influential Catholic journal, *Commonweal*, underlined the clerical criticism, and the editors of the Protestant magazine, *The Christian Century*, commented, "A man has a right to make a fool of himself, but people don't have to listen. . . . Tune him out! He is through."[16]

Father Coughlin tried to ignore the attacks of these churchmen, but he could not ignore the mid-October visit to the United States by Eugenio Cardinal Pacelli, the Vatican Secretary of State. The news media were alive with rumors that Cardinal Pacelli's mission in Amer-

---

[14] "Vatican Voices," *Time*, XXVIII, No. 11 (September 14, 1936), 61–63.

[15] *New York Times*, September 15, 26, 1936.

[16] *Ibid.*, September 26, 1936; McCoy, p. 151; *Commonweal*, XXV, No. 2, 45; and "Father Coughlin Says The Last Word," *The Christian Century*, LIII, No. 41 (October 7, 1936), 1309–1310.

ica was to "do something about Coughlin." The radio priest's campaign briefly faltered once again: he canceled a Newark speech for no apparent reason and called off another because of "throat trouble." Around the same time he stated, "Roosevelt has done many things that are commendable. . . . If Lemke weren't in the field, I'd tell you to vote for Roosevelt." [17]

Coughlin recovered in time to end his Union Party effort with a fresh torrent of biting anti-New Deal rhetoric. But the problem of his relations with Church superiors clouded the issues and impaired his efforts right up to election eve. On October 30, Bishop Gallagher forced Coughlin to make a public apology for having called FDR a "scab President." Throughout the first three days of November the Bishop issued equivocal public statements about his controversial priest, on one occasion calling Coughlin "a national institution, invaluable to safeguarding genuine Americanism," and on another, implying that after election day, the priest would no longer be allowed to take an active part in politics.[18]

The pressure exerted on Father Coughlin by other churchmen, then, was clearly a second important reason why the Union alliance was experiencing heavy weather in the later stages of the campaign. A final source of major tension resulted from the partial defection of Dr. Francis E. Townsend.

The old doctor had been struggling with a series of unhappy developments during the late summer and early fall. In August, he was forced to oust both the Reverend Clinton Wunder, eastern regional director of his movement, and the southern regional director, Nathan Roberts, after these two men had bitterly denounced the endorsement of Lemke and complained about the role of Gerald L. K. Smith in the organization. Following their dismissal, Wunder and Roberts joined other disgruntled ex-Townsendites, led by the Reverend Alfred J. Wright, as plaintiffs in an unsuccessful suit asking the ouster of the doctor as President of the Townsend National Recovery Plan, Ltd., and demanding an audit of the corporation's books.[19]

At about this time, the old man's troubles were compounded by the poor showing of candidates he had endorsed in primary contests across

[17] *The Nation*, CXLIII, No. 16, 434; *New Masses*, XXI, No. 4, 9; and *New York Times*, October 10, 1936.

[18] *Ibid.*, November 1, 2, 3, 1936; "Father Coughlin's Friends," pp. 6–7; and General Jewish Council, *Father Coughlin: His "Facts" and Arguments* (New York: General Jewish Council, 1939), p. 7.

[19] *New York Times*, August 13, 25, 1936.

the country. The Kansas primary was the scene of a general rout of state Townsend forces, and pension promoters suffered bad beatings also in Idaho, Oklahoma, Washington, and Oregon. Only the victory of Charles O. Andrews — a man who advocated relief for the aged but would not commit himself to the Plan — in the Democratic primary for Senator in Florida, offset the downward trend of Townsend's fortunes in the political arena.[20]

In September and October, the physician started receiving disturbing reports about the reaction of his large California following to the Lemke candidacy. State Chairman Edward Margett forwarded the results of a presidential preference poll of fifty thousand California Townsendites, which showed 28 per cent for Roosevelt, 52 per cent for Landon, 4 per cent neutral and only 6 per cent favoring Lemke. When William Lemke failed to win a place on the ballots of several strong Townsendite states, Dr. Townsend decided to act.[21]

On October 7, he telegraphed Margett instructions to switch the California organization to the support of Landon. Townsend told the press, "I shall cast my vote for an untried man . . . in the hope that he may prove of greater value to the nation than the incumbent. . . . I do this because I will not be permitted to vote for Mr. Lemke, my choice for the office."[22]

Now the doctor initiated an energetic campaign to "support the lesser of the two evils." Rejecting as "utterly foolish and futile" the Union national chairman's suggestion that a write-in campaign for Lemke electors be launched in California, Townsend gradually widened his appeal for Landon support to all fourteen of the states in which Lemke's name would not appear on the ballot. "This is the only course for us to follow," he announced. "Lemke has my endorsement and I hope he will win, but remember, Roosevelt is our sworn enemy. . . . He must be beaten."[23]

Obviously, Francis E. Townsend's last-minute decision to back Landon as well as Lemke put further strains on the Union alliance.

By election eve, it was clear that the third party campaign was losing

[20] *Ibid.,* August 6, 23, 1936; "Pensions and Ballots," *Literary Digest,* 122, No. 8 (August 22, 1936), 6; and "Pension Senator," *Time,* XXVIII, No. 8 (August 24, 1936), 22.

[21] Baker to Farley, October 8, 1936, McAdoo Papers; and Henry B. R. Briggs to Farley, July 27, 1936, National Committee Correspondence.

[22] *New York Times,* October 8, 1936.

[23] *Ibid.,* October 8, 12, 26, 1936. Desperate for votes, Landon helped elicit this Townsend support by promising to meet the pension leader if elected. See *ibid.,* October 8 and November 3, 1936.

headway. Reports flowing into Democratic national headquarters revealed that in key Unionite areas, more and more voters were switching from Lemke to Roosevelt. Even the national preference polls, notoriously inaccurate in this election, reflected the decline in Union support. In the *Literary Digest* poll, Lemke's percentage of the straws fell steadily throughout October, and totaled but 2.7 per cent in the final report on October 31. The more trustworthy Gallup Poll gave the North Dakotan as much as 5 per cent of the total predicted vote in early September but charted a similar slump in subsequent weeks.[24]

As the fateful first Tuesday in November approached, newsmen who had once termed the Union appeal formidable now wrote of its dwindling power. The *New York Times's* Duncan Aikman suggested that while Lemke could have polled five million votes if election day had come earlier in the campaign, by mid-October he could be expected to receive three million at best. Other observers gave the third party candidate something less than two million votes and dismissed any possibility that he might carry even a single state. A widely reprinted cartoon on November 1 showed Lemke on a bedraggled horse stopped in its tracks, with a railbird describing his major party opponents: "They Went That Way."[25]

In the last week of October, Union headquarters in Chicago was still bravely claiming five to ten million votes and six to eight states for its nominee. But Coughlin and Lemke were more candid. The radio priest admitted that the ballot defeats in New York and California had not only ended any possibility of a Lemke victory, but his own prediction of nine million votes was "based upon returns from 48 states." Hailing a Landon bandwagon invisible to everyone else, Coughlin insisted that he had helped the GOP defeat Roosevelt. But in a moment of clear perception hours before the polls opened, he told reporters that "the National Union for Social Justice might have to be a martyr in this fall's election."[26]

[24] For Democratic campaign reports, see, for example, Keinath to Farley (Ottawa, Ohio), September 10, 1936, and Moore to Farley (Cleveland, Ohio), September 24, 1936, in National Committee Correspondence; "Reports of The Literary Digest's 1936 Presidential Poll," *Literary Digest*, CXXII, Nos. 10, 14, 15, 16, 17, 18 (September 5, October 3, 10, 17, 24, 31, 1936), 7–9 (in each issue); and report of the Gallup Poll in *Los Angeles Times* (September 20, 1936). The final report of the *Literary Digest* poll showed Lemke with 83,000 votes (55,000 of which were Democratic) compared with Landon's 1,290,000 and Roosevelt's 970,000.

[25] *New York Times,* October 18 and November 1, 1936; and Mitchell, *New Republic,* LXXXVIII, No. 1132, 10.

[26] *New Masses,* XXI, No. 7, 9; and *New York Times,* October 18, 30, 1936.

William Lemke also had to face reality. Although campaigning furiously to the very end, he no longer spoke of "carrying Ohio, all of New England, and most of the Middle-West"; he no longer even alluded to throwing the election into the House of Representatives. The best he could manage was the weakly defiant: "We've scared the two old parties to death." Late in the day Lemke even began to show grave concern about the one contest he had a chance to win, his congressional reelection race. Supporters in North Dakota, warning him that constituents were resentful over his lack of interest in the congressional election, called on him to come home for fence mending if he wanted to remain in the House of Representatives. Lemke obligingly returned to North Dakota in the final days of the campaign.[27]

On election eve, both Father Coughlin and Dr. Townsend delivered final radio appeals to the nation. Coughlin implored his listeners not to allow Franklin D. Roosevelt the opportunity to "sovietize" the United States. Townsend, in a rare oratorical display, proclaimed that "democratic government itself is at stake here."[28]

The campaign was at last over. Now the Union Party leaders had only to await the counting of the ballots. And all of them knew that the returns could bring but one result: crushing defeat.

[27] *Ibid.*, November 1, 1936; *Newsweek*, VIII, No. 16, 16; and *Newsweek*, VIII, No. 19, 9.
[28] *New York Times*, November 3, 1936.

PART VII

DEFEAT AND DISSOLUTION

The minority is now purely theoretical. We
have a one party system now. . . . Franklin
D. Roosevelt has more power than any man
ever had in history. . . . But this is not a
time for continuation of carping, criticizing,
or badgering. . . . If the people want these
things, as their votes indicate they do, let
them have them. — Charles E. Coughlin
(November 4, 1936)

20

Defeat

The headlines told the story. The day after the election, the *New York Times* announced: "Union Party Vote Far Below Expectations; William Lemke Makes Scarcely A Dent." Coughlin, Lemke, Smith, and Townsend had been inflationists in more than one sense in the 1936 campaign; they had grossly overestimated the size, or at least the political allegiance, of their followings. When all returns were in, Union candidate Lemke had polled only 892,378 votes—just under 2 per cent of the national total—and had not even come close to carrying any single state. He had been swept aside by the Unionites' hated enemy, Franklin D. Roosevelt, who scored the most one-sided victory to date in American political history. It was an awesome display of vote-getting appeal: the President's 27,751,597 votes dwarfed Landon's total of 16,679,583, and made a mockery of the new third party's efforts. FDR's electoral vote total of 523 was a record; he fell but eight votes shy of completely blanking his GOP opponent.[1]

When he first heard the results, Father Coughlin sat stunned in his Royal Oak office, the tears streaming down his cheeks. It was beyond comprehension. A few hours passed before he had sufficiently composed himself to issue a public statement: "President Roosevelt can be a dictator if he wants to; I hope that God will bless him and the Holy Ghost will inspire him not to misuse his power. . . . I expected that Roosevelt would be elected, but was surprised at the magnitude of the vote." Of course, Coughlin was taking liberties with the truth, for only

---

[1] *New York Times*, November 4, 1936; and Murray S. Stedman, Jr. and Susan W. Stedman, *Discontent At The Polls* (New York: Columbia University Press, 1950), pp. 34, 162.

a few minutes before the polls opened, he had maintained, "I am positive Mr. Roosevelt will not be re-elected." Yet in the aftermath of the landslide, all predictions could be forgotten.[2]

For a brief period, the radio priest regained his optimism. The National Union for Social Justice had fared better than the Republican Party, he told reporters, because "at least we are not bankrupt in intelligence." Indeed, in his most accurate prediction in months he said of the GOP: "They can never make a comeback under their present organization. . . . Rugged individualism will never return." Coughlin compared his NUSJ to boxer Joe Louis after the fight with Schmeling: "We took a thorough-going, good knockout for the count of 10, but there is still a possibility of a comeback. . . . What we have ahead of us now is a trip to the showers, and a new training camp for the comeback, if and when it is required. . . . If the Constitution of the United States is preserved, we have a chance."[3]

But three days later, after having studied the dimensions of his defeat, Charles E. Coughlin was in a state of deep depression. The National Union, he admitted to a radio audience, had been "thoroughly discredited by the recent election." While the movement would not die and would "live as long as the truth lives, because the 16 principles are immortal," it must follow in the future "a policy of silence. . . . It must become inactive." The priest acidly noted that "fewer than 10% of the membership had lived up to their promises to vote for the Union candidate." Without loyalty, said the founder, there could be no purpose in continuing. And so, with a flick of his hand, Father Coughlin disbanded his national organization.[4]

As for himself, the priest told newsmen, he would live up to a pre-election promise to retire if his campaign proved unsuccessful. In a dramatic farewell address to his radio following, he began, "I hereby withdraw from all radio activity in the best interests of all the people." And petulantly managing to turn both cheeks at once, he declared, "I love my country and my church too much to become a stumbling block to those who have failed to understand." In a wave of self-pity, he concluded: "A few hearts will be saddened, many others elated, a vast majority totally indifferent to my departure . . . , but I hold not even a small degree of animosity. Good by and God bless every one, friends and

[2] Kramer, *Harper's Magazine*, 191, No. 9, 390; "Prophets," *Newsweek*, VIII, No. 18 (November 14, 1936), 9; and *Detroit News*, November 4, 1936.

[3] *Ibid.;* "Third Parties," *Time*, XXVIII, No. 20 (November 16, 1936), 28; and *New York Times*, November 5, 1936.

[4] *Ibid.*, November 8, 1936; and *Social Justice*, November 16, 1936.

opponents. You are all friends tonight." If Coughlin's critics were un-impressed by this noble gesture of forgiveness of those whom he had been vilifying, the cleric's mail continued to pour in. It seemed clear that Father Coughlin still had his disciples, but it was equally clear that he considered the National Union for Social Justice and the Union Party personal disasters which must be permanently shelved.[5]

William Lemke's response was different. He shared Coughlin's initial despair over the returns but not his repudiation of the party. On election night, he defiantly told the newsmen, "We have no apologies. The Union Party was not defeated. We just lost the first skirmish. Right is never defeated—it may only be postponed."[6]

The candidate was confused and unhappy over the size of his vote. "I don't know how many people told me that they voted for me and then I found out that I had no votes at all in their precincts." Yet he insisted that his party would persevere and even talked of winning fifteen to twenty Congressional seats in 1938 and "making a sweep in 1940." Publicly he avowed, "We are the only ones offering the solution for the new America coming"; privately he confided to friends that his own victory in the North Dakota congressional race provided a platform from which to continue to lead and promote a potentially powerful third force.[7]

Party Chairman John Nystul echoed Lemke's words. "The party made tremendous strides in the few months of its existence," Nystul insisted, "and it did so entirely without the help of the 'big money' that supports the other major parties. . . . Even the size of the vote has been a tremendous gratification to me and the other Union executives and managers."[8]

But those other founders of the party were not available for comment. Gerald L. K. Smith, just released from a New Orleans jail, was silent. Dr. Francis E. Townsend declined to make a public statement on the Lemke vote, content merely to predict gains for his plan in Congress as a result of the election of "66 Representatives favorable to old age pensions." Yet Townsend was obviously unhappy about his Union Party experience. He announced that Edward J. Margett, a strong supporter

[5] New York Times, November 8, 15; "Father Coughlin Commits Hara-Kiri," The Nation, 143, No. 20 (November 14, 1936), 563; and "The Total Eclipse of Father Coughlin," The Christian Century, LII, No. 47 (November 18, 1936), 1517.

[6] Statement by William Lemke, November 3, 1936, copy in Lemke Papers.

[7] Minutes of National Union Party Conference, December 19, 1936, copy in ibid.; and New York Times, November 19, 1936.

[8] The Leader, November 12, 1936.

On the day after the election, Smith was arrested in New Orleans on charges of using obscene language, disturbing the peace, and reviling police. He declined parole and remained in jail for two hours. *Wide World*

of FDR and the most prominent man in the movement opposing the endorsement of Lemke and the coalition with Coughlin and Smith, had agreed to leave California and come to Chicago to run the new national headquarters of the Townsend Plan. There would be no third party adventures for the old doctor in the near future.[9]

Of all the original allies, then, only William Lemke — acting more on blind hope than anything else — planned to remain active in the party after the debacle of November, 1936. The disastrous electoral defeat not only had blasted the dreams of the radical leaders, it had all but destroyed their new third party. How could they have been so wrong? Was there anything in the returns to buoy their flagging spirits?

The answer to the last question was an emphatic "no." To review the presidential vote was to see at once that the Union candidate ran poorly everywhere. Only in New Hampshire did the total of Lemke and Landon ballots barely equal Roosevelt's, and obviously not every Union voter would have gone to the Republican had not the new party been in the field. As Farley had guessed, Lemke's largest state vote, 132,212, came in Ohio; his best showing, 13 per cent of the presidential totals, predict-

[9] *New York Times*, November 5, 6, and 15; and *Time*, XXVIII, No. 20, 28.

ably came in his home base of North Dakota, the only state in which he controlled over 7 per cent of the vote. His next strongest showings were in Minnesota, Massachusetts and Rhode Island, with 6.5 per cent; in Oregon, 5.5 per cent; and Ohio, Wisconsin, Illinois, Pennsylvania and Michigan, where he won between 4 and 4.8 per cent of the total.[10]

State by state, with those starred in which the candidate was not on the ballot, this is how William Lemke fared:

	Roosevelt	Landon	Lemke
Alabama	238,195	35,358	549
Arizona	86,722	33,433	3,307
*Arkansas	146,765	32,039	4
*California	1,766,836	836,431	
Colorado	295,081	181,267	9,962
Connecticut	382,129	278,685	21,805
Delaware	69,702	54,014	442
*Florida	249,117	78,248	
Georgia	255,364	36,942	141
Idaho	125,683	66,256	7,684
Illinois	2,282,999	1,570,393	89,439
Indiana	943,974	691,570	19,407
Iowa	621,756	487,977	29,687
*Kansas	464,520	397,727	494
Kentucky	541,944	369,702	12,501
*Louisiana	292,894	36,791	
Maine	126,333	168,823	7,581
*Maryland	389,612	231,435	
Massachusetts	942,716	768,613	118,639
Michigan	1,016,794	699,733	75,795
Minnesota	698,811	350,461	74,296
*Mississippi	157,318	4,435	
Missouri	1,111,403	697,891	14,630
Montana	159,690	63,598	5,549
Nebraska	347,454	248,731	12,847
*Nevada	31,925	11,923	
New Hampshire	108,460	104,642	4,819
New Jersey	1,083,549	719,421	9,405
New Mexico	105,838	61,710	924
*New York	3,293,222	2,180,670	
*North Carolina	616,141	223,283	2
North Dakota	163,148	72,751	36,708

(Continued on page 268)

[10] Stedman, Jr., and Stedman, p. 34. No Union candidate for state or local offices was elected. Lemke, endorsed by the Republican Party as well as the Nonpartisan League, was re-elected to Congress from North Dakota along with Usher Burdick, the two men winning their races easily. See Masters, p. 293; and Blackorby, p. 520.

	Roosevelt	Landon	Lemke
Ohio	1,747,122	1,127,709	132,212
*Oklahoma	501,069	245,122	
Oregon	266,733	122,706	21,831
Pennsylvania	2,353,788	1,690,300	67,467
Rhode Island	165,238	125,031	19,569
*South Carolina	113,791	1,646	
South Dakota	160,137	125,977	10,338
Tennessee	327,083	146,516	296
Texas	734,485	103,874	3,281
Utah	150,246	64,555	1,121
*Vermont	26,124	81,023	
Virginia	234,980	98,366	233
Washington	459,579	206,982	17,463
*West Virginia	502,582	325,358	
Wisconsin	802,984	380,828	60,297
Wyoming	62,624	38,739	1,653
Totals	27,751,597	16,679,583	892,378 [11]

The total and distribution of the Lemke vote tells a great deal about the appeal of the Union Party. On the most superficial level of analysis, it is clear that the Unionites, by establishing themselves as the predominant "third" party in the United States in 1936, were recipients of the protest vote always reserved in any major election for a strong but peripheral political organization. Lemke recorded more than four times the 188,000 votes given the next most popular minor party candidate, Socialist Norman Thomas. Yet Thomas, running in 1932 as the leading minor party aspirant, had polled 873,000 votes, just short of the Union figure for 1936 and an even larger percentage of the total vote. In Wisconsin, Oregon and several other states, the figures for Lemke in 1936 correspond with those for Thomas in 1932.[12]

But if the vote of protest was an obvious factor in the Union appeal, there is lively controversy concerning the economic, ethnic, and religious components of that vote, while hovering behind all attempts to categorize it is the complex of factors which weakened the Union cause late in the campaign, thus making the Lemke totals only a shadow of what they might have been.

Does, for example, the Union vote belong directly in that stream of

[11] Edgar Eugene Robinson, The Presidential Vote: 1936 (Stanford, California: Stanford University Press, 1937), pp. 3–91.

[12] Harry Hansen (ed.), The World Almanac, 1962 (New York: New York World-Telegram and The Sun, 1962), pp. 418–46; and Richard M. Scammon, America at the Polls: A Handbook of American Presidential Election Statistics, 1920–1964 (Pittsburgh: University of Pittsburgh Press, 1965), pp. 337–38, 371–72, 503–05.

farmer and labor parties whose history traces back to the nineteenth century? While there is no doubt that a significant ideological tie bound Coughlin, Lemke, and to a certain extent, Smith, to the radicals of an earlier period, there is nonetheless only scanty evidence in the 1936 returns to document this connection. For Lemke received fewer than one-quarter of a million votes in the farm districts of twenty-four middle western states, areas in which the old radicals had shown their strength. He won only a handful of votes in the South, where the Populists had been powerful (but, of course, difficulties with the ballot in this region render the comparison less significant). Only in North Dakota, Minnesota, Wisconsin, Oregon, South Dakota, and Iowa is there even a slim correlation between the Union record in 1936 and the Populist vote in 1892. This cannot be the single key to the meaning of the Union Party.[13]

The case for Unionites as isolationists is a stronger one. In *The Future of American Politics*, Samuel Lubell argues that foreign policy rather than economics explains the Lemke record, for in the Union Party one can see the first crack in the leftist-isolationist alliance which created the Wisconsin Progressives and Minnesota Farmer-Laborites. Tracing the origins of the Union vote, he shows that outside of North Dakota, Lemke got more than 10 per cent of the presidential vote in thirty-nine counties, twenty-one of which had a Catholic majority. In twenty-eight of these thirty-nine counties, the predominant nationality was German. The four cities in which Lemke received more than 5 per cent of the vote — St. Paul, Dubuque, Boston and Cincinnati — were all heavily German and Irish Catholic. Lubell attributes the Union vote to the Anglophobia of isolationists who feared that Roosevelt would lead the United States into war against Germany and on the side of Ireland's old antagonist, Great Britain.[14]

This provocative thesis has several shortcomings. First, it overlooks the relatively strong third party performance in several western states —

[13] Murray S. Stedman, Jr. and Victor Ferkiss have tied the Unionites to the Farmer-Labor tradition. See, particularly, Stedman, Jr. and Stedman, p. 52. Nick Arthur Masters utilizes scattergrams to compare Union and Populist votes, finding only a slight correlation of between 2 per cent and 10 per cent. See Masters, pp. 296–300, and *New York Times*, November 5, 1936. Michael Paul Rogin's thorough study of northwestern voting patterns does reveal a relatively high correlation coefficient between the likely Populist vote in North Dakota and the Union vote. He attributes this to the "social support" for an agrarian protest leader and not the "authoritarian character" of the party, a point essential to his thesis that Populism was a non-authoritarian radical movement. See Rogin, pp. 131–33.

[14] Lubell, pp. 150–54.

Oregon, Washington, and Idaho—where Townsend Plan members were the most vociferous Lemkeites and ethnic bias was absent. In addition, it overemphasizes foreign policy as a determinant in 1936, a year in which it was not at all clear that the New Deal was aligned with the British against the Germans in a struggle for Europe; indeed, the inevitability of such a struggle was anything but certain at the time. A review of the North Dakota returns, which show Lemke running strongest in the northwestern sections and weakest in the northeastern, heavily Germanic counties, suggests that isolationism was not the important factor in the state friendliest to Unionites. A review of reports from Minnesota, where the German-American population was pictured as badly divided on the Lemke candidacy, with Catholics supporting him but Lutherans in bitter opposition, also suggests other elements at work in the data on which Lubell built his case. Finally, a review of the isolationist vote in 1940, in which a state with a large Germanic population such as North Dakota would give President Roosevelt only 44 per cent of its vote as opposed to the 69 per cent it delivered in 1936, suggests that the year of the Union Party was simply not the year of the real break in the ethnic-isolationist vote. That leading isolationists, such as Senator Gerald P. Nye, refused to support the new party simply underlines the fact.[15]

More important than any other consideration, however, in analyzing the Lubell thesis is the nature of the Union campaign. The new party's leaders simply did not concentrate on isolationist themes. They discussed the evils of international banking, of course, and on a few occasions hinted that election of either major party candidate would lead to war to protect the bankers. But the main thrust of the argument was aimed at domestic issues: the cruel Depression caused by ruthless Wall Streeters abetted by FDR and his Eastern, intellectual Brain Trust and the foolproof solutions offered by the radicals themselves. If those who voted for Lemke did so because of an isolationist impulse, they must have been prophets. Lemke, Coughlin and Smith did become isolationists years after their Union adventure, but in 1936 they were concerned with a different order of problem.

[15] Blackorby, pp. 515–20; John F. Wilde to Harry Peterson (St. Paul, Minnesota), August 22, 1936, Williams Papers; Rogin, pp. 103, 131; Edward C. Blackorby, "William Lemke: Agrarian Radical and Union Party Presidential Candidate," *Mississippi Valley Historical Review*, XLIX, No. 1 (June, 1962), 80; and Bean, pp. 96–101, 195. Isolationist ex-Mayor Thompson did lead the Union ticket in Illinois, with over 128,000 votes, but this was surely due as much to his familiar name as his peculiar "program." See *Illinois Blue Book*, 1937–1938, p. 672.

If foreign policy was not, then, at the heart of the Union vote, why the numbers of German and Irish-Americans backing Lemke? Perhaps the answer involves a consideration of American xenophobia, which, as Edward A. Shils has pointed out, is a complicated affair. It seems to consist of a violent denial of the value of being foreign and at the same time a lingering attachment to what is still foreign; it is hatred of the alien coupled with a persisting attachment to the country of origin. And so the Irish or German American can gratify his attachment to the European homeland through an Anglophobia which need have nothing to do with foreign policy, for it can be directed against Americans of English origin. Indeed, if one of the problems plaguing the hyphenate Americans is a chronic insecurity over the degree of assimilation achieved in the polyglot American milieu, then anger at Americans of English origin can serve a dual purpose—providing a scapegoat for frustrations in social and economic relationships while at the same time expiating any lingering guilt attached to leaving the homeland. Thus, the Irish and German vote for Lemke can be seen as a response to the Union leaders attack on the real hidden enemy: the Anglicized Wall Streeters, Brain Trusters and Ivy Leaguers.[16]

This analysis could also modify the claims of those theorists who hold that the third party appeal was directed primarily to the Catholic vote. For if ethnic as well as religious factors steered American Catholics into the new party, then the strong correlation between Catholic presence and Union strength in certain districts of Massachusetts, Rhode Island, Ohio, and Pennsylvania has a different meaning.[17]

It is indisputable that Catholicism played an important role in shaping Union fortunes. Reports from Pennsylvania that avowedly anti-Catholic Townsendites were deserting Lemke because they feared his domination by a priest left no room for doubt that Father Coughlin's powerful personality had injected a religious theme that affected many of the dissident elements in the Union alliance. Indeed, Democratic workers frequently sent national headquarters the cheery news that Roosevelt was picking up strength among radical Protestants who "could not stomach" the political priest. But was the Union Party really a Catholic Party? The third party's appeal to non-Catholic voters in areas of Oregon, Wisconsin, North Dakota, and other states where agrarian and

[16] Shils, pp. 82–83.
[17] For the views of one political scientist who regards the Union Party as a primarily Catholic organization see Masters, pp. 292–310. But Rogin, p. 103, demonstrates the lack of Catholic support in Wisconsin.

old age pressure politics were operating, the well-advertised opposition to the party by most influential Catholic leaders as well as the suggestive ethnic component in the Presidential vote, is all evidence to the contrary.[18]

Each of the claims made about the Union Party appeal is, however, at least partially valid. For the disparate radical leadership was casting a wide net among angry and frustrated Americans who might seek to solve their depression-bred woes in one stroke. The German and Irish Catholic supporters of Coughlin, the agrarian radicals of the Midwest who looked to William Lemke as their champion, the old people who pinned their hopes on Dr. Townsend and his plan, the poor-white southern farmers who had once followed Huey Long, were all part of that consensus of despair which the Union organizers dreamed of making. In the end, the election returns indicated that the party's appeal was most successful among the Coughlin following, but there was evidence that some Townsend and Lemke backers also had joined the abortive crusade. Still, the cold figures of the presidential race could never be an accurate thermometer of the intense heat that these radicals had generated earlier in the election year. The problems of financial backing and ballot placement, of internal jealousies and external pressures, of amateurs battling the shrewd professionals in the other parties, of an uninspiring candidate facing a magnetic President, of irresponsible leaders failing to sense the conservative temper of the public, all conspired to emasculate the Union appeal and by November to turn what seemed certain to be a powerful performance at the polls into a laughable charade. The party had been trounced, but the postelection headlines would never tell the full story. They were enough only to spell the end for the Union Party of 1936.[19]

---

[18] For reports on anti-Catholicism in Union ranks see, for example, Charlotte F. Jones to Lemke (Philadelphia, Pa.), February 15, 1937, Lemke Papers; and Kloeb to Farley (Cleveland, Ohio), September 4, 1936, National Committee Correspondence. That most Catholic clergy opposed Coughlin has not been disputed, one priest writing the White House following the election about "the 103 of 106 Bishops in the U.S." who voted for FDR. Quoted in Shenton, *Political Science Quarterly*, LXXIII, No. 3, 367.

[19] Anthony Downs has described the powerful argument in a two-party democracy against "wasting" a vote on a party without chance of success. This was another deadly problem for the Unionites. Anthony Downs, *An Economic Theory of Democracy* (New York: Harper & Row, 1957), p. 48.

21

The Death of the Party

Only William Lemke was interested in keeping the party alive after its black Tuesday at the polls. The only real professional in the leadership quartet, this rugged veteran of the political wars was best prepared to weather the disappointment which came with disastrous defeat. Late in the campaign he had told a newsman that if the party was badly beaten, Father Coughlin would reject it and he and his associates would fall heir to the machinery. In one of the rare moments of candor during that trying autumn, he had added the hopeful thought that the party would then be democratized and transformed into a genuine mass movement.[1]

Lemke's first prediction was accurate. For while Coughlin announced soon after the election that "we are going forward. . . . We are planning to devote our entire energies toward the end of building a greater and stronger Union Party in the future," the priest had no intention of flailing what he now considered a dead horse. Soon indignant friends were writing to Lemke about Coughlin's public statements on the subject: that the Union cause was hopeless and that all politicians, "good and bad," were the same. But the Congressman refused to rebuke the priest publicly. He explained that it was not necessary to read Coughlin out of the party officially; the cleric was not interested and the party machinery had fallen to him by default. By 1937, Union Party stationery was carrying the legend "Founded by William Lemke" under the organization's name.[2]

[1] Mitchell, *New Republic*, LXXXVIII, No. 1132, 10.

[2] *The Leader*, November 12, 1936; Joseph M. Hefferman to Lemke, October 4, 1938, Lemke to Hefferman, November 11, 1938, and Backus to Lemke, December 21, 1937, Lemke Papers.

Once he had secured total control, Lemke moved quickly to build the much needed grass roots structure. With National Chairman John Nystul, he proposed the formation of a National Federation of Union Party Clubs and spoke hopefully of establishing a club in every rural community and every city precinct and eventually organizing Congressional district councils and state-area boards. His hope was that large numbers of flourishing clubs could remedy the fatal flaws in the 1936 party—lack of financial support and failure to enlist local candidates and workers.[3]

The drive to establish the Union Clubs was kicked off at a National Conference of the Union Party, convening in Chicago on December 19, 1936. Delegates from fourteen states (all in the midwest except for California, Maryland, and Florida) heard Lemke report that the party's national headquarters would be maintained in Chicago. Nystul would stay on as chairman, dividing his time between Chicago and his Fargo, North Dakota, home and business. State chairmen were appointed for a number of eastern and midwestern states, and there were lively discussions of ways and means of organizing youth and women, as well as wiping out the $6,400 campaign deficit. It was clear that the leaders were putting their hopes on the formation of local clubs.[4]

But these hopes would never materialize. Only a handful of Union Clubs were formed, most of them short-lived. The party remained little more than a national headquarters with no national substructure. Lemke was to learn the truth of the oft-quoted remark of Theodore Roosevelt after the defeat of his more powerful third party in 1912: "You can't hold a party like the Progressive party together. There are no loaves and fishes." Without the promise of patronage, there was no incentive for local support. The Congressman soon admitted, in a letter to an Arizona follower, that "the Union Party has no organizers and each state must take care of itself. . . . No one has volunteered and the national headquarters has no funds for organizers."[5]

Like a drowning man grasping wildly for any straw of hope, Lemke tried to retain a cheerful façade by talking of a "merger of the various liberal factions in the country" into his party and even promising a national convention in 1940. He counseled supporters to "put up a full

[3] John Nystul to All Charter Members of the Union Party (Circular Letter), December 8, 1936, *ibid.*

[4] Minutes of the 1936 National Conference of the Union Party, December 19, 1936, *ibid.;* and *New York Times*, December 20, 1936.

[5] Henry F. Pringle, *Theodore Roosevelt* (New York: Harcourt, Brace and Company, 1956), p. 400; and Lemke to W. S. Young, April 4, 1938, Lemke Papers.

ticket in 1938 and make a real fight" but cautioned that the national party could not help state and local members who took this advice.[6]

There was no chance of survival. Facts are more important than dreams, and the facts were that both party name and existing state and local machinery lay subject to capture by anyone who wished to seize it. In North Dakota, William Langer "stole" the Union Party from Lemke himself by filing "dummies" on the party ticket in 1938; in Illinois, various Nazi groups took over local party units and used the Union name in distributing anti-Semitic literature. While the organization was dismembered, national headquarters could only stand helplessly by.[7]

The death blow for the Union Party was delivered by that old bugaboo, insolvency. By January, 1938, Vice-chairman Clyde Backus wrote Lemke that "we have pawned everything we had and borrowed from the loan sharks to keep this thing alive." He reported that the national office could no longer afford a stenographer and was having trouble meeting rent payments. It could not even afford postage to answer mail. Lemke tried to help out by sending five hundred copies of his inflationist tract, *You and Your Money*, to national headquarters. But the book had never been very popular, and the skeleton staff was unable to raise any money through its sale. Informed of this, the "founder" wrote, "I sincerely hope that there is a brighter side to the future of the organization. Personally I went the limit myself."[8]

By late 1938, it was clear that the end was near. John Nystul, recently recovered from a nervous breakdown and having exhausted his personal funds, wrote a troubled letter to Lemke: "It is my judgment that immediate steps should be taken to close party headquarters. . . . If we continue, the deficit will only steadily rise." Within months, the Chicago office was shut down.[9]

William Lemke was now resigned to the death of his party. At long last he had learned the painful lesson that organizing a successful third party in a state such as North Dakota was vastly different from trying to do the same on a national scale. He finally was forced to agree with Theodore Roosevelt, who had instructed his followers that beaten insurgents must always return to the major party. He wrote to one

[6] Lemke to D. A. Sherman, January 22, 1938, and Lemke to Fullerton Brown, December 27, 1937, *ibid.*

[7] Lemke to H. W. Rosevold, August 16, 1938, and Lemke to Myrtle Ellsworth, October 22, 1937, *ibid.*, and Blackorby, p. 520.

[8] Backus to Lemke, January 28, 1936, and Lemke to Backus, February 2, 1936, *ibid.*

[9] M. Voxland to Lemke, February 28, 1938, Nystul to Lemke, November 3, 1938, Nystul to Lemke, March 3, 1939, and Lemke to Nystul, March 8, 1939, *ibid.*

friend, "When you have had the experience I have had trying to organize new parties, you will be satisfied to stick to the same 87 varieties we now have." He told another, "The truth is that the liberals must get together under one of the existing parties." Lemke regretfully closed the books on the Union Party and rejoined the ranks of the Republicans.[10]

The party was declared officially dead in 1939, but Lemke was burying a long-dead corpse. The Union Party really had died when the radicals' bid for power had been so dismally unsuccessful in the election of 1936.

[10] Lemke to John D. Stinger, September 29, 1938, and Lemke to Hefferman, May 13, 1938, *ibid.*

22

The Later Years

For the four men whose lives and hopes had fused briefly in the Union Party, there would never be a time like 1936. But such were their ambitions and persuasive powers, their sense of commitment or their drive for fame, that none of them could retire from the scene or renounce their roles as social and political activists.

Their later careers would provide a striking symmetry with the parts they had played in 1936 and earlier. The pattern had been established long before the birth of their party: two of the men had been leaders in search of movements, the other two had been both symbol and organizer of well-established interest groups with deep roots in the socio-economic conditions of the times. After the Union alliance was dissolved, Coughlin and Smith continued to scheme for power through demagoguery; Lemke and Townsend reverted to the sincere, if radical, reformers that they had been before.

Father Coughlin found that he could not keep his promise to "retire in obscurity if Lemke loses." After an abortive effort to propound a new sixteen-point program for something he called "neighborhood Social Justice Councils," the priest finally allowed his National Union for Social Justice to die, letting it lie dormant until 1944, at which time it was formally disbanded. But he could not stay away from his radio audience, where the bitter people who were his hard core followers awaited his return, unchastened by the Union Party disaster.[1]

[1] Newton, *The Southwestern Social Science Quarterly*, 41, No. 3, 348–49; and Charles J. Tull, *Father Coughlin and the New Deal* (Syracuse, N.Y.: Syracuse University Press, 1965), pp. 177–188. Mr. Tull's book is a slightly expanded version of his dissertation, with the new material on Coughlin's career after 1936. See pp. 173–238.

On January 1, 1937, after a "retirement" of only six weeks, Coughlin delivered a New Year's radio message, hinting that if enough people wanted him to return to the air on a weekly basis, he might do so. On January 18, he promised to return if the circulation of *Social Justice* (which had continued publication without interruption) was built from 600,000 to 1,250,000. On January 24, despite the fact that his newspaper's circulation still stood far below one million, he was back on the nationwide hookup.[2]

Those who heard his mellow voice that day were told of the death of Coughlin's friend, benefactor, and ecclesiastical superior, Bishop Michael G. Gallagher. The Bishop's last request before he died on January 20, Coughlin told his forty-three-station audience, was that the radio priest return to the microphone. But if his superior's demise provided the impetus for a new radio career, it also meant trouble for the controversial cleric from Royal Oak. The Most Reverend Edward Mooney, new Archbishop of Detroit, was, unlike his predecessor, a man with little sympathy for Coughlin's causes. When Coughlin, attempting to aid Henry Ford in his battle against auto industry unionization, accused the CIO of "Communist-domination" and tried to establish a rival "Christian" union, Archbishop Mooney angrily cracked down. In the October 1937 issue of *Michigan Catholic*, the Archbishop scolded the priest for his language, took issue with his reasoning, and disclosed that he had refused to allow Coughlin to publish a rebuttal. The radio priest cancelled his season of broadcasts and complained through a spokesman that he preferred silence to censorship.[3]

But public silence had always been intolerable for this man, and he continued to communicate with his national flock through *Social Justice*. Both his ideas and his plans grew blacker with the passing months. In November, 1937, he issued a vicious attack on democracy, calling it "the new king set upon the throne . . . , the magic of numbers through which the majority shall prevail." Early the next summer he announced formation of a new organization to combat the "Red menace," to be called the Christian Front Against Communism. He was moving ever closer now to the theories and tactics of contemporary European fascists: using the threat of Communism as an excuse for rejecting democracy and writing off certain races and religions as "dangerous" to the American state.[4]

    [2] *Social Justice*, January 18, February 1, 1937.
    [3] *Ibid.;* George Seldes, *Facts and Fascism* (New York: New Union Press, 1943), pp. 129–30; *New York Times*, October 8, 1937; and "Coughlin Silenced," *Time*, XXX, No. 16 (October 18, 1937), 52.
    [4] Chase, Jr., p. 93; *Social Justice*, July 25, 1938; and Ferkiss, pp. 250–52.

As his ideology became more totalitarian, his audience slowly changed. In 1934, it was estimated that his following was 65 per cent non-Catholic and that many liberals and radicals of Protestant and Jewish faith were regular listeners. His behavior during the Union campaign led to the departure of many of these supporters, and the creation of the Christian Front narrowed his following even more. Of the 1,200 members enlisted in his new movement — in cells of twenty-five — most were young, unemployed Irish-Americans in the big eastern and mid-western cities. He decided to give these angry and frustrated young men a familiar scapegoat: the Jews. At long last, the ancient symbols of anti-Semitism would become a major weapon in this modern American demagogue's armory.[5]

In January, 1938, Father Coughlin suddenly announced the resumption of his radio series. Whether he was braving the wrath of his superior or accepting Mooney's supervision remained unclear, but by the spring his sermons were setting new standards for defamation of character. He began attacking bankers, Communists and New Dealers with unmistakably Jewish names. In July, *Social Justice* began printing *The Protocols of the Elders of Zion*, a notorious anti-Jewish forgery detailing an alleged "international Jewish conspiracy." Then, on November 20, in a remarkable radio address, he launched a slashing, full-scale, anti-Semitic crusade, accusing the Jews not only of devising Communism but also of imposing it on Russia, and excusing Nazism as an understandable effort to block the Jewish-Communist plan for subjugating Germany.[6]

Now it became open season on all things Jewish. Coughlin attacked Jews for believing they were the chosen people, for having a double-standard toward non-Jews, for thinking of themselves as messiahs. He accused them of starting Freemasonry and the French Revolution, of destroying medieval Christian civilization and of threatening modern Christianity. Echoing an earlier theme, he played most heavily on the contradictory notion that Jews were both international bankers (decadent, evil capitalists) and international Communists. He warned that if Jews did not "change their ways," they would get no sympathy for conditions in Hitler's Germany. Indeed, he praised the "social justice" dispensed by the Third Reich and his newspaper began to reprint speeches of Paul Josef Goebbels, distributed by the Nazi propaganda agency, the World Press Service.[7]

[5] Leighton (ed.), pp. 249–50; and Kramer, *Harper's*, CLXXXIII, No. 9, 384.

[6] General Jewish Council, pp. 5–8; and Donald S. Strong, *Organized Anti-Semitism In America* (Washington, D.C.: American Council on Public Affairs, 1941), pp. 57–59.

[7] *Social Justice*, March 27, April 3, 1939; and Masters, pp. 152–70.

In 1939, Father Coughlin turned full attention to "the problem of the American Jews." He was instrumental in setting up a "Christian Index," through which Jewish merchants in New York City were boycotted. Young toughs bragging of their membership in the Christian Front incited fights with teen-age Jews and destroyed stores and other property owned by Jews in a series of incidents in Boston and New York. These activities evoked from all sides bitter counterattacks upon the radio priest. The General Jewish Council published several emotion-charged works repudiating Coughlin and his "facts." Chicago's Cardinal Mundelein and other prominent members of the Catholic clergy publicly rebuked him, but the cleric cleverly dissociated himself officially from the Christian Front by claiming that as merely a "friend and counsellor" of the movement, he could not be held accountable for any acts of violence attributed to it.[8]

Why Charles E. Coughlin turned to virulent anti-Semitism in 1938 remains a mystery. In his earlier career as a mass leader, only very infrequently had he traded on racial or religious bigotry of any kind. Perhaps the Nazi literature had finally convinced him of the "Jewish threat." But it is more likely that the radio priest, always a man with his eye on the main chance, hoped to find in a new anti-Semitic crusade a way of recouping his losses from the Union Party fiasco and a way of returning to the national spotlight. Whatever the motive, he must have been satisfied with the new campaign. The year 1938 proved one of his best ever in terms of finances, with $574,416 collected from devoted followers. While his radio audience of 3.5 million was less than half the size it had been in 1935, it was apparently composed of true believers. A Gallup Poll in January, 1939, revealed that almost 70 per cent of the priest's weekly listeners agreed with everything he said.[9]

In mid-1939, Father Coughlin renewed his call for the establishment of a "corporate state" in America, devoting several broadcasts to describing a new system of government based on vocational representation. This quasi-fascistic plan took on a new dimension with the outbreak of war in Europe. The priest pictured Hitler's Germany as "an innocent victim of a sacred war declared against her nine years ago by the Jews," and railed against intervention by the United States on the side

[8] *Ibid.*, pp. 174–80; *New York Times*, August 16, 1939; General Jewish Council, pp. 5–59; and *Social Justice*, August 14, 1939.

[9] Francis Biddle, *The Fear of Freedom* (Garden City, N.Y.: Doubleday & Company, 1952), p. 79; Morris Schonbach, "Native Fascism During the 1930's and 1940's: A Study of Its Roots, its Growth, and its Decline" (unpublished Ph.D. dissertation, Department of History, University of California at Los Angeles, 1958), pp. 292–93; and Spivak, p. 160.

of "the Communists" and the British bankers. He was popular at Fritz Kuhn's German-American Bund meetings, although he roundly denied rumors that his Christian Front would be merged with the Bund. But the Nazi newspaper, *Der Stuermer*, praised Coughlin as "one of the few men in the United States who has the courage to speak his conviction that National Socialism is right." [10]

As the United States moved closer to entry into World War II, the priest retreated to an increasingly hysterical isolationism. One day he would endorse "traditional American neutrality"; a short time later he would scoff at the idea of international law — calling it a "ghost which no one obeys." He supported Japan's bid for a "Monroe Doctrine" for Asia and applauded the German invasion of the Soviet Union as "the first strike in the holy war on Communism." Counseling Americans to leave the Axis powers alone, he lauded the work of the America First Committee. [11]

Even after Pearl Harbor, Coughlin continued to side with those nations who were now the enemy. His arguments constituted a potpourri of all the fantasies he had entertained at one time or another: the war had been caused by a British-Jewish-Roosevelt conspiracy; Germany and Italy were innocent "have-not" nations engaged in a struggle with the antichrists; America was fighting only to save Britain and Britain was going Communist; Roosevelt was "run by Jews," and the increased taxes he ordered were not for defense but to solidify Jewish power and to build the New Deal bureaucracy. But now the priest had gone too far. Several members of his Christian Front were arrested for trying to overthrow the government. In April, 1942, Attorney General Francis Biddle charged *Social Justice* with a violation of the Espionage Act, and Postmaster General Frank Walker simultaneously barred it from the mails. Coughlin discovered that even his most loyal followers were finally turning away, and an appeal for funds brought in only a trickle of money. With radio stations reluctant to deal with a man opposing the war effort and giving aid and comfort to the enemy, the end of the radio priest's spectacular career was near. [12]

It was an order from a church superior that finally silenced the golden voice. Attorney General Biddle sent an emissary to Archbishop Mooney

[10] Shenton, *Political Science Quarterly*, LXXIII, No. 3, 372; McCarten, *American Mercury*, XLVII, No. 186, 140; William C. Kernan, *The Ghost of Royal Oak* (New York: Free Speech Forum, 1940), p. 22; and *New York Times*, January 15, 1940.

[11] Ferkiss, pp. 242–45, 351–60; and *Social Justice*, November 11, 1940.

[12] *Social Justice*, December 8, 22, 1941, February 9, 1942; and Leighton (ed.), pp. 253–55.

with word that the only alternative to a demoralizing sedition trial would be the suppression of Coughlin's activities. In mid-1942, the radio priest told the dwindling band of bitter men who remained faithful that he had "bowed to orders from Church superiors" and was dissociating himself completely, personally and morally, from *Social Justice* and the movements which it promoted.[13]

Charles E. Coughlin remained in retirement even after victorious conclusion of the war. His name appeared in the news briefly in late 1953 after he publicly urged Catholic laymen's groups to support the guaranteed annual wage, which was being backed that year by the United Auto Workers. But the aging cleric was no longer interested in notoriety. When a national magazine sent reporters to interview him in 1955, the resulting story was entitled "Calm For a Stormy Priest." Coughlin told his visitors he was totally engrossed in the affairs of his parish; he still filled the massive Shrine of the Little Flower for Sunday sermons and boasted of having six assistant priests and a modern dormitory in which to house them. He expressed remorse about the activities of earlier years and admitted that "it was a horrible mistake to enter politics . . . and intemperate of me, unbecoming a priest, to call the President a liar." He remembered the Union Party with regret, making a particular point of saying that he "was frightened of Smith, a professional anti-Semite and an anti-Christian." When other newsmen sought him out in 1962, he repeated his disavowals of his political adventures, calling them "a young man's mistake."[14]

Father Coughlin remained on active duty as a parish priest until the mid-1960's, living quietly and refusing to discuss the career that had brought him fame and misfortune. Time robbed him of his anger and his ambition; as retirement approached, he apparently sought only peace. The man who led the masses was a demagogue no longer.

The activities of Gerald L. K. Smith in the years following 1936 bear a striking resemblance to those of Coughlin, but with one exception. Smith was also involved in a variety of anti-Semitic and isolationist movements in the late 1930's and 1940's, but, unlike the priest, age never mellowed the man.

After leaving the Union Party, Smith tried to breathe life into his new Committee of One Million. The Committee was based on seven nebu-

---

[13] *New York Times*, May 5, 1942; and Tull, *Father Coughlin and The New Deal*, pp. 234–37.

[14] *Ibid.*, pp. 237–38; "Father Coughlin's Reappearance," *The Nation*, CLXXVIII, No. 1 (January 2, 1954), 1; and "Calm For A Stormy Priest," *Life*, XXXIX, No. 20 (November 14, 1955), 119–23.

Father Coughlin with children of his parish school at the Shrine of the
Little Flower, 1955. *John Zimmerman, Life Magazine (c) Time Inc.*

lous "principles," such as wiping out Communism, protecting American
institutions, and defending a white, Christian nation. Perhaps because of
this lack of focus, the movement never got off the ground. For a while,
the former minister worked with a fellow native demagogue, Gerald
Winrod, in still another anti-Communist "crusade." Needing money,
he recruited financial backing from wealthy dowagers and retired stock-

brokers, people who feared the power of the masses in a depression era. But soon he lost the support of what he called "the Park Avenue crowd" and found himself for the first time in many years broke and hungry. He toured the country peddling his faith cure for Communism and occasionally won a commission by an industrialist to act as an antiunion speaker, especially in the midwestern auto assembly plants where the CIO was making inroads. He even set up a "Federation of Americanization" in Detroit in 1938, and was doing well until he became *persona non grata* with Henry Ford and was out of work once again.[15]

The approach of World War II was a windfall for Gerald L. K. Smith, for it opened a host of new demagogic opportunities. As an outspoken isolationist, he displayed his remarkable platform style at numerous rallies held by the America First Committee. He made national news by presenting a petition to Congress with a million signatures of people who opposed for any reason America's entry into war. Attacking the policies of Great Britain and lauding those of Hitler, he was swiftly returning to the racist arguments with which he had flirted during the Silver Shirt period. Now he began calling the Negroes a "child race," and now he was intensifying his attacks upon the Jews. He was taking the same path as Coughlin.[16]

Smith interrupted his antiwar campaign long enough to return to Louisiana in 1940 at the invitation of Earl Long, who was engaged in a bitter battle for the Democratic gubernatorial nomination. Gerald's "homecoming" turned out to be a mistake for both him and Long; the audience hooted the former minister off the stage and Huey's brother was rejected by the electorate in a primary runoff.[17]

After Pearl Harbor, the self-styled messiah tried several new ventures. First, he annexed a score of small women's clubs and set up the Mothers of American Heroes and the Mothers of Sons Forum. When these groups failed, he turned once more to the idea of a third political force, experimenting first with the Christian National Party before establishing the America First Party. Soon he was extravagantly claiming three million members with "120,000 cells in 32 states." Hoping to fill a vacuum he thought was created by the retirement of Father Coughlin and the death of *Social Justice*, Smith began publishing, in

[15] Ferkiss, pp. 287, 318; Huie, *American Mercury*, LV, No. 224, 149–50; and House Committee on Un-American Activities, *Investigation of Gerald L. K. Smith*, 1946, p. 19.

[16] *Ibid.*, p. 22; *Current Biography, 1943*, p. 709; and Sindler, p. 112. Smith's racism was not a factor in the mid-1930's. There were no racial barriers in the Share-Our-Wealth Society, and the minister did not use racist arguments in the Union Party campaign.

[17] Kane, p. 447; and Martin, p. 179.

mid-1942, a weekly newspaper, *The Cross and The Flag*. In an effort to enlist the leaderless Coughlinite following, he lavishly praised the radio priest and made as the first plank of his America First Party platform: "Free speech for all good Americans, including Father Charles E. Coughlin."[18]

Smith prospered for a short time. He received 100,000 votes in the Republican primary for United States Senator in Michigan in 1942. His income rose to $1,500 a week, and he purchased a comfortable house in Detroit. Attracting xenophobes, anti-Semites and appeasers, he continued to promote his party and ran for President in 1944, but this time with almost no success at the polls. Smith, like Coughlin, was going too far. At this point he was saying, "If we'd herd all Reds and Communists into concentration camps and outlaw about half of the movies and then turn to Christian statesmanship, our problems would be solved," and "This is an unnecessary war. . . . Nobody wanted it but the power mad internationalists operating under the direction of international Jewry." The Justice Department finally listed his newspaper as a propaganda vehicle for alleged seditionists.[19]

With the end of the war, Smith hurriedly established an organization called the Christian Veterans of America. But once again he had misread the temper of the times and the effort failed miserably when it became clear that returning veterans were not, as Smith had hoped, bitter, angry, and unemployed. Searching desperately for a cause, he settled on that old standby for aspiring dictators—anti-Semitism. Throughout the postwar period, Gerald L. K. Smith was to seek fame and fortune through an incredibly fierce hatred of the Jewish population. Launching a Christian Nationalist Crusade in 1947, he set out on a nationwide speaking tour with the support of Theodore Bilbo. In 1948, he accused General Dwight D. Eisenhower of being a Jew and headed a "Stop-Ike-the-Kike" campaign before the presidential primaries (when it was widely speculated that Eisenhower might be the Democratic nominee). In the election that year, Smith ran for President himself, this time on the Christian Nationalist Party ticket, having failed to win Dixiecrat backing after being repudiated by Senator J. Strom Thurmond. In 1952 and 1953, Smith busied himself with distributing charts purporting to trace "Roosevelt's Jewish Ancestry," leading a conference on the abolition of the United Nations (he called it the "Jew-United Nations"),

---

[18] Davenport, *Collier's*, CXIII, No. 10, 15, 60–62; and Roy, pp. 62–63.

[19] House Committee on Un-American Activities, *Investigation of Gerald L. K. Smith*, 1946, p. 21; Huie, *American Mercury*, LV, No. 224, 153; and Ferkiss, p. 288.

and spreading racist literature at the national nominating conventions in 1952.[20]

Gerald L. K. Smith claimed that his *The Cross and The Flag* had a circulation of 100,000 in the early 1950's, but the B'nai B'rith's Anti-Defamation League, a close student of his activities, put the number at 25,-000. Smith clearly was losing ground steadily by 1953. Although he publicly praised the actions of Senator Joseph R. McCarthy, he was undoubtedly unhappy over the spate of concern with an internal Communist threat represented by the controversial lawmaker. For as the numbers of nationalistic and fundamentalistic agitators steadily grew throughout the decade, the now aging former minister tended to get lost in the crowd.[21]

Gerald L. K. Smith never stopped trying to lead the masses, never ceased trying, in his words, "to teach 'em how to hate." Moving his headquarters to Los Angeles, he continued into the 1960's to use the mails to spread his vicious anti-Negro and anti-Semitic literature. But virtually everyone ceased to listen. The demagogue had lost his flamboyance. He had become just another bitter old man.[22]

The public career of William Lemke following the campaign of 1936 was strikingly different from that of Gerald Smith. Lemke never again resorted to the tactics of the rabble rouser. He returned to Congress and continued his efforts to aid the western farming regions.

Lemke was hurt in at least three important ways by his participation in the 1936 presidential race. First, his national reputation was badly tarred. While the North Dakotan had been considered a back-country neophyte upon his arrival in Congress in the early 1930's, his drafting of the Frazier-Lemke bills and his persistent and persuasive handling of them in the House had won him great respect in Washington's legislative circles. But that hard-won respect evaporated with the Union disaster, for now he was dismissed as a crank, a nut, a fanatic. Furthermore, his defection from the GOP in November inevitably meant punishment by congressional Republicans when he returned to the House for the next term: both Lemke and his colleague Usher Burdick, when they came back to the Capitol in 1937, found they had been stripped of

---

[20] *Ibid.*, p. 318; and Roy, pp. 13, 15–16, 60–67.

[21] *Ibid.*, pp. 65, 70–74.

[22] In 1965, Smith described himself as "for all practical purposes, the senior advisor and liason contact for something over 1,700 right-wing organizations." See his essay in Simon (ed.), pp. 47–48.

committee seniority and demoted to the bottom rank of their committees, even beneath newly elected Representatives.[23]

Finally, Lemke's role in the Union Party inadvertently strengthened his archenemy in North Dakota politics, William Langer. Langer, running as an independent for the United States Senate in 1936, won a tight three-cornered race with a plurality of some four thousand votes over his regular Republican opponent. Many observers credited this narrow margin to Lemke, for the new Senator almost certainly benefited from his listing in the same ballot column (marked "independent") as the popular congressman. Such a triumph gave this old Lemke foe the opportunity to rebuild his political machine. In 1940 he would defeat William Lemke—running that year as an independent—by less than eight thousand votes for the pivotal office of governor.[24]

The North Dakotan's dream of winning influence and power through the third party adventure had proved not only a romantic illusion, but a serious political miscalculation. But the resilient Lemke never surrendered to despair, never stopped trying in Congress to promote the interests of his beloved agrarians. In 1939, he teamed once again with Senator Frazier to introduce a "cost of production" bill, proposing that the government fix prices of certain farm products and compel dealers and handlers of these commodities to pay a set amount on the share of that crop sold in the United States, the rest to be disposed of abroad at whatever price it could bring. But while debate still raged on this measure, war came to Europe, and all farm prices rose abruptly.[25]

The coming of World War II also turned Lemke down the path of isolationism. He favored neutrality legislation prohibiting the shipment of arms or war materials during peace or war to any foreign nation and endorsed an absolute embargo on food and clothing to any wartime belligerent. He supported the building of powerful armed forces as a means of deterring aggression against America, but as for wars in Europe and Asia: "We cannot stop them . . . but we can stay out of them." Unimpressed by the argument that the United States had to fight to help other democratic states, he pointed out that "it wasn't so very long ago that a certain democracy stole the Boer Republic and another one . . . the Panama Canal." [26]

---

[23] *Washington Post,* January 15, 1937; and Blackorby, p. 518.

[24] *Ibid.,* p. 563; and Blackorby, *Mississippi Valley Historical Review,* XLIX, No. 1, 82–84.

[25] Salutos and Hicks, p. 532; and Blackorby, p. 525.

[26] *Ibid.,* p. 530; Lemke to Joe T. Rensch, January 21, 1939, and Lemke to Robert S. Field, January 20, 1939, Lemke Papers.

Lemke returned to Congress in 1942, and is shown here in 1949, a year before his death, with Rep. Toby Morris of Oklahoma. *United Press International*

Like most other isolationists in Congress (and unlike Coughlin and Smith), Lemke forgot his objections and rallied behind the war effort after the attack on Pearl Harbor. Out of public office for two years following his unsuccessful gubernatorial bid in 1940, the agrarian leader returned to the House of Representatives in 1942 to participate in important wartime and postwar legislative actions and served in the House until his death in 1950 at the age of 72. His later career was unmarked by controversy, but William Lemke remained until the end what he had been all of his adult life, a dedicated spokesman for the radical farmers of the American West.

Dr. Francis E. Townsend's post-Union Party career closely paralleled that of Lemke's. He too suffered as a result of his association with the party, but he too continued to work diligently for his interest group.

Shortly after the 1936 election, United States Attorney Leslie C. Garnett announced from Washington that Dr. Townsend would be prose-

Dr. Townsend was saved from going to jail for contempt of Congress by a pardon from President Roosevelt in April, 1938. In 1948, at the age of 83, he worked at his home in Los Angeles, still confident that Congress would enact his program. *Wide World*

cuted on the contempt citation voted against him when he had defiantly walked out of the Bell Committee hearings in the spring. With the Democratic victory safely won, it was possible to risk the wrath of the Townsend following. The elderly physician was convicted of contempt of Congress in early 1937 and fined $100. Only a barrage of pleading letters from those who remained faithful moved the President to commute the prescribed jail sentence.[27]

Dr. Townsend remained a free man, but his organization was faltering. The presence of Coughlin and Smith—however brief—had cast a destructive aura of demagoguery over it, and the election had exposed it as an ineffective political pressure group. It had no real power —it could not defeat a President or even intimidate the major parties. Membership fell off, and from the decay of the plan sprang other panaceas, such as the "Thirty Dollars Every Thursday" clubs in California.[28]

Still the old man pushed on. In the 1938 campaign he tried to rally his followers against the New Deal, calling social security a "snare and a delusion" and exclaiming, "No New Dealers can be full-blooded Townsendites." In 1940 he worked for the election of Wendell Wilkie, but this time even his trusted lieutenants defied him and announced for Roosevelt. By 1948, the leader of the aged was once again on the quixotic third party trail, endorsing the Progressive candidacy of Henry Wallace.[29]

Dr. Townsend continued to lead his movement, publish his newspaper and maintain a national headquarters throughout the postwar years. He vainly tried to modernize his plan and to remove the stigma of naive utopianism that it had acquired by no longer calling for a $200 monthly pension, only a "substantial" one. But nothing could reverse the growing tide of unconcern among the elderly toward the movement and its founder. The end of the Depression and the prosperity of the 1940's and 1950's eliminated the fear and privation upon which the plan had fed. Yet Dr. Townsend carried on until 1960, when, still speaking hopefully of the future, the man who had found a new career when most men think of retirement, died in Los Angeles at ninety-three.[30]

The later years were not kind to any of the four leaders of the Union Party. Coughlin and Smith continued to pursue power through rabble

---

[27] *Time*, XXVIII, No. 20, 28; and Wecter, p. 204.
[28] *Ibid.*
[29] Cantril, p. 185.
[30] David H. Bennett, "The Year of the Old Folks' Revolt," *American Heritage*, XVI, No. 1 (December, 1964), 107.

rousing until official sanctions or old age robbed them of all hope. Lemke and Townsend failed to make an impact with pressure group politics, but perhaps it was the humiliating defeat of 1936 that caused these two to reexamine their motives and their tactics and to become again the humane reformers they had been before. If their subsequent records were unimpressive, they were, at least, honorable. In the end, however, they would all be best known to history for their efforts in the futile Union alliance. The year was 1936 — the year of the radicals' bid for power.

Epilogue: Yesterday's Radicals and American History

Just as the past often serves to illuminate the present, so do contemporary events elucidate history by casting new shadows on the old. The 1960's have been a time of social and political upheaval in America, and a fresh and indigenous breed of young radicals has come on the scene to raise "new" questions and propose "new" solutions. But in many ways, today's burning issues are the same as those which animated the leaders of the Union Party and which gave their social movements national impact.

Everywhere there are parallels. One sees the widespread concern about the plight of the poor in the United States of the 1960's, with a federally financed "war on poverty" spearheading a drive to help the culturally and economically deprived, while more ambitious schemes for guaranteed annual incomes, negative income taxes, and government rent subsidies wait in the wings. One then remembers Father Coughlin and Dr. Townsend, William Lemke, and Gerald L. K. Smith (with his mentor, Huey Long) years ago trumpeting their anger at the wealthy and self-satisfied people who turned their backs on "the other America." Three decades before the "Great Society" was born or the "new left" was created, yesterday's radicals were calling for bold new programs to help the underprivileged. Was not Long and Smith's Share-Our-Wealth plan really a precursor of the guaranteed annual income? And Dr. Townsend's old age program a first shot in the battle that has resulted in Medicare and proposals for expanded social security benefit?

In the very motive forces of political organization, there are interesting similarities between the protest and reform groups of past and present. The mass movements of the Depression decade which de-

293

manded changes in political and economic affairs worked, like today's
civil rights, peace, and antipoverty movements, both as pressure groups
for certain special interests and as instruments for more general and
widespread change. Moreover, the protest groups of the present practice a kind of politics of morality—an emphasis on the inherent right-
ness of their cause and a distrust of the pragmatic, compromising, "hypocrisy" of traditional "consensus" politicians. So too did the supporters
of the National Union for Social Justice and the Old Age Revolving Pension Plan fervently believe that the truth and justice of their position
would bring victory, and that they would not need to "sell out" to the
moderate reformers of the age, who offered only half a loaf. The cru-
sading spirit was present in all of the leaders and movements joining
forces in the election of 1936. Indeed, two of these leaders were ministers—pioneers for an age which finds many clergymen moving into
the political arena to demand moral solutions for public problems.

But perhaps most important, the all-pervasive concern about alienation, which forms the backdrop for the rise of so many social movements of the sixties, was evident in the earlier period. William Lemke
crying out against the loss of individualism in a bureaucratic America
where agrarian traditions had been forgotten, Charles Coughlin de-
ploring the suffocating power of big institutions, be they "capitalist"
or "socialist," Francis E. Townsend lamenting the callous materialism of
his time, with the concomitant loss of family solidarity, respect for age,
and a sense of purpose for the elderly, Huey Long damning the exploiters and promising to make every man a king, were all calling for a
revaluation of American values and a rebirth of concern for the individual. They all appealed to their followers' feelings of frustration and
powerlessness in industrialized and urbanized America, and they all
promised the "little man" another chance to master his environment and
find a unique place in the sun. If their specific programs pointed to an
even more complex and powerful welfare state, it was a paradox they
would share with later radicals.

Along with these similarities, however, there are compelling differences between the men and movements of the two eras. The passing
years have brought striking changes in the economic climate of the
nation. In the late sixties, the gross national product has grown in
quantum jumps until it stands at more than ten times the figure for the
midthirties. In an America experiencing the fruits of the greatest
period of sustained growth in the history of capitalism, the national
poverty and declining economic indices of the earlier period are only
dim memories. The change of setting brings with it a change in attitude toward what the men of the past considered radical, Utopian,

and even dangerous programs. In an affluent society, it is possible to plan massive federally financed rent subsidies, medical care, and farm benefits without fear of bankrupting the nation or seriously disturbing that complex set of relationships which govern the market in a free enterprise economy. Moreover, as the standard of living for many moves steadily upward, it is necessary to redefine the luxuries of yesterday as the necessities of today. Where reality suggested that radical programs in the Depression were all too often truly unworkable, the new realities make similar plans feasible or at least debatable today.

There is an even greater dissimilarity in technique than in program, and a more suggestive one, for there are only a few parallels in contemporary social reform movements for that strain of malignant demagoguery which was all too often the hallmark of the Union Party leadership. Most groups on the new radical left shun charismatic leadership as antidemocratic. But character assassination and scapegoating, grandiose promises for the future and a sustained effort to intensify the irrational elements in political unrest in order to seduce potential followers into an emotional attachment to themselves were the daily fare of Father Coughlin and Gerald L. K. Smith. In order to fulfill their own cravings for power and position, these men constantly ignored those traditions of civility and rational discourse upon which democracy rests. William Lemke and Dr. Francis E. Townsend were marginal figures in this regard, for their main concern was not really the aggrandizement of personal power. They were merely reformers unafraid of radical ideas. Yet in the hectic and bitter days of the 1936 campaign, when their burden of personal disappointment and political failure had become almost too great to bear, both men took on the coloring of their messianic allies, Coughlin and Smith. Townsend, buoyed by the adulation of his devoted followers, and Lemke, blinded by his sudden rise to national prominence, became, as it were, demagogues for a season as they converted their bitterness and frustration into angry speeches that bore the unmistakable demagogic stamp.[1]

---

[1] Some scholars, uncomfortable with its pejorative tone, dislike the word "demagogue." T. Harry Williams, who disapproves of its use, reminds us that it comes from the Greek, the original definition being "a man of loose tongue, intemperate, trusting to tumult, leading the populace to mischief with empty words." The Union Party leaders, whatever their difficulties or motives in 1936, seem to fit even this definition in that critical year. See Williams, *The Journal of Southern History*, XXVI, No. 1, 17. But their great enemy, Franklin D. Roosevelt, does not. Accused by many of being a demagogue, Roosevelt did personalize public issues (especially in 1936) but did not, in Paul K. Conkin's words, "picture his enemies as overwhelming dangers to the country, threatening its very survival." See Paul K. Conkin, *The New Deal* (New York: Thomas Y. Crowell Co., 1967), pp. 85–87.

In the end, the differences between the men of the Union Party and today's "new left" supporters of social and economic reform, despite the violence of their protests or the moral authoritarianism of their rhetoric, are as important as the similarities. Which raises the question: should these radicals of the past be considered "leftists" or "rightists" in the context of American life?

In this land of unmatched opportunity and diverse peoples, with its political system geared to compromising the clashing interests of a vast nation and to obfuscating their differences, the sharp black and white marking the extremes of the political spectrum in other states often have been blurred into mild shades of gray. And yet it is possible to suggest the rough outlines of the dichotomy, for the men of both the right and the left are idealists, who have opposing visions of the ideal America they are striving to reach. In the case of the right, it is usually a kind of re-creation, for here the vision is a memory and the movement a backward reach to the Utopia that was once believed to be reality. The men of the right rail against the betrayal of the old American dream and seek to build their Utopia in history. For the men of the left, conversely, the vision is a prophecy and whether it be the dream of a Marxist millennium or some other one, the leftists have their eyes set forward.

In terms of this definition, the Union Party leaders are more easily located on the right than on the left. William Lemke's efforts represented a longing for the past, a quest to save the "old" America of his agrarian Northwest, whose rugged frontier values were being ignored and discarded by a preponderant industrial society. Dr. Townsend's nostalgic vision was of his own boyhood, and his dream was to give the old people of his day the security that their fathers had known. Gerald L. K. Smith's Share-Our-Wealth sermons always contained the reminder that accumulation of wealth and power in the big cities and especially in the East had disrupted the historic opportunity and freedom of those "ideal" Americans, the rural folk of the South, who could trace their heritage far back in the nation's past. Even Charles E. Coughlin shared this theme, for he continuously denounced the evil few who were conspiring to sour the old American dream by blocking the aspirations of the Coughlinite following. Like traditional messianic leaders, they "preached the return of the old order, or rather a new order in which the old will be revived.[2]

To describe the Unionites as "re-creators," however, does not ex-

---

[2] Bernard Barber, "Acculturation and Messianic Movements," *American Sociological Review*, Vol. 6, No. 5 (October, 1941), pp. 663–65.

plain their radicalism. For in this sense they can be seen only as conservatives, albeit very different from the established conservatives of their time. Where the Liberty Leaguers and old guard Republicans sought to conserve the status quo of the twenties, the Union leaders were concerned with an American ideal which had been on the wane for years and looked farther back in history for their model. Yet these militant men of the Depression were clearly more than conservative; they were radicals who preached extremism and eschewed the moderate conservative approach. In their radicalism, they manipulated some of the symbols and proposed some of the programs traditionally associated with the left in the United States, but the main thrust of their activity constituted a kind of radicalism of the right.

To understand this process, one must consider the forces shaping the whole history of extremism in America. Two essential and complementary factors seem to be at work here. One relates to something which might be called the "sameness of American society." The other has to do with the variety of America's people—the polyglot nature of the United States population and the "antialienism" that has developed among its citizens.

The first of these factors was suggested by Louis Hartz in *The Liberal Tradition in America,* when he observed that "the basic ethical problem of a liberal society is not the danger of the majority, which has been its conscious fear, but the danger of unanimity, which has slumbered unconsciously behind it, the 'tyranny of opinion' that Tocqueville saw unfolding."[3]

There has always been a real consensus concerning social goals and mores among the American people. The fetish for equality that Tocqueville noted 130 years ago has been discovered again and again by perceptive social critics. (Even the members of the New Left in the 1960's, while challenging the humanness of the competitive system and the viability of contemporary democracy, share some of the goals of an avowedly open and egalitarian society.) But this consensus has been perverted when the nation has undergone times of trial—when, for example, it has had to confront economic depression at home or ideological and/or military challenge abroad. Then this consensus has become for many a tyranny of opinion, an assumption that to *be* an American means not only that certain values are shared but that certain ideas *must* be held in common.

In such periods of tension, aspiring demagogues, using extremist

[3] Hartz, p. 11.

arguments, have been able to play upon the fears and frustrations of millions of Americans. They have issued the clarion call that enemy ideas are everywhere in evidence, which really has meant that those citizens of other than conventional political and social persuasions are fair game. In this century alone several men have effectively utilized such tactics. In 1919 Attorney General A. Mitchell Palmer took advantage of the unhappiness in post-World War I America by helping to raise the cry that Communists were about to make a revolution in the country as they had in Russia. In a setting of economic depression, labor unrest, disillusion with the peace treaty, and distress over the success of the Bolsheviks in the new Soviet Union, Palmer shrewdly encouraged a red scare, in which thousands of men and women were jailed, deported, or harassed because they had allegedly espoused radical views. The new red scare of the early 1950's and the continuing fear of Communist infiltration into high academic and governmental positions in the 1960's reflected the same kind of perversion of the American consensus.

This process was at work in the 1930's. When the great Depression cast its black shadow across America, desperate millions were willing to believe—indeed, eager to believe—that behind their sorry plight lay the machinations of a few evil men. The charming and articulate Father Coughlin appeared on the scene to provide the scapegoats that so many wanted to attack. When the radio priest accused Roosevelt's Brain Trusters and Wall Street financiers alike of being part of an international conspiracy which had created the Depression and oppressed the common man, he was playing upon fears of "alien" ideas in almost every sermon. He, too, was riding the tide of the tyranny of opinion.

Gerald L. K. Smith's clever harangues, in which Communist-hunting was tied to promises of universal affluence, were also variations on this destructive theme. Even Lemke and Townsend, in the heat of the campaign summer of 1936, occasionally engaged in excoriations of Communist or "Mussolini Fascist" ideas (i.e., foreign ideas) in Washington. The crusade against un-American ideas, then, was part and parcel of the Union Party rhetoric.

Present also was that other factor which has shaped radical movements in America—the crusade against un-American peoples, better known as nativism.

The roots of nativism also lay in the remarkable consensus in American society. For although there has been a striking agreement, as it were, about the American way of life, there also have been nagging questions concerning who *are* the Americans. The compelling attractions of the United States, its freedom, its wealth, its opportunities, brought endless waves of immigrants to its shores in the last three and one-half centuries. For many of these immigrant millions and their off-spring, the first years in the new nation were often difficult and heart-breaking. The Irish, the Germans, the Jews, the Italians, and the Puerto Ricans have all been accused of being alien and inferior, of being out of the mainstream of American life, of being somehow less American than earlier settlers. (For Afro-Americans, with their heritage of slavery and racial prejudice antialienism all but prevented that assimilation which now some young Negroes reject.)

The great American melting pot has not melted away all the anxiety felt by the later arrivals; the distinctive ethnic traits have been marks of alienation and reasons for exclusion. The disquieting question, who are the Americans, has arisen in muted, even perverted forms across the years to haunt both those who would exclude others from the community and those who would seek full acceptance into it.

In the 1850's, the Native American or Know-Nothing Party was the instrument of self-proclaimed nativists who feared those whose religious, linguistic, and social practices were outside the tradition that they had known. The target of the time was Irish Catholics, a group who had immigrated in large numbers to America during the potato famine years of the 1840's. In the tension-filled period preceding the Civil War, there was a sustained and occasionally violent attack on the foreign "Papists" who threatened American institutions. A similar reaction could be seen half a century later, in the tumultuous 1890's, when organizations such as the American Protective Association issued the old cry: America for the Americans! The nativistic radical right was at work once again.[4]

In the 1920's the old poison was injected into the bloodstream of American society in two waves. The red scare at the dawn of the decade was directed not only at "leftists" — men with alien ideas — but at men with alien "blood" as well. The members of the real or alleged radical organizations were for the most part Jews, Ukranians, South Slavs, and other newly immigrated groups. They were easy bait; they satisfied the need for "cleansing" the land of foreign influences. And they would be the scapegoats a few years later as well, when the rise of the modern

[4] For nineteenth and early twentieth century nativism see Ray Allen Billington, *The Protestant Crusade, 1800-1860* (Chicago: Quadrangle Books, 1964), and John Higham, *Strangers in the Land* (New Brunswick; Rutgers, 1955); and Donald L. Kinzer, *An Episode in Anti-Catholicism: The American Protective Association* (Seattle: University of Washington Press, 1964).

Ku Klux Klan testified to the resiliency of nativism. As the Klan spread across the Midwest, the Rocky Mountain states and the South, its spokesmen celebrated Anglo-Saxonism and damned the "cross-breeding hordes" of new immigrants. The frustrated Protestant townsmen of native stock who felt themselves overwhelmed and overawed by the rise of the city, the growth of big business and big labor, and the rapidly changing nature of an urbanized and industrialized society which seemed to have passed them by, tried to find succor in destroying churches, beating rabbis, and terrorizing those whose names were strange and whose ways were different.[5]

In the Depression decade, a host of organizations like Pelley's Silver Shirts promoted the old antialien themes. But in those years the most significant, the most virulent form of nativism was a curiously inverted one. It came in the growth of Father Coughlin's National Union for Social Justice.

Coughlin was concerned with the alien thinker. But who was the alien to the radio messiah? In the late 1930's, when Coughlin's bid for power had long since failed and he had become just another voice crying in the wilderness, the alien would be the Jew. But in mid-decade, when the National Union was at its peak and when the priest was a power to be reckoned with in American politics, the alien was the white Anglo-Saxon Protestant "aristocrat"—the man of money and power. Coughlin appealed to a large Irish and German Catholic audience, working men and women living in large eastern and midwestern cities, whose suffering in the Depression was as severe as that of any group of Americans and for whom the economic crisis had opened old social and psychological wounds. Thus did the priest offer members of his movement more than a panacea for the economic problems which beset them, for when he struck out at the international bankers and international Communists who were destroying America, he made it clear that these evil men were the eastern financiers, federal government advisers and Ivy League intellectuals. These were the groups who had in the past oppressed his people. In this way did Coughlin preside over a new kind of antialien-

---

[5] Richard Hofstadter describes the "paranoid style" of many men on the radical right, and suggests the difference between some older groups of last century and organizations such as the modern Klan. The former felt that they were still in power, the latter felt dispossessed. See Richard Hofstadter, *The Paranoid Style in American Politics* (New York: Alfred A. Knopf, 1965), pp. 4 and 23. See also Daniel Bell's essay, "The Dispossessed" in Bell (ed.); Robert K. Murray, *Red Scare: A Study in National Hysteria, 1919–1920* (Minneapolis: University of Minnesota Press, 1955); David M. Chalmers, *Hooded Americanism* (Garden City, N.Y.: Doubleday & Co., 1965); and Kenneth T. Jackson, *The Ku Klux Klan in the City, 1915–1930* (New York: Oxford University Press, 1967).

ism, for if he could convince his listeners that the Anglo-Saxon establishment, the men controlling access to status and affluence in America, were aliens, were Communists or international capitalists, then his followers' long journey to assimilation might at last be complete. Those who had been victimized by the Know-Nothings, the APA, and the Klan were given the means of turning the tables; in this neonativist organization they were offered security in their place in America.

The other radical leaders who joined Coughlin in the Union Party also occasionally traded on nativist themes, albeit more conventional ones. Lemke's appeal to his farmer followers was often couched in a soothing prose that assured the faithful (most of them second generation Americans) that the agrarian type was the ideal American and that the city folk were somehow out of the mainstream of the national experience. Dr. Townsend's nostalgic lectures on the virtues and values of the aged, those who carried the "true" American tradition out of the nineteenth century, smacked of the same antipathy for "foreign" elements. Gerald L. K. Smith was particularly interested in this theme and skilled in exploiting it. Long before his blatantly nativist activities of the war and postwar years, Smith was dramatizing the superiority of the "poor but honest" dirt farmer over the immoral and vaguely alien forces of the eastern seaboard and southern city.

Nativism or antialienism—the assault on un-American people, and the tyranny of opinion—the assault on un-American ideas, thus have been twin themes played out in dramatic counterpoint for over a century in the radicalism of the right. The frantic efforts to preserve or resurrect the past at the expense of some elements within the society have been the hallmarks of those groups whose anger has converted conservatism to extremism.[6] Such efforts were made by the men of the Union Party, who were all, to some extent, purifiers and exclusionists, hoping to protect their nation from evil and dangerous ideas and/or people.

A case can be made, of course, for the Unionites as radicals of the left. The party platform, with its call for a national bank and its demand that wealth be more evenly distributed, seems not only in the tradition

[6] Radicalism of the left has been affected by these same forces in America. The history of the Communist Party in the United States is a story of a program bent or broken by these themes: Communism's most prosperous years were during the Popular Front, 1935–1939, when the party eschewed revolution, claiming "Communism is Twentieth Century Americanism." Thus the charge of un-American activities was muted and limited success followed. The New Left of the 1960's has also escaped this charge. Rejecting Orwell's "smelly little ideologies," it represents indigenous American radicalism. Indeed, the search for an ideology which blueprints anything beyond the existential act of breaking up the old order has been one of its major problems.

of today's militant poverty warriors, but the child of a long history of monetary extremism of the left in America. Coughlin, Lemke, and Smith were all, in part, products of the Populist heritage of monetary radicalism. But what does this mean? Some scholars (the counterrevisionists) see Populism as a liberating and eminently progressive force, at best a "class movement which accepted industrialism but opposed its capitalistic form, seeking instead a more equitable distribution of wealth," and at least a product of "interest politics," concerned with solutions and remedies to very real economic problems. Yet the opponents in this heated historical debate (the revisionists) would disagree, placing the Populists in a retrogressive rather than progressive matrix and seeing in the movement a kind of status politics that was often destructive in its attacks on foreigners and urbanites, a politics which provided the seedbed for many kinds of xenophobia, anti-intellectualism, conspiracy-hunting and authoritarianism in succeeding years.[7]

The most satisfactory solution to the problem of Populism probably lies in a synthesis of the progressive and retrogressive elements in the agrarian crusade. The same is true of the Union crusade, although here the balance is more clearly on the side of the radicalism of the right. For if it shared the class and interest orientation which marked, in part, the Populist movement as well as some new left groups today, it was more influenced by the reactionary tradition of status politics which came not only from Populism, but from many nativist groups which predated and antedated the 1890's. And it manifested, moreover, a pandering to the tyranny of opinion which became the calling card of Communist-baiters throughout the twentieth century.[8]

In the end, there are stronger ties between the Unionites and the postwar radicals of the right than contemporary leftists. Many of the same themes can be found in the speeches of Senator Joseph R. McCarthy and those of Father Coughlin. The setting was different in the two

[7] Counter-revisionist scholars on this point, other than C. Vann Woodward, are Norman Pollack, Chester M. Destler, Walter K. Nugent, and Michael Paul Rogin. See especially Rogin, pp. 7, 168–82; Woodward, *American Scholar*, Vol. 29, No. 1, p. 63; Norman Pollack, *The Populist Response to Industrial America* (New York: W. W. Norton & Company, Inc., 1962), pp. 11–12; and Chester McArthur Destler, "Western Radicalism, 1865–1901: Concepts and Origins," *Mississippi Valley Historical Review*, Vol. XXI, No. 3 (December, 1944), 351–55. Revisionists include, of course, Hofstadter as well as Peter Viereck, Edward Shils, and Victor Ferkiss.

[8] Seymour Martin Lipset, in his essay, "Three Decades of the Radical Right," in Bell, ed., implies that Coughlin's appeal might be viewed largely in terms of class politics because of the economic conditions and the low incomes and high unemployment rates of his followers. While it is true that part of the Coughlin success can be attributed to his economic arguments, the nature of his enemies and the style of his attacks suggest that a new kind of status politics was at work as well, even in the Depression.

cases—McCarthy came on the scene in a period of relative prosperity and did not have to wed his anticommunist crusade to an economic program as did Coughlin in the Depression. And a number of political scientists have argued that McCarthy's success was due not to status politics or any latent appeals to the hidden fears and frustrations of his audience, but to the political vulnerability of his opponents during the cold and Korean wars, the demands of a desperate Republican Party and the fundamentalist conservative impulse within it, and the man's shrewd manipulation of the mass media. Still, the scapegoating technique was similar in both cases, for the Junior Senator from Wisconsin was vilifying many of the same devils and may have been playing upon many of the same social and psychological (if not economic) frustrations as had his predecessor. In both cases, the followers apparently enjoyed their leader's means as well as his ends—the attack on the enemy as well as the financial program or anticommunist exposure. Indeed, their audiences may not have been very dissimilar if status politics worked the same side of the street in both decades. And if the members of a contemporary organization like the John Birch Society or George Wallace's American Independent Party would not respond to some of the ethnic biases of these earlier groups, it is clear that such organizations' fetish for individualism and assaults on big government are congenial with Coughlinite and McCarthyite doctrine. It was Coughlin, the monetary radical, who had the distinction, however, of assailing the ever-growing "bureaucracy" while proposing programs which would lead to even greater power for the central government. This paradox haunted all four Union leaders.[9]

Although William Lemke and Francis Townsend were truly radical in their monetary theories, these two Unionites can be compared with later extremists only in the period of their reckless radicalism of 1936. But for another Union organizer, Gerald L. K. Smith, it is not difficult to find a niche among today's lunatic fringe. A comparison between the Smith of 1936 and a contemporary fundamentalist political figure such as Billy James Hargiss, the leader of a recent Christian Crusade against Communism, might reveal the same kind of striking similarity as a Coughlin-McCarthy pairing.

Yet all the lines that can be drawn backward and forward in history

[9] Lipset, Ferkiss, Viereck and others have traced a line from Coughlin to McCarthy. See, for example, *ibid.,* p. 440, and Ferkiss, p. 360. The attack on McCarthyism as status politics has come from Rogin, pp. 30–51, 248–50; Nelson W. Polsby, "Toward an Explanation of McCarthyism," *Political Studies,* Vol. 8 (October, 1960), pp. 250–71; and Earl Latham, *The Communist Controversy in Washington from the New Deal to McCarthy* (Cambridge, Mass.: Harvard University Press, 1965), pp. 416–23.

from the political messiahs of the Depression decade may ultimately obscure the central questions concerning their activities. More important than the light they can shed on movements past or future is the result of their own experience in their own time.

What conclusions can be drawn from this experience? The most obvious is that no mandate from heaven protects Americans from the siren song of the demagogue. In the critical years of the thirties, a number of factors combined to drive millions of United States citizens into the arms of those self-styled leaders who offered simple solutions to complex problems. Each of the men who helped form the Union Party was appealing to a desperate and frightened population. For many of these potential followers, the Depression had abruptly halted movement up the social and economic ladder of success; for others, the economic catastrophe had wiped out savings and obliterated fixed incomes, suddenly hurling those who had long been in the middle classes into a state of near indigency. It was estimated that four out of five families with incomes below $4,000 yearly listened to either Father Coughlin or Senator Huey Long regularly in 1935.[10]

Yet whether it was the ambitious urban poor who supported the radio priest, the restive agricultural underclass of the South who rallied behind Long and his lieutenant, Gerald Smith, or the newly impoverished supporters of Dr. Townsend, there was more to the Union appeal than class or interest politics. It was not enough that Coughlin and Long promised a world of wealth-sharing for the underdog or that Townsend and Lemke offered protection for the special interests of the elderly and the farmer. In a time in which the Roosevelt Administration was recruiting millions for a war on depression-bred poverty, these radicals needed another and more subtle theme with which to attract the masses. The New Deal may not have moved strongly enough to eliminate racial discrimination or the hard core pockets of economic inequality which would plague later generations, but its crisis-bred programs of relief, recovery and reform did lead to a new relationship between the public and private sectors of American life. It marked a new beginning in the struggle to adjust industrial capitalism to democratic values and the powerful "Roosevelt coalition" of poor or displaced groups responding to it was evidence that most citizens were voting with their feet as well as their ballots for a government they felt was anything but static. Some have argued that failure to join radical, even millenarian, movements during times of dire troubles might imply an

---

[10] Chase, Jr., p. 82.

"abject adjustment to suffering and want," an impaired sense of reality. But in 1936, when politics had been polarized by the new liberal reformers, many of those who rallied to the radical movements did so not because the traditional parties offered no hope for change, but because their angers went beyond economics.[11]

It was their wedding of social and psychological panaceas to the more obvious economic ones that gave their movements a distinctive and successful stamp. Coughlin's shrewd manipulation of the frustrations felt by his Irish and German Catholic followers, Lemke's populistic promise to save and enhance the position of the American farmer, Smith's oft-repeated vow to put the little man in the seat of power, and Townsend's desire to restore the way of life his aging supporters had once known were central to the success of each of these leaders. Their different brands of status politics added to their much advertised economic programs made the winning combination. Indeed, it is this combination which raises central questions for the student of radical politics. Rejecting foreign ideologies, these leaders came out of the "Americanist ethos" and were not neofascists. Their achievements cannot be dismissed as an aberration of the Depression or the work of a few fanatics, and concern about the nature of their mass following goes beyond the pluralist's preference for the stability of group politics or the liberal's "suspicion of the people" and "fear" of radical action.[12]

But none of these four crusaders of despair was capable alone of making a bid for national influence. William Lemke's base of power was limited to the agricultural northern plains and Smith's influence declined rapidly with the death of his mentor Long. Even Coughlin and Townsend, despite their devoted millions, could not convert their ideas into legislation without outside support.

It was the alliance of the four leaders—with Charles E. Coughlin the driving force—which proved to be so formidable in the Depression. The tie that bound these disparate men and movements together, in addition to a shared hatred of President Roosevelt, was the inflationary nature of the four panaceas. None of the leaders called for revolutionary

[11] E. P. Thompson, *The Making of the English Working Class* (New York: Vintage Books, 1966), pp. 49–50, discusses realistic responses to suffering. Barton J. Bernstein in Bernstein (ed.), pp. 781–82, argues that the Roosevelt Administration failed to endorse meaningful egalitarianism and "seduced" the "marginal men trapped in hopelessness . . . by rhetoric . . . style and movement." See also Howard Zinn's introduction to his *New Deal Thought* (New York: The Bobbs Merrill Co., 1966).

[12] Hartz, p. 279, and Rogin, pp. 103, 213–15, 278–82. Rogin places the Union Party on the radical right, but ties it to "neo-fascism." He defends some mass movements (i.e., Populism) as useful in overcoming the political conservatism of leadership.

answers to the problems of the times; none of them made basic attacks on the fundamental tenets of the American political or economic system. Coughlin, Lemke, Smith, and Townsend all sought to work miracles through the magic of the manipulation of money. And they all were willing to accuse a small group of evil and powerful men of having usurped power by refusing to make their brand of cheap money available—in this sense they were all practitioners of "the paranoid style" in American politics.

Initial success greeted the coalition of the radicals, the tumultuous Townsend and Coughlin national conventions serving as stunning showcases of the emotional appeal of the new party, but it soon became obvious that serious internal and external problems were proving harder to handle than any of the organizers had dreamed. The November returns revealed the disastrous result of the failure to meet these problems.

Perhaps the most damaging failure came in the realm of organization. Unionites could not build a grass roots party capable of recruiting precinct workers or nominating local and even statewide candidates in the few short months available. They also failed to win a place on the ballot in fourteen states. There were too many amateurs and too few professional politicians with national experience in the ranks.[13]

Almost as destructive was the inability of party leaders to cooperate in building a coherent campaign. Smith's defiant behavior and subsequent expulsion, Townsend's belated decision to support Landon in some states, and Coughlin's wavering attitude toward the New Deal opponent as a result of Church pressure all created tension in the leadership circle and sowed confusion in the minds of followers and potential followers.

Even when they were hard at work for their party, Coughlin and Smith created trouble. The priest's slanderous attacks on the President and the minister's wild charges and sinister plans proved counterproductive by exacerbating the difficulties of meshing interests of urban Catholic workers and western and southern agrarians and by repelling even those who disagreed with Roosevelt. Indeed, the spectacular nature of the Coughlin and Smith speaking tours served to underline another Union weakness: candidate Lemke's inability to project an image of strength and presidential stature. The North Dakotan's fumbling platform style and earnest but uninspired campaign techniques sug-

[13] The party not only failed to get on the ballot in some key states, but won a poor place on the ballots of others. In Iowa, Lemke was listed seventh. See Hill to Farley, August 20, 1936, National Committee Correspondence.

gested that he could not lead his own party, to say nothing of the nation. Newspapers soon chose to ignore the candidate in favor of the colorful antics of his allies.[14]

Yet even a more efficient effort by Unionites would not have overcome the reluctance of many Americans to "throw away" their vote. Radical parties with demagogic leaders prosper best in a setting of extreme crisis, and by 1936, the direst Depression days were long past. The slowly reviving economy was an evil omen for the party; New Dealers drove home the message that a vote for Lemke was a vote for Roosevelt's Republican opponent and all the attendant dangers of a return to the grimmer conditions of the recent past. Leaders of labor, agrarian, and progressive organizations rebuked the Union alternative and rallied behind a President whose creative leadership had brought change and hope to the land and whose policies had stolen the thunder of his critics.[15]

The charismatic appeal of FDR was an added nail in the radical coffin; this charming and dominating figure made mockery of Unionite claims that the election presented a choice between their kind of salvation and the old order. Indeed, the dynamic Roosevelt had traveled so far down the road of reform that he left GOP opponents, burdened with the blame for crisis, pathetically far behind in his militantly liberal 1936 campaign. This was the most critical aspect of the Union plight: minor parties have traditionally been most effective when the major parties are more or less evenly divided, for in such a situation a vote given to an important swing group need not be considered thrown away. In 1936, the Democratic sun was at its zenith.[16]

Yesterday's radicals were taught at last the lesson painfully learned by many earlier political outsiders. The institutional arrangements in America make it virtually impossible for any man or movement to capture a major party, and when a single demagogue tries to challenge both major parties with a third force, he is likewise tilting at windmills;

[14] Jerome G. Locke to Williams, September 1, 1936, Williams Papers.

[15] Lemke claimed that FDR got "seven million votes of people who feared Landon." See the Minutes of the 1936 National Union Party Conference, December 19, 1936, copy in Lemke Papers.

[16] President Roosevelt's appeal was so effective that even a majority of Townsendites defied their leader and supported the man who had given them social security. One study estimates that over 70 per cent of the pensioneers voted for FDR. See Cantril, p. 209. But did Roosevelt overemphasize his personal appeal in 1936? Did he foster a "cult of personality" in the campaign which bypassed debate on some major issues, and, failing to educate the electorate, led to a weakening of the New Deal and the defeat of the Roosevelt coalition in the midterm election of 1938? See Conkin, pp. 88–89.

in this vast and diverse nation, no one self-styled leader can meet the requirements for support from a substantial sector of the population. And even when several aspiring messiahs join forces, the vitality of the major parties combined with the built-in organizational bias against third parties almost predetermines failure. Add to this the very problems of alliance and the dismal prognosis is complete. For there is nothing so damaging to one panacea as another on the same platform; for one demagogue to admit even in a whisper that another has any part of the truth is to demoralize the whole Utopian market. Faced by a hostile press which dismissed them as eccentrics, fanatics, or, even worse, fascists, the Union leaders found that even fanatic followers were undependable on election day.

The devastating defeat at the polls was dramatic evidence that the leading radicals of the Depression could stir the air with their rhetoric but could never influence the outcome of a national campaign. Yet they did have an effect on some of the legislative programs of the time. President Roosevelt once said, years after the demise of the Union Party, that "you sometimes find something pretty good in the lunatic fringe." Friends of the New Deal will note that the actions of articulate men calling for extreme government action helped shape the drafting and passage of certain Rooseveltian measures. Dr. Townsend has been credited with stimulating quick action on Social Security, Long (and his aide Smith) may have helped along the steeply graduated income tax in 1935, and William Lemke certainly forced the White House to pay closer attention to the needs of drought-plagued states in the West. On the negative side, Father Coughlin was partially responsible for the defeat of the bill allowing the United States to join the World Court.[17]

All of this seems to be a rather small mark, made on the margins of events, by men who created such a furor in their time. And so perhaps it was their very presence — not their success or failure — which is, in the end, their most enduring monument. "It is dissatisfaction with the attainable," Raymond Gram Swing has written, "which leads to fanaticism and at last to social fury. . . . When great masses are ready to believe

---

[17] President Roosevelt's Press and Radio Conference, May 30, 1944, Roosevelt Papers, PPF, L-P, #952; Douglas, p. 73; Mason, p. 331; and Blackorby, p. 497. Seymour Martin Lipset suggests that Father Coughlin might have been much more influential, attributing the drop-off in Democratic support in 1938 and 1940 to the issues raised by the radio priest and the loyalty of his supporters. He bases this speculation on the results of Gallup Polls measuring attitudes toward Father Coughlin conducted in April and December, 1938. The date of the survey, the size of the sample, and the percentage differentials cast serious doubt on Lipset's sweeping conclusions. See Bell, ed., pp. 388–89.

the impossible, that is an ominous political fact." The radical leaders of the Depression decade played upon the desperation and anxiety felt by millions caught up in a great national crisis. They promised their supporters riches, they promised them that their oppressers would be punished, and, in James M. Burns' words, "following Hitler's advice, they burned into the little man's soul the proud conviction that although a little worm, he was nevertheless part of a great dragon." The fiercely angry, dangerously credulous, and pathetically eager men and women who trooped blindly after the messiahs of the Union Party, therefore, were walking with history. If the radical leaders of their time could elicit such devotion, it could happen again and again. Certainly the forces molding the mind of the extremist would not pass from the American scene.[18]

Still, there are built-in safeguards in the great democracy against a successful bid for power by any combination of radicals, not the least of which is that traditional American conservatism at the polls. No matter how much they may applaud the extremist when he speaks on the radio or in the auditorium, many Americans become suspicious when they enter the voting booth. Perhaps this is simply a natural timidity, but perhaps it is something more. In 1936, citizens who lost their taste for panaceas before they marked their ballots seemed instinctively to sense what Winston Churchill wrote about so eloquently when he crossed the Atlantic to observe the Union Party leaders. "The specious promises of the prophets of an unearned plenty," Churchill stated, "are a mirage which beckons and lures us, not to the millennial city, but into the deserts of disillusion and ruin. And perhaps we shall even lose our liberties on the way." [19]

[18] Swing, *Forerunners of . . .* , pp. 131–32; and Burns, p. 209.
[19] Churchill, *Collier's,* 97, No. 25, 46.

Bibliography

BOOKS

Allen, Frederick Lewis. *Since Yesterday*. New York: Harper & Brothers, 1940.

Ashton E. B. *The Fascist, His State and His Mind*. New York: William Morrow & Co., 1937.

Baldwin, Hanson W., and Shepard Stone (eds.). *We Saw It Happen*. New York: The World Publishing Co., 1941.

Beals, Carleton. *The Story of Huey P. Long*. Philadelphia: J. B. Lippincott Co., 1935.

Bean, Louis H. *How to Predict Elections*. New York: Alfred A. Knopf, 1948.

Bell, Daniel (ed.). *The New American Right*. New York: Criterion Books, 1955.

———— (ed.). *The Radical Right*. Garden City, N.Y.: Doubleday & Co., Inc., 1963.

————' *The End of Ideology*. Glencoe, Illinois: The Free Press, 1960.

Bendix, Reinhard, and Seymour Martin Lipset (eds.). *Class, Status and Power*. Glencoe, Illinois: The Free Press, 1953.

Berle, Adolf A., Jr., and Gardner C. Means. *The Modern Corporation and Private Property*. New York: The Macmillan Co., 1933.

Bernstein, Barton J. (ed.). *Towards a New Past: Dissenting Essays in American History*. New York: Pantheon Books, 1968.

Biddle, Francis. *The Fear of Freedom*. Garden City, N.Y.: Doubleday & Co., 1952.

Bingham, Alfred M. *Insurgent America*. New York: Harper & Brothers, 1935.

Blackorby, Edward C. *Prairie Rebel: The Public Life of William Lemke*. Lincoln, Nebraska: University of Nebraska Press, 1963.

Bruce, Andrew D. *The Non-Partisan League*. New York: Macmillan Co., 1921.

Burns, James MacGregor. *Roosevelt: The Lion and The Fox*. New York: Harcourt, Brace and Co., 1956.

Cantril, Hadley. *The Psychology of Social Movements*. New York: John Wiley & Sons, Inc., 1941.

Chalmers, David M. *Hooded Americanism*. Garden City, N.Y.: Doubleday & Co., 1965.

Chase, Francis, Jr. *Sound and Fury: An Informal History of Broadcasting*. New York: Harper & Brothers, 1942.

Cohn, Norman. *The Pursuit of the Millennium*. New York: Harper Torchbooks, 1961.

Committee On Old Age Security of the Twentieth Century Fund. *The Townsend Crusade*. New York: The Twentieth Century Fund, Inc., 1936.

Conkin, Paul K. *The New Deal*. New York: Thomas Y. Crowell Co., 1967.

Coogan, Gertrude M. *Money Creators*. Chicago: Sound Money Press, Inc., 1935.

Coser, Lewis A. (ed.). *Political Sociology*. New York: Harper & Row, 1967.

———. *The Functions of Social Conflict*. New York: The Free Press, 1964.

Coughlin, Charles E. *By The Sweat of Thy Brow*. Detroit: The Radio League of the Little Flower, 1931.

———. *Driving Out the Money Changers*. Detroit: The Radio League of the Little Flower, 1933.

———. *The New Deal in Money*. Royal Oak, Michigan: The Radio League of the Little Flower, 1933.

———. *Eight Lectures on Labor, Capital and Justice*. Royal Oak, Michigan: The Radio League of the Little Flower, 1934.

———. *A Series of Lectures on Social Justice*. Royal Oak, Michigan: The Radio League of the Little Flower, 1935.

———. *A Series of Lectures on Social Justice, 1935–1936*. Royal Oak, Michigan: The Radio League of the Little Flower, 1936.

———. *Money! Questions and Answers*. Royal Oak, Michigan: Social Justice Publishing Co., 1936.

Crane, Milton (ed.). *The Roosevelt Era*. New York: Boni & Gaer, Inc., 1947.

Davis, Forrest. *Huey Long*. New York: Dodge Publishing Co., 1935.

De Grazia, Sebastian. *The Political Community, A Study of Anomie*. Chicago: The University of Chicago Press, 1948.

Destler, Chester M. *American Radicalism, 1865–1901*. New London, Conn.: Connecticut College Press, 1946.

Dorman, Morgan J. *Age Before Booty: An Explanation of the Townsend Plan*. New York: G. P. Putnam's Sons, 1936.

Douglas, Paul H. *Social Security in the United States*. New York: McGraw-Hill Book Co., Inc., 1936.

Downs, Anthony. *An Economic Theory of Democracy*. New York: Harper & Row, 1957.

Ellis, John Tracy. *American Catholicism*. Chicago: The University of Chicago Press, 1955.

Farley, James A. *Behind the Ballots*. New York: Harcourt, Brace and Co., 1938.

———. *Jim Farley's Story*. New York: McGraw-Hill Book Co., Inc., 1948.

Father Coughlin's Friends. *An Answer to Father Coughlin's Critics*. Royal Oak, Michigan: The Radio League of the Little Flower, 1940.

Flynn, John T. *The Roosevelt Myth*. New York: The Devin Adair Co., 1948.

Fossum, Paul. *The Agrarian Movement in North Dakota*. Baltimore: Johns Hopkins Press, 1925.

[Franklin, John Carter]. *American Messiahs*. New York: Simon and Schuster, 1935.

Galbraith, John Kenneth. *The Great Crash: 1929*. Boston: Houghton Mifflin Co., 1954.

Gaston, Herbert G. *The Non-Partisan League*. New York: Harcourt, Brace and Co., 1920.

General Jewish Council. *Father Coughlin: His "Facts" and Arguments*. New York: General Jewish Council, 1939.

Gerth, H. H., and C. Wright Mills (eds.). *From Max Weber: Essays in Sociology.* New York: Oxford University Press, 1958.

Glazer, Nathan and Daniel Patrick Moynihan. *Beyond the Melting Pot.* Cambridge, Mass.: The M.I.T. Press, 1963.

Handlin, Oscar. *Race and Nationality in American Life.* Boston: Little, Brown and Co., 1957.

Heberle, Rudolf. *Social Movements.* New York: Appleton-Century-Crofts, Inc., 1951.

Hesseltine, William B. *The Rise and Fall of Third Parties.* Washington, D.C.: Public Affairs Press, 1948.

Hicks, John D. *The Populist Revolt.* Minneapolis: The University of Minnesota Press, 1931.

Higham, John. *Strangers in the Land. Patterns of American Nativism, 1860–1925.* New Brunswick, N.J.: Rutgers University Press. 1955.

Hoffer, Eric. *The True Believer.* New York: Harper & Brothers, 1951.

Hofstadter, Richard. *The Age of Reform.* New York: Alfred A. Knopf, 1956.
———. *The Paranoid Style in American Politics.* New York: Alfred A. Knopf, 1965.

Holtzman, Abraham. *The Townsend Movement: A Political Study.* New York: Bookman Associates, 1963. Ickes, Harold L. *The Secret Diary of Harold L. Ickes.* Vol. I: *The First Thousand Days, 1933–1936.* New York: Simon and Schuster, 1953.

Jackson, Kenneth T. *The Ku Klux Klan in the City, 1915–1930.* New York: Oxford University Press, 1967.

Johnson, Walter. *1600 Pennsylvania Avenue: Presidents and the People, 1929–1959.* Boston: Little, Brown and Co., 1960.

Kane, Harnett T. *Louisiana Hayride.* New York: William Morrow & Co., 1941.

Kernan, William C. *The Ghost of Royal Oak.* New York: Free Speech Forum, 1940.

Key, V. O., Jr. *Southern Politics In State and Nation.* New York: Alfred A. Knopf, Inc., 1950.

Kinzer, Donald. *An Episode in Anti-Catholicism: The American Protective Association.* Seattle: University of Washington Press, 1964.

Kramer, Dale. *The Wild Jackasses, The American Farmer in Revolt.* New York: Hastings House, 1956.

Latham, Earl. *The Communist Controversy in Washington From the New Deal To McCarthy.* Cambridge, Mass.: Harvard University Press, 1966.

Lee, Alfred McClung, and Elizabeth Briant Lee. *The Fine Art of Propaganda: A Study of Father Coughlin's Speeches.* New York: Harcourt, Brace and Co., 1939.

Leighton, Isabel (ed.). *The Aspirin Age.* New York: Simon and Schuster, 1949.

Lessa, William A. and Vogt, Evan Z. (eds.). *Reader in Comparative Religion: An Anthropological Approach.* New York: Harper & Row, 1965.

Leuchtenburg, William E. *Franklin D. Roosevelt and the New Deal.* New York: Harper & Row, 1963.

Lipset, Seymour Martin and Leo Lowenthal (eds.). *Culture and Social Character.* Glencoe, Illinois: The Free Press, 1961.

Long, Huey P. *Every Man A King.* New Orleans: National Book Co., Inc., 1933.
———. *My First Days in the White House.* Harrisburg, Pa.: The Telegraph Press, 1935.

Lubell, Samuel. *The Future of American Politics.* Garden City, N.Y.: Doubleday Anchor Books, 1956.

Luthin, Reinhard H. *American Demagogues.* Boston: The Beacon Press, 1954.

Martin, Thomas. *Dynasty: The Longs of Louisiana.* New York: G. P. Putnam's Sons, 1960.

Marx, Leo. *The Machine in the Garden: Technology and the Pastoral Ideal in America.* New York: Oxford University Press, 1964.

Mayer, George H. *The Political Career of Floyd B. Olson.* Minneapolis: The University of Minnesota Press, 1951.

McCoy, Donald R. *Angry Voices: Left-Of-Center Politics in the New Deal Era.* Lawrence, Kansas: University of Kansas Press, 1958.

Merton, Robert K. *Social Theory and Social Structure.* Glencoe, Illinois: The Free Press, 1957.

Milne, Richard. *That Man Townsend.* Los Angeles: Prosperity Publishing Co., 1935.

Mitchell, Broadus. *Depression Decade.* New York: Rinehart & Co., Inc., 1947.

Moley, Raymond. *After Seven Years.* New York: Harper & Brothers, 1939.

Morlan, Robert L. *Political Prairie Fire: The Nonpartisan League, 1915–1922.* Minneapolis: University of Minnesota Press, 1955.

Mugglebee, Ruth. *Father Coughlin: The Radio Priest of the Shrine of the Little Flower.* Garden City, N.Y.: Garden City Publishing Co., Inc., 1933.

Murray, Robert K. *Red Scare: A Study in National Hysteria, 1919–1920.* Minneapolis: University of Minnesota Press, 1955.

Neuberger, Richard L., and Kelley Loe. *An Army of the Aged.* Caldwell, Idaho: The Caxton Printers, Ltd., 1936.

Opotowsky, Stan. *The Longs of Louisiana.* New York: E. P. Dutton & Co., 1960.

Parrington, Vernon Louis. *Main Currents in American Thought.* Vol. III: *The Beginnings of Critical Realism in America, 1860–1920.* New York: Harcourt, Brace and Co., 1930.

Perkins, Frances. *The Roosevelt I Knew.* New York: The Viking Press, 1946.

Pollack, Norman. *The Populist Response to Industrial America.* New York: W. W. Norton & Company, 1962.

Rauch, Basil. *The History of the New Deal.* New York: Creative Age Press, Inc., 1944.

Reeve, Joseph E. *Monetary Reform Movements: A Survey of Recent Plans and Panaceas.* Washington, D.C.: American Council on Public Affairs, 1943.

Robinson, Edgar Eugene. *The Presidential Vote: 1936.* Stanford, Cal.: Stanford University Press, 1938.

———. *They Voted for Roosevelt.* Stanford, Cal.: Stanford University Press, 1947.

Robinson, Henry Morton. *Fantastic Interim.* New York: Harcourt, Brace and Co., 1943.

Rogin, Michael Paul. *The Intellectuals and McCarthy: The Radical Specter.* Cambridge, Mass.: The M.I.T. Press, 1967.

Roosevelt, Elliott (ed.). *F.D.R.: His Personal Letters.* Vol. I. New York: Duell, Sloan and Pearce, 1950.

Roy, Ralph Lord. *Apostles of Discord.* Boston: The Beacon Press, 1953.

Saloutos, Theodore, and John D. Hicks. *Agricultural Discontent in the Middle West, 1900–1936.* Madison, Wisconsin: University of Wisconsin Press, 1951.

Sanford, Charles L. *The Quest for Paradise.* Urbana, Illinois: The University of Illinois Press, 1961.

Scammon, Richard M. *America at the Polls: A Handbook of American Presidential*

Election Statistics, 1920–1964. Pittsburgh, University of Pittsburgh Press, 1965.

Schlesinger, Arthur M., Jr. *The Politics of Upheaval.* Boston: Houghton Mifflin Co., 1960.

Seldes, George. *Facts and Fascism.* New York: In Fact, Inc., 1943.

Shils, Edward A. *The Torment of Secrecy.* Glencoe, Illinois: The Free Press, 1956.

Simmel, Georg. *Conflict & The Web of Group Affiliations.* New York: The Free Press, 1964.

Simon, Rita James (ed.). *As We Saw the Thirties.* Urbana, Illinois: University of Illinois Press, 1967.

Sindler, Allan P. *Huey Long's Louisiana.* Baltimore: The Johns Hopkins Press, 1956.

Smith, Henry Nash. *Virgin Land: The American West as Symbol and Myth.* New York: Vintage Books, 1950.

Spitz, David. *Patterns of Anti-Democratic Thought.* New York: The Macmillan Co., 1949.

Spivak, John L. *Shrine of the Silver Dollar.* New York: Modern Age Books, 1940.

The Statistical History of the United States. Stamford, Conn.: Fairfield Publishers, 1965.

Stedman, Murray S., Jr., and Susan W. Stedman. *Discontent at the Polls: A Study of Farmer and Labor Parties, 1827–1948.* New York: Columbia University Press, 1950.

Stokes, Thomas L. *Chip Off My Shoulder.* Princeton, N.J.: Princeton University Press, 1940.

Strong, Donald S. *Organized Anti-Semitism In America: The Rise of Group Prejudice During the Decade 1930–1940.* Washington, D.C.: American Council on Public Affairs, 1941.

Swing, Raymond Gram. *Forerunners of American Fascism.* New York: Julian Messner, Inc., 1935.

Thomas, Norman. *After the New Deal, What?* New York: The Macmillan Co., 1936.

Thompson, E. P. *The Making of the English Working Class.* New York: Vintage Books, 1966.

Townsend, Francis E. *The Townsend National Recovery Plan.* Chicago: Townsend National Weekly, Inc., 1941.

———. *New Horizons: An Autobiography.* Chicago: J. L. Stewart Publishing Co., 1943.

[Trivanovitch, Vaso]. *The Townsend Scheme.* New York: National Industrial Conference Board, Inc. 1936.

Tull, Charles J. *Father Coughlin and the New Deal.* Syracuse, N.Y.: Syracuse University Press, 1965.

Viereck, Peter. *The Unadjusted Man: A New Hero for Americans.* Boston: The Beacon Press, 1956.

Ward, Louis B. *Father Charles E. Coughlin: An Authorized Biography.* Detroit: Tower Publications, Inc., 1933.

Wecter, Dixon. *The Age of the Great Depression, 1929–1941.* New York: The Macmillan Co., 1948.

Wells, H. G. *The New America, The New World.* New York: The Macmillan Co., 1935.

Woodward, C. Vann (ed.). *The Comparative Approach to American History*. New York: Basic Books, 1968.

Zinn, Howard (ed.). *New Deal Thought*. New York: The Bobbs-Merrill Co., 1966.

ARTICLES

Abel, Theodore. "The Pattern of a Successful Political Movement," *American Sociological Review*, II, No. 3 (June, 1937), 347–52.

Aikman, Duncan. "Townsendism: Old Time Religion," *The New York Times Magazine*, March 8, 1936, pp. 5, 25.

———. "Lemke's New Party, and Three Key Men," *The New York Times Magazine*, July 26, 1936, pp. 6, 7, 18.

"Al Smith to Right of Them, Coughlin to Left of Them," *The New Republic*, LXXXVII, No. 1126 (July 1, 1936), 226.

Barber, Bernard. "Acculturation and Messianic Movements," *American Sociological Review*, VI, No. 5 (October, 1941), 663–69.

Barnes, Joseph. "The Social Basis of Fascism," *Pacific Affairs*, IX, No. 1 (March, 1936), 24–32.

Bennett, David H. "The Year of the Old Folks' Revolt," *American Heritage*, XVI, No. 1 (December, 1964), 48–51, 99–107.

Berthoff, Rowland. "The American Social Order: A Conservative Hypothesis," *The American Historical Review*, LXV, No. 3 (April 1, 1960), 495–514.

Blackorby, Edward C. "William Lemke: Agrarian Radical and Union Party Presidential Candidate," *The Mississippi Valley Historical Review*, XLIX, No. 1 (June, 1962), 67–84.

Broun, Heywood. "Broun's Page," *The Nation*, CXLIII, No. 8 (August 22, 1936), 213.

"Calm for a Stormy Priest," *Life*, XXXIX, No. 20 (November 14, 1955), 119–23.

"Campaign Blares at Door of Voters," *The Literary Digest*, CXXII, No. 7 (August 15, 1936), 3–4.

Cantril, Hadley. "Educational and Economic Composition of Religious Groups," *American Journal of Sociology*, 47, No. 5 (March, 1943), 570–85.

Carter, Hodding. "How Come Huey Long? (I. Bogeyman)," *The New Republic*, LXXXII, No. 1054 (February 13, 1935), 11–14.

"Charles Edward Coughlin," *Current Biography, 1940*, pp. 198–201.

Childs, Marquis W. "Father Coughlin: A Success Story of the Depression," *The New Republic*, LXXVIII, No. 1013 (May 2, 1934), 326–27.

Churchill, Winston. "Soapbox Messiahs," *Collier's*, XCVII, No. 25 (June 20, 1936), 11, 44–46.

Colony, David Carl. "Dictator Coughlin," *The Forum*, XCIII, No. 4 (April 1, 1935), 196–201.

Coughlin, Charles E. "Inflation and Silver," *Today*, I, No. 11 (January 6, 1934), 6–7, 22–23.

———. "How Long Can Democracy and Capitalism Last?" *Today*, III, No. 10 (December 29, 1934), 6–7.

———. "What I Think Congress Should Do," *Today*, V, No. 9 (December 21, 1935), 6–7, 18.

———. "A Third Party," *Vital Speeches of the Day*, II, No. 20 (July 1, 1936), 613–16.

Creel, George. "The Old Homesteader," *Collier's*, XCVIII, No. 14 (October 3, 1936), 22.

Crowell, Chester T. "The Townsend Plan: A Challenge to Congress," *The American Mercury*, XXXIV, No. 136 (April, 1935), 456–60.

"Dangers of Demagogy," *The Commonweal*, XIX, No. 6 (December 8, 1933), 144.

Davenport, Walter. "The Shepherd of Discontent," *Collier's*, XCV, No. 18 (May 4, 1935), 12–13, 57–60.

———. "Mr. Lemke Stops To Think," *Collier's*, XCVIII, No. 16 (October 17, 1936), 7–8, 25–26.

———. "The Mysterious Gerald Smith," *Collier's*, CXIII, No. 10 (March 4, 1944), 14–15, 60–62.

Davis, Forrest. "Father Coughlin," *The Atlantic Monthly*, CLVI, No. 6 (December, 1935), 659–68.

Destler, Chester M. "Western Radicalism: 1865–1901: Concepts and Origins," *The Mississippi Valley Historical Review*, XXI, No. 3 (December, 1944), 335–68.

Deutsch, Herman B. "Huey Long: The Last Phase," *The Saturday Evening Post*, CCVIII, No. 15 (October 12, 1935), 27, 82–91.

Eubank, Earle Edward. "Father Coughlin Triumphs in Cincinnati," *The Christian Century*, LII, No. 48 (November 27, 1935), 1514–1516.

"Father Coughlin," *Fortune*, IX, No. 2 (February, 1934), 34–39, 110–12.

"Father Coughlin and Ex-Governor Smith," *The Christian Century*, L, No. 51 (December 13, 1933), 1564.

"Father Coughlin at the Garden," *The Nation*, CXL, No. 3648 (June 5, 1935), 644.

"Father Coughlin Commits Hara-Kiri," *The Nation*, CXLIII, No. 20 (November 14, 1936), 563–64.

"Father Coughlin Denounced by Father Ryan," *The Nation*, CXLIII, No. 16 (October 17, 1936), 434.

"A Father Coughlin Forum," *The Nation*, CXL, No. 3637 (March 20, 1935), 332.

"Father Coughlin's Position," *The Commonweal*, XXII, No. 10 (July 5, 1935), 265.

"Father Coughlin's Reappearance," *The Nation*, CLXXVIII, No. 1 (January 2, 1954), 1.

"Father Coughlin Says the Last Word," *The Christian Century*, LIII, No. 41 (October 7, 1936), 1309–1310.

"Father Coughlin Walks Again," *The Nation*, CXLIII, No. 8 (August 22, 1936), 201–02.

"Four Preachers in Political Arena," *The Literary Digest*, CXXII, No. 5 (August 1, 1936), 5–6.

Frank, Gerold. "Huey Long the Second," *The Nation*, CXLIII, No. 4 (July 25, 1936), 93–94.

———. "Father Coughlin's Fish Fry," *The Nation*, CXLIII, No. 8 (August 22, 1936), 203–04.

"Gerald Lyman Kenneth Smith," *Current Biography, 1943*, pp. 707–10.

Goldstein, Morton S. "The New Party and the Ballot," *The New Republic*, LXXXVII, No. 1122 (June 3, 1936), 99–100.

Harris, Herbert. "Dr. Townsend's Marching Soldiers," *Current History*, XLIII, No. 2 (February, 1936), 455–62.

Harris, Herbert. "That Third Party," *Current History*, XLV, No. 1 (October, 1936), 77–92.

Hicks, John D. "The Third Party Tradition in American Politics," *The Mississippi Valley Historical Review*, XX, No. 1 (June, 1933), 3–28.

Higham, John. "Another Look at Nativism," *The Catholic Historical Review*, XLIV (July, 1958), 147–58.

"How Europe Views Our Candidates," *The Literary Digest*, CXXII, No. 3 (July 18, 1936), 8.

Huie, William Bradford. "Gerald Smith's Bid for Power," *The American Mercury*, LV, No. 224 (August, 1942), 145–57.

"The Impassioned Preacher of Royal Oak," *The Living Age*, CCCL, No. 4435 (April, 1936), 169–70.

Kolodin, Irving. "Propaganda On the Air," *The American Mercury*, XXXV, No. 139 (July, 1935), 293–300.

Kramer, Dale. "The American Fascists," *Harpers Magazine*, CLXXXI, No. 9 (September, 1940), 380–93.

Lake, Stuart N. "If Money," *The Saturday Evening Post*, CCVII, No. 45 (May 11, 1935), 12–13, 121–27.

Linton, Ralph. "Nativistic Movements," *American Anthropologist*, XLV (1943), 230–40.

Lovett, Robert Morss. "Huey Long Invades the Middle West," *The New Republic*, LXXXIII, No. 1067 (May 15, 1935), 10–12.

Magil, A. B. "Father Coughlin's Army," *New Masses*, XIV, No. 1 (January 1, 1935), 11–15.

———. "Can Father Coughlin Come Back?" *The New Republic*, LXXXVII, No. 1125 (June 24, 1936), 196–98.

McCarten, John. "Father Coughlin: Holy Medicine Man," *The American Mercury*, XLVII, No. 186 (June, 1939), 129–41.

Milliken, Seymour J. "$200 a Month at Sixty," *The Forum*, XCII, No. 5 (November, 1934), 326–29.

Mitchell, Jonathan. "Liberty Bill Lemke," *The New Republic*, LXXXVIII, No. 1132 (August 12, 1936), 8–10.

———. "Father Coughlin's Children," *The New Republic*, LXXXVIII, No. 1134 (August 26, 1936), 72–74.

Moore, Harry Thornton. "Just Folks in Utopia," *The New Republic*, LXXXV, No. 1093 (November 13, 1935), 9–10.

Neuberger, Richard L. "The Townsend Plan Exposed," *The Nation*, CXLI, No. 3669 (October 30, 1935), 505–07.

Neumann, Franz. "Anxiety in Politics," *Dissent*, II, No. 2 (Spring, 1955), 133–43.

"News and Comment from the National Capital," *The Literary Digest*, CXIX, No. 11 (March 16, 1935), 12.

Newton, Craig A. "Father Coughlin and His National Union for Social Justice," *The Southwestern Social Science Quarterly*, XLI, No. 3 (December, 1960), 341–49.

Niebuhr, Reinhold. "Pawns for Fascism—Our Lower Middle Classes," *The American Scholar*, VI, No. 2 (Spring, 1937), 145–52.

Owen, Russell, "Townsend Talks of His Plan and Hopes," *The New York Times Magazine*, December 29, 1935, 3, 15.

Parsons, Wilfrid, "Father Coughlin and Social Justice," *America*, LIII, No. 6 (May 18, 1935), 129–31.

Parson, Wilfrid. "Father Coughlin and the Banks," *America*, LIII, No. 7 (May 25, 1935), 150–52.

———. "Father Coughlin's Ideas on Money," *America*, LIII, No. 8 (June 1, 1935), 174–76.

———. "Father Coughlin: The Aftermath," *America*, LIII, No. 12 (June 29, 1935), 275–77.

"Pensions and Ballots," *The Literary Digest*, CXXII, No. 8 (August 22, 1936), 5–6.

"Political X," *The Literary Digest*, CXXII, No. 1 (July 4, 1936), 6.

Polsby, Nelson W. "Towards an Explanation of McCarthyism," *Political Studies*, VIII (October, 1960), 250–71.

"Recovery Pensions," *The Literary Digest*, CXXII, No. 4 (July 25, 1936), 5–6.

"Reports of The Literary Digest's 1936 Presidential Poll," *The Literary Digest*, CXXII, Nos. 10, 14, 15, 16, 17, 18 (September 5, October 3, 10, 17, 24, 31, 1936), 7–8 (in all issues).

Rice, Stuart A. "Is the Townsend Plan Practical?" *Vital Speeches of the Day*, II, No. 38 (January 27, 1936), 50.

Richberg, Donald R. "The Townsend Delusion," *Review of Reviews*, XCIII, No. 2 (February, 1936), 24–27.

Rodman, Selden. "The Insurgent Line-Up for 1936," *The American Mercury*, XXXV, No. 137 (May, 1935), 77–83.

Ryan, John A., and James J. Carberry. "The Ryan-Coughlin Controversy," *The Commonweal*, XXV, No. 2 (November 6, 1936), 44–46.

"The Ryan-Coughlin Controversy," *The Commonweal*, XXIV, No. 26 (October 23, 1936), 597–98.

"Salvation from the Bible Belt," *The Nation*, CXLIII, No. 4 (July 25, 1936), 88–89.

Sayre, Wallace C. "Political Groundswell," *Current History*, XLIV, No. 3 (June, 1936), 53–60.

Shaw, Albert. "As the Campaign Gets Under Way," *Review of Reviews*, XCIV, No. 1 (July, 1936), 15–22.

Shaw, Roger. "Third Parties of 1936," *Review of Reviews*, XCIV, No. 2 (August, 1936), 30–32.

Shenton, James P. "The Coughlin Movement and the New Deal," *Political Science Quarterly*, LXXXIII, No. 3 (September, 1958), 352–73.

Smith, Gerald L. K. "How Come Huey Long? (Or Superman)," *The New Republic*, LXXXII, No. 1054 (February 13, 1935), 14–15.

Strack, Celeste. "Whither Townsendism?" *New Masses*, XX, No. 5 (July 28, 1936), 7–9.

"Strategy Behind Coughlin's Campaign," *Business Week*, No. 361 (August 1, 1936), 44.

Swing, Raymond Gram. "Father Coughlin: The Wonder of Self Discovery," *The Nation*, CXXXIX, No. 3625 (December 26, 1934), 731–33.

———. "Father Coughlin: The Phase of Action," *The Nation*, CXL, No. 3626 (January 2, 1935), 9–11.

———. "Dr. Townsend Solves It All," *The Nation*, CXL, No. 3635 (March 6, 1935), 268–70.

———. "The Build-Up of Long and Coughlin," *The Nation*, CXL, No. 3637 (March 20, 1935), 325–26.

"Third Party Threat," *The Literary Digest*, CXXI, No. 26 (June 27, 1936), 5–6.

Thorning, Joseph F. "Senator Long on Father Coughlin," *America*, LIII, No. 1 (April 13, 1935), 8–9.

"The Total Eclipse of Father Coughlin," *The Christian Century*, LIII, No. 47 (November 18, 1936), 1517.

Townsend, Francis E., and Nicholas Roosevelt. "Townsend Pensions: Sense or Nonsense," *The Forum*, XCV, No. 5 (May, 1936), 282–87.

"Townsend Plan: Rift and Inquiry," *The Literary Digest*, CXXI, No. 14 (April 4, 1936), 6–7.

"Townsend Plan's Change of Drivers," *The Literary Digest*, CXXI, No. 15 (April 11, 1936), 5.

"Union Party Economics," *The Saturday Evening Post*, CCIX, No. 8 (August 22, 1936), 22.

Ward, Paul W. "Lemke: Crackpot for President," *The Nation*, CXLIII, No. 2 (July 11, 1936), 34–36.

"Washington Notes: Coughlin Calls the Tune," *The New Republic*, LXXXVII, No. 1122 (June 3, 1936), 100–01.

"Washington Notes: Representative Bell Stalks Fame and Townsend," *The New Republic*, LXXXVII, No. 1123 (June 10, 1936), 128–29.

"Washington Notes: Father Coughlin's Union Party," *The New Republic*, LXXXVIII, No. 1127 (July 8, 1936), 265–66.

"Washington Notes: The Old Folks Crusade," *The New Republic*, LXXXVIII, No. 1133 (August 19, 1936), 45–46.

"Washington Notes: Coughlin in the Papal Doghouse," *The New Republic*, LXXXVIII, No. 1138 (September 23, 1936), 182–83.

Wilcox, Benton H. "An Historical Definition of Northwestern Radicalism," *The Mississippi Valley Historical Review*, XXVI (December, 1929).

Williams, Michael. "The Priest of the Radio," *Today*, I, No. 6 (December 2, 1933), 17.

Williams, T. Harry. "The Gentleman From Louisiana: Demagogue or Democrat," *The Journal of Southern History*, XXVI, No. 1 (February, 1960), 4–21.

Winner, Percy. "Fascism at the Door," *Scribner's Magazine*, XCIX, No. 1 (January, 1936), 33–38.

Woodward, C. Vann. "The Populist Heritage and the Intellectual," *The American Scholar* (Winter, 1959–1960), pp. 55–72.

PAMPHLETS

Jones, Ellis O. *Lemke's the Man for President*. Los Angeles: Ellis O. Jones Publisher, 1936.

Kennedy, Edward E. *The Farmer and the Three Major Parties*. Chicago: The Union Party, 1936.

Lemke, William. *America Self-Sustained*. Chicago: The Union Party, 1936.

Magil, A. B. *The Truth About Father Coughlin*. New York: Workers Library Publishers, 1935.

Noble, Robert. *How Lemke Can Be Elected*. Los Angeles: The Robert Noble Series, 1936.

―――. *Lemke and the Union Party*. Los Angeles: The Robert Noble Series, 1936.

Townsend, Francis E. *Old Age Revolving Pensions*. Long Beach, California: Old Age Revolving Pensions, Ltd., 1934.

Townsend, Francis E. *Dr. Townsend Tells Why He Is Supporting William Lemke.* Chicago: J. W. Brinton, 1936.

Townsend, Francis E., and Robert E. Clements. *The Townsend Plan.* Los Angeles: Old Age Revolving Pensions, Ltd., 1935.

A University of Chicago Round Table. *The Economic Meaning of the Townsend Plan.* Chicago: The University of Chicago Press, 1936.

Walker, Mabel L. *The Townsend Plan Analyzed.* New York: Tax Policy League, 1936.

West, George E. *The Spotlight of Truth on the Townsend Plan.* Chicago: P. W. Treloar, 1936.

Wolfe, Richard W. *Lemke or Stalin—Which?* Chicago: The Union Party, 1936.

——— (ed.). *On to Victory.* Chicago: The Union Party, 1936.

——— (ed.). *The Union Party Will Win With Lincoln Legal Tender Monay.* Spokane, Washington: The Union Party, 1936.

Public Documents

Illinois Blue Book, 1937–1938.

Massachusetts Blue Book, 1937.

The North Dakota Blue Book, 1937.

Pennsylvania Blue Book, 1937.

U.S. Congress, House, Committee on Un-American Activities. *Investigation of Un-American Propaganda Activities in the United States: Gerald L. K. Smith.* 79th Cong., 2d Sess., January 30, 1946.

U.S. Congress, House, Committee on Ways and Means. *Hearings, Economic Security Bill.* 74th Cong., 2d Sess., 1935.

U.S. Congress, House, Select Committee Investigating Old Age Pension Organizations. *Testimony of Robert E. Clements.* 74th Cong., 3d Sess., 1936, Part I.

The Wisconsin Blue Book, 1937.

Unpublished Material

Blackorby, Edward C. "Prairie Rebel: The Public Career of William Lemke." Unpublished Ph.D. dissertation, Department of History, University of North Dakota, 1958.

Brudvig, Glenn Lowell. "The Farmers' Alliance and Populist Movement in North Dakota." Unpublished Masters thesis, Department of History, University of North Dakota, 1956.

Ferkiss, Victor C. "The Political and Economic Philosophy of American Fascism." Unpublished Ph.D. dissertation, Department of Political Science, University of Chicago, 1954.

Holtzman, Abraham. "The Townsend Movement: A Study in Old Age Pressure Politics." Unpublished Ph.D. dissertation, Department of Government, Harvard University, 1952.

Mason, Bruce Bonner. "American Political Protest, 1932–1936." Unpublished Ph.D. dissertation, Department of History, University of Texas, 1953.

Masters, Nick Arthur. "Father Coughlin and Social Justice: A Case Study of Social Movement." Unpublished Ph.D. dissertation, Department of Political Science, University of Wisconsin, 1955.

Schonbach, Morris. "Native Fascism During the 1930's and 1940's: A Study of

Its Roots, Its Growth, and Its Decline." Unpublished Ph.D. dissertation, Department of History, University of California, Los Angeles, 1958.

Tull, Charles J. "Father Coughlin, the New Deal, and the Election of 1936." Unpublished Ph.D. dissertation, Department of History, Notre Dame University, 1962.

MANUSCRIPT COLLECTIONS

Democratic National Campaign Committee: Correspondence of James A. Farley, Chairman, 1936. Franklin D. Roosevelt Library, Hyde Park, New York.

Franklin D. Roosevelt Papers. Franklin D. Roosevelt Library, Hyde Park, New York.

    Official File 300 (Democratic National Committee.)

    Official File 306 (Charles E. Coughlin.)

    Official File 494-A (Old Age Pensions.)

    Official File 1038 (Frazier-Lemke Bill.)

    Official File 1403 (Huey P. Long.)

    Official File 1542 (Dr. Francis E. Townsend.)

    President's Personal File I-P (Press Conferences.)

    President's Personal File 2338 (Charles E. Coughlin.)

    President's Personal File (Additional Items.)

Henry G. Teigan Papers. Minnesota Historical Society, St. Paul, Minnesota.

Howard Y. Williams Papers. Minnesota Historical Society, St. Paul, Minnesota.

Oral History Research Project. Columbia University, New York, New York.

William Gibbs McAdoo Papers. Library of Congress, Washington, D.C.

William Lemke Papers. Orin G. Libby Historical Manuscripts Collection, University of North Dakota, Grand Forks, North Dakota.

NEWSPAPERS AND NEWS MAGAZINES

Age of Plenty (St. Paul, Minnesota)

American Progress (New Orleans, Louisiana)

Boston Evening Transcript

Chicago Daily Tribune

Chicago Herald and Examiner

Cincinnati Enquirer

Cincinnati Post

Cleveland Plain Dealer

Davenport Democrat (Davenport, Iowa)

Detroit Evening Times

Detroit Free Press

Detroit News

Fargo Forum (Fargo, North Dakota)

The Leader (North Dakota Nonpartisan League, Bismark, North Dakota)

Lemke Leader (Los Angeles, California)

Los Angeles Examiner

Los Angeles Times

Minneapolis Journal

Minneapolis Star

Minneapolis Tribune

Modern Crusader (The Townsend Movement, Long Beach, California)
New York Herald Tribune
The New York Times
Newsweek
The Philadelphia Record
Portland Oregonian
San Francisco Examiner
St. Paul Pioneer Press
Sioux Falls Argus Leader (Sioux Falls, South Dakota)
Social Justice (Royal Oak, Michigan)
Time
Times Picayune (New Orleans)
Townsend National Weekly (Los Angeles, California)
Union Party Advocate (Elkhart, Indiana)
The Washington Post

Index

Advertising, 172

Age, 8, 147, 155, 172, 179, 293; Long and, 120, 121, 141; population of, 156, 157–58; social change and, 22, 163–66, 167–68, 305; Townsend on, 6, 7, 105, 145, 150, 151, 152–53, 156, 290, 304, 308; Union Party and, 193, 194, 243, 251, 258, 272, 290

Agrarianism, *see* Farmers

Agricultural Adjustment Act, 38, 77, 158; Lemke and, 93, 94, 95, 237

Aikman, Duncan, 259; quoted, 201

Alabama, 125, 128, 238, 267

Albany, New York, 92, 94

Allen, Oscar K., 131–32, 136

America First Committee, 281, 284

America First Party, 284–85

American Association for Social Security, 173

American Business Surveys, 162

American Federation of Labor, 17–18, 52; Lemke and, 100, 235

American Independent Party, 303

American Institute of Public Opinion, 156–57, 176

American Jewish Congress, 106

American Liberty League, 78

American Progress, The (periodical), 124, 125

American Protective Association, 299, 301

Amlie, Thomas, 205

Andrews, Charles O., 258

Anglophobia, 246, 269, 270, 271; Coughlin, 75, 76, 281, 300–301

Anti-alienism, *see* Nativism

Anti-Catholicism, 57, 221, 222, 271, 272n18; Catholic responses to, 31, 37n26, 58, 63–64, 65, 228, 254, 299, 300–301

Anti-Communism, 10, 23, 247; Coughlin use of, 21, 33, 35, 51, 69, 75, 76, 78, 227, 228, 229, 230–31, 235, 254, 278, 279, 281, 300–301, 302–303; Smith use of, 11–12, 19, 139, 143, 238, 239, 252–53, 283–86, 298

Anti-intellectualism, 159, 302; Coughlin use of, 63, 69, 70, 197, 298, 300; Lemke use of, 235, 270, 271; Smith use of, 19, 124

Anti-Semitism, 49n15, 106, 275, 299, 300; of Coughlin, 52–53, 63, 255n13, 278–82, 300; of Long, 132–33; of Smith, 282, 284, 285–86; of Thompson, 247

Arizona, 174, 267, 274

Arkansas, 125, 128, 267

Assumption College, Sandwich, Ontario, 30

Austria, 60

Autocracy, 253–54, 269n13, 302; Coughlin and, 17, 71, 78, 208, 230–31; Long and, 119, 122, 123, 208; Townsend and, 169–70, 171, 181, 199, 208

Backus, Clyde, quoted, 275

Baker, Ray Stannard, 81

Baltimore, Maryland, 76, 139

Banking, 11, 18, 34, 36, 38, 62–63; central, 6, 15, 43, 49, 50, 51, 76, 95, 96, 105, 193, 207, 233, 301; Detroit